The Red Rose and the White

The Red Rose and the White

The Wars of the Roses, 1453–1487

John Sadler

Longman
is an imprint of

Harlow, England • London • New York • Boston • San Francisco • Toronto • Sydney • Singapore • Hong Kong
Tokyo • Seoul • Taipei • New Delhi • Cape Town • Madrid • Mexico City • Amsterdam • Munich • Paris • Milan

PEARSON EDUCATION LIMITED

Edinburgh Gate
Harlow CM20 2JE
United Kingdom
Tel: +44 (0)1279 623623
Fax: +44 (0)1279 431059
Website: www.pearsoned.co.uk

First edition published in Great Britain in 2010

ISBN: 978-1-4058-2360-9

British Library Cataloguing in Publication Data
A CIP catalogue record for this book can be obtained from the British Library

Library of Congress Cataloging in Publication Data
Sadler, John, 1953–
   The red rose and the white : the Wars of the Roses, 1453–1487 / John Sadler.
      p. cm.
   Includes bibliographical references and index.
   ISBN 978-1-4058-2360-9 (hardcover : alk. paper) 1. Great Britain—History—
Wars of the Roses, 1455–1485. 2. Great Britain—History—Wars of the Roses,
1455–1885—Campaigns. 3. Great Britain—History—Lancaster and York,
1399–1485. 4. Great Britain—History, Military—1066–1485. 5. Lancaster,
House of. 6. York, House of. I. Title.
   DA250.S23 2009
   942.04—dc22
                                                                      2009029004

10 9 8 7 6 5 4 3 2 1
13 12 11 10 09

Typeset in 10/14 pt Galliard
Printed and bound in China (GCC)

The Publisher's policy is to use paper manufactured from sustainable forests.

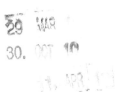

Contents

CONTENTS

Acknowledgements

The author's particular fascination with the Wars of the Roses can be traced back to afternoons of black-and-white television in the early 1960s, and the BBC's *Age of Kings* – Shakespeare's History Plays, subsequently and still in black and white, interpreted in *Wars of the Roses*, which I think was shown in three episodes on Thursday evenings. Both of these landmark series were based on *Henry VI* Parts I, II and III, together with *Richard III*. That Shakespeare could be enjoyable, indeed rivetingly so, came as something of a revelation to one reared on the standard (as it then was) GCE diet of the Bard as purely exam fodder, presented with painstaking dullness. An immediate debt of gratitude is therefore due to the producers and cast.

As a young lad I found the frequent, virtually non-stop, bloodletting particularly appealing if, sequentially, rather hard to follow. Who was killing who this time, and why? The search for answers has occupied a considerable amount of my time since. What follows is therefore a military study, rather than a full political and social history; the wider context has been covered by a number of distinguished authors, and the present writer would not attempt to improve upon their many excellent studies.

Thanks are due first to my agent Duncan McAra and to my editors at Pearsons, Christina Wipf-Perry, Mary-Clare Conellan and Mari Shullaw – this book owes a great deal to all. I am also very grateful to Dr Maureen Meikle of Sunderland University, Dr Richard Britnell of Durham University, Professor Tony Pollard of the University of Teesside, Professor Gordon Batho, to Chloe Rodham for producing the maps and battle plans, Adam Barr for the photographs, Richard Groocock of the National Archives, Dr Joan Harvey of the University of Newcastle upon Tyne, Dr Constance Fraser, the late Professor George Jobey, Jennifer Gill and Liz Bregazzi of County Durham

Record Office, Joe Ann Ricca of the Richard III Foundation Inc., Philip Albert of Royal Armouries, Nicola Waghorn of the National Gallery, Matthew Bailey of the National Portrait Gallery, the staff of the 'Lit. & Phil.' in Newcastle upon Tyne, Adrian Waite of the Red Wyverns, Duncan Brown of EH Photo Library, Anthea Boylston and Jo Buckberry of Bradford University, Winnie Tyrell of Glasgow Museums, Rosie Serdiville of the Society of Antiquaries of Newcastle upon Tyne.

Lastly, and as ever, thanks are due to my wife Ruth for her unfailing patience and support. Any errors and omissions remain entirely the responsibility of the author.

John Sadler, Belsay, Northumberland

Publisher's Acknowledgements

We are grateful to the following for permission to reproduce copyright material:

Photographs in central plate sections by Adamskii Bespoke Photography; figures 1–6 © National Portrait Gallery, London.

In some instances we have been unable to trace the owners of copyright material, and we would appreciate any information that would enable us to do so.

List of Illustrations

Plates

(In central plate sections)

1. Towton Battlefield
2. Towton – 'Lord Dacre's Cross'
3. Hedgeley Moor Battlefield
4. Hedgeley Moor – *Percy's Leap*
5. Tewkesbury Abbey
6. Tewkesbury – the battlefield plaque
7. Tewkesbury Battlefield
8. Bosworth Battlefield
9. Bosworth Field
10. Bosworth – the view from Ambion Hill
11. Middleham Castle, Yorkshire
12. Middleham Castle, inside
13. Dunstanburgh Castle, Northumberland
14. Alnwick Castle, Northumberland
15. Bamburgh Castle, Northumberland
16. York Micklegate Bar

Figures

List of Maps

Abbreviations

'The Arrivall' 'The Historie of the Arrivall of King Edward IV in England and the Final Recoverye of his Kingdomes from Henry VI A.D. 1471' (ed. J. Bruce) Camden Society vol. 1 1838

Chastellain G. Chastellain, 'Chronique des derniers Ducs de Bourgogne' in *Panthéon Littéraire* vol. 4 Paris (n.d.)

Croyland 'Croyland Abbey Chronicle' (ed. H. T. Riley) 1854

Croyland Continuator 'The Croyland Chronicle Continuation 1459–1486' (ed. N. Pronay and J. Cox) Gloucester 1986

CS Camden Society

CSPM 'Calendar of State Papers and Manuscripts existing in the Archives and Collections of Milan' (ed. and trans. A. B. Hinds) 1912

Davies 'An English Chronicle of the Reigns of Richard II, Henry IV, Henry V and Henry VI' (ed. J. S. Davies) 1856

De Commynes Phillippe de Commynes, 'The Memoirs of the Reign of Louis XI 1461–1483' (trans. M. Jones) 1972

EH English Heritage

Fabyan Robert Fabyan, 'The New Chronicles of England and France' (ed. H. Ellis) London 1809

Froissart 'Froissart's Chronicles' (ed. G. Brereton) Harmondsworth 1968

GCL 'The Great Chronicle of London' (ed. A. H. Thomas and I. D. Thornley) London 1938

Gregory	William Gregory's Chronicle of London in 'Historical Collections of a Citizen of London in the Fifteenth Century' (ed. J. Gairdner) CS New Series vol. 17 1876
Hall	Edward Hall 'The Union of the Two Noble and Illustre Famelies of Lancastre and Yorke' 1548
KG	Knight of the Order of the Garter
London Chronicles	Chronicles of London (ed. C. L. Kingsford) Oxford 1905
Mancini	Mancini Dominic, 'The Usurpation of Richard III' (ed. C. A. J. Armstrong) Oxford 1969, reprinted Gloucester 1984
NCH	Northumberland County History
NPG	National Portrait Gallery
PL	'The Paston Letters 1422–1509' (ed. J. Gairdner) 3 vols. 1872–75
PV	'Three Books of Polydore Vergil's English History' (ed. H. Ellis) 1844
RA	Royal Armouries
Rose of Rouen	'Rose of Rouen', *Archaeologia* 29, pp. 344–7
RP	'Rotuli Pariamentorum' (ed. J. Strachey et al.) 6 vols 1767–77
SAM	Scheduled Ancient Monument
SS	Surtees Society
TNA	The National Archives
Warkworth	John Warkworth, 'A Chronicle of the First Thirteen Years of the Reign of Edward IV 1461–474' (ed. J. O. Halliwell) CS vol. 10 1839
Waurin	Jean de Waurin, 'Recueil des Chroniques D'Angleterre' (ed. W. Hardy and E. L. C. P. Hardy) 1891
Whethamstede	'Registrum Abbatis Johannis Whethamstede' in 'Registra quorandum Abbatum Monasterii S. Albani' (ed. H. Riley) 2 vols Rolls Series 1872–3
Worcester	William of Worcester, 'Annales Rerum Anglicarum' in 'Liber Niger Scaccarii' (ed. J. Hearne) 2 vols Oxford 1728
Year Book	The Year Book de Termino Paschae 4 Edward IV' in 'Priory of Hexham' SS vol. 1 1864

Timeline

1461 17 February, Second Battle of St Albans

1461 March, Earl of March proclaimed Edward IV

1461 29 March, Battle of Towton

1462 War in Northumberland; Lancastrians hold coastal fortresses; Berwick surrendered

1463 War in the North splutters on; castles surrender; Margaret of Anjou flees to France

1464 25 April, Battle of Hedgeley Moor; 14 May, Battle of Hexham; Montagu created Earl of Northumberland

1465 July, capture of Henry VI

1469 Warwick plots to overthrow Edward IV; The Duke of Clarence marries the Earl's daughter

1469 26 July, Battle of Edgecote

1469 Edward IV regains control

1470 12 March, Battle of 'Losecote Field' (Empingham)

1470 July, Warwick and Clarence in exile in France; the Earl comes to an agreement with Margaret of Anjou

1470 September, Edward and the Duke of Gloucester flee Warwick's coup

1471 March, return of Edward IV and Gloucester

1471 14 April, Battle of Barnet

1471 4 May, Battle of Tewkesbury/death of Henry VI; Gloucester assumes Warwick's offices as warden, begins his tenure in the north

1475 July, Edward IV launches French expedition

1478 February, killing of the Duke of Clarence

1482 Gloucester launches Scottish campaign, recovers Berwick and occupies Edinburgh

1483 April/June, death of Edward IV; Gloucester seizes power, eliminates the Woodvilles, executes Lord Hastings, assumes the throne; Edward V and the Duke of York (the Princes in the Tower) are confined

1483 October, the Duke of Buckingham's rebellion

1484 Richard III rules an uneasy realm

1485 August, landing of the Lancastrians under Henry Tudor; 22 August Battle of Bosworth

1487 16 June, Battle of Stoke

Dramatis Personae

Edmund Beaufort, [1st] 2nd Duke of Somerset (1406–1455)   4th son of John Beaufort, the 1st Earl; he was involved in the French wars and the recapture of Harfleur, KG in 1436, Earl of Dorset 1442, then a year later Marquess and, in 1444, succeeded his father as 4th Earl. After Suffolk's removal and murder he became leader of the Lancastrian faction at court, handsome and urbane (he was rumoured to have had a clandestine affair with Queen Katherine in 1427) he was, nonetheless, totally unscrupulous. Killed at First St Albans, on 22 May 1455.

Edmund Beaufort, titular 4th Duke of Somerset (1438–1471) younger brother of the 3rd Duke, led the Lancastrians in the campaign and Battle of Tewkesbury, taken from sanctuary and beheaded the day after the defeat.

Henry Beaufort, 3rd Duke of Somerset (1436–1464)   previously Earl of Dorset; wounded at First St Albans, a prime mover in the Lancastrian revival after the constitutional settlement of 1460, he fought at Wakefield and Second St Albans, where his generalship proved superior. Defeated at Towton, he maintained the war in the north and though he capitulated in 1463, reverted the following year and was executed after the debacle at Hexham.

Thomas Bourchier (1404–1486)   younger son of William Bourchier, Count of Eu and Anne of Gloucester (half brother to Humphrey Stafford, 1st Duke of Buckingham); educated at Oxford, Thomas entered the Church, where he rose with dizzying rapidity; Bishop of Worcester in 1434, of Ely in 1443 and finally Archbishop of Canterbury in 1454. At first he was neutral in the wars, inclining to the court, though an advocate for peace. After 1459, however, he became a Yorkist partisan and went on to crown

Edward IV and Elizabeth Woodville (he became Gloucester's emissary for the surrender of the young Duke of York in 1483), and he then crowned the usurping Richard III before an effortless transition to the Tudor camp, crowning Henry VII.

William Catesby (1450–1485) one of Richard III's loyal adherents, vilified in the famous doggerel, a lawyer and leading figure in Parliament, he was executed at Leicester, two days after Bosworth.

George, Duke of Clarence (1449–1478) sixth son of Richard of York and Cicely Neville, one of four to reach maturity, elevated to his dukedom in 1461, married Warwick's elder daughter and joined in the conspiracies of 1469–70. He reverted to his allegiance prior to Barnet but was eventually 'privately' executed in 1478. Brilliant and charismatic, he was also unstable, jealous and treacherous.

Sir William Conyers of Marske (d. 1469) he, with his brother Sir John, were firmly of the Earl of Warwick's affinity, centred on his great power base of Middleham. It is possible that Sir William was the true 'Robin of Redesdale' or 'Robin Mend-all'. He led the rebel forces that confronted the Herbert brothers at Edgecote and perished in the melee.

John de Clifford, 9th Baron Clifford (1435–1461) a long-established family, holding the lordships of Appleby and Skipton. After his father, Thomas de Clifford, the 8th Baron (1414–1455) was killed at the First Battle of St Albans, Clifford became a savage paladin of the House of Lancaster. He fought at Wakefield and is credited with the slaying of Richard, Duke of York's second son, Edmund, Earl of Rutland. He was, in turn, killed in the skirmish at Dintingdale prior to the Battle of Towton, and his followers, 'The Flower of Craven', were decimated around him.

John de La Pole, Earl of Lincoln (1464–1487) a nephew of Edward IV, son of Elizabeth Plantagenet and John de la Pole, who held a number of high offices in the Yorkist administration of the 1480s. After the death of Edward of Middleham, Richard III's only son, in 1484, he became heir-presumptive. Subsequently he engineered the Lambert Simnel conspiracy and fell in the defeat at Stoke.

John de la Pole, 2nd Duke of Suffolk (1442–1491) son of the 1st Duke, and first husband of Margaret Beaufort (she did not recognise the marriage, which was annulled by Henry VI in 1453), brother-in-law of Edward IV and father of the Earl of Lincoln. Though he fought for York at First St Albans, he remained largely inactive thereafter.

William de la Pole, 1st Duke of Suffolk (1396–1450) one of Henry VI's chief ministers and blamed for the loss of the French territories, subsequently impeached and murdered whilst attempting to quit the realm. He was the second son of the 2nd Earl, Michael de la Pole; his older brother (Michael) fell at Agincourt. William became 4th Earl, later Marquess and 1st Duke. He held joint command at Orleans after the death of Salisbury.

John de Vere, 12th Earl of Oxford (*c*.1408–1462) a Lancastrian by sentiment, did not fight at First St Albans, arriving a day late, and was executed in 1462 for alleged plotting against Edward IV.

John de Vere, 13th Earl of Oxford (1443–1513) a dedicated Lancastrian and something of a swashbuckler, he took Mont St Michel in a daring coup de main and held it through an embarrassingly long siege. Imprisoned on his surrender at Hammes, he was able to join with Henry Tudor and was instrumental in the victory. He also led the van successfully at Stoke, two years later.

Duke Humphrey of Gloucester (1390–1447) youngest son of Henry IV and something of a quixotic character; able enough in arms under his brother Henry V, he became the leader of the 'War' faction during the minority of Henry VI. At odds with Cardinal Beaufort and the 'Peace' faction, he met his death in suspicious circumstances.

Thomas Grey, Marquess of Dorset (1451–1501) Elizabeth Woodville's son by her first, Lancastrian, husband, remained loyal to Edward IV. He competed with Lord Hastings for the affections of a number of mistresses, including the celebrated Jane Shore. After the usurpation of Richard III he fled to join Henry Tudor, but his loyalty was never certain.

William, Lord Hastings (*c*.1430–1483) a stalwart Yorkist, he fought at Towton, Barnet and Tewkesbury, in the latter two engagements commanding a wing of Edward IV's army. He was a favourite crony of the King, Lieutenant of Calais and much disliked by the Woodville faction. A staunch ally of Gloucester, after Edward's death, it may have been his doubts as to the Duke's intentions that led to his summary execution.

Sir William Herbert, Earl of Pembroke (d. 1469) Herbert was a partisan of Edward IV. A Marcher lord in Usk and Caerleon, his elevation to the earldom in 1468 was a slap for Warwick, with whom he clashed. His difficult temperament led to the row which weakened the King's army before Edgecote and, after the fight both he and his brother Sir Richard Herbert were executed on Warwick's orders.

Henry VI of England (1422–1471) came to the throne as a minor on the death of his father Henry V, his reign witnessed the steady decline of English fortunes in France and a growing crisis at home. He married Margaret of Anjou in 1445 and was captured by the Yorkists after 1465, briefly reoccupying the throne during the 'Re-adoption' engineered by Warwick. He was killed in 1471, whilst a captive in the Tower, after the Battle of Tewkesbury.

Henry VII of England (1457–1509) son of Edmund Tudor, Earl of Richmond and Lady Margaret Beaufort, nephew to Jasper Tudor, Earl of Pembroke; was a leading Welsh Lancastrian. His claim to inherit the mantle of the House of Lancaster was more expedient than real.

Henry Holand, 3rd Duke of Exeter (d. 1475) despite his wedding to one of York's daughters he came to be implicated in the disturbances of 1453 as a partisan of the Percies. He fought at Blore Heath, Wakefield, Second St Albans, Towton and Barnet, where he was left for dead on the field but escaped (his Yorkist wife had abandoned him, some time before!). He escaped to the Continent, where he was reduced to beggary, though he met his end as a prisoner in the Tower in dubious circumstances.

Lord John Howard, Duke of Norfolk (1430–1485) a dedicated Yorkist, he fought at Towton and rose to Earl Marshall in 1483; loyal supporter of Richard III, he fell leading the Yorkist van at Bosworth. His son Sir Thomas Howard (d. 1524) was likewise unshakeable in his affinity. He fought at Barnet and became Earl of Surrey in 1483. Under a cloud and imprisoned after Bosworth, he was rehabilitated and regained his estates, a loyal councillor to both Henry VII and his son. At the age of 70 he scored his greatest triumph when he led an English army to an overwhelming victory against the Scots at Flodden in September 1513.

Edward of Lancaster (1453–1471) only child of Henry VI and Margaret of Anjou (some questions were asked as to his legitimacy). He was raised in exile in readiness for an attempt to recover his father's throne. Allied to the Kingmaker, by marriage to a younger daughter, his chance came, and went, together with his life, at Tewkesbury.

Francis Lovell, 9th Baron, 1st Viscount Lovell (144?–1487) a key figure in the administration of Richard III, he survived Bosworth and joined in the Lambert Simnel conspiracy. He was said to have met his end after the disaster at Stoke, possibly drowned or, even more mysteriously, dying of starvation in a hidden cellar of his property at Minster Lovell. Less prosaically, we know from the Scottish Treasury Calendars that he was in Scotland during 1488!

Edward, Earl of March (1442–1483), King of England 1461–1470 and 1471–1483 'The Sunne in Splendour', eldest son of the Duke of York and Cicely Neville, ('The Rose of Raby'), victor of Mortimer's Cross, Towton, Empingham, Barnet and Tewkesbury. He secretly married Elizabeth Woodville on 1 May 1464. Courageous on the field, with a flair for both strategy and tactics, he was rightly regarded as the leading captain of his day.

Margaret of Anjou (1429–1482) daughter of the impecunious Rene I of Sicily, Duke of Anjou, King of Naples and Sicily; married to Henry VI of England at the age of 15. Beautiful and vivacious, she was strong minded and with her favourite, the Duke of Somerset, dominated the Lancastrian court faction and, until 1463, was the mainspring of resistance in the north, where she had been prepared to swap the twin bastions of Berwick-upon-Tweed and Carlisle in return for Scottish arms. She was kept in the Tower after the disaster at Tewkesbury until finally being released in 1475. She spent her final years in Anjou.

John Mowbray, 3rd Duke of Norfolk (1415–1461) it was Norfolk's arrival on the field of Towton, at the eleventh hour, which turned the tide, he was already terminally ill at this point. York's nephew, he had previously fought at First St Albans.

George Neville (d. 1476) brother of John, Thomas and Richard, entered holy orders and became Bishop of Exeter and then Archbishop of York, sided with his brother in the rising against Edward IV in 1469. The Archbishop appeared in full harness on presenting himself before the king as the latter was, effectively captured.

John Neville, Lord Montagu (d. 1471) the Earl of Warwick's younger brother, an able soldier and administrator, principal architect of the Yorkist victory in the north from 1461–64. Temporarily installed as Earl of Northumberland, he was later stripped of the title and, though partly compensated, joined his brother in the coup of 1470, dying with him at Barnet.

Richard Neville, Earl of Salisbury (1400–1460) younger son of the Earl of Westmorland, his mother was Joan de Beaufort and he married Alice Montacute, Countess of Salisbury. KG in 1438, he received the lesser share of the family estates on the east side of the Pennines. In addition to his feud with the Percies he was at odds with the senior branch of the Nevilles (from west of the hills). Brother-in-law to the Duke of York, he was active in Yorkist councils and a senior statesman in the cause; killed after Wakefield with one of his sons Sir Thomas Neville (d. 1460), whose marriage to Maud Stanhope fanned the flames of the Percy–Neville feud.

Richard Neville, Earl of Warwick (1428–1471) known as 'The Kingmaker', mightiest of the 'overmighty subjects' and a pivotal figure in the period. He was Salisbury's eldest son and York's nephew; married a daughter of the de Beauchamp Earl of Warwick. He fought at First St Albans, Northampton, Second St Albans and Towton. Seeing himself as the power behind the throne, he was increasingly alienated from Edward IV, following the Woodville marriage. His final manipulation led to the 'Re-adeption' of Henry VI in the coup of 1470. He, with his brother Lord Montagu, was killed at Barnet in the following spring.

Thomas Neville, 'Bastard' of Fauconberg (d. 1471) Fauconberg's illegitimate son, something of a swashbuckler and buccaneer, awarded the freedom of the City of London in 1454 for his actions against pirates in the Channel. Following Warwick's switch of allegiance, he was active on the Lancastrian side in 1471 and, though pardoned, suffered execution later in that year.

William Neville, Lord Fauconberg (*c.*1410–1463) younger son of Ralph, Earl of Westmorland, brother of the Earl of Salisbury, and a veteran of the French Wars. Knighted in 1426, castellan of Roxburgh, KG 1440, captured in 1449 and subsequently ransomed, he, like York, was owed substantial sums by the crown. Though a staunch Lancastrian prior to 1455, he successfully led the Yorkist van at Northampton and Towton, acquired his title by right of his wife (who lacked mental capacity), became Earl of Kent and Lord Admiral.

Henry Percy, 2nd Earl of Northumberland (d. 1455) son of the famous Henry Percy ('Hotspur') killed at Shrewsbury in 1403. He gradually clawed back the family lands after his father's attainder; involved in the rivalry with the Nevilles and killed at First St Albans.

Henry Percy, Lord Poynings, later 3rd Earl of Northumberland (d. 1461) Border Warden after his father, he was one of the leading northern Lancastrians, fighting at Wakefield, Second St Albans and Towton, where he fell. The title was, once again attainted after his death, passing to John Neville, Lord Montagu. Edward IV subsequently restored his son, who became the 4th Earl. A far slipperier character than his father, determined to be on the winning side. He appeared to work well with Richard III, as Duke of Gloucester from 1471–83, though his role at Bosworth was ambivalent. He flourished briefly under Henry VII but was murdered by a mob protesting over taxation near Thirsk.

Sir Ralph Percy (d. 1464) Margaret of Anjou's champion in the North from 1461 to 1464, though prone to switching allegiance; he reverted to Lancaster for the last time before the rout at Hedgeley Moor, where he died fighting.

Thomas Percy, Lord Egremont (1422–1460) younger son of the 2nd Earl of Northumberland, created Lord Egremont in 1445, violent and thuggish; an actor in the Percy–Neville feud of the early 1450s. He was killed at Northampton.

Humphrey Stafford, 1st Duke of Buckingham (1402–1460) married to York's sister Anne, perceived as a peacemaker, champion of the 'Loveday' accord, fought at First St Albans and died at Northampton. He was the son of Edmund Stafford, 5th Earl of Buckingham, and Anne of Gloucester, a granddaughter of Edward III. Knighted 1421, KG 1429, active on the Royal Council from 1429, served extensively and with distinction in France, created Duke in 1444.

Henry Stafford, 2nd Duke of Buckingham (1454?–1483) married, against his will, to one of Elizabeth Woodville's seemingly endless line of sisters, he became a prime mover in the counsels of the Duke of Gloucester leading up to and during the usurpation. Disappointed, he later rebelled, a still-born affair, leading to his execution.

Thomas, Lord Stanley, Earl of Derby (1435–1504) fourth husband of Margaret Beaufort and a leading magnate in the north-west, he at first served but, at Bosworth, betrayed Richard III, his intervention being decisive in the King's defeat, a defection which earned him a peerage.

Sir William Stanley (d. 1495) younger brother of Thomas, led the Stanley affinity into the fight at Bosworth; an inveterate plotter, he later conspired against Henry VII and was subsequently beheaded; famed as 'the richest commoner in England'.

John Tiptoft, Earl of Worcester (d. 1470) held the office of Constable of England 1462–1467 and again in 1470, noted both for his extensive literary tastes, his outstanding library and his severity. He was universally reviled, and Warwick had him executed in 1470, primarily as a sop to widespread clamour.

Sir Andrew Trollope (d. 1461)   successful soldier who fought in the French Wars, appointed as Master Porter of Calais, and acted at first as an advisor to York; his defection provoked the collapse of morale and subsequent 'Rout' of Ludford. He may have been instrumental in the Lancastrians' winning tactics at Wakefield and fought with distinction at Second St Albans. His luck finally ran out at Towton.

Edmund Tudor, Earl of Richmond (1430–1456)   the son of Owen Tudor (d. 1461, executed after Mortimer's Cross), and Katherine of Valois, widow of Henry V; he married the formidable Margaret Beaufort and fathered Henry Tudor, the future Henry VII, before succumbing to a bout of the plague.

Jasper Tudor, Earl of Pembroke (1431–1495)   brother of Edmund, a diehard Lancastrian, he fought at First St Albans and Mortimer's Cross but avoided Towton. After an unsuccessful attempt to relieve Harlech, he fled in 1468 to Brittany. After Bosworth subsequently married Buckingham's Woodville widow.

Lord Wenlock (c.1400–1471)   a venerable survivor of the French wars, he proved a steadfast Yorkist, fighting at Mortimer's Cross and Towton. He, nonetheless, supported Warwick in 1470 and survived to be killed at Tewkesbury, possibly felled by Somerset himself in a fit of suspicion.

Anthony Woodville, 2nd Earl Rivers (1442–1483)   brother of Queen Elizabeth Woodville, he fought for his brother-in-law with some distinction at both Barnet and Tewkesbury, notable in the lists and something of a poet. He was a victim of Richard of Gloucester's coup in 1483. Despite early reassurances from his brother-in-law, he was subsequently and summarily executed.

Queen Elizabeth Woodville (1437–1492)   married to the Lancastrian knight Sir John Grey of Groby, and then widowed; Edward IV married her in secret to the great consternation of his supporters, most particularly Warwick, who had been seeking to broker a French alliance. Noted for her ruthless avarice and rapacity, her family were excoriated for their shameless greed.

Richard Woodville, 1st Earl Rivers (d. 1469)   Elizabeth's father, married to Jacquetta of Luxembourg, widow of the Earl of Bedford, Henry V's brother and regent after his death. Initially an adherent of Lancaster, fighting at Towton, he held high office under his son-in-law, earning the powerful enmity of the Earl of Warwick, who had him executed after the defeat at Edgecote.

Elizabeth of York (1466–1503) eldest daughter of Edward IV and Elizabeth Woodville, possibly pursued by her uncle, Richard III, after his widowhood, she eventually married Henry Tudor, thus effecting the symbolic union of Lancaster and York.

Margaret of York, Duchess of Burgundy (1446–1503) sister of Edward IV, she was married to the quixotic Charles the Bold, Duke of Burgundy (d. 1477); she remained a Yorkist intermeddler after the death of her brother at Bosworth.

Richard, 3rd Duke of York (1411–1460) the senior member of the Yorkist faction, with a strong claim to the throne, active in the later stages of the French wars, a bitter opponent of Somerset. He was Lord Protector on two occasions, claimed the throne in 1460 and was killed at Wakefield at the end of that year.

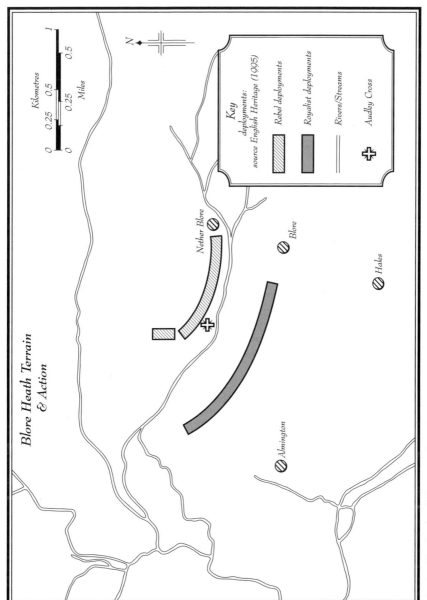

Blore Heath Terrain & Action

Key

deployments:
source English Heritage (1995)

▨ Rebel deployments

▬ Royalist deployments

| Rivers/Streams

✠ Audley Cross

Kilometres
0   0.25   0.5   0.5   1

Miles
0   0.25   0.5

N

Nether Blore

Blore

Hales

Almington

Map 1: The Battle of Blore Heath, 1459

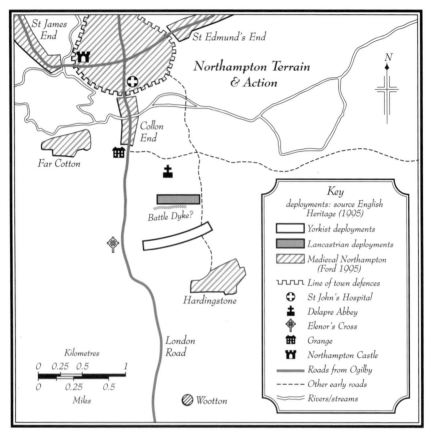

Map 2: The Battle of Northampton, 1460

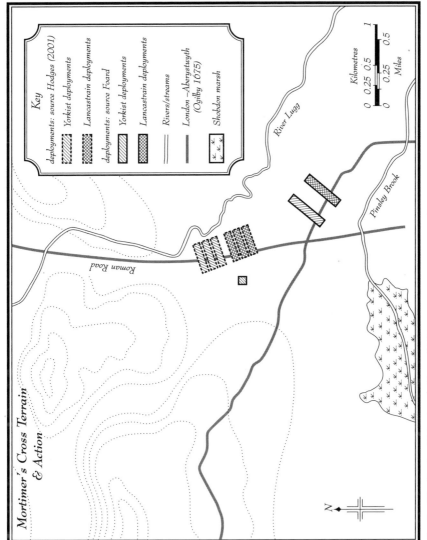

Map 3: The Battle of Mortimer's Cross, 1461

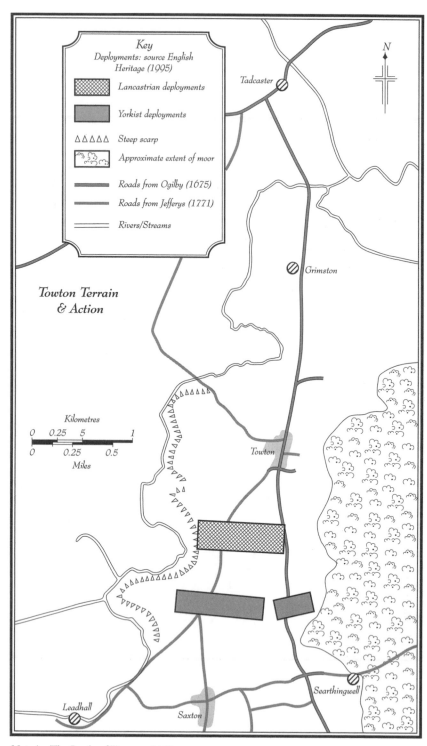

Map 4: The Battle of Towton, 1461

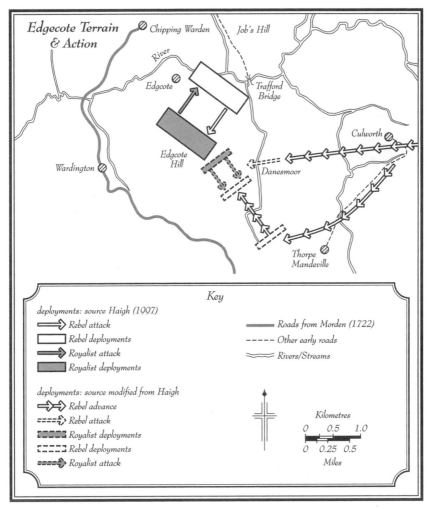

Map 5: The Battle of Edgecote, 1469

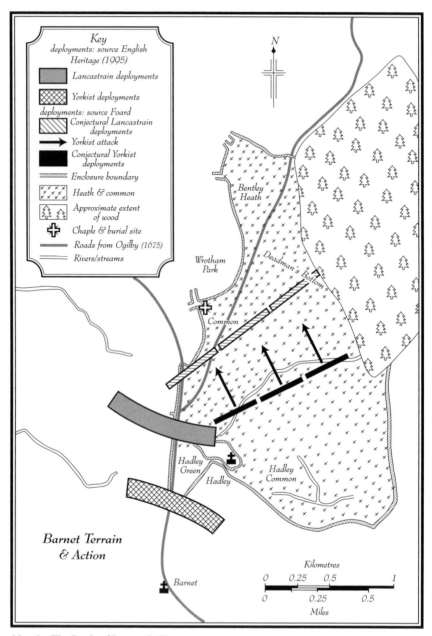

N

Bentley
Heath

Wrotham
Park

Deadman's Bottom

Common

Hadley
Green

Hadley

Hadley
Common

Barnet Terrain
& Action

Barnet

Kilometres

0   0.25   0.5   1

0   0.25   0.5

Miles

Map 6: The Battle of Barnet, 1471

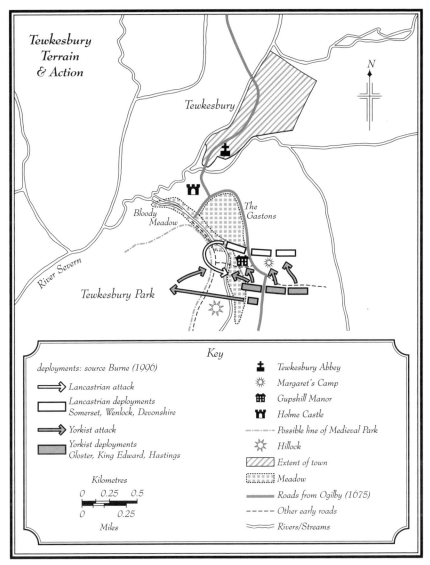

Map 7: The Battle of Tewkesbury, 1471

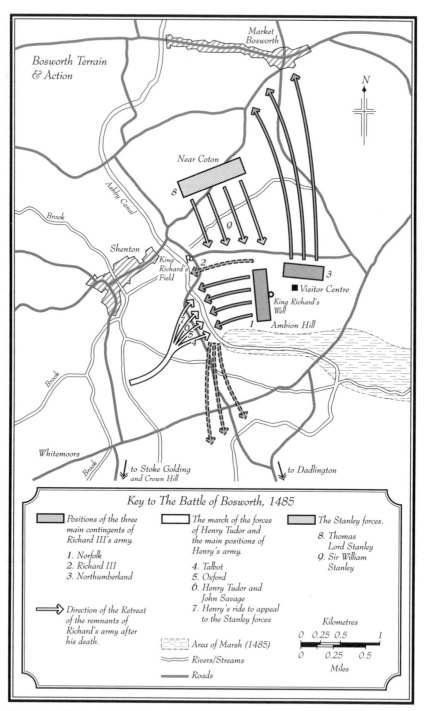

Map 8:   The Battle of Bosworth, 1485

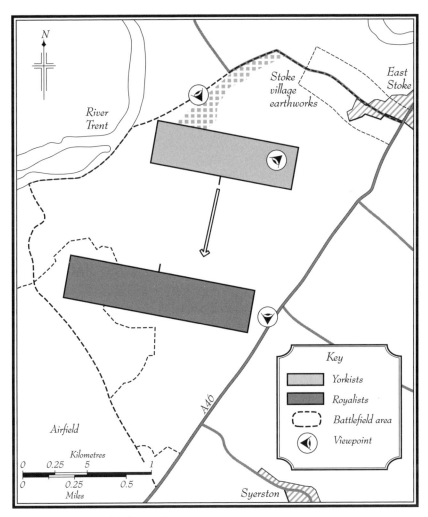

N

River
Trent

Stoke
village
earthworks

East
Stoke

Key

Yorkists

Royalists

Battlefield area

Viewpoint

A46

Airfield

Kilometres
0   0.25   5   1

0   0.25   0.5
        Miles

Syerston

Map 9:   The Battle of Stoke, 1487

Being Introductory

The reader may ask why it is necessary to have yet another book on the Wars of the Roses; many excellent studies already exist: Gillingham, Lander, Carpenter, Pollard and Haigh, to name but several. The mere fact that the present writer has a fascination with the subject cannot be sufficient warrant. Most aspects have been explored and, in many ways, there is little new to say; save for this writer's explanation of the Battle of Hexham, which differs significantly from the conventional interpretation, there is little that has not appeared before. One of the author's prime objectives has been to provide an account of the whole period which is accessible to the general reader, to the military historian, and to the reader who may wish to walk the ground of some or all of the battles.

Martin Bell, writing in 2003, *Through Gates of Fire*, asserts there are only two categories of war in the twenty-first century, one of these being 'wars of collapsed states'. The Wars of the Roses (and here I adopt the convention of bundling the range of dynastic conflicts from 1453 to 1487 into one generic band) could be said to represent a war of this sort. A series of linked campaigns of civil discord, which arose primarily because of the failure of the Lancastrian dynasty and the particualar incapacity of Henry VI. One must always be wary of pushing the contemporary analogy too far, but there are parallels.

My purpose therefore is to provide a coherent narrative of the military campaigns, beginning with disturbances in the north in 1453, the initial, deadly, clash at First St Albans two years later, and the spates of open warfare which followed: 1460–64, 1469–71, 1485, and 1487. For these to be understood it is necessary to support the account of military matters with a political and social framework; we need to understand not only how men performed on the field but what it was that brought them there. For the same reason I have included, as an opening chapter, an account of the art of war in the mid fifteenth century; a fascinating subject in itself and one which is essential for the reader to gain a true understanding of how battles were fought, by whom, employing what strategic/tactical doctrines, and the level of weapons technology which obtained at the time.

A Glossary on pages 278–81 explains some possibly unfamiliar terms.

Chapter 1

The Art of War in the Fifteenth Century

Arguably the first clash in the series of dynastic conflicts later to be described as the Wars of the Roses occurred in 1453 when the Percies prepared an ambush for the Neville affinity attending the wedding of Sir Thomas Neville.[1] First blood was not properly shed until the First Battle of St Albans in May 1455 and much of that was gentle; in civil war, traitors carry no promise of ransom.

> *King Edward told me that in all the battles which he had won, as soon as he had gained victory, he mounted his horse and shouted to his men that they must spare the common soldiers and kill the lords of which none or few escaped.*[2]

In the long bloody Battle of Towton, the Lancastrians, as their army disintegrated, suffered very badly. John, Lord Clifford, 'the Butcher' had been killed in the skirmish at Dintingdale the day before; Northumberland, Lord Dacre of Gilsland and Sir Andrew Trollope, fell on the field. With the rotting skulls of their own families grinning down from Micklegate Bar it is no wonder that the Yorkists were unmoved by notions of chivalry.[3]

Raising Armies

In order to provide a reliable supply of trained fighting men, Edward III had developed the contract system, whereby the monarch, as commander-in-chief, entered into formal engagements and indentured contracts in writing with experienced captains, who were then bound to provide an agreed number of men at established rates for a given period. The protracted and wide-ranging campaigns in France made the reputations of famous captains, such as Robert Knollys and John Chandos. Frequently it was the magnates who acted as main contractors, sub-contracting knights, men at arms and archers in turn.[4] To what extent the end of the French wars and the dashing of final hopes, with the consequential glut of unemployed men at arms, fuelled the rise of magnatial thuggery, remains questionable. It is certain, however, that a swelling reservoir of trained manpower offered recruits to gentry affinities. The provision of indentures and annuities was, it appears, also employed by lords to bind their retainers. Humphrey Stafford, 1st Duke of Buckingham, killed at Northampton in 1460, had 10 knights and 27 esquires in his service. One of the former, Sir Edward Grey, was granted a life annuity of £40 in 1440. Those further down the social scale might receive annual emoluments of £10–£20.[5]

In addition to his professional retainers the lord could call out his tenantry, many of whom might also have military experience. To these he might add, if numbers were sought, a following of masterless men happy to have the protection of a great man's livery. A surviving indenture, dating from 1452, and entered into by the Earl of Salisbury and his tenant Walter Strickland, knight of Westmorland, lists the complement which Sir Walter was to muster: billmen – 'horsed and harnessed', 74; mounted bowmen to the number of 69; dismounted billmen 76; with 71 foot archers – an impressive total of 290.[6] Archers, in most companies were still the predominant arm, outnumbering bills by anything between 3 to 1 and 10 to 1.

When Sir John Paston was preparing to sail for Calais, he begged that his brother recruit 4 archers: 'Likely men and fair conditioned and good archers and they shall have four marks by year and my livery'.[7] In short, these were to be permanent retainers, paid an annual wage. A particularly skilled archer belonging to a lord's household might command equal remuneration to a knight. In 1475 Edward IV was raising an army to intimidate France, and the great magnates each contributed to his muster as follows:

- Duke of Clarence: 10 knights, 1,000 archers
- Duke of Gloucester: 10 knights, 1,000 archers
- Duke of Norfolk: 2 knights, 300 archers
- Duke of Suffolk: 2 knights, 300 archers
- Duke of Buckingham: 4 knights, 400 archers.[8]

The king still had the capacity to issue what were termed 'Commissions of Array', which empowered his officers to call up local militias who, in theory at least, were to be the best armed and accoutred men from each village in the county. This system, though time honoured, was much open to abuse. The antics of Falstaff provide a comic parody.[9] Contemporary letters from the Stonor correspondence, relating to the Oxfordshire half hundred of Ewelme, comprising some 17 villages in the county, show that the catchment yielded 85 recruits, 17 of whom were archers. The village of Ewelme itself provided 6:

> Richard Slyhurst, a harness and able to do the King service with his bow, Thomas Staunton [the constable] John Hume, whole harness and both able to do the King service with a bill. John Tanner, a harness and able to do the King service with a bill. John Pallying, a harness and not able to wear it, Roger Smith, no harness, an able man and a good archer.

Those without any armour are described as 'able with a staff'.[10]

Surviving muster rolls from the period also provide an insight into the local levy. One held at Bridport in Dorset on the 4 September 1457, before the King's officers, reveals that a man was expected to possess a sallet, jack, sword, buckler and dagger. Of those on parade that day around two thirds carried bows and had arrows. Other weapons on show included poleaxes, glaives, bills, spears and axes, staves and harness.[11] Dominic Mancini has left us a vivid, eyewitness account of the appearance of the troops that Gloucester and Buckingham brought into London in 1483 to provide encouragement for any citizen who might be tempted to think of resisting the usurpation:

> There is hardly any without a helmet, and none without bows and arrows; their bows and arrows are thicker and longer than those used by other

nations, just as their bodies are stronger than other peoples, for they seem to have hands and arms of iron. The range of their bows is no less than that of our arbalests; there hangs by the side of each a sword no less long than ours, but heavy and thick as well. The sword is always accompanied by an iron shield . . . they do not wear any metal armour on their breast or any other part of their body, except for the better sort who have breastplates and suits of armour. Indeed the common soldiery have more comfortable tunics that reach down below the loins and are stuffed with tow or some other soft material. They say the softer the tunics the better do they withstand the blows of arrows and swords, and besides that in summer they are lighter and in winter more serviceable than iron.[12]

Attitudes to War

Civil wars do not promote chivalric conduct, vendettas tend to mar fair play, and the decline in knightly values was much bemoaned by contemporary chroniclers, though vestiges persisted. In his work 'Le Jouvencel' the chronicler Jean le Beuil, writing around 1466, gives an insight into the mind of the fifteenth-century gentleman:

What a joyous thing is war, for many fine deeds are seen in its course, and many good lessons learnt from it . . . You love your comrade so much in war. When you see that your quarrel is just and your blood is fighting well, tears rise in your eyes. A great sweet feeling of loyalty and pity fills your heart on seeing your friend so valiantly expose his body to execute and accomplish the command of our Creator. And then you prepare to go and live or die with him, and for love not abandon him. And out of that there arise such a delectation, that he who has not tasted it is not fit to say what a delight is. Do you think that a man who does that fears death? Not at all; for he feels strengthened, he is so elated, that he does not know where he is. Truly, he is afraid of nothing.[13]

Fine sentiments indeed, but the list of slaughters which accompanied battles or which mired the wrack of defeat does not bear this out. The thirst for revenge, fear, greed and sheer expediency were all powerful realities. Salisbury was handed to the mob, or so it appears, after Wakefield and, in the same battle, his nephew Rutland was murderously slain by Clifford. Battles, such as Hexham and Tewkesbury, were immediately followed by a savage round of executions. At Shrewsbury in 1403 the English had discovered what it was like to be on the receiving end of the missile storm. During the Wars of the Roses both sides employed the longbow, and many battles opened with an archery duel; as a consequence, casualties would be high, and it was usually the side which fared worst in the opening exchanges that first advanced to contact. The armourer's art may have developed to a point where good quality harness could deflect a clothyard shaft, but the commons, relying on jacks, were less protected. At Stoke in 1487 the Earl of Lincoln's Irish, ill-harnessed kerns were shot down in droves.[14]

Improved armour did not render a knight invulnerable. When Lord Clifford unwisely removed his bevor to gulp water in the extended skirmish at Dintingdale he was pierced through the throat. A similar fate befell Lord Dacre. It has been estimated, again with reference to Palmsunday Field that, if each archer loosed four dozen arrows, then over a million shafts with a gross weight of 40 tons fell across the field.[15] In all probability archers, like billmen, remained posted with their own companies, rather than being formed into a separate arm. Most likely, at the start of the fight, all would advance a few paces from the line to shoot, and then retake their places for the melee which was bound to follow. As a contemporary chronicler observed: 'After the third or fourth, or at the very most the sixth draw of the bow, men knew which side would win.'[16]

Strategy

Strategy tended to be based purely upon the offensive. Conversely, tactics often assumed the defensive. Command was most frequently exercised by the magnates themselves: York at St Albans and Wakefield, Warwick at Second St Albans and Barnet, Henry Beaufort 3rd Duke Somerset at Wakefield, Second St Albans, Towton and Hexham. Divisional commanders would often be family or high-ranking members of the commander-in-chief's affinity. Thus Richard of Gloucester commanding a wing of his brother's forces at Barnet and Tewkesbury; Oxford and Exeter leading divisions of Warwick's army at Barnet. Commanders might and did rely upon the advice of seasoned professionals such as Sir Andrew Trollope. Though many of the older generation of protagonists, such as York, 2nd Duke of Somerset, Buckingham and Fauconberg, had seen service in the French wars, their sons and successors, for the most part, had not.

Campaigns were of short duration, avoiding the need to keep forces vict-ualled and in the field through the harshness of winter. Commanders tended to seek a decisive encounter, rarely was the offer of battle refused (Warwick at Coventry in 1471 is an obvious if rare exception). When one side faced hopeless odds, the temptation was simply to flee the realm – as did the Yorkist leaders after Ludford Bridge, Warwick and Clarence after Empingham and Edward IV in 1470. As Professor Hicks points out, in each case the exiles made a successful return bid. To force the issue, then, was the preferred course. Once strong forces were in the field, attempts at mediation invari-ably foundered. If a ruling monarch was unable to prevent his enemies from effecting a lodgement, then it was essential to move quickly to destroy his forces before he could recruit sufficient contingents: thus Richard III has-tens to confront Henry Tudor. Major field engagements therefore dominate the course of the conflicts; long sieges (Harlech being an exception here, and the sieges of the Northumbrian Castles 1461–3), are rare; territory is not held or ceded, manoeuvre to contact is far more the norm. Where a magnate raised the flag of rebellion he would seek to confront the reigning monarch in the field before the forces owing loyalty to the Crown might be fully mustered. Thus Warwick hastens to bring the army of Henry VI to a decisive moment at Northampton before the northern Lancastrians could add their strength to the muster.

Grand Tactics

Subtlety is lacking. In the majority of campaigns the two sides simply square up: Somerset's flanking manoeuvre before Second St Albans evidences a rare degree of strategic and tactical innovation. To stake all on the outcome of a single battle is a high-risk strategy. Once forces are committed on the field, the commander has little prospect of decisively influencing events. The soundest of tactics can be undone by the fog of war – Edmund Beaufort at Tewkesbury, and a want of intelligence as to the numbers arrayed against could lead to disaster. York's end at Wakefield being a salutary lesson.

Knights and men-at-arms dismounted to fight on foot, horses were sent to the rear, to be mounted only when the enemy was in rout;[17] pursuit of the beaten foe was rigorous and merciless, the slaughter indiscriminate. A wealthy captive in the French wars could be the making of a yeoman's fortune but a lord whose lands stood to be attainted by the victors had no commercial value. Personal animosities were a constant factor; even in victory, Edward IV and his supporters would have seen the ghastly remains of their relatives. Fixed on high, as they rode in triumph into York. Hobilars or light horsemen, sometimes called 'prickers', were deployed for scouting and vedette work. But, once battle was joined, a commander could exercise little direct control. Armies were still marshalled into three divisions or 'battles': the van, or vaward, main battle and rear or rearward. Deployment was in linear formation, knights and men-at-arms dismounted and ready, archers moving to the fore to shoot, all beneath the banner of captain or lord.

Battle was a most hazardous enterprise. In the fifteenth century a commander had limited forces at his disposal, a single, significant defeat in the field would likely ruin his cause and not infrequently his person. Defeated generals fared badly in the Wars of the Roses (Somerset at First St Albans, York at Wakefield, Northumberland at Towton, the younger Somerset at Hexham, his brother at Tewkesbury, Warwick at Barnet, Richard III at Bosworth, and Lincoln at Stoke). Communications were dependent upon flags, supply and victualling a constant headache, and the spectre of treachery as omnipresent as Banquo's ghost.

With the impetus and fury of the opening arrow storm, both sides would tend to move swiftly forward to contact but, on several occasions, such as Salisbury's stand at Blore Heath, defensive tactics worked well. Warwick's complex network of defences proved to be a veritable Maginot Line at Second St Albans, and the Lancastrian entrenchments at Northampton failed miserably primarily, it has to be said, due to treachery abetted by adverse weather. Treachery and subornment were the random cards that could wreck any strategy: Lord Grey at Northampton and Trollope's defection at Ludford Bridge precipitated a rout in each case. Warwick chose to blame the disaster at Second St Albans on the treachery of his Kentish captain, Lovelace; 'False Perjured Clarence' betrayed first his brother, then his father-in-law.

Good intelligence was, as always, vital – all armies fielded scouts or 'scourers' – and bad intelligence, such as York's failure before committing to battle at Wakefield, could prove fatal. Once the decision to engage in battle was taken and the army marshalled accordingly, it was a most difficult business to reverse. In the dangerous game of cat and mouse which unfolded during the Tewkesbury campaign, Margaret of Anjou several times avoided contact, leaving the army of Edward IV drawn up in battle array, but without an enemy in sight! The King also had his scouts, however, and by dint of gruelling marches in the heavy heat, followed by a dash through the short spring night, he succeeded in frustrating the Lancastrian attempt to cross the Severn at Gloucester, and brought Somerset to bay at Tewkesbury.

Although armies deployed in line with opposing divisions aligned, this neat arrangement could go awry, depending upon weather and terrain – as in the fog of Barnet. A commander with a good eye for ground might try to deploy an ambush party for a flank attack: Somerset attempted this at Towton, and Edward the same at Tewkesbury. Such tactics were not new: the Scottish flanking move at Otterburn in 1388 had proved decisive, as had Prince Henry's attack at Shrewsbury fifteen years later.

Late-medieval captains were, for the most part, literate and familiar with the tenets of their trade. Many, if not most, would have read the classical authors, such as the late-Roman theorist Vegetius, whose *Epitoma Rei Militaris* was revised in the fifteenth century by Christine de Pisan. She also wrote the *Livre des fais d'armes et de chevalerie,* subsequently translated and popularised by Caxton as *The Book of the Fayttes of Armes and Chyvalrye*. At this time the continental system of 'lances' was not popular in England. Companies were led by captains and formed up according to their chosen arms. Banners were important, as morale boosters, signalling devices and rallying points. The use of liveries did, at least, promote some degree of uniformity. In practice this consisted of a loose tunic or tabard which the soldier wore over his jack or harness in the lord's colours. The Percies, for instance, fielded a livery of russet, yellow and orange, with the badge of the Percy Lion rampant sewn onto the shoulder. The system could still produce moments of confusion, perhaps most tellingly, in the fatal mist of Barnet, where Lord Montagu's men mistook Oxford's badge of the star and stream for King Edward's sun and stream, with disastrous consequences.

Arms and Armour

The late fifteenth century saw the final flowering of the armourer's art, fine plate armours that could resist even the deadly arrow storm. Italian harness of this era was skilfully and beautifully constructed to maximise deflection. Defences for the vulnerable areas at the shoulder, elbow and knees were strengthened, fashioned ribs on exposed parts were constructed to deflect a killing blow.[18] German armourers moved this concept toward the angular perfection of the Gothic style with its emphasis on uncompromising lines, swept by heavy fluting. A harness of this period might weigh around 60 lbs (30 kilos) and would not greatly inhibit the mobility of a robust man, trained since boyhood to move and fight in armour.[19]

Medieval knights, even when fighting on foot, frequently bore a less onerous burden than the average 'Tommy' of World War One, burdened with rifle and pack, ammunition bandoliers, wire and tools. The Italian and German styles came together in Flanders, a flourishing centre of manufacture, where Italian armourers produced a hybrid style that features the flexible, fluted plates of the Gothic combined with the more rounded pauldrons (shoulder defences) and tassets (thigh guards) of their native style. Such armours were sold in quantities in England as evidenced by their regular appearance in funerary monuments. For head protection the stylish sallet form of helmet was popular from mid-century onwards, the rear of the elegantly curved brim swept downwards into a pointed tail to provide extra deflection to the vulnerable areas at the back of the head and neck. Usually provided with a fixed or moveable visor, the sallet was accompanied by the bevor, which afforded protection to the throat and lower face. Although knights could move freely, even in full plate, thirst and heat exhaustion were constant threats even in winter campaigning. The swift end meted out to Butcher Clifford by an alert archer was the penalty for unstrapping the bevor in the heat of the press. Dressing for battle was best achieved at leisure, before the enemy was in the field, as a contemporary author, writing *c*.1450 explains:

> *To arme a man.Ffirste ye must set on Sabatones* [armoured over-shoes] *and tye hem up on the shoo with small points* [laces] *that woll not breke. And then griffus* [greaves, plate defences for the calves] *and then cuisses* [thigh defences] *and ye breche* [leggings] *of mayle. And the Tonlets. An the Brest and ye Vambras* [upper arm defences] *and ye rerebras* [lower arm] *and then gloovis* [plate gauntlets]. *And then hand his daggere up on his right side. And then his shorte sworde on his lyfte side in a round rynge all naked to pull it out lightli* [the sword is carried without a scabbard, hung in a ring for quick release]. *And then put his cote upon his back. And then his basinet* [bascinet – a form of helmet in use prior to the sallet] *pyind up on two greet staples before the breste with a dowbill bokill* [double buckle]

behynde up on the back for to make the basinet sitte juste. And then his long swerd [sword] *in his hande. And then his pensil in his hande peynted of St George or of oure ladye to bless him with as he goeth towarde the felde and in the felde.*[20]

Whilst knights and men-at-arms would wear full harness, archers tended to favour padded jacks or brigandines, as the account from Dominic Mancini, quoted earlier, suggests. The fabric garment was finished with plates of steel or bone riveted between the inner and outer layers or, as in the cheaper version, simply padded and stuffed with rags and tallow. The ubiquitous jack was far cheaper, lighter and, for many purposes, more practical. Some were fitted with sleeves of mail to afford protection to the arms. Though archers traditionally eschewed leg harness, billmen and men-at-arms would wear whatever they could afford or were able to loot, the seasoned campaigner augmenting his kit from the spoil of dead and captives. As an alternative to the expensive sallet, the foot might rely on the basic 'kettle' hat.

One of the most popular knightly weapons of the age was the fearsome poleaxe; a heavy axe blade on a stout ash shaft, some four to six feet in length, a hefty 'beak' or hammer head on the reverse of the blade, and the head tapering to a wicked spike. This tool was designed to defeat the armourer's art by 'opening up' a harnessed opponent, in the manner of a crude but deadly can opener. Popular in the tourney and judicial duel, the blade was secured by steel strips or 'languets' intended to frustrate the action of lopping off the head of the weapon. The doomed Somerset, cornered at First St Albans, fought valiantly and brought down a quartet of Yorkist opponents before a blow from a poleaxe felled him. Swiss peasants had already proved the worth of the halberd, and English bills had contributed to the glorious victories in France. The horseman's lance, grown heavier than the original Norman spear, was carried couched under the arm and used for thrusting. The weight was such the weapon had to be held with the point angled across the saddle, a difficult business that could only be accomplished with plentiful training. When used on foot, the shaft was generally cut down in length to make for easier handling.

At this time the medieval knight's sword reached the apex of its development prior to its eclipse, in the next century, by the rapier. Blades were designed for both cut and thrust, long and elegantly tapering, with a full grip that could be hefted in one or two hands, in section resembling a flattened diamond; simple quillons, curved or straight, a wheel, a pear- or kite-shaped pommel. This was the hand and a half or 'bastard' sword, the very 'King of Swords'. Such precision instruments were reserved for the gentry, extremely expensive to buy. The commons carried a simpler, lighter and considerably cheaper sidearm, a short single edged blade with the quillons curving around up to the hilt to provide a form of crude knuckle guard. Gentlemen and commons both bore daggers; the long-bladed rondel with tapering triangular blade, hardwood grip, disc guard and pommel, was a popular style. The ballock knife, whose wooden handle featured two rounded protuberances of suggestive form, rather resembles the later Scottish dudgeon dagger. As handy as a tool as a weapon, daggers were carried by all ranks and might be used to stab an opponent or plant vegetables, as the situation required. In battle the thin-bladed knife could be used to deliver the coup de grace to an armoured enemy, either thrust directly through the eye slit of the steel visor or into the more vulnerable areas of armpit or genitals.

The Arrow Storm

It was only later, during the sixteenth century, that the term 'longbow' came into usage; a plainer expression – 'bow' or 'livery bow' – was more commonplace during the fifteenth. Retained or liveried archers normally carried their own bows but, in the long continuance of the French wars, the Office of Ordnance began issuing standardised kit on campaign to replace those lost or damaged. Thus quantities of bows were manufactured to a standard or government pattern, like the infantry musket of following centuries. Yew was the preferred timber, though ash, elm and wych-elm were also favoured. The weapon was usually between 5ft 7in. (1.675 m) and 6ft 2in. (1.850 m) in length, the cross section corresponded to a rounded 'D' with a draw weight of between 80 and 120 lbs (40–60 kilos), a modern target bow has an average draw of around 45 lbs (22.5 kilos).

Arrows were crafted from a variety of woods. Roger Ascham, tutor to Elizabeth I and a noted sixteenth-century authority, advocated aspen as the most suitable, though ash, alder, elder, birch, willow and hornbeam were also used. The shafts were generally around 2ft 6in. (75 cm) in length, the fletching formed from grey goose feathers. Arrowheads came in a variety of forms – flat, hammer headed, barbed or wickedly sharp needle-pointed piles or bodkins – designed to punch through plate and mail. Livery quality arrows were issued to retainers, 'standard' grade was just that and 'sheaf' arrows came in bundles of two dozen.[21] At each extremity the bow was tipped with cowhorn, grooved to take the linen string and, when not in use, the stave was carried unstrung in a cloth cover. To draw, the archer gripped the bow with his left hand, about the middle, where the circumference of the wood was around 4.5in. (22.5 cm). Then he forced the centre of the bow away from him to complete the draw, using the full weight of his body to assist, rather than relying on the strength in his arms alone. Such strength, stamina and expertise demanded constant drill; practice at the butts was compelled by statute. The bow could kill at 200 yards, the archer wore a leather or horn 'bracer' strapped to his wrist to protect against the vicious snap of the bowstring.

Properly deployed, the bow had proved to be a battle-winning weapon. Many who fought for Lancaster or York would have already seen active service in the French wars. Few who had encountered the deadly hail of the arrow storm could have forgotten the experience. If gentlemen, secure in fine plate, enjoyed greater protection than their predecessors, then the rank and file were less fortunate. As the armies faced each other at Towton, in the bitter sleet, cunning Fauconberg took advantage of the poor visibility to advance his Yorkist archers before they loosed, the mass of shafts flicking into the tightly packed Lancastrians. Having shot, his men then smartly stepped back whilst Somerset's archers, gauging the range, shot into empty ground! Their arrows were swiftly returned by their opponents and so galling were the Yorkist volleys that the Lancastrians had no recourse other than to advance to contact.

The Gunner's Art

By the early years of the fifteenth century artillery was steadily becoming the dominant arm in siege warfare. In April 1464 as King Edward IV was preparing to march north, he caused his siege train to be made ready and this included 'the great ordnance of England' – the bombards 'Dijon', 'London', 'Newcastle', 'Edward' and 'Richard Bombartel'.[22] This new science of gunnery had begun to surpass that of the military architect. Henry V had deployed his train against the walls of Harfleur in 1415, and had subsequently breached the formidable walls of Le Mans after a few days' bombardment.[23] 'Bombard' was a generic term, used to describe a large siege gun; in this era there was, as yet, no standardisation of calibres.[24]

These monsters were fired from ground level and from behind a hinged, timber shutter rather like a very much larger version of the archer's mantlet. This provided some cover for the gunner, his mate and matrosses. Most guns loaded at the breech, having a removable block shaped not unlike a commodious beer mug. By the 1460s trunnions were coming into use and even the heavier pieces were being equipped with wheeled carriages; elevation was achieved by the use of wedges.[25] Transportation was an area of major difficulty; large teams of draught horses or oxen were required, a section of pioneers had to be added to the train, their task to level and fill the generally appalling roads over which the guns must pass. Larger pieces were still manufactured on the hoop and stave principle (hence the term 'barrel'), though casting in bronze was, by mid-century, commonplace.[26] Another arm, growing in significance and potency, was the smaller handgun or 'gonne'. These were little more than a miniature cannon lashed onto a basic wooden stock. Such 'hagbuts' were held underarm, or over the shoulder, rather than pressed into the shoulder as with a modern firearm. Once loaded with powder and shot, the gun was fired by means of a lit length of slow match, the burning end of which was applied to a touchhole, drilled in the side of the breech.

Although artillery had radically diminished the status of castles as centres of resistance, guns remained frightfully expensive to procure and difficult to move. The various sieges of the Lancastrian-held strongholds in Northumberland during 1461 to 1464 were conducted with an artillery train in attendance, but only once were the great guns deployed in earnest, at Bamburgh in the closing stages of the final year's campaigning. Here the ordnance was brought into play with considerable reluctance. Bamburgh was a major bastion against the Scots and slighting such a key fortress was best avoided.[27] In 1473, John de Vere, Earl of Oxford launched a lightning strike against the Yorkist regime, by seizing St Michael's Mount in a coup de main. With no more than a couple of companies of foot, the Earl captured and held the fortress. Perhaps the most prolonged and celebrated siege of the Wars of the Roses was the investment of Harlech which resisted for the best part of seven years, holding out even when Jasper Tudor, as castellan, fled to Ireland.

Field fortifications featured in a number of the battles. Salisbury, caught with inferior numbers at Blore Heath by Lord Audley's Lancastrians in September 1459, sought to consolidate an already strong defensive position by digging a ditch to cover his rear and erecting a palisade to the front. The labour proved worthy of the effort. Nearly a year later, in a miserable July, it was the Lancastrians at Northampton, who placed their faith in a wet ditch and a timber palisade studded with guns. They were doubly unfortunate; unseasonal rainfall flooded the gun pits and soaked their powder, treachery surmounted the fieldworks. Warwick, the victor, also placed great trust in elaborate entrenchments when preparing to meet Queen Margaret's host by St Albans, scene of his earlier triumph, in February 1461. A quantity of pre-pared positions were dug, augmented by a liberal sowing of caltraps – the anti-personnel and anti-equine devices of their day with an array of spiked nets, hinged mantlets and other elaborate contrivances. Bad intelligence, slow thinking and possibly yet more treachery comprised the whole com-plex scheme, turned by a flank attack.

The Face of Battle

Time and romance have, over the intervening years, cast a shroud of pageantry over the harsh realities of medieval combat. The truth is some-what less attractive. Though lacking the scale and widespread devastation of modern wars, devoid of the full horror of industrialised conflict, warfare, in the fifteenth century, was every bit as frightful. As discussed, many battles opened with an archery duel, regular volleys thudding home into tightly packed ranks, inflicting numerous fatalities and wounds. These preliminaries probably lasted only a short time before that side which was suffering the most was compelled to advance. The movement would be ordered rather than swift, the sergeants bellowing orders to keep the ranks dressed. Cohe-sion was all important; the divisions that could maintain both order and momentum stood the best chance of breaking a more disordered foe. A commander with an eye for ground would always seek the position of best advantage, though elements in the topography, adverse weather, mist and darkness could combine to upset the best laid plans and, as at Barnet, each side might find themselves equally confounded. Once battle was joined in earnest the combat became an intensely personal affair – a hacking, stamp-ing melee of bills and other polearms, sword, and axe.

Men, half blind in plate, soon assailed by raging thirst and swiftly reaching exhaustion, would become disorientated. Dust and the steam from thousands of sweating men would further obscure any wider view. Few would be killed by a single blow, but a disabling wound, bringing the sufferer to his knees, would expose him to a further flurry, his skull then shattered, pierced through the visor or groin by daggers, hacked by bills, stamped on, kicked and slashed. Not a swift death, nor an easy one. Illustrations from the period show the field heaped with the press of the slain; garnished by a slew of severed limbs, blood would run in great rivulets, splattering the living.

Once one side broke in rout, casualties would begin to mount; armoured men trying to flee toward horses tethered at a distance would be easy prey. Those less encumbered or not enfeebled with wounds might survive the race, others would not. The victors, their horses brought forward by the grooms, would be swooping and circling like hawks. Abbot Whethamstede, who may have been an eyewitness, graphically chronicles the fate of some of Warwick's men, fleeing from the debacle at Second St Albans:

> *The southern men, who were fiercer at the beginning, were broken quickly afterwards, and the more quickly because looking back, they saw no one coming up from the main body of the King's army, or preparing to bring them help, whereupon they turned their backs on the northern men and fled. And the northern men seeing this pursued them very swiftly on horseback; and catching a good many of them, ran them through with their lances.*[28]

A mass grave excavated during the 1990s on the field of Towton, has provided a grim insight into the sheer nastiness of fifteenth-century warfare. Some 37 skeletons were unearthed; most of these had suffered a series of horrific head injuries, puncture wounds and calamitous fractures with evidence of specific and deliberate dagger thrusts to the back of the skull, either a coup de grace or cold-blooded execution. In either event the victim would have been stripped of head protection at the fatal moment.[29]

By contemporary standards the available medical services were both rudimentary and sparse. The perceived presence of evil humours was the source of copious bleedings, quacks cast horoscopes and peddled bizarre potions. Wounds, sensibly, were cauterised with hot pitch; anaesthesia, with solutions mixed from herbs, was by no means unknown, however, and surgical techniques were perhaps more sophisticated than might be assumed. Gerhard von Wesel, travelling in England in 1471, has left an eye-witness account of the army of King Edward IV as the survivors of Barnet trudged wearily back into London: 'Many of their followers were wounded, mostly in the face or the lower part of the body, a very pitiable sight.'[30] These, it must be remembered, were the victors.

Campaigns of the period tended to be highly mobile and of relatively short duration, adequate logistical provision for keeping large bodies in the field, was a particular problem, as was the need to find cash to pay wages. In common with other periods, men undoubtedly died from disease and want. Dysentery was a major killer, as were cholera and typhus. Plague also stalked the armies. The late-medieval era has been described as 'the golden age of bacteria'[31] with perhaps thirty-odd outbreaks occurring between the first onslaught in 1348 and 1487. French mercenaries in the service of Henry Tudor were blamed for introducing the 'sweating sickness' that killed off two mayors of London and six aldermen in barely a week in 1485.[32]

Notes

1 Of those who took part in the apparently bloodless fracas at Heworth, Lord Egremont was killed at Northampton in 1460; Sir Thomas Neville and his father, the Earl of Salisbury, fell at Wakefield at the end of that year; Richard Percy died at Towton in 1461; John Neville, Lord Montagu, later Earl of Northumberland, was killed at Barnet in 1471.

2 Philippe de Commynes 'The Memoirs for the Reign of Louis XI, 1461–1463' trans. M. Jones, 1972, p. 187.

3 P. A. Haigh, *The Military Campaigns of the Wars of the Roses* (London 1995), p. 59.

4 T. Wise, *The Wars of the Roses* (London 1983), p. 22.

5 Ibid., p. 23.

6 Sir Charles Oman, *The Art of War in the Middle Ages* (London 1924), vol. 2, p. 408; cited in Wise, op. cit., p. 29.

7 Wise, op. cit., p. 27.

8 Ibid., p. 27.

9 In *I Henry IV*, IV. ii. 11: 'If I be not ashamed of my soldiers, I am a sous'd gurnet. I have misused the King's press damnably' (Falstaff).

10 Wise, op. cit., p. 27. The Stonor correspondence is that of an Oxfordshire family in the Middle Ages – see C. L. Kingsford (ed.) 'The Stonor Letters and Papers 1290–1483', CS 3rd series 29, 30m, London 1919.

11 Wise, op. cit., p. 27.

12 Cited in Wise, op. cit., p. 27.

13 Cited in A. W. Boardman, *The Medieval Soldier in the Wars of the Roses* (London 1998), p. 173.

14 Wise, op. cit., p. 29.

15 Boardman, op. cit., p. 167.

16 Ibid., p. 167.

17 When a lord sent his horse to the rear and took his place amongst the foot, this was perceived as having an effect on morale as the gentleman was placing himself in equal peril.

18 C. Blair, *European Armour* (London 1958), p. 77.

19 A. V. B. Norman and D. Pottinger, *English Weapons and Warfare 449–1660* (London 1966), p. 114.

20 R. E. Oakeshott, *A Knight and his Weapons* (London 1964), p. 51.

21 C. Bartlett, *The English Longbowman 1330–1515* (London 1995), pp. 23–30.

22 'Edward' is featured in an inventory of 1475; the Master of Ordnance, John Sturgeon, handed into store at Calais 'divers parcels of the King's Ordnance and artillery, including a bumbardell [bombard] called "The Edward"', see H. L. Blackmore, *The Armouries of the Tower of London – Ordnance* (HMSO 1976), p. 33.

23 Norman and Pottinger, op. cit., p. 137.

24 A survivor from this period and still to be viewed in Edinburgh Castle is 'Mons Meg' which may be considered not untypical of the heavy guns of this period, cast in Flanders around 1460.

25 H. C. B. Rogers, *Artillery Through the Ages* (London 1971), p. 19.

26 Norman and Pottinger, op. cit., p. 141.

27 P. Warner, *Sieges of the Middle Ages* (London 1968), p. 198.

28 H. T. Riley (ed.) 'Registrum Abbatis Johannis Whethamstede' 1872, vol. 1, pp. 388–92.

29 Boardman, op. cit., pp. 181–3.

30 Bartlett, op. cit., p. 51.

31 S. L. Thrupp, 'The Problem of Replacement rates in late Medieval English Population' *Economic History Review* 2nd series (1965), p. 18.

32 Ibid., p. 18.

Chapter 2

The Nature of Kingship and the House of Lancaster

On a hot summer's day in August 1485, Richard III, last Plantagenet King of England, died on the field of battle, our final reigning monarch to suffer such an end, his short, controversial reign brought to a close in a Wagnerian flourish. Of his three immediate predecessors two had likely met their deaths through foul play.

The Nature of Kingship

Kings and kingship were the foundation of English polity in the medieval period: The King stood at the head of the social and economic pyramid, supported by a sophisticated legal and fiscal framework which had been evolving since the Conquest.[1] From 1337 to 1453 England was at war with France and, not infrequently during this period with Scotland too. The financial burden imposed by the Hundred Years War had had an effect upon the economic framework surrounding the position of the Crown. The king was responsible for maintaining law and order at home and for securing the realm against external threat; Edward III had campaigned aggressively and with considerable outward success against both Scots and French, holding both kings captive after 1356.[2] A successful monarch, such as Edward I or

Henry V, needed to work closely with his leading magnates. They represented the landed interest, and ownership of land was all-important. Since Magna Carta and the constitutional reforms of Henry III's reign the king's conduct was held to be subject to the law – a king such as Richard II, who arbitrarily confiscated the estates of his greatest peer, would forfeit the obedience of others. The king's rule might be ordained by God but this did not excuse or exonerate tyranny.

Should the king, however, behave in an authoritarian and unjust manner, he nevertheless remained king. The subject owed him an absolute duty of obedience. In such an instance, which had arisen in the rule of Edward II and latterly, in that of Richard II, there was no certainty about what should be done to bring the monarch to account. His removal was contrary to God's law, usurpation a crime against the laws of man and of God.

That kings of England were frequently at war with external enemies, in Wales, Ireland, Scotland and France gave rise to the reality of taxation – a constitutional acceptance that the burden of these conflicts should be borne collectively. The process was by no means swift or absolutely certain but, by the reign of Edward III, there was a general acceptance that the sovereign had the right to levy tax, due as a portion of the individual subject's wealth, due when legitimised by Act of Parliament. Royal finances were complex but essentially revolved around the concepts of 'ordinary' revenue which the king derived from customs revenues plus the income from his estates, and 'extraordinary' which was voted as a tax. The former was expected to cover his normal household and administrative expenses, the latter to extend to defence of the realm, frequently and in practice implying armed expeditions abroad.

By far the most influential class, in political terms, were the magnates, the great landowners. Not only did they control vast acres but they provided the military 'muscle' which the Crown required to enforce its will. There was no standing army as such (unless we include the Calais garrison); the magnates with their household men and retainers formed the nucleus of any military force the monarch needed, either to deal with civil discord or to fight abroad. Through the web of nobility controlling, and scattered throughout, the shires, the King could exercise control over the whole and raise forces for his campaigns. Even the development of the contract system under Edward III had not destroyed this: the magnates frequently acted as the king's captains in recruiting companies – Henry of Derby and, latterly, Richard, Duke of York, being but two examples. Throughout the period, the nobility, if the Crown was weak, might elect to settle their disputes by force of arms rather than through the medium of the courts; the Courtenay–Bonville; Percy–Neville, Stanley–Harrington feuds are merely some instances. The plain fact was that the administrative authority of the king, in terms of available force, was upheld by privately raised contingents which he did not directly control.[3]

To be successful, the king needed to be accessible and receptive. His status might be conferred by God but the magnates were not overly deferential, most had opinions and were forthright in expression. Even stern, authoritarian figures like Edward I faced magnatial opposition; peers were not cowed by the royal rage, impressive and volcanic as it might be. When rulers such as Edward II or Richard II chose to ride roughshod over the advices and privileges of their magnates, they invited stern opposition. As a class the nobility were generally well educated, experienced and skilful in the management of their estates and were frequently well versed in war which was, after all, the gentleman's trade. If the authority of the Crown was very considerable, then the obligation to use those powers both wisely and justly was implicit. When royal authority was weakened, then internal discord could fester, and foreign enemies strike. The failure of Edward II to ensure the defence of northern England after his defeat at Bannockburn in 1314 was a case in point. The harrying of the north by the Scots imposed such an intolerable burden that some of the gentry, at least – Sir Gilbert de Middleton being perhaps the most notorious – defected.

What then to do with a king whose tyrannies proved intolerable? John and his son Henry III were not deposed but a form of constitutional settlement was forced upon them; Edward II, by 1327, had clearly shown himself unfit but he was still not actually deposed. He was, to be sure, removed from power, but this was carefully orchestrated as an abdication, the succession passing immediately to his legitimate heir Edward III. The magnates soon tired of the overbearing regency of Isabella and her paramour Roger Mortimer, whose pretensions and oppression quickly came to rival those of Edward II. In the case of Richard II the matter was both more complex and more dangerous. The King had no immediate heir and Henry Bolingbroke's claim was not necessarily paramount. Many historians, taking a traditional view have, following Tudor chroniclers, seen the roots of the Wars of the Roses as lying in the fact of the Lancastrian usurpation of 1399. More recent writers have inclined away from this, preferring to see the conflict more as the consequence of administrative failures of the 1450s and the consequential rise of aristocratic discord.

Richard II, son of martial Edward, the Black Prince, and grandson of Edward III came into his inheritance whilst still a minor. His reign witnessed a resumption of both the French and Scottish wars and in both cases the English cause faltered. A preference for unsuitable favourites, pressing economic needs and an inability to develop a firm affinity amongst the nobility spread disaffection. His attempt to sequester the vast estates of the Duchy of Lancaster on the death of his uncle John of Gaunt, provoked a rising led by the exiled Henry Bolingbroke, Earl of Derby, old Gaunt's heir. Richard was dispossessed, dying very soon thereafter and Derby became Henry IV. The new king was thus a usurper and the crown sat uneasily, his reign being disturbed by a series of rebellions in 1399–1400, 1403, 1405 and 1408. Later writers, beginning in Tudor times, were to ascribe the subsequent dynastic upheavals as being a direct consequence of this usurpation – God's judgement on those who offended against the Lord's annointed.

Henry V, by contrast, is considered one of medieval England's most able and successful rulers. He dealt swiftly with the Southampton plotters in 1415 and resumed the war with France. His arms won towering victory at Agincourt in 1415 and he campaigned relentlessly to conquer Normandy, reducing towns and fortresses, however seemingly impregnable, with brilliant siegecraft. By 1422 he had reduced the French to terms, secured the hand of the King of France's daughter and was within a hairbreadth of the succession. The great warrior-king succumbed, not to the swords of his enemies, but to the commonplace scourge of dysentery, his vision tantalisingly near but incomplete. He left a legacy of success, a French widow and an infant son, now Henry VI.

> *He was, like a second Job, a man simple and upright, altogether fearing the Lord God, and departing from evil. He was a simple man, without any crook of craft or untruth, as is plain to all. With none did he deal craftily, nor ever would say an untrue word to any, but framed his speech always to speak truth . . .*[4]

Thus John Blackman, Henry VI's chaplain, describes the character of the King: such hagiography might be viewed in the light of Henry's potential for canonisation after his death in 1471. Admirable as such traits may appear, they were not those expected of, or needed by, a strong medieval ruler. It would be hard to imagine a starker contrast between father and son: Henry V

Figure 1: King Henry VI
(© National Portrait Gallery, London)

had been the very epitome of chivalry, a ruthlessly successful field commander under whose able leadership the prestige of English arms had ascended
to dizzying heights. Equally, Henry took pleasure in the rigours and ferocity
of combat. War without fire, he is said to have opined, is like sausages without mustard.[5] If we fully accept all that his chaplain asserts, then Henry VI
was obsessively pious, his equal obsession with chastity, which appears to
have manifested itself in excessive prudery, suggests a degree of narrow-
minded instability. The hagiography was certainly effective, for the King's
tomb at Windsor became a shrine and, to support a bid for sainthood a list of
over one hundred of his miraculous cures was compiled. Though Blackman's
view might be coloured by his own agenda, there is perhaps considerable
validity in his appreciation of the King's character and that the failure of his
reign was caused not by bad rule but by a total absence of rule.

The Lancastrian Administration

There was a long-held view that Henry VI, after he had assumed control of his sceptre in 1437, remained a tool in the sway of a clique of unscrupulous magnates. This idea has, however, been challenged and an alternative, perhaps more credible view is that the King, after attaining his majority, simply failed to rule effectively and that his advisers were obliged to rule by proxy. That some, such as William de La Pole, Duke of Suffolk, may have compromised duty with venality, may not detract from the fact that their core actions were driven by necessity. The Lancastrian administration was not unduly corrupt and inefficient, though both failings may have arisen, but was essentially damned due to the King's inability to rule. The fruits of the failure of the sovereign to govern became more apparent after 1450 and thus paved the way toward disorder.

Henry VI has been somewhat harshly judged by many subsequent writers. One of the charges laid at his door was of fiscal incompetence. During the reign of Richard II, the annual income of the Crown stood at around £120,000; by the 1450s this had declined sharply to no more than £40,000.[6] In part, Henry himself was to blame for this failure to manage his own household expenses, but core revenue was also plummeting and this was due to factors beyond his control. The yield from Crown lands, a major source of revenue, had tumbled, and customs dues had also dwindled. A slump in agriculture and a trade recession, which had begun to bite from the 1350s, fuelled the economic collapse. The King was not the only one to suffer, the same decline threatened to impoverish the magnates and it has been suggested that the financial pressures created by recession prompted the lords to compete more vigorously for crown appointments.[7] A further agricultural slump in the years 1438–40 caused yields to fall even more and provided an additional stimulus to the burgeoning Percy/Neville rivalry, a dispute that was to have a telling impact on the descent into lawlessness and civil war after 1453. It has been suggested that the Wars of the Roses were fought, not because magnates were recruiting soldiers, but because they could not afford to pay those already in their employ![8]

During the King's minority from 1422 to 1437 his uncle John, Duke of Bedford, continued the policies of Henry V. He and Cardinal Beaufort broadly agreed that the correct course was to maintain the steady acquisition of territories and establish the full authority of the English Crown in

France. Until the collapse of the Burgundian alliance in 1435 and Bedford's death, this appeared entirely feasible; English armies continued to win more victories, though the emergence of Joan of Arc and defeat at Orleans showed that victory was by no means assured. The role of the late King's other surviving brother, the Duke of Gloucester, of a volatile and mercurial temperament, was restricted to that of protector, defender and chief councillor, a rather shapeless remit. His authority only lasted whilst Bedford was engaged in affairs overseas and he was unable to exercise full sway over the Council, which was increasingly dominated by Cardinal Beaufort, Bishop of Winchester.

This great prelate enjoyed the considerable resources of his see and was, further, a feoffee of the Duchy of Lancaster – the revenues of the Duchy of Lancaster had, since the King's death, devolved into the control of stakeholders who were responsible for paying off his debts and legacies. Thus the Crown had no direct call on these revenues and was obliged to rely upon loans from the feoffees. Beaufort was a major lender, whose fiscal support was invaluable. Parliament was not generally inclined to fund the maintenance of the French territories through taxation as it was expected that these could be self-financing. Equally there was a reluctance to alienate the Normans in particular by excessive demands. In the early years this did not create a crisis situation as royal income and expenditure could be roughly made to balance. The rift with Burgundy, however, which reduced customs dues on the vital wool trade, exacerbated the position greatly.

We have been left with a view that fifteenth-century England was prone to increasing lawlessness but, whilst violence did flare among magnates and gentry, the minority rule did not witness any major breakdown in royal authority, despite the mounting antipathy between Gloucester and Beaufort. Indeed, Bedford, on several occasions and in addition to being the butt of his brother's bile, sided with the Cardinal to curb the Duke's perceived excesses. Gloucester's enthusiasm for picking a quarrel with Burgundy (seen as a commercial rival by the urban bourgeoisie) and his determination to defend Calais at the expense of other, more pressing strategic options, won him a measure of popular support. Bedford was obliged to intervene when Duke and Cardinal quarrelled openly in 1425, and he was constrained to intermeddle again in 1433. From 1429, when young Henry was crowned, first in England and, two years later, in France, Gloucester's influence waned; his protectorate time expired.

Henry VI remained, even for a number of years after his marriage, childless. Excessive chastity and distaste for the lures of the flesh may have been a contributing factor but a king without an heir was vulnerable, failing in his dynastic duty. This weakness was exacerbated by the fact that, should Henry die childless, then the Duke of York was heir presumptive.[9] The House of Lancaster had not, of course, obtained the throne by legitimate or constitutional means. Henry Bolingbroke, son of John of Gaunt, third son of Edward III, had usurped the sceptre from his cousin Richard II, son of Edward, Prince of Wales. Gaunt's innocuous, younger brother Edmund of Langley, Duke of York, took little part in national affairs. His son Richard, Earl of Cambridge, married Anne Mortimer, descended from the old King's second son Lionel of Clarence, and was executed for his part in the abortive Southampton Plot. Nonetheless, the fact remained that this branch of the family could claim seniority over John of Gaunt's line, and York was the dead traitor's son.

In 1437 the real difficulties of the reign were not entirely apparent. Despite internal divisions the Council had done much to maintain the English position in France and maintain the rule of law at home. Bedford and Beaufort had seen themselves as legatees of Henry V's policies. They had striven, not without success, to maintain these, but a holding policy cannot be indefinite; at some point a new direction must be forthcoming and this could only emanate from the person of the King himself. It was time for Henry VI to take control of the affairs of state, high time in fact; a number of elements now combined to demand strong evidence of effective kingship:

- Law and order was beginning to be affected; disputes such as that which arose in Bedfordshire between Lord Grey of Ruthyn and Lord Fanhope, disturbed the English polity.
- The collapse of the Burgundian alliance and the death of John, Duke of Bedford indicated a new direction was needed in the conduct of affairs in France.
- The situation of the royal finances was becoming critical.[10]

The Adult Rule of Henry VI 1437–1453

A question which has dogged historians is the extent to which, if any, Henry VI ruled in his own right; was he a contributor to the gradual collapse of the regime or was he a hapless pawn in the hands of a venal cabal? It may be assumed that Henry's active role declined after his mental breakdown in 1453 and was minimal after the end of the second protectorate in 1456. The King was certainly old enough to wield the sceptre after 1437 – princes came into their own at a young age: Edward IV was still in his teens when he won his decisive victory against the Lancastrians at Towton in 1461. Despite this devolution of power onto the royal person, the Council appears to have reasserted a measure of control in 1441, possibly due to the young king's continuing inexperience or, far more serious in implication, his perceived inability to rule. Recent scholars such as John Watts, followed by Carpenter, have put forward the notion that the King showed a marked disinclination for kingship. This was potentially disastrous in a society where the king stood at the apex of the social and economic pyramid. It therefore became necessary for a group of magnates, based around the household, initially guided by Cardinal Beaufort then, successively, the Dukes of Suffolk and Somerset, to rule by proxy. The facade of royal administration was preserved, remarkably so. Current thinking would dictate that the differences between York and Somerset did not arise until after the crisis of 1450 and that York was a functioning member of the English polity throughout the 1440s.[11]

Humphrey of Gloucester remained something of a loose cannon and tended to clash with Cardinal Beaufort. The rising Beaufort dynasty represented the legitimised offspring of John of Gaunt's long-term romantic liaison with his mistress Katherine Swynford. Richard II had provided these able newcomers with ample opportunities for advancement, even if they were specifically excluded from any pretensions to the throne itself. Henry Beaufort, Bishop of Winchester was appointed Chancellor in 1422 (five years thereafter he attained his cardinal's hat). He and Humphrey were already antipathetic. Henry V appointed yet another Beaufort as guardian of the infant ruler: the Duke of Exeter; a third brother was Earl of Dorset (later Duke of Somerset). Regency Councils were, throughout the whole of the medieval period, notoriously prone to factionalism and, from the outset, the Beaufort affinity carried a loud voice. His relations with Gloucester were far from cordial. So fractious was the rivalry that adherents of both Duke and Prelate had attended the Leicester Parliament on 1426 bearing cudgels; the assembly was dubbed 'The Parliament of Bats'.[12] Whilst the Regency Council bickered in England John, Duke of Bedford was attempting to maintain his nephew's cause in France. The death of Henry V might have seriously undermined the motive for and direction of the war but the English position showed no immediate signs of deterioration. Charles VII, no longer Dauphin since the death of his father in October 1421, could not manage to raise a sufficient force or find generals who could effectively challenge the English in open field. Most important, the vital Burgundian alliance held. Bedford, a highly competent commander in his own right and endowed with the levels of patient diplomacy needed to deal with his slippery brother-in-law who controlled Paris and the north, maintained the English hegemony in Normandy and Aquitaine.

Humphrey of Gloucester had begun his own feud with the Duke of Burgundy when he championed the cause of Jacqueline, Countess of Hainault, a client of Philip the Good, who fled to England in 1421.[13] The lady succeeded in obtaining a divorce, wed her English paladin and urged him to take possession of Hainault by force. Humphrey ignored both the pleadings of his brother and the admonitions of the Beauforts, and crossed the Channel. His campaign achieved little, Jacqueline was captured and escaped but the Pope decided her union with Gloucester was unlawful. Whilst Bedford was distracted by his mercurial brother, Burgundy, inevitably piqued, was continuing his dialogue with Charles. In 1427, with the Duke in England, the Bretons defected from a concord of four years earlier. Threatened now with an attack upon Normandy from the west, Bedford deemed it necessary to extend his sway into the central Loire by taking the great city of Orleans.[14] In a vigorous campaign, Bedford swiftly cowed Jean V of Brittany; William de la Pole, Earl of Suffolk raided through his lands; Salisbury took Le Mans and in the summer of 1428 entered Paris in triumph, trumping his Burgundian allies. The English tide had reached its high water mark. Suffolk, who was to become a key figure, had excellent credentials: his father died before the walls of Harfleur, his elder brother on the field of Agincourt; Suffolk himself had later been captured.

By the start of October 1428 Salisbury was before the walls of Orleans. The siege began well but the Earl was mortally wounded by a stray roundshot, and Suffolk assumed command. The arrival of Joan of Arc seemingly galvanized the defenders who broke the siege in a series of daring attacks on the ring of English forts and culminated in a telling defeat at Patay. The Congress of Arras opened in July 1435. Bedford, already a very sick man, died in September and it was Cardinal Beaufort who led the English delegation. Burgundy now agreed terms with Charles VI, abandoning his former allegiance. In 1436 the French recovered Paris whilst Philip hastened to show his enthusiasm by making an attempt on Calais. Gloucester, in charge of the defence, soon saw him off and harried Burgundian lands. The English were not yet beaten; Richard, Duke of York, appointed as Bedford's successor, took Dieppe. The loss of the Burgundian alliance was a severe blow to English hopes. The policy Beaufort and Bedford had been pursuing was one of caution; maintaining the overall position in France till the young king came into his own and could assume direction of the war. Losing Burgundy dramatically undermined that strategy.

At this time of mounting difficulties England had a boy king, a divided Council and a resentful Parliament, whose willingness to continue levying taxes was waning. Cardinal Beaufort, with Suffolk and others of his affinity, was in favour of a pragmatic approach; peace with honour. It appeared obvious to the peace faction that England was no longer able to add to her French territories, the pendulum had swung too far the other way. It was more a matter of clinging to such gains as could be salvaged. Henry VI had, in fact, been crowned King of France in Paris on 2 December 1431; a good show no doubt but something of a sham, for the true King of France was always crowned at Rheims where he was anointed with St Remy's Holy Oil. In the circumstances a negotiated peace was the only viable option and Cardinal Beaufort was adopting a pragmatic approach. In this he was undoubtedly correct; both he and Suffok, whose role was expanding, appeared to agree. Humphrey of Gloucester, in remaining loudly bellicose, fast became an anachronism.

Beaufort favoured a dynastic marriage alliance as the cement to bind a ceasefire; he had proposed a match between Henry VI and a princess of the Valois but this idea was rejected during the acrimonious exchanges at Arras. Gloucester had in mind a Gascon alliance with the daughter of Jean IV, Count of Armagnac. For a while this seemed a distinct possibility, the union would serve to shore up the English position in Aquitaine. By the summer of 1442, Charles had, however, assembled sufficient military might to cow Count Jean who, realising in which direction the wind was now blowing, broke off negotiations. The English forces engaged in propping up the remains of the Plantagenet empire in France, whilst slender, were still effective, but were reliant on the same tried-and-tested tactics which had proved so succesful in the past.

It was rapidly becoming clear to those around the young king that Henry VI was not likely to espouse his father's martial stance; his finances were becoming parlous.[15] Fresh campaigns, such as that in Guyenne in 1439, proved most difficult to fund – the glory days were clearly over. In this new mood of pragmatism Beaufort attempted further negotiations at Calais in 1439 and offered to release the captive Duke of Orleans who had languished since 1415. This was expressly contrary to the late king's policy. Gloucester managed to get the initiative blocked in Council; the commons were still loud for the war and Duke Humphrey achieved a measure of popular acclaim but he and his supporters were blinding themselves as to the current realities. The business in France was no longer about making fresh gains but simply about hanging on. With Paris once again back in French hands, English outposts were cleared from the Île-de-France and the country north of the Seine. King Charles VII, if he was not a great soldier, was certainly a ruthlessly efficient politician and a sound administrator. In England Gloucester was attacked obliquely when his current wife, the beauteous former lady-in-waiting to Jacqueline of Hainault, was arraigned on charges of witchcraft. This was all trumped-up nonsense, of course, but, as it turned out, credible nonsense – the Duchess was convicted, publicly humiliated and imprisoned. With her husband apparently incapable of protecting her, few rushed to his aid.

In the early 1440s Cardinal Beaufort's influence, now dented by policy failures, waned, and Suffolk assumed a more pivotal role. If the Duke was not a great man and prone, like many of his contemporaries, to some level of venality, he was in a very difficult position, trying to carry out policy which should properly have been directed by the King, but hamstrung by a king who appeared disinterested. The Duke of York was sent to France as Lieutenant for a further five-year term in 1440. There is no direct evidence, at this time, that York was in any way disadvantaged or that he was anything other than a functioning member of the English polity; he does not appear to have been at odds with Suffolk. Before the Cardinal's death in 1447 something of a rift had opened between him and the Duke. Buoyed by his great personal wealth, Beaufort still had an eye for opportunities which might arise to confer estates upon his nephews Edmund of Dorset and John of Somerset. Unlike York's these Beaufort siblings did not inherit any vast patrimony. In 1442 Somerset was given an independent command and turned loose on Maine and Anjou. Beyond robbing York and Shrewsbury of resources little was achieved. John received his dukedom but died in May 1444, possibly by his own hand.

Whether this ill-judged intervention prompted York to conceive an active resentment of the Beauforts at this stage is unclear; quite possibly it did not. He was owed substantial arrears but, due to the Crown's crippling indebtedness, most officers were awaiting payment. The Beauforts may have been compensated sooner but it does seem likely that York's resentment was effectively 'backdated' after 1450 and that, during the 1440s there was actually no palpable rift, nor was the Duke in any way marginalised. His subsequent appointment to the Lieutenancy in Ireland was a normal progression – his family had a long history there and he was endowed with new and extended authority. Current perceptions, based on an analysis of the chronicle evidence, would tend to support the view that York was working in harmony with Suffolk and the Beauforts. These magnates were, whatever their failings, men who had been schooled in a tradition of public service, of doing their duty, and in the absence of proactive regal instruction, this meant pulling together to maintain the machinery and form of government. The gentry and commons appear to have accepted this in so far as they were aware of the situation. It was only after 1450 that the cracks became all too visible and harmony disappeared.

In France, the energetic Shrewsbury (Shakespeare's Bull Talbot) husbanded his meagre resources but used them well, winning some neat, if ultimately inconclusive, little actions. A new peace initiative was launched and discussions began at Tours in the spring of 1444. Suffolk acted as the principal English negotiator, and the Truce of Tours, finally sealed in 1446, confirmed English possession of the lands they still held – a tacit admission that the rest were lost. By way of a dynastic marriage, the best that the young King of England could achieve was the hand of the 16-year-old Margaret of Anjou, daughter of Duke Rene of Bar and Lorraine, the titular if impecunious King of Sicily, unable even to fund a dowry. This young and spirited Princess arrived in England during April 1445. Her sea passage, though her fleet was magnificent, was turbulent and she required several days of rest at Portsmouth. She had yet to meet her new husband, though already officially married a month earlier at Nancy, with Suffolk standing as proxy for the absent groom. Raffaeolo de Negra, an Italian correspondent, recalled a story current at the time:

When the Queen landed in England the king dressed himself as a squire, and took her a letter which he said the king of England had written. While the queen read the letter the king took stock of her, saying that a woman may be closely observed while she is reading, and the queen never found out that it was the king because she was so engrossed in the letter that she never looked at the king in his squire's dress.[16]

During the negotiations at Tours Suffolk may have offered to trade Maine, as an expedient to win the truce. Subsequently Henry, in the course of personal correspondence with Charles VII, offered to return the district, the effective date of handover to be 22 December 1445.[17] There was no direct military pressure which could account for this retreat; English forces were still tying down Gascony, Anjou, Maine and Normandy. The decision appears to have been dictated by pure pragmatism. Such realpolitik could not be publicised – neither Council nor Parliament would have stood for what appeared as mere appeasement. Consequently, the King did not broadcast his intention and even Suffolk, upon whom the brunt of public opprobrium fell, sought to distance himself from the surrender by offering a formal disclaimer.

Humphrey of Gloucester was predictably outraged: intellectually gifted, he was never a skilled politician and his following amongst the magnates was at best limited. The attempt, in 1442, to silence him had, as we saw above, involved accusations of witchcraft hurled against Duchess Eleanor, who was charged with attempting to procure the King's death by sorcery. He was thus diminished but not fully reduced. In February 1447 Gloucester was summarily arrested as he entered Bury St Edmunds, where Parliament was due to convene. None raised a voice in his defence and in less than a week Duke Humphrey died whilst still in confinement. It may well be that his demise was entirely through natural causes.[18] Despite strenuous denials, Suffolk was widely suspected of foul play, and his dead opponent gained a higher stature in death than he had ever enjoyed in life. The legend of 'Good Duke Humphrey' probably arose posthumously and even York, who was later to assume the mantle of opposition, remained supine at the time – he was even a beneficiary of the dead man's estate. The plain fact was that with matters in France at such a critical pass Gloucester's stirring of the commons was intolerable; York whatever he may have broadcast later, expressed no reported concerns at the time.

In the event, abandonment of Maine achieved nothing. The Fougères incident[19] merely provided Charles VII with the pretext he had been seeking to recover Normandy. The increasing burden of taxation imposed by English rule had alienated local opinion to the extent that many of the Norman towns simply threw open their gates to welcome their countrymen as liberators. Verneuil, Mantes and Vernon swiftly capitulated before Jean Dunois, Bastard of Orleans, crossed the Seine and moved against Argentan. From the west, Duke Francis led the Bretons in a sweep through the Lower Cotentin, to mop up St Lo, Carentan and Valognes. Rouen was besieged and, after only three days, the local populace rose and opened the town's gates. By October 1449 the castle of Rouen had fallen. Bull Talbot was again a prisoner. Before the following summer was out the English presence in Normandy was expunged. Once more Suffolk, supposed architect of the Fougères fiasco was blamed. In fact it was Suffolk who had attempted to mount a counter stroke, landing Sir Thomas Kyriel and three thousand men at Cherbourg on 15 March. Several forts were retaken and a juncture effected with Somerset's two thousand soldiers from Caen. On 15 April, a bare month after their arrival, the English were utterly defeated in a fight at Formigny against a smaller French force under the Count of Clermont.

Though popular outrage focused on Suffolk, the fault was by no means his: the collapse of the Anglo-Burgundian entente, the fiscal burden and the King's lack of effective leadership had combined to fatally damage the English position. The country no longer had the means, or, in reality, the stomach to continue the fight, and the subject towns and provinces groaned under a harsh and arbitrary rule. Money was a continual worry: the mounting cost of maintaining a losing war was massively exacerbated by the King's difficulties in controlling his personal finances. Henry's annual income amounted to some £33,000, even as early as 1433 his indebtedness stood at £164,000, a sum which, by 1450, had rocketed to £372,000.[20] Since his marriage, expenditure on the King's household had increased more than threefold, from £8,000 to some £27,000 per annum, with Parliament expected to make up the shortfall. The manifesto put about by the Kentish rebels in 1450 complained of the parlous state of the royal purse 'the king himself is so beset that he may not pay for his meat and drink and he owes more than ever any king of England ought, for daily his traitors about him, when any thing should come to him by his laws, at once ask it from him'.[21]

Swelling anger against 'these traitors' focused on an influential cabal, a 'gang of three' – the King's principal advisors: Suffolk, William Ayscough Bishop of Salisbury, Henry's spiritual advisor, and Adam Moleyns, Bishop of

Chichester. The latter was done to death by a disgruntled mob in the course of violent disturbances at Portsmouth in January 1450. Unrest swiftly spread to the capital[22] and though order was restored the spirit of protest could not be extinguished, the lords clamouring after the commons. On 28 January Parliament successfully ousted Suffolk who found himself in the Tower. Two formal indictments were laid – first that he was guilty of treason by virtue of his dealings with the French, secondly that he was guilty of widespread corruption. The former was a calumny but the latter had significantly more substance, though the traditional evidence, derived largely from the Paston correspondence may, itself, be subject to contemporary bias:

> The said duke [Suffolk], in the 16th year of your reign, then being next and priviest of your council, and steward of your honourable household, then and many years sith, for covetise of great lucre of good singularly to himself, stirred and moved your Highness, the said 16th year, ye then being in prosperity and having great possessions, to give and grant much partie of your said possessions, to divers persons in your said realm of England, by the which ye be greatly impoverished . . .[23]

Not that this really mattered; it was Suffolk's head his enemies wanted. In a bid to stave off the inevitable conviction, the advisors managed to fix the sanction at five years' exile. On 30 April 1450, the Duke took ship from Ipswich: he was not destined to reach sanctuary on the continent. A carefully prepared ambush at sea had been laid and Suffolk found himself as a prisoner aboard *Nicholas of the Tower* – he can have had few illusions as to what would follow. The Paston correspondence reveals his dismal end:

> And Suffolk asked the name of the ship, and when he knew it, he remembered a prophecy that said, if he might escape the danger of the Tower, he should be safe; and then his heart failed him for he thought he was deceived, and in the sight of all his men he was dragged out of the great ship into a boat; and there was an axe, and a stroke, and one of the lewdest of the ship bade him lay down his head, and he should be fairly dealt with and die on a sword; and took a rusty sword and smote off his head with half a dozen strokes, and took away his gown of russet and his doublet of mailed velvet and laid his body on the sands of Dover.[24]

Suspicion of the deed fell on the men of Kent, though the catalogue of the murdered Duke's enemies was so extensive as to make identification problematic. Reprisals against the entire county were bruited, which served only to spark another bout of disturbances. Jack Cade,[25] brandishing the rebels' manifesto 'Complaint of the Commons of Kent', led an army of citizens as far as Blackheath. The government appeared impotent, its paltry forces scattered and the King seeking refuge at Kenilworth. On 29 June Bishop Ayscough, only surviving member of the triumvirate, was dragged from the altar and butchered. The people of Edington committed the murder 'and spoiled him unto the naked skin, and rent his bloody shirt into pieces and bare them away with them, and made boast of their wickedness'.[26] The treasurer, Lord Saye, equally unpopular with his son-in-law William Crowmer, the County Sheriff of Kent who had, injudiciously, bragged of their likely reprisals against the county, suffered a similar fate. It seemed as thought Henry's government could now collapse completely in the face of such determined unrest:

> And after that the commons of Kent arose with certain other shires, and they chose them a captain, the which captain, compelled all the gentles to arise with them. And at the end of the parliament they came with a great might and a strong host unto the Blackheath, beside Greenwich, the number of 46,000; and there they made a field, dyked and staked well about, as it had been in the land of war, save only they kept order among them, for alls good was Jack Robin as John at the Noke, for all were as high as pigs' feet, unto the time that they should commune and speak with such states [lords] and messengers as were sent unto them; then they put all their power unto the man that named him captain of all their host.[27]

However, the Kentishmen soon angered Londoners and the tide began to ebb as swiftly as it had surged. Concessions were made and a Royal Commission established to examine local grievances. Fresh disturbances bubbled through the summer but did not anywhere explode into large-scale violence; a semblance of calm returned. The crisis of 1450 was one of the most serious to afflict the Crown in the medieval period.[28] For a decade the magnates around the throne, including York had managed to rule in the King's name, masking the vacuum that existed. The final collapse in Normandy fractured the illusion; the commons were suddenly jolted into the realisation that there was an emptiness at the heart of the English polity. They chose to blame the perceived incompetence and avarice on the King's advisors who, whilst they might and probably were to some degree feathering their own nests, were nonetheless striving in an impossible situation.[29] The kingdom was effectively without a king; 'keeping the show on the road' had worked in the 1440s but could not continue indefinitely – the debacle in Normandy merely exposed the fiction. Somerset, as commander, had been unable to stem the rot; it is doubtful if any could have done better. After the defeat at Formigny both Vire and Bayeux fell; Caen held out for only three weeks. Somerset was taken and then released, retreating into the great fortress of the Calais Pale. On 11 August, the port of Cherbourg, the very last English toehold in Normandy, capitulated without any attempt at relief.[30]

Richard of York – the Unlikely Rebel

It was perhaps York's good fortune that his tenure across the Irish Sea put him, both literally and figuratively, at a distance from the crisis. He was able to escape the rush of opprobrium that descended on Suffolk and those closest to the throne as Normandy was lost. This providential distance afforded him the opportunity to create a platform and it is from this time that he appears as the inheritor of Good Duke Humphrey, in whose fall he had at least been complicit. The nobility were reeling from the collapse of the edifice so carefully tended during the preceding decade; gentry and commons had reacted with violent outrage to their perceived failures. York, having spent little of his life within his own estates, lacked a solid affinity; a number of his retainers, men like Fastolf and Oldcastle, had served him in France and suffered loss when Normandy fell. Somerset, despite having been the defeated general, managed to attach himself to the King's household and, effectively, replace Suffolk. His job would be that much harder because the pretence of direct royal command had faltered. Before York returned in September 1450, he had taken steps to at least begin the return to stability.

Having assumed Gloucester's mantle, York's platform was essentially anti-household, broadly populist, drawing support from some magnates but also from gentry and bourgeois. As the King was still, at this point, childless, York stood to be recognised as heir-presumptive. In fact Somerset was nearer in blood but was debarred by statute. Somerset was hamstrung in that he was adopting a mode of governance that had failed, and failed badly: York stood for 'collective conciliar action'[31] and also for the continuance of the French war. He was the man who might have saved France; in practice this was unlikely but it added to his manifesto. Somerset acted as the King's proxy, as had Suffolk. Like his predecessor he was, to an extent, a hostage of the household. His authority was never absolute and this was particularly noticeable in the rash of local magnate disputes that flared after 1450 and which contributed in bringing him and the 'court' faction into disrepute.

Despite any alarm which York's unlooked-for and unauthorised return provoked – and it may be that the Duke saw enemies where perhaps none existed – he had not come to seek a fight. Half-hearted efforts were made to detain him, but he sidestepped these to arrive at Westminster with a substantial following. His purpose, aside from stating his grievances, was to affirm his loyalty to Henry VI and promote his suitability for the post of chief advisor. His protestations were by no means divorced from self interest. York was launching his own manifesto as the most suitable candidate for the role he coveted. For the commons, infuriated at the perceived failure to maintain the Crown's position against the French and concerned at the apparent breakdown in law and order, York, apparently untainted, seemed the perfect nominee. For the Duke to base his platform on the roarings of the mob was most impolitic; a man who holds himself out as the restorer of order cannot rise on the back of disorder.[32] Whatever the popular acclaim, York did not enjoy a following amongst the aristocracy.

Correspondence from William Wayte[33] to John Paston on 6 October 1450 indicates that York and those of his affinity, like Sir William Oldhall, were apparently successful in getting the better of the rump of Suffolk's affinity in East Anglia – in particular, John Heydon and Thomas Tuddenham, both Norfolk gentlemen, the latter Clerk of the Great Wardrobe in the second half of the 1440s. York, through the early autumn, was assiduous in canvassing support in both East Anglia and the East Midlands. Henry, or Somerset on his behalf, rejected his cousin's bill – he averred he would rather be advised by a body of counsellors than rely upon a single chief minister. York, for all his efforts and widespread sympathies, did not command any significant faction among the magnates, only Norfolk and Devon lent overt support and that mainly guided in each case by self interest.

Nonetheless, in Parliament the Duke had a number of sympathisers, Oldhall was elected speaker, and certain reforms did reach the statute books. However, this support only obtained for as long as the House was in session. York, whose eye for timing was never good, sought to engineer the passage of a bill whereby the King would formally recognise the Duke as his heir. This proved a step too far and Parliament was promptly dissolved.[34] Somerset, meantime, had acquired the office of Captain of the Calais garrison, a significant appointment and one which placed him in control of the country's largest standing force. That there was a need for a strong hand to enforce law and order was amply demonstrated in 1451 when a simmering rivalry which had been brewing in the south west during the 1440s burst into open discord. Leadership in that corner of the kingdom had, for generations, been the preserve of the Courtenay Earls of Devon. Latterly, they had been offered a challenge by the Lord Bonville of Chewton. William Bonville was a capable officer who had served both Henry V and his brother the Duke of Bedford in France, where he had risen to high office as seneschal of Gascony. Since returning he had occupied himself energetically in local matters and had married a Courtenay, the 12th Earl's aunt.

This move, outwardly politic, did not ingratiate him with the Earl as the Courtenays were themselves divided. Worse, Henry VI appointed Thomas Courtenay as Steward of the Duchy of Cornwall, an office previously awarded to Bonville. Throughout the 1440s the feud festered, Bonville was perceived as Suffolk's creature, therefore favoured by the court faction and so, inevitably, the Earl gravitated toward York's affinity. In September 1451, matters reached a head when the Earl, with his confederate, Lord Cobham, took up arms and marched against Bonville, bottling him up in Taunton Castle, which they besieged. The administration was ignored whilst the nobles made private war. It was York who, on his own initiative, relieved Taunton, calmed the Courtenay faction and compelled the warring parties to their senses. Whilst this was highly effective policing, there may also have been a private motive in so far as York would not wish to see Devon, his ally, brought to account and incarcerated.[35]

Such a signal success emboldened the Duke who, still finding himself thwarted by Somerset, resolved to enforce his right by more direct means. The situation was exacerbated by yet more defeats in France. Having regained Normandy and at so little cost, Charles VII naturally turned his eyes southwards toward the ripe plum of Gascony. Bordeaux was presently threatened as the French swept through the province and the castellan agreed to lower his flag should relief not arrive by 14 June 1451. None came and the city surrendered; three centuries of English domination came to an end. The loss of Bordeaux constituted a disaster of the first magnitude and there appeared no hope of its recovery. Sir William Oldhall was detailed to act as his master's tool in laying the foundations for a possible coup, though he quickly developed a bad case of cold feet and sought sanctuary, from whence he did not fully emerge until 1455![36]

York had canvassed support fom amongst both commons and gentry by widespread circulation of his manifesto; however, he had again misread the mood of the country. Aside from areas under his direct control, or that of his affinity, there was no general uprising. He commanded respect, there was sympathy for the preceived wrongs which had been done to him, but he simply did not have a sufficient power base amongst his fellow magnates. King Henry may not have been suited to rule and the party around him, seeking to prop up the administration, had largely foundered, yet there was no stomach for a direct revolt against the authority of the Crown. Neither London, nor even Kent would lend him support; the men who had marched with Jack Cade refused to come out for Richard of York. As he made his camp at Dartford, the Duke could count only upon Devon and Lord Cobham. Even the prominent Nevilles were to be found in the King's great army mustering at Blackheath. The confrontation of March 1452 did not result in a fight; York was heavily outnumbered but, neither his brother-in-law, Salisbury, nor his nephew, Warwick, wished to see him defeated:

> And on Thursday at afternoon there was made a pointment between the king and the Duke of York by the mean of lords. And on the morrow, that was Friday, the king ensembled his host on the Blackheath afore noon; and there abode the coming of the Duke of York after the pointment made over even. And in the king's host was numbered 20,000 fighting men, and men said the Duke of York came with forty horse to the king about noon, and obeyed him to his liegance; and with [him] the earl of Devonshire and the Lord Cobham, the which held with the Duke of York and were in host with him. And the king took them to grace and all.[37]

York was not minded to compromise. It is likely that, behind the scenes, he believed the Nevilles lent his way and he insisted on Somerset's removal and indictment as conditions precedent to any accord. By the close of play the Duke was convinced the meeting, with the King's acquiescence, had agreed to these terms; consequently he disbanded his forces and the matter appeared settled. In this he was mistaken. York, whatever his qualities, was not a skilled politician; Somerset certainly appears as the more astute and York found himself treated, if not as a traitor, then as something very close.

He was humiliated when the royal train returned to London, compelled to ride before the royal party as though a mere felon. Both of his followers, Devon and Cobham, were kept in detention for a period, though the Duke himself was restored to liberty on 10 March, amidst rumours that a large force of Welsh adherents was set to march on London and procure his liberty, if necessary by force. Though unscathed, he was not undamaged – being made to swear a strict oath of allegiance in the very public arena of St Paul's, whilst Somerset, later that year, conducted trials of certain of York's retainers implicated in the abortive rising – proceedings which were conducted at Ludlow, in the very heart of the Duke's estates. York was largely corralled; Somerset remained as chief councillor. If, however, York was sidelined and his challenge defused, the magnates were not prepared to allow Somerset to destroy him.

In France matters took a turn for the better when, in the autumn, Bull Talbot recovered Bordeaux and, in the spring, the Queen was at last with child. By the summer of 1453, the brief English recovery ended for good when Talbot, fighting valiantly, was overwhelmed and killed, his small force decimated at Castillon on 17 July.[38] This was bad but, even worse, whilst at Clarendon the King suffered a complete mental collapse. Try as they might, the court faction could not hide the King's disability and without his sovereign power behind them, the court faction's authority evaporated. The crisis of 1450 had exposed the weakness at the core of the English polity; York, previously acquiescent, had leapt onto a particular bandwagon, but his intervention appeared abortive. What had now changed was that there was a clear division – the outward amity of the 1440s had disappeared; York had rewritten his role during the decade and the rift was palpable; lawlessness was mounting and the realm inexorably drifting closer to civil strife.

Notes

1 C. Carpenter, *The Wars of the Roses – Politics and the Constitution in England c.1437–1509* (Cambridge 2002), p. 27.
2 David II was captured at the Battle of Neville's Cross in 1346, the King of France a decade later at the Battle of Poitiers.
3 Carpenter, op. cit., p. 35.
4 J. Gillingham, *The Wars of the Roses* (London 2001), pp. 53–4.
5 D. Seward, *Henry V as Warlord* (London 1987), p. 41.
6 A. J. Pollard, *The Wars of the Roses* (London 2001), p. 55.

7 Ibid., p. 54.
8 Ibid., p. 54.
9 York had only been four years old when his father was executed for treason.
10 Carpenter, op. cit., pp. 95–6.
11 Ibid., p. 97.
12 Ibid., p. 79.
13 Gloucester had unwisely become embroiled with Jacqueline of Hainault, whose aspirations clashed with the Burgundian influence, much to his brother's horror.
14 Charles of Orleans was a prisoner awaiting ransom – he had been captured at Agincourt!
15 Carpenter, op. cit., p. 95.
16 Gillingham, op. cit., p. 58.
17 Ibid., p. 57.
18 Carpenter, op. cit., p. 102.
19 Fougères: an important Breton fortress; captured from the French by Francois de Surenne, an Aragonese mercenary captain in Somerset's service.
20 C. Ross, *The Wars of the Roses* (London 1976), p. 26.
21 Ibid., p. 26.
22 The leaders took rather colourful names, such as; Robin Hood, Bluebeard, the King and Queen of the Fairies; see Gillingham, op. cit., p. 62.
23 RP v 177–81.
24 PL i pp. 124–5.
25 Not a great deal is known about Jack Cade, though he was most probably an ex soldier, who sometimes called himself John Mortimer as though identifying himself with the Duke of York. There is no evidence linking the two.
26 Cited in Gillingham, op. cit., p. 62.
27 Gregory, pp. 190–4.
28 Carpenter, op. cit., p. 117.
29 Ibid.
30 R. Neillands, *The Hundred Years War* (London 1990), pp. 281–3.
31 Carpenter, op. cit., p. 121.
32 Ibid.
33 The writer was clerk to William Yelverton, who sat on the King's Bench; see J. R. Lander, *The Wars of the Roses* (London 1990), p. 44n.
34 Thomas Young, the Bill's proposer, was an ally of pro-Yorkist Oldhall; his presumption, however, landed him in the Tower!
35 Gillingham, op. cit., p. 72.
36 Oldhall sought sanctuary in the Church of St Martin-le-Grand, Dover.
37 Lander, op. cit., pp. 46–7.
38 Gillingham, op. cit., p. 74.

Chapter 3

The Path to Conflict
1453–1455

If Somerset had succeeded in maintaining his control of the administration, the problems inherent in any situation where a weak monarchy existed were unlikely simply to disappear. However even-handed someone in the Duke's position might appear to be, he would, to a degree, be bound to support those who supported him and thus lack the full impartiality of the Crown when it came to resolving local disputes. There is no real evidence to suggest that the nobility and gentry of the mid fifteenth century were more quarrelsome or more inclined to resort to arms than their predecessors. Nonetheless, the lack of a royal will opened the gates to a series of local disturbances which were to assist in propelling the magnates along the path to open conflict.

In Derbyshire a slew of gentry families – Blounts, Gresleys, Vernons and Longfords – were openly feuding; Richard Neville as Earl of Warwick was experiencing difficulties in exercising sway over his late father-in-law's wide lands in Warwickshire. Despite Suffolk's taking off, his widow and Lord Scales kept stirring the brew in East Anglia. The Courtenay–Bonville fracas had erupted. In Gloucestershire the Talbots and Berkeleys were at odds and the Duke of Exeter was sparring with Lord Cromwell. The events in

Warwickshire had been causing tension between the Earl of Warwick and the Duke of Buckingham; the Earl was also at odds with Somerset over various portions of the Beauchamp inheritance.

Percy v. Neville

On 24 August 1453 Thomas Percy, Lord Egremont, younger son of the 2nd Earl of Northumberland, lay in ambush by Heworth Moor, just north-east of York. With him he had perhaps a thousand men-at-arms and archers; their intended quarry the bridal party attending Sir Thomas Neville and his new wife Maud Stanhope. The bride and groom were accompanied by Sir Thomas's parents, the Earl and Countess of Salisbury, and Thomas's brother John, the future Lord Montagu. All were travelling north from Tattershall Castle in Lincolnshire where the marriage had been celebrated. The Nevilles were neither unguarded nor unaware and, when the Percy affinity swarmed from ambush, the bridal party acquitted themselves more than adequately and the attack was vigorously repulsed.

Though this affair, on the surface, may appear as little more than a local and largely bloodless brawl, it could be said to represent the first significant, armed clash between the two pre-eminent northern magnates, who were also active in the wider movement to reform and ultimately remove the Lancastrian administration.[1] Some commentators have seen the Percy–Neville feud as the catalyst which led mere factionalism to degenerate into civil war. Since the heady days of the late fourteenth century, when the power of the Percies was unrivalled in the north, the Nevilles had risen to challenge and indeed eclipse that supremacy.[2] The almost princely independence of the Percies confirmed a quasi-regal status in the north: 'the dominant individual in northern society was Henry Percy 4th Earl of Northumberland'[3] – a view which persisted even after the end of the immediate conflicts, and when the Nevilles were crushed.

This view is not without its detractors who view the rebellions of the 1st Earl and his eldest son Henry Percy ('Hotspur'), as attempts to throw off the yoke of royal control, which both Richard II and then Henry IV had sought to exercise. The family ultimately failed in their bid to regain the measure of independence they had enjoyed in the 1360s and 1370s. Hotspur's rebellion ended in defeat and a traitor's death at Shrewsbury in

1403. By the time the dead man's son, yet another Henry (the Percies enjoyed the regal distinction of having the numerous Henries numbered sequentially by historians), was able, in 1416, to reverse his father's attainder, the rising star of the Neville dynasty had risen, at least in part, to fill the void.[4]

Under the steady, if grasping, hand of Ralph Neville, 1st Earl of Westmorland, the family had remained staunchly loyal to the House of Lancaster and had gradually increased their estates and spheres of influence. The Earl died in 1425 and his effigy in Staindrop Church, County Durham, shows him wearing the distinctive 'S' collar of a solid Lancastrian.[5] Having held the north for Henry IV when the Percies rebelled, he cemented his relationship with the Crown by marrying Joan Beaufort, Salisbury's mother and herself a daughter of John of Gaunt. With the Beaufort clan high in the Council of Henry VI, the Neville allegiance seemed secure.[6]

A policy, begun by John of Gaunt, of buttressing the power of the Nevilles as a counterweight to the Percies, was continued by Henry VI and the expanse of the affinity of the former was, not infrequently, at the expense of the latter.[7] The prestige of the Nevilles was particularly high in County Durham, where the influence of their rivals was noticeably weaker. William, Lord Fauconberg ('Little Fauconberg'), the Earl of Salisbury's brother, together with others of the Neville affinity – George, Lord Latimer; Edward, Lord Abergavenny; and his son Sir Thomas – are consistently named in commissions of the peace. At various times Fauconberg, a veteran of the French and Scottish wars, was seneschal, steward, justice of assize and justice of gaol delivery; Latimer acted as chamberlain, and Thomas also held similar offices to those of his uncle, including that of commissioner of array for the wards of Chester, Darlington, Easington and the Wapentake of Sadberge.[8]

Richard, Earl of Salisbury inherited the bulk of the Neville holdings in Yorkshire, centred on the valuable estates of Middleham and Sheriff Hutton. The worth of this legacy, Salisbury being the son of the Earl of Westmorland's second wife, sparked a deep division with the senior branch, which retained the title and lands in the north-west. Undisturbed by this family rift, Salisbury went on to steadily build up the scale of his holdings. His own eldest son, another Richard, added the dazzling Beauchamp inheritance and the earldom of Warwick to his titles and was to mature into a key figure of the political landscape, bringing the power of his name to its ultimate zenith before crashing to ruin: 'Warwick the Kingmaker'. Always something of a swashbuckler, he

> *had energy, dash and courage. A skilful propagandist, he had great success in rousing the common people to his cause and was well noted for his open handed generosity. Yet he was also self-interested and arrogant . . . acquisitive and unscrupulous to a degree . . . unusually ruthless in his treatment of defeated enemies.*[9]

The three ridings of Yorkshire were parcelled out, in terms of land owner-ship, between four of the greatest magnates of the realm, including the Crown as Duchy of Lancaster, the Percies, Nevilles and the Duke of York, Salisbury's brother-in-law. The Percy holdings east of the Pennines were interspersed with those of Salisbury and York, though the latter showed scant interest in his northern estates.[10] Having taken the years from 1416–40 for the Earl of Northumberland to recover the bulk of his father's lost inheritance, Salisbury, who had been elevated to his earldom in 1429, had had ample time to consolidate his hold on manors in Cleveland, West-morland, Cumberland and the important lordship of Raby.[11]

His bickering with the senior branch continued over this period, and even a negotiated settlement of 1443 did not appease the bitterness. Salisbury cer-tainly could not depend on his kin to back him in a feud with the Percies.[12] In the course of that year Salisbury was appointed to the West March wardenry, a prestigious office which allowed him to increase his affinity through Cumber-land and Westmorland. By the early 1440s his annual income could have reached the very substantial amount of £3,000, only £500 behind the Bishop of Durham, but perhaps as much as a £1,000 more than Northumberland could garner.[13] For decades the Percies had been active and pre-eminent in border affairs; Hotspur's fight at Otterburn in 1388 and the signal victory of Homildon 14 years later, had provided the inspiration for stirring border balladry, and the 2nd Earl's second son, another Henry, Lord Poynings, held the East March from 1440. After a decade in office, Salisbury retained his post, now held jointly with Warwick. One of the significant benefits of the warden's office was the right to raise forces. These were, ostensibly, to be arrayed for the defence of the frontier against the Scots, but a warden's swollen retinue could be a useful boost to his family's muscle, should the need arise.[14]

At one level, the state of the borders in the 1400s appears to have been less turbulent than during the preceding century. The period of over a hundred years between the disaster at Homildon and the death of James IV at Flodden saw long phases of minority rule on the Scottish side. The majority of James II (he of the 'fiery face'), witnessed a sudden upsurge in the tempo of aggression. The young King attempted to take Berwick in 1455 and again two years later. During the intervening year he led a destructive chevauchee through Northumberland. He was finally and, from the English perspective fortuitously, killed at the siege of Roxburgh in 1460.[15] The office of warden, which had its origins in the earlier medieval period, was, by the mid fifteenth century, well established with the power and burden of the holder clearly defined. Having enjoyed the privileges of the wardenry for so long, the Percies tended to rely on the robust thuggery of border practice. In January 1453, a band of Percy tenants could feel sufficiently confident that no sheriff or other Crown official could wield power within, specifically, the manor of Tocliffe and, more generally, on any land held by the Percies.

This aggressive posturing was fed by the conduct of Lord Egremont who had threatened the life of the Sheriff of Cumberland, Thomas de la Mare, an adherent of Salisbury.[16] Egremont, who had gained his lordship in 1449 at the age of 25, typified all the adverse traits of his name: 'quarrelsome, violent and contemptuous of all authority, he possessed all the worst characteristics of a Percy for which his grandfather is still a byword'.[17] Salisbury's sister Eleanor was married to Northumberland, but the ties of blood counted for little in a game with such high stakes. Both families possessed mature and ambitious patriarchs, each with a brood of young, restless and potentially lawless sons, and no shortage of available manpower.[18]

When Thomas Neville married Maud Stanhope, this proved a provocation too far for the volatile Egremont. The bride had been married before, to Robert, Lord Willoughby of Eresby, who had died the previous summer. She was also, and significantly, the niece and co-heiress of Ralph, Lord Cromwell, a choleric character himself but one who had acquired the leases on two choice manors at Wressle and Burwell in Lincolnshire, previously in the hands of the Percies. In February 1440 Cromwell had purchased the reversionary interest. Northumberland, whose line had spent lavishly on Wressle, had litigated in vain. When Cromwell married his niece to a Neville he was adding insult to injury.[19] Tension had been mounting throughout the early summer of 1452. In June the King had summoned both Egremont and John Neville; by the end of that month, Neville was laying pans for an ambush of his own. On 2 July, Henry dissolved Parliament and journeyed north to confront his quarrelsome vassals. He proposed that Percy and his affinity should gird themselves in readiness for service in Gascony, where their martial spirit might be more usefully deployed, however, the proposal came to nothing.

Disturbances in the North

On 12 July the King established a Commission of Oyer and Terminer, the membership of which included both the rival earls, Viscount Beaumont and some fourteen others.[20] A fortnight later, the commission was reissued, but to little effect. Salisbury who, unlike Northumberland, sat in the Council, undoubtedly used his influence to pack the membership with allies, whose ranks included such Neville stalwarts as Sir James Pickering, Sir Henry Fitzhugh and Sir Henry le Scrope of Bolton.[21] Despite the commission's excellent credentials, it proved ineffective amidst a rising tide of disorder and, by the end of July, a new and perhaps less overtly partisan body was set up under the guidance of Sir William Lucy, a knight of Northamptonshire and Council member, his leadership supported by leading counsel. Immediately Sir William set to work, summoning Ralph Neville, Sir John Conyers, Sir James Pickering, Sir Ralph Randolf, Sir Thomas Mountford, Richard Aske, Thomas Sewer and John Alcombe. On 10 August, nine Percy adherents were summoned, together with both Sir Ralph and Sir Richard Percy.[22]

York, as the economic and cultural capital of the north, was equally important to both factions in the escalating disturbances, both of whom made moves to court the citizenry. The city, as a major mercantile centre, was suffering from the general recession of the 1450s. The loss of Gascony had seriously affected the all-important wine trade, the North Sea was infested with pirates, relations with the Hanse were difficult and the defeat of English hopes at Castillon only worsened the situation.[23] Recession and unemployment provided a further reservoir of available manpower, which could be drawn into factionalism. Egremont, in seeking to spring his trap of 24 August was presumably aiming to decimate the Nevilles. Of the 710 persons named on indictments laid before the Duke of York the following summer, some 94 per cent of these came from the northern gentry and yeomen, and slightly more than 15 per cent were citizens of York.[24]

Undeterred by the failure at Heworth, Richard Percy and a band of unruly adherents now embarked on a spree of vandalism, culminating in the kidnapping of Lawrence Catterall, the bailiff of Staincliff Wapentake, who was roughly dragged from his devotions in Gargrave Church on 9 September. He was subsequently incarcerated, at first in Isel Castle and, later, at Cockermouth. Obviously the luckless man had, in some unrecorded way, offended the Percies.[25] The unrest continued: on 25 September a brace of Percy retainers – a John Catterall and Sir John Salvin – pillaged the house of William Hebdon, vicar of Aughton. This may have been in reprisal for John Neville's plundering of the Earl of Northumberland's property at Catton.[26]

On 8 October King Henry wrote plaintively to both earls, enjoining them to exercise some degree of control over their headstrong siblings. At this time the King's mental health was already causing concern, he had no history of instability and his Queen, with the court faction, were not inclined to advertise the fact. The exact nature of the King's malady has never been definitively diagnosed, though catatonic schizophrenia has been

Figure 2: Margaret of Anjou

(© National Portrait Gallery, London)

favoured. Whatever the cause, the plain fact was that Henry's deteriorating mental condition contributed to his administration's grip on law and order. By 17 October Egremont had assembled perhaps 50 harnessed retainers, who mustered at Topcliffe. Rather less than half of these were from the Percy heartland of Northumberland or the City of Newcastle.[27] Heedless of the feeble royal admonitions, both sides were squaring up for a further brawl, and a confrontation of sorts probably occurred at Sandhutton on 20 October.

Here, Salisbury and Warwick, joined by Sir John and Sir Thomas Neville, were bolstered by such trusty friends as Sir Henry Fitzhugh and Sir Henry le Scrope. Not to be outdone, the Percy affinity were led by the Earl and Lord Poynings, Lord Egremont and Sir Richard Percy. The stand-off seems to have amounted to little more than bravado on both sides, but the magnates themselves had now clearly shown their hands in the fracas. Battle lines had been drawn, even if very few blows had yet been struck.[28] As the tempo of strife rose, the King's grasp on reality declined and it had, by now, become impossible to hide the fact of his condition. Matters were further stirred by the birth, on 13 October of a son, Edward of Lancaster. With this, York's hopes of securing the succession from a childless monarch vanished like the mist. Increasingly vociferous, the Duke, as the senior magnate, was clamouring to be appointed as regent during the term of the King's illness, a demand the Queen and Somerset were equally determined to resist. On 25 October the Council convened at York with both Salisbury and Warwick in attendance. Northumberland and Lord Poynings were pointedly absent.[29]

The Duke of York had married Salisbury's sister Cicely, the celebrated 'Rose of Raby'. His career in the public service had been worthy if undistinguished. His efforts to secure Normandy had been wasted by Somerset's subsequent mishandling. Much of his endeavours had been self-financed and the Duke was owed substantial sums by the Crown. His posting to Ireland was, in all but name, a form of exile, yet he had done good service in that unruly province. As a man he was: 'a somewhat austere, remote and unsympathetic figure, with little capacity or inclination to seek out and win support from his fellow noblemen or from the wider public'.[30]

York had no love for Somerset, whom he perceived, almost certainly correctly, as the main block to his inclusion in the King's inner circle. The loss of the French territories had led to the confrontation at Blackheath. It was here that Salisbury and Warwick undertook the roles of honest brokers. None can have been impressed when the promises made were contemptuously put aside. The King's breakdown dramatically altered the balance of power and York, fully supported by his brother-in-law and nephew, secured the protectorate. Despite his Beaufort blood, Warwick maintained a separate quarrel with Somerset, over title to a portion of the vast Beauchamp inheritance. The Duke's greed surpassed his judgement – making an enemy of the Earl was downright folly with the balance of power so delicately poised. No sooner was York in office than his former rival was consigned to a sojourn in the Tower.[31]

Undoubtedly, some of those returning from the wrack of the French wars would seek employment in the households of the great magnates and, in the north, the Anglo-Scottish border had witnessed generations of endemic, low-intensity warfare. A surviving indenture from 1452 and entered into by Salisbury and Walter Strickland, a Westmorland knight, provides, inter alia, that the latter will supply 74 billmen 'horsed and harnessed', 69 bowmen likewise arrayed, 76 dismounted billmen and 71 foot archers – an impressive company.[32] Lord Cromwell, notoriously litigious, had been at odds in the courts with Henry Holand, Duke of Exeter. The matter had become so heated between these two choleric peers that, in July 1453, both had been temporarily incarcerated. With the Neville marriage, Cromwell found an ally in Salisbury; Exeter, inevitably, sought common cause with the Percies.[33] On 27 March 1454 the Duke of York was formally installed as Protector and, less than a week later his brother-in-law was appointed as Chancellor.

Secure in his high office, Salisbury summoned Egremont and Richard Percy to attend upon his convenience on pain of forfeiture and outlawry.[34] Whereas the Percies might disdain the King's feeble complaints, Salisbury, in the mantle of Chancellor, could not be ignored. York's appointment marked a period of more decisive governance, though the Nevilles were clearly, as ever, motivated by self-interest. Sensing the mood, Sir Thomas Neville of Brancepeth (not Salisbury's son but a younger brother of the Earl of Westmorland, and no friend to his cousins), took the opportunity to 'take up' the property of Sir John Salvin at Egton in Eskdale. This was accomplished with a body of two dozen armed retainers who lifted some £80 worth of 'gear' (valuables and household goods).[35]

In May 1454 York, as Protector, sent a strongly worded summons to the Earl of Northumberland, ordering him to appear before the Council on 12 June. Lord Poynings and Ralph Percy were summoned to appear ten days

beforehand. Already, on 3 April, Exeter had been removed from his lucrative and prestigious post of Lord Admiral.[36] Not unsurprisingly, the Percies
were not minded to follow the path of humility. On 6 May, they showed
what respect they had for the new Chancellor by vandalising his house in
York and roughing up one of his tenants, John Skipworth. Many of these
now involved in this fresh rash of disturbances had been 'out' upon
Heworth Moor the previous summer. By the middle of May Egremont was
mustering his affinity at Spofforth and there, on the 14th, he was joined
by Exeter, bridling at his humiliation. Riotous behaviour broke out in the
streets of York, alarming the burgesses, especially after the mob had brutally
assaulted the Mayor and the Recorder. A wave of anarchy now swept through
the North Riding, whilst Exeter, not to be outdone, busily stirred up trouble
in Lancashire and Cheshire.[37] Needless to say, the invigorated Council,
supported by York, as Protector, were not inclined to remain inert whilst
these troubles flared. Sir Thomas Stanley, the Duchy of Lancaster's Receiver
for the counties of Lancashire and Cheshire, ably assisted by Sir Thomas
Harrington, saw Exeter off in short order. The Protector himself entered the
City of York on 19 May – the rioters fled the streets.[38]

Exeter, whose thuggish traits matched those of Egremont, was, nonetheless, one of King Henry's closest blood relations, tracing his line through
John of Gaunt. It is conceivable that he perceived, in this localised brawl, the
chance to light a fuse that might unseat York and see him appointed in his
stead.[39] On 21 May, with Egremont and his affinity, he reappeared in York
and set about further intimidation of the much abused Mayor and burgesses.
Disorder flared once again through the shire. Egremont was sufficiently
inflamed to solicit aid from James II of Scotland. The Scots had recently
violated the previous year's truce, and the herald dispatched to Edinburgh
to register the Council's protest was kidnapped at Spofforth. This smacked
of rebellion, and the rebels, as they could now be termed planned to lure
the Protector into an ambush beneath the walls of York.[40]

York summoned both the ringleaders to appear on 25 June, and used the
interval to consolidate his position and build up local forces. By the 15th of
the month he was reinforced by Warwick and Lord Greystoke; a week later
Lord Clifford, the Earl of Shrewsbury, and Sir Henry Fitzhugh added their
retinues. A number of summonses had been issued and, several individuals
suffered forfeiture or even outlawry, Exeter, Egremont and Sir Richard
Percy all failed to appear.[41] For all their violent posturing the rebels had

completely failed to achieve any serious objective. Exeter crept back to London. By 8 July he was in captivity, and by the 24th he had been safely incarcerated in Pontefract Castle. The snake might appear to have been scotched, but was still writhing, York did not feel sufficiently secure in the north with the Percies still at large to return to the capital.[42] Matters continued in this tense vein until the autumn, when a further confrontation took place; this time at Stamford Bridge, heavy with ancient blood, some miles east of York and held by the Nevilles. Whether any actual fighting occurred is doubtful, but the Percy faction were confounded by treachery when one of their own bailiffs, Peter Lound, with some two hundred followers deserted. The Nevilles, led by Thomas and John pounced on their discomfited enemies and captured both Egremont and Sir Richard Percy.

The prisoners were sent, probably via Middleham, into safe custody in Newgate Gaol. Arraigned before the Protector on 4 November both were penalised by the imposition of swingeing fines. Salisbury was to be compensated in the amount of 8,000 marks, and other members of the Neville clan were awarded lesser amounts. The total burden was some 16,800 marks, an indebtedness the Percies could not, in the short term, hope to discharge, and thus, as was no doubt intended, they remained behind bars.[43] If the Nevilles felt they had cause for satisfaction, their triumph was short-lived for, in December 1454, Henry VI recovered his wits and was deemed able to resume the reins of government; the office of Protector was thus redundant. On 7 February Somerset was freed from the Tower and reinstated to all his many offices. A month later Salisbury bowed to the inevitable, and resigned as Chancellor. A mere seven days after his departure, Exeter was set at liberty. Somerset and the Queen would be in the mood for retribution rather than compromise; a further and greater trial of strength now appeared inevitable.

What had changed since the earlier showdown at Blackheath was that York was not now entirely isolated – true, the Courtenays, disgruntled at the Duke's handling of their feud with Bonville, had switched their allegiance to the court faction. Now, however, York had the powerful support of the Neville earls, Salisbury and Warwick, with their large affinities. Somerset had blundered in allowing the alienation of the Nevilles who, with York, now believed the Duke with Wiltshire, Exeter, Beaumont and Northumberland, was at the head of a faction intent upon their destruction. The situation was considerably more volatile than that which had obtained in 1450; the scene was thus set for armed confrontation.

Notes

1 R. A. Griffiths, 'Local Rivalries and National Politics: The Percies, the Nevilles and the Duke of Exeter, 1452–1455', *Speculum,* vol. 43, 1968, p. 589. I am indebted to Griffiths's groundbreaking monograph for much of the information in this chapter.

2 A. J. Pollard, 'Percies, Nevilles and the Wars of the Roses', *History Today* September 1992, p. 42.

3 M. E. James, 'The Murder at Coxlodge on 28th April, 1489', *Durham University Journal,* vol. 42, 1965, p. 80.

4 H. Weiss, 'A Power in the North? The Percies in the Fifteenth Century', *Historical Journal* 19.2, 1965, pp. 501–9.

5 Pollard, 'Percies, Nevilles and the Wars of the Roses', p. 42.

6 Ross, op. cit., p. 31.

7 Weiss, op. cit., p. 503.

8 Ibid., p. 504.

9 Ross, op. cit., p. 31.

10 Griffiths, op. cit., p. 589.

11 Ibid., p. 590.

12 Ibid., p. 591.

13 Ibid., p. 593.

14 Ibid., p. 591.

15 G. Ridpath, *The Border History of England and Scotland* (Berwick 1776), pp. 288–9.

16 Griffiths, op. cit., p. 592.

17 Ibid., p. 591.

18 Ibid., p. 592.

19 Ibid., p. 594.

20 Ibid., p. 594.

21 Ibid., p. 595.

22 Ibid., p. 595.

23 D. Seward, *The Wars of the Roses* (London 1995), pp. 23–5.

24 Griffiths, op. cit., p. 592.

25 Ibid., p. 602.

26 Ibid., p. 603.

27 Ibid., p. 604.

28 Ibid., p. 605.

29 Ibid., p. 605.

30 Ross, op. cit., p. 28.

31 Ibid., p. 29.

32 Oman, op. cit., vol. 2, p. 408, cited in Wise, op. cit., p. 29.

33 Griffiths, op. cit., p. 608. The dispute between Exeter and Cromwell arose over the manor of Ampthill in Bedfordshire.
34 Ibid., p. 609.
35 Ibid., p. 610.
36 Ibid., p. 610.
37 Ibid., p. 611.
38 Ibid., p. 612.
39 Ibid., p. 613.
40 Ibid., p. 616.
41 Ibid., p. 620.
42 Ibid., p. 621.
43 Ibid., p. 622.

Chapter 4

First Blood – First St Albans 22 May 1455

And so do I. Victorious Prince of York,
Before I see thee seated in that throne
Which now the house of Lancaster usurps,
I vow by heaven these eyes shall never close,
This is the palace of the fearful King,
And this the regal seat. Possess it York;
For this is thine, and not King Henry's heirs.

William Shakespeare, 3 Henry VI, *I. i. 21–7*

The Court Party Revived

Somerset and the revived court party were minded to deal decisively with their Yorkist opponents. As the winter of 1455 turned to spring, York and his affinity stayed safe in the north, building their strength. Somerset could not allow this process to continue and we may assume that his was the guiding hand behind the decision, taken on 21 April, to summon a Council, ostensibly to seek resolution of the current impasse. A date, one month hence was fixed, and the notice contained the provision 'that they should meet to discuss the safety of the King against anyone who would threaten it'.[1] This contained a clear intimation that more than a whiff of treason was in the air. York cannot be blamed for concluding that to attend, without a substantial show of strength, would be to invite a similar fate to that of Humphrey of Gloucester. The Duke thus resolved upon a bolder strategy, possibly urged by his nephew, the Earl of Warwick: that the Yorkists should head south, down the track of the Great North Road and confront the royal train before it reached Leicester. In so doing, they would free the person of Henry VI from the evil counsellors around him, particularly Somerset, for whom York nursed a particular animosity: Beaufort's mishandling of affairs in France was blamed for the collapse. He had behaved deceitfully and cynically after Blackheath, and had gleefully humiliated his rival.

Matters had, of course, changed for the Yorkists since Margaret of Anjou had provided her husband with a male heir. Henry's long hiatus in conforming to dynastic duty might have given York grounds for optimism. The birth of Edward of Lancaster appeared to finally confound any hopes the Duke might have entertained. Worse, with the court faction thus immeasurably boosted, York was simply a rival claimant. The Queen and Somerset would be far safer if he were to be dispensed with altogether. It would appear that Somerset and the King were unaware, as they set off for Leicester, that York was on the march and under arms. Perhaps even at this stage they expected him to arrive humbly like Gloucester before him. The 'official' version of events as subsequently dictated by the victorious Yorkists and agreed by King Henry, by then in their power, seeks to justify this aggressive posture:

> Our said cousins [York, Salisbury and Warwick] understanding and considering as they say, the labours made against them . . . addressed them toward our presence, to declare them our true liegemen, the better accompanied for their surety, and to resist such malice as they verily deemed was purposed to have been executed against them . . .[2]

The northern army, which now followed the banners of York, Salisbury and Warwick southwards, numbered perhaps three thousand men, not a huge force, but large enough should a trial of arms ensue.[3] Within the English polity, matters were now more finely balanced than they had been at Blackheath: Warwick and Salisbury were fully alienated, had nailed their colours to the Yorkist mast, and the Duke could count on Devon as before. His redoubtable uncle, Sir William Neville, Lord Fauconberg, was with the King but his sympathies were likely elsewhere. Somerset could rely on his son

Henry Beaufort, Earl of Dorset, Northumberland, Lord Clifford of Skipton, Jasper Tudor, Earl of Pembroke and a particular royal favourite James Butler, Earl of Wiltshire. The veteran Duke of Buckingham, though attached to the court faction, was a respected moderate who constantly sought to broker an accord.

Once it became clear that York was advancing under arms, a sharp reminder was sent to him that failure to disband his brigade forthwith would be deemed an act of treason. No reply was forthcoming and, on 21 May, the day fixed for the Council hearing, the King, together with Somerset and a substantial body of retainers marched north from the capital. Three days earlier a general summons had been sent to the magnates to lend their banners to the royal cause. Some time had passed since Blackheath, and Somerset's perceived misgovernment had alienated many peers whom, whilst they would baulk at outright defiance, were in no rush to comply. York did, finally, write, intimating that he was unfairly excluded from the Council and that the detested Somerset must be removed from office forthwith. This correspondence, begun on 20 May, was initially addressed to Canterbury, as Chancellor, protesting at the Yorkist peers' exclusion from an earlier Council meeting at Westminster and affirming their loyalty to the King. The following day a copy of this letter was sent to the King with a covering note.

The King received this communication whilst at Kilburn, the Duke being already in Royston. Nonetheless, despite having fewer numbers, Henry marched on to Watford, whilst York moved up to Ware. From here, he dispatched a further communication, which largely reiterated the content of the previous message, there could be no reconciliation whilst the hated Beaufort remained at the King's table. Barely a score of miles now separated the two forces. Finally, the threads which had wound through the English polity for several decades were about to coalesce, the process of dissent, begun by the mercurial Gloucester, was finally to break out into armed dispute. Whether we accept the Tudor view that this process had been set in train by the Lancastrian usurpation of 1399, or whether we incline to the opinion that the causes were far more recent, as Abbot Whethamstede had observed, the point of no return was fast approaching.

It cannot be ascertained if the King and Somerset with the lords they had in attendance intended to fight from the outset, as some commentators have suggested. This seems unlikely; with no more than 2,000 men, their force was small. It is quite true that the Duke of Somerset was anxious to avoid any confrontation in the south near London, where Yorkist sentiment ran high, but may well have clung to the belief that he could face York down as the court faction had done at Blackheath. The Duke, however, had imbibed the bitter lesson of that humiliation. For him there was no question of backing down or even temporising. In the warm spring dawn of 22 May, the King received intelligence that the northerners were approaching St Albans. Thus, before continuing his march, King Henry summoned an urgent meeting of his officers. Somerset showed no desire to avoid a fight. The northern Lancastrians, Percy and his affinity, were not shy of a showdown with their Neville rivals. It was the moderate, Buckingham, who sought, by cautious counsel, to deflect the hotheads, advising a more conciliatory approach aimed at negotiation rather than confrontation. This was sage advice; Buckingham, loyal to the King, had no personal quarrel with York.

At this point Henry, who preferred to avoid the prospect of bloodshed, heeded the Duke's more objective advice and appointed him commander-in-chief, doubtless to the chagrin of Somerset who had, until the meeting, held that office. There was sound logic in this: Buckingham was related by marriage to York and was known as an honest broker, his presence at the head of the King's forces would surely reassure the northerners that battle could be avoided. The sight of Somerset's banners can only have had the opposite effect. By 9.00 a.m. both armies were circling the town, and the King was the first to enter, planting his royal standard in the market place whilst his forces consolidated their grip on the streets. At this time, St Albans, Roman Verulamium, was a thriving market town. It had played a role in the Peasant's Revolt of 1381 when there had been brewing tension between the townsmen and the Abbey. Nonetheless, the ecclesiastical establishment brought in travellers and pilgrims who funded numerous inns and ale houses, including the George, the Fleur-de-Lys and the Tabard.

The First Battle of St Albans

The town lay mainly on the north bank of the River Ver. The streets, comprising timber-framed dwellings, liberally spaced with ale houses, were protected not by a wall, but by a defensive ditch that circled the ground to the east, crossed by three lanes. From the north these were Cock Lane, then

Shropshire Lane (now Victoria Street) and Sopwell Lane – the modern London Road runs more or less squarely between the two. The spread of the abbey and its attendant structures stood to the west of Hollywell Street which ran northwards to the Market Place and to the main thoroughfare of St Peter's Street, dominated by the parish church. Whilst Henry made his HQ centrally, his officers spread their forces judiciously around the existing defences, manning the two gateways on Sopwell and Shropshire Lanes.[4] As the Lancastrians deployed, the superior Yorkist contingents were marshalling in open ground on Key Field, east of the outskirts. Here they were facing the long gardens of the houses on Hollywell Street, the square and St Peter's Street, running southwards toward the River Ver.

York's position was on the crest of a shallow ridge, overlooking the buildings; he himself occupied the right flank with a tried-and-trusted captain, Sir David Hall. Warwick led the Yorkist centre, supported by Sir Robert Ogle and with his numbers bolstered by a Mowbray contingent, though Norfolk himself was absent. Salisbury and Sir Thomas Neville took the left flank. The town's defensive fosse or ditch ran in front of the Yorkist line with the several lanes crossing. Both of the two most southerly were defended, and Cock Lane, to the north, crossed the ditch before it wound around the top of the town in a north-westerly direction. In his immediate entourage the King kept Lord Fauconberg and his favourite Wiltshire; the willing Buckingham scurried back and forth, carrying terms. York would not be budged from his position on Somerset's future – the terms employed made no bones about what fate awaited the Duke should he come into the northerners' power. Stung by the harshness of his dissenting lords, the King, with a flourish of bravado, bid them damnation, threatening to hang, draw and quarter all those who opposed his will. Professor Lander quotes some contemporary correspondence, the so-called Dijon Relation, penned certainly within a week of the fight:

> *The reply made was that he [York] was not coming against him thus, [he] was always ready to do him obedience but he well intended in one way or another to have the traitors who were about him so that they should be punished, and that in case he could not have them with good will and fair consent, he intended in any case to have them by force. The reply that was made from the king's side to the said Duke of York was that he [the King] was unaware that there were any traitors about him were it not for the Duke of York himself who*

had risen against the crown. And even before this reply came to the Duke of York there begun the skirmish before the village by one side and the other.[5]

This advance to contact was a momentous step. York, Salisbury and Warwick were amongst the leading magnates of the realm, with wide estates and great fortunes at risk. For the magnate to take up arms directly against the King was not only treason at law but a mortal sin, in an age when the sanction of the Church would weigh heavily on noble and commons. Once swords were drawn in anger, there could be no going back. Protest as they might that they had taken up arms only to deliver the person of Henry VI from evil counsellors, they now made war on the throne. There had not been an armed confrontation in half a century, since Hotspur fell at Shrewsbury. The Yorkists advanced along Sopwell and Shropshire Lanes to probe the defences. It was now mid-morning. As the northerners surged towards the gates, more Lancastrians appeared, to shore up the defenders and, in the narrows, they maintained the advantage. Having witnessed Buckingham's parley the Lancastrians, holding the inner flank of the ditch, seem to have adopted a somewhat relaxed approach, thinking the business would finish without recourse to arms. Only when these men heard York address a hurried harangue to his troops, before giving the order to advance, did they suddenly realise this was not to be a repeat of the sham at Blackheath.

For the first time in the course of the struggle, Englishmen now fought each other in earnest. The Lancastrians appear to have been caught slightly off guard by the sudden push toward the barriers, but the thin ribbon of road and the gates were sufficient to slow the attackers, to deny them the advantage their numbers might otherwise confer. The fight was a confused affair of hacking bills and random volleys, the savage melee of hand to hand in confined space, no room hardly for the dead to fall or the wounded to crawl free. Any man who went down to wounds, could count on being hewed and stamped on as he writhed, the narrow way soon puddled in blood. It seemed as though the defences would hold up indefinitely, but the Earl of Warwick, having wisely judged the tactical stalemate, now led the uncommitted portion of his forces in an outflanking move. The attackers swarmed over the ditch, filtering through the gardens to break through the ribbon of houses and gain the square.[6]

This proved to be a sound move.[7] His men burst through with a proud flourish and shouts of 'a Warwick, a Warwick'. It was now that the uncertainty of battle in a jumble of lanes told against the Lancastrians as their men perceived they were taken in rear. The defenders, who had so resolutely defended the two contested entrances, broke ranks and withdrew, allowing York and Salisbury to follow Warwick's initiative. For the King's officers, all they could do was attempt a rally in the square itself, around the talisman of the royal personage. Henry, if he was no soldier, displayed considerable sangfroid and is said to have remained calmly seated beneath the shade of a tree throughout, whilst the fight raged around. Warwick's archers were presented with a fine target as their remaining opponents crowded the square. Both Buckingham and the King himself sustained wounds. Abbot Whethamstede, witnessing these events from his incomparable vantage above the abbey entrance, breathlessly observed: 'Here you saw one fall with his brains dashed out, there another with a broken arm, a third with a cut throat, and a fourth with a pierced chest, and the whole street was full of corpses.'[8]

The commons were perhaps fortunate, the gentry less so, being particular targets for their enemies. Warwick's retainers cut down Lord Clifford, the Earl of Northumberland fell shortly after, possibly trying to seek refuge in the Castle Inn, which occupied the corner of Shropshire Lane.[9] Henry Beaufort, Earl of Dorset, was taken and spared, though sore wounded, as were the injured Buckingham and captured Tudor. The Earl of Wiltshire, who was to demonstrate something of a genius for survival, made good his escape;[10] Lord Fauconberg, who had, at least nominally, been in the King's host, departed unmolested. The Dijon Relation reports the action:

> The battle began on the stroke of ten hours in the morning but because the place was small few of the combatants could set to work there and matters reached such great extremity that four of those who were of the king's bodyguard were killed by arrows in his presence and the king himself was struck by an arrow in the shoulder, but it penetrated only a little of the flesh.[11]

One man for whom there could be no expectation of clemency was Edmund Beaufort, 2nd Duke of Somerset. He sought temporary sanctuary inside the Castle Inn[12] but, being denied any hope of quarter, resolved to die bravely. Whatever the Duke's shortcomings he did not fail as a knight. Sallying out, he accounted for a quartet of opponents before the hacking blade of a poleaxe brought him down. The Dijon Relation confirms the Duke's fate:

> [T]he Duke of Somerset seeing that he had no other remedy took counsel with his men about coming out and did so, as a result of which incontinent

[helpless] he and all his people were surrounded by the Duke of York's men. And after some were stricken down and the Duke of Somerset had killed four of them with his own hand, so it is said, he was felled to the ground with an axe and incontinent being so wounded in several places that there he ended his life.[13]

So, the man who would control the polity of England, coughed up his life's blood over the cobbles of St Albans, though his son, at least, survived. The Dijon Relation suggests the fight lasted till around half past two in the afternoon, and under two hundred casualties were sustained by both sides. The battle in the streets, if it ended in a clear-cut Yorkist triumph, was obviously not easily won. Even when the attackers had, at length, broken the main knot of Lancastrian resistance in the square, Somerset and a handful of diehards held out in the inn for some time. It would not have been an entirely quick or bloodless victory.

Soon, the only Lancastrian left alive in the square was the reigning monarch. Even his standard bearer, Sir Philip Wentworth, had joined the stampede to escape. The King, wounded by an arrow, was led from the bloodied streets, taken perhaps first to a tanner's dwelling to have his wound dressed and conveyed next to the more suitable surroundings of the abbey. Presently his Yorkist subjects craved an audience and begged forgiveness on bended knee for so discommoding their sovereign, expressing the desire that he should share their relief at his favourite's deserved demise! In the circumstances Henry proved sufficiently politic to ameliorate his previous harsh and uncompromising attitude to the rebels, who were now a ruling junta, and gave them his dispensation. Again, the Dijon Relation picks up the thread:

Wherefore the king agreed freely to allow him to arrest the said two lords [Buckingham and Wiltshire] and so he did, in particular the Duke of Buckingham. The treasurer could not be found for disguising himself he fled in a monk's habit . . . And when all these things were done the Duke of York enterd within the abbey and went before the king's person and there went on his knees to him crying mercy.[14]

For the Yorkists it had been a clean sweep: the fulcrum of opposition was removed with Somerset's death, the Nevilles appeared to have resolved their dispute with the Percies, and both the Earl of Northumberland and his ally Clifford lay dead – a senior generation of the court party taken off at a stroke. But these dead men had sons and brothers and had left intact affinities anxious to pick up the gage. St Albans was a victory but not a conclusion. For the first time since his bitter humiliation after the virtual surrender at Blackheath, three years earlier, the Duke of York rode into London alongside his King, but now he rode on the right, with his brother-in-law Salisbury trotting on the left hand and his nephew Warwick in front, bearing the sword of state. It seemed as though his day had finally arrived. He was Defender of the Land, Protector and de facto ruler, the man who wore the crown reduced to a puppet, his faction decimated. Some days after the fight, John Paston was appraised of the events, that had occurred at St Albans:

> Right worshipful and most well-beloved sir, *I commend myself to you desiring with all my heart to hear how you are. This is to let you know that the news we have here is that three lords are dead; the duke of Somerset, the earl of Northumberland and Lord Clifford; as for any other well known men I know of none except Watton of Cambridge-shire. As for the other lords, many of them are hurt; as for Feningley, he is alive and well, as far as I can find out.*[15]

There is no particular reason to doubt the contemporary correspondent's assessment of the total dead as around 120. The fight had been fairly short, the numbers involved not significant, there was no organised pursuit. The Yorkists had achieved their purpose with a degree of surgical precision. Power, after the years of chafing against the bile of the court faction, was now theirs. All they now had to do was hang on to it – and this would prove the greater test.

Notes

1 Haigh, op. cit., p. 8.
2 RP v 250–251.
3 Haigh, op. cit., p. 8.
4 Ibid., p. 12.
5 This correspondence was discovered in the Archives de la Cote d'Or at Dijon, quoted in Lander, op. cit., pp. 52–3.
6 At least Warwick was quick to claim the credit for the initiative which might have, in fact, come from Ogle; nonetheless this manoeuvre, which decided the course of the fight, confirmed the Earl's reputation as a commander of note; see Haigh, op. cit., p. 13.
7 Sir Charles Oman takes the view that Warwick was a general of genius, though other writers have been less confident.

 8 A. H. Burne, *TheBattlefields of England* (London 1950), p. 81.

 9 Haigh, op. cit., p. 12.

10 The Earl of Wiltshire assumed the guise of a monk and, thus attired, slipped cleverly past the Yorkists.

11 Lander, op. cit., p. 53.

12 There is a legend ataching to Somerset that he had a particular fear of castles, as a fortune-teller had foretold he would perish under the shadow of one; if so, then the prediction proved correct.

13 Lander, op. cit., p. 53.

14 Ibid., p. 55.

15 PL p. 71.

Chapter 5

Blore Heath 23 September 1459 and the Rout of Ludford Bridge 12/13 October 1459

Now you see the deaths of so many great men in such a brief space of time, men who have worked so hard to grow great and to win glory and have suffered so much from passions and cares and shortened their lives, and perchance their souls will pay for it.

Philippe de Commynes

The Protectorate

If the history of the Wars of the Roses was to demonstrate any single fact concerning sovereignty it was that gaining control of the Crown was frequently a deal easier than its retention. Warwick would discover this in 1469 and again, during the 'Re-adeption' of Henry VI. In the summer of 1455 it was York, flush with the triumph of First St Albans, who was to discover this inconvenient truth. In the first heady rush of success this difficulty remained unperceived. The dead and discredited Lancastrians were stripped of their offices, now parcelled out amongst the winners. The Duke appointed himself Constable and the plum of Calais went to Warwick; Viscount Bourchier replaced Wiltshire as Treasurer. With Somerset dead, the blame for the fray could be laid alongside his corpse. The deceased Duke, with two of his affinity, Thomas Thorp and William Joseph, were portrayed as the chief troublemakers – accused of suppressing York's correspondence to the King, sent on the eve of battle. By dumping the blame squarely on the losers these could be seen as the chief instruments of discord bringing about, by their perfidy, a confrontation which could otherwise have been avoided. The Bill of Attainder, passed on 18 July, fully cleared the Yorkist faction of any treasonable conduct.

Other moves followed – a series of measures,[1] nicely calculated to appeal to a broad constituency. Stringent new fiscal procedures were put in place to curb the perceived profligacy of the King's Household, and Humphrey of Gloucester was fully rehabilitated in law, martyr to the excesses of the court party. Encouraging and sound as these actions were, the plain fact was the Yorkists had secured their ascendancy by force of arms, and the ripples of alarm inevitably radiated outward, disturbing the limited calm of the realm. Richard, Duke of York constantly needed to shore up his position, to be seen to be acting within the law and with the acquiescence of Parliament. In November 1455 he sought MP's support for a further term in office as Protector. The Commons, orchestrated by the Duke's retainer William Burley, proved compliant, the Lords less so – but a providentially timed outbreak of fresh disturbances in the south west, where the Courtenay Earl of Devon was once again at odds with his old adversary, Lord Bonville, added a note of urgency.

Burley was able to make much of the trouble:

> And also here there had been great and grievous riots done in the West Country, between th'Earl of Devonshire, and the Lord Bonvile, by the which some men have been murdered, some robbed, and children and women taken. It is thought that if such Protector and Defensor were had, that such riots and injuries should be sooner punished, justice largely ministered, and the law more duly to proceed.[2]

The threat to law and order, if largely localised, was nonetheless very real. Bonville, previously an ardent Lancastrian, had prudently decided to swap allegiance, and secured a marriage alliance with the Nevilles.[3] This manoeuvring alarmed the Courtenays, who reacted with vigour and force. Nicholas Radford, whose role in the affair was no more than to have acted as

Bonville's lawyer, was one of the first victims. The events leading to his murder were graphically described by his cousin and executor John Radford in a petition, subsequently laid before the King:

> *And the said Nicholas P, Thomas P and John Amore and other forthwith turned upon the said Nicholas Radford, and then and there the said Nicholas P with a glaive [a polearm] smote the said Nicholas Radford a hideous deadly stroke overthwart the face, and felled him to the ground, and then the said Nicholas Philippe gave him another stroke upon his head behind so that the brain fell out of the head. And the said Thomas Philippe that time and then with a knife feloniously cut the throat of the said Nicholas Radford, and the said John Amore that time and there with a long dagger smote the said Nicholas Radford behind on his back to the heart. And so the said Nicholas P, T.P., and John Amore thus gave the said Nicholas Radford several deadly wounds, and him then and there feloniously and horribly slew and murdered.*[4]

John Radford, in his subsequent petition, goes on to aver that the Earl of Devon sheltered Sir Thomas and his murderous confederates who proceeded to hold a sham inquest in the dead man's chapel, in the presence of his mutilated remains. The process was, inevitably, a farce and returned a decision that their victim had killed himself! Still not satisfied, they heaved the corpse from its coffin and chucked the remains into a pit wherein the mangled body was pelted and broken with stones, 'having no more compassion nor pity than though it had been a Jew or a Saracen'.[5]

Worse was to follow. Exeter was occupied by the Earl, his sons and an armed company, whilst Powderham Castle, home to a rival sept of the Courtenays and its castellan Sir Philip, was besieged. Efforts by Lord Bonville to raise the siege were repulsed. Low-intensity war raged throughout parts of Devon for weeks without Crown or Parliament being able to exercise any check. Such a state of affairs constituted dire precedent, the breakdown of law and order, and could be as contagious as the plague – and near as deadly. All of this was ample proof that only a strong Protector could compel the violent Courtenays, themselves members of York's affinity, to heel. Burley had made much of the lawlessness in the west, and the Lords, with some reluctance, accepted York as Protector. For decorum's sake the Duke protested his unworthiness, but the list of conditions and caveats governing his acceptance of office was very quickly to hand.[6] In mid December, after Bonville's latest reverse at Clyst, York began to march. The Courtenays, in no hurry to alienate their patron, the Protector, submitted meekly. The Earl of Devon surrendered after a parlay at Shaftesbury and was sent to cool his ardour in the Tower. The feud, like an autumn gale, blew itself out and calm returned to the county. York had proved worthy of his high office.

It would naturally seem that the bloodletting at First St Albans had effectively polarised the two factions and that the future battle lines had now been irrevocably drawn. This may not necessarily be the case: Christine Carpenter argues that the final split may have come later and that, between the years 1455 and 1458, a broad sweep of the nobility was working to find a constitutional settlement. York had a very narrow base, dependent upon the Nevilles, and even Salisbury and Warwick may not have been completely committed to an unswerving Yorkist stance. St Albans had witnessed the destruction of both Somerset and Northumberland, thus any local rivalries had been resolved in their favour. Henry Beaufort, 2nd Duke of Somerset, was still a very young man and was perhaps less openly confrontational than his father. The powerful coalition of younger northern Lancastrains had not yet come into focus. The difficulty that faced York as Protector was that it was impossible for any magnate of the day to represent a 'loyal' opposition – this, almost by definition, was treasonable. The royal will was still supreme and at least Somerset appeared to act with the King's authority, even if he was actually the source of most of the decision making. Removing Henry VI was not an option the peers would yet countenance – this remained contrary to God's will. Henry, after all, was not a tyrant, his offence was one of default. He was not a bad king, he just wasn't really a king at all.

Calais

Calais and the Pale[7] was a problem of far greater magnitude. The garrison was necessary, but also very expensive. In the three years from mid 1451 the wages bill topped £17,000. This was without the additional outlay on supply and maintenance. The Pale was now the final English bastion, all that remained of the proud inheritance of Edward III, the final thorn in the flesh of the French King. A likelihood of fresh French aggression, as Charles VII sought to finally clear the hated English from the last scrap of French soil, came at a particularly bad time. This was when revenues from Calais were declining and the cost of its defence no longer capable of self-financing.

When the Crown could not meet the cost of paying its soldiers, as was not infrequently the case, then the garrison was in the habit of simply impounding the wool supply in lieu of wages.

When, in the previous year (1454), York had ousted Somerset and assumed his office of Captain, the mood of the garrison was so sour that the Duke was denied entry, truculence that soon flared into outright disobedience. York had been too distracted by other matters to effect a settlement with the troops who received neither their arrears nor an assent to dispose of the wool they had seized to make good the deficiency. Now, it was Warwick's turn to encounter the same impasse, the only difference being that the arrears had accrued steadily in the interval. Protracted negotiations followed, aimed at ending the deadlock, but the matter was not resolved until January 1456.[8] Warwick did not formally enter into his command until that summer and by then York had lost his tenuous grip on power in England. Henry VI, addressing Parliament, formally withdrew the Duke's authority as Protector. The Yorkists were not yet marginalised, their control of the Council did not waver and the King lacked sufficient allies to breathe full defiance.

Margaret of Anjou, with Somerset gone, was the natural focus for any resurgent court faction. Dynamic and utterly determined to secure her son's rightful inheritance, she feared York's dynastic ambitions. The Duke's faction held sway amongst the mercantile classes in London, so the Queen shifted her court to the Midlands, to the heartland of the Duchy of Lancaster and the lands of Prince Edward's earldom of Chester. This was a carefully and cleverly calculated move. It enabled Margaret to escape the confinement of a pro-Yorkist capital and build up new centres of influence in the shires. Historians have tended to regard Margaret as a remorseless intriguer, whose obduracy removed any hope of reconciliation between the factions.[9] This may be unduly pejorative. She was naturally and understandably fearful of the Yorkist claim; there are suggestions that Henry was not the true father of Edward of Lancaster and that Somerset may have done his dynastic duty by proxy. Her child was a defenceless minor, her husband of little practical assistance.

More recent authors have pointed out that she was an ambitious woman in a male orientated and dominated society; a foreign princess, lacking native affinity. That she should seek to assert herself and develop a power base, harnessing the resentment of the sons of those peers who spilled their blood in the streets of St Albans, would tend to show she was both astute and calculating. At no point did she attempt to usurp her husband's authority and rule in his stead.

> ... she allied unto her all the knights and squires of Cheshire for to have their benevolence, and held open household among them; and made her son called the Prince give a livery of Swans[10] to all the gentlemen of the country, and to many others throughout the land.[11]

This emergence of the person of the young Queen as the leader of the court faction was the final step toward factional polarisation. Had the rump of the old Suffolk–Somerset party remained headless, then some degree of equilibrium might have been maintained. At this point York represented no overt, dynastic threat to the Crown, and the Lancastrian succession stayed secure. Had the reasonable balance, toward which moderates like Buckingham and the King himself strove, survived then St Albans might have been the single battle, rather than the curtain raiser for a list of others. At the same time, proxy rule by the court party was a poor substitute for a strong and able monarch. Margaret could promote a faction; she could not impose a universal peace. Only the King could achieve that, fairly but forcibly. Henry was inclined to fairness but lacked the strength of character necessary to impose fairness on others as an act of royal will. Bad governance was the root cause of strife and, whilst this malaise endured, peace between the factions was fragile in the extreme.

Loveday

Henry joined Margaret at Kenilworth and, steadily, the Queen clawed back the reins of power, using the King's authority to stuff the offices of state with her nominees. Laurence Booth, Margaret's able chancellor, was created Keeper of the Privy Seal.[12] When the Prince Bishop,[13] a Neville, died in 1457 Booth was appointed to the powerful and prestigious see of Durham. Soon, the Yorkists had lost the offices of Treasurer and Chancellor, Shrewsbury replacing Bourchier and it was he who with Exeter and Henry Beaufort (now Duke of Somerset) set out to assassinate the Earl of Warwick. Wiltshire was another who enjoyed a fresh spell in office as Treasurer. Ominously for the Yorkists, the thuggish Egremont was soon, like his old ally Exeter, at liberty, whilst his brother Lord Poynings (now

3rd Earl of Northumberland) was appointed as East March Warden, a traditional Percy sinecure.

None of these men were friends of the York–Neville faction. Egremont and Exeter, both of volatile dispositions, were instigators of the troubles of 1453–4. The 2nd Duke of Somerset and 3rd Earl of Northumberland were the sons of those lords who had fallen at First St Albans; they had scores to settle. Exeter was appointed as Lord Admiral though he was, doubtless much to his chagrin, soon supplanted by Warwick. The Duke of York had lost his grip on the English polity but, if he had not added to his enemies he had at least made a few friends: the merchants of the Staple were drawn within his broader affinity. These mercantile entrepreneurs were most useful allies, and Calais continued as a secure and vital base.

If Queen Margaret was demonstrating some success in rebuilding a viable Lancastrian affinity, the Yorkists were still the ones with the sharpest teeth. York and Warwick were respected as men of probity and action, important assets in an age of alarums. The French 'took up' Sandwich in late August 1457, in a daring amphibious operation, prompting fears of an invasion.[14]

A lone but powerful voice for moderation, and indeed for reconciliation, was that of the Duke of Buckingham, senior statesman of the age. He was unflinchingly loyal to his sovereign Henry VI, in whose cause he had sustained serious wounds at First St Albans, yet he was untainted by any particular amity toward the court faction as such. Buckingham was unquestionably sincere in his actions and genuine in his desire to avoid a further lurch toward renewed civil strife.

Buckingham appeared to have a constant ally in the King himself. Henry, like the Duke, was equally concerned to avoid further bloodshed; the carnage in the streets of St Albans had clearly taken its toll on his brittle personality. It is an element of Henry's tragedy that he was a dove in a martial age, when a desire for peace and amity was not a characteristic much sought after in a king. Had he been a man of blood and iron like his illustrious father, then history would, undoubtedly, have given him a more glowing obituary. The culmination of the peacemakers' efforts was a singular ceremony of reconciliation which took place in St Paul's on 24 March 1458, 'Loveday'. The title is ironic as there was little of love in the air when the principal antagonists – Somerset, paired with Salisbury, Northumberland with Warwick and York with Margaret – joined hands in a symbolic series of gestures. Previously the Yorkists had conceded that they would endow a chantry in St Albans to celebrate masses for the souls of the dead and that, more practically, they would pay compensation to both Percy and Clifford.

As an effort to paper over the cracks, Loveday was a fine show. Those not prone to cynicism might have discerned the dawn of a new era, others might have chosen to note the quantities of liveried soldiery that followed in the magnates' trains. There might be gestures of peace, but the capital was an armed camp with the Mayor and burgesses sweating mightily for fear that some spark might ignite a conflagration that could transform the streets of London into a second St Albans. As Christine Carpenter points out, however, Loveday may in fact mark the point at which the continuation or development of the existing factional discord slid into the abyss of civil war. The ceremony, however hollow, clearly recognised that two separate factions existed and that one could not prevail without encompassing the destruction of the other. There were two clear sources of authority surrounding a supine king, and a sustained trial of arms was the only remedy. Fear of this polarisation irrevocably pushed the Nevilles toward York.

In the Channel, the Earl of Warwick, secure in the Captaincy of Calais, pursued his swashbuckling career as a privateer. Queen Margaret, fretting that the Nevilles should cling to such an important post, continued a policy of withholding the garrison's salaries. Warwick was ready for this; the deficiency could be made good through piracy – far from bringing opprobrium, the Earl's naval forays met with widespread approval. During the course of May 1458, Warwick attacked a superior Spanish squadron in the Channel. His fleet was tiny – five warships, some armed merchantmen and a quartet of diminutive pinnaces; but, after a sharp and bloody fight, he won the day, taking half a dozen valuable prizes.

Even the trading vessels of the great Hanseatic League were not safe, their fat-bellied, salt-laden convoy proving altogether too tempting. Brigandage and expediency do not necessarily imply a lack of policy. The Earl's buccaneering was, in all probability, far from random. First, he needed to counter the Lancastrians' attempt to starve him from office; secondly he built up a personal loyalty amongst the regular garrison, which would furnish him with a standing army. Thirdly, he was playing to the commons, especially those in the south-eastern counties, the natural gateway from Calais to London. Lastly, it did not unduly damage the Yorkists to provide diplomatic embarrassment to the rival, court faction. His actions, flagrant, bold and hubristic, made the Queen and her affinity appear impotent.

The Davies Chronicle, written in the 1460s or early 1470s, paints a dismal picture of bad governance during this earlier period, with the court faction perceived to be as incompetent as in the days of Somerset:

The queen with such as were of her affinity ruled the realm as she liked, gathering riches innumerable. The offices of the realm, and specially the Earl of Wiltshire treasurer of England for to enrich himself, peled the poor people, and disinherited rightful heirs, and did many wrongs. The queen was defamed and dislandered, that he that was called Prince, was not her son, but a bastard gotten in avoutry [adultery].[15]

Blore Heath

Later in that year (1458) Warwick deigned to answer a royal summons to explain his assault on the Hanse ships. In London the Earl's party became involved in a fracas with royal retainers. This swiftly degenerated into a brawl and the Neville party claimed they were obliged to fight for their lives, to break free and escape by water. From now on Warwick held his post in Calais in defiance of the King. Battle lines were drawn once again.

Moderation was the first casualty; the middle ground was completely eroded. Buckingham, no admirer of Warwick, with whom he was personally at odds,[16] refused to shift his core loyalty away from the throne. When Margaret summoned a council to Coventry in June, prominent Yorkists were pointedly excluded, including George Neville and Bourchier. Richard, Duke of York, was fully aware of this manoeuvring and prepared to resist what he perceived as the inevitable application of force to reduce his affinity. He planned to gather his strength in the Yorkist heartland at Ludlow; Warwick would bring over a strong detachment from the Calais garrison,[17] whilst Salisbury would muster his northern retainers.

Even at this stage York did not necessarily intend to fight. He and those of his fellowship were painfully aware, however, that only a strong show of force would deter the Lancastrians who now viewed themselves as being in the ascendancy. The court faction could still emerge victorious from a confrontation if it could prevent the Yorkists from achieving their full muster, defeating their presently scattered detachments in detail. Warwick's Calais contingent had to run the full gauntlet of England but did so with elan, neatly sidestepping Somerset's attempt to block them. The main Lancastrian force, mustering in the Midlands, was commanded by Buckingham, whilst Queen Margaret had moved to Eccleshall to join the strong de-tachent under James, Lord Audley, fast approaching Market Drayton. This was a very substantial force. Jean de Waurin, our most complete chronicler, puts Audley's numbers at 10,000, the majority mounted.

Salisbury was marching for Ludlow; with him his sons Sir John and Sir Thomas, together with Sir John Conyers, Sir Thomas Harrington and Sir John Parr. His numbers were considerably inferior to the Lancastrian contingents that were poised to intercept him, though, as skilful on the march as his son, he avoided Buckingham. If Margaret was to frustrate a full Yorkist muster she would have to deploy Audley's army to stop Salisbury. By the chill dawn light on 23 September, the two forces were already jockeying for position, prickers on both sides covering the ground. The Yorkists were advancing along the line of the road that runs from Newcastle-under-Lyme to Market Drayton, their movement screened by Burnt Wood straddling the highway. The Lancastrians marching to meet them. As the Yorkists passed through the belt of trees, scouts brought intelligence that the Queen's forces were near, marshalling in battle array behind a substantial 'forest hedge'.

With the woodland to their rear, also protected by a hastily dug trench, Salisbury's officers completed their deployment. As their right flank was 'in the air', the Earl commanded a wagon leaguer be positioned so as to create both an anchor and obstacle. Knowing the odds were unfavourable, Salisbury intended to stand on the defensive and threw out a line of stakes along his front. A stream, the Wemberton Brook, ran along the left flank then bore diagonally through a valley running between two shallow ridges; it was along the line of the easterly eminence that the Yorkists had taken position. During the remainder of the morning there was something of a stand-off. It would be obvious to Audley that, though his force was the greater, the Yorkists were strongly posted. Besides, Salisbury and his officers were seasoned soldiers and their men, in many instances, veterans. The situation changed in the early afternoon when the Lancastrians appear to have come to the erroneous con-clusion that the Yorkists were seeking to disengage.

This, as Colonel Burne, writing in *More Battlefields in Britain* in the 1950s argues, was purely a ruse, intended to prompt Audley into attacking. Whether it was only the centre of the Yorkist line that was involved in this Parthian retreat, or whether the flanks also showed signs of withdrawal, is unclear. The impression was convincing enough to persuade Audley it was time to advance his cavalry – there are certainly similarities between Blore

Heath and some of the battles of the Hundred Years War. The Lancastrians trotted down the slope and negotiated the stream, by no means a major obstacle, but a distinct hindrance to so great a press of mounted men. With no attempt at manoeuvre, Audley cantered toward the Yorkist line. Salisbury and his men, having received the unction and commended their souls to God, strung their bows and began to shoot. Audley may have been supported by a contingent or contingents of his own archers but the cavalry fared badly, perhaps as many as 500 falling to the arrow storm.

Disconcerted, Audley's survivors from the first wave fell back, leaving a field piled with fallen riders and horses. He re-formed and came on again, with similar consequences, except that Audley himself also fell dead (the spot where he died now the site of the battle stone). With their commanding general lost, the Lancastrians experienced both a change of commander and a shift in tactics: John, Lord Dudley dismounted his horsemen and formed a foot column which he led to renew the attack, skirting or stumbling over the mounds of dead or moaning men and mounts. This field, uncannily similar to Poitiers,[18] now became a slogging match, an infantry melee of hacking bills, the noise of battle rolling like thunder over the ground. The fight dragged on for several bloody and exhausting hours, neither side gaining significant advantage, men swaying in the ritual dance of slaughter, the lines shifting and heaving. The Lancastrians' final reserve was a mounted rearguard that could be thrown in to exploit any gaps that the foot might open in the Yorkist line – the day could yet be won.

For whatever reason, perhaps a failure of morale, the rearguard chose to quit the field as lost, their defection spreading like a contagion to the infantry who now gave way. A body of the defeated avoided the horrors of pursuit by a timely shift of allegiance; the rest were harried mercilessly. The Yorkists were particularly energetic in the chase, the hunt becoming confused and disorganised. Squads of the victors looted the dead, pelted after fresh victims, and generally engaged in indiscriminate pillaging. A number of the vanquished were brought to ground some two miles west of the main fight, at a place known as 'Deadman's Den', by the little River Tern.[19] Aside from Lord Audley himself, a rash of knights were slain – Sir Hugh Venables of Kinerton, Sir Thomas Dutton of Dutton, Sir Richard Molineux of Sefton, Sir John Dunne and Sir John Haigh, with perhaps as many as two thousand of the commons. The Yorkists escaped without the loss of any gentry and with only a handful of dead amongst the rank and file.

This intemperate pursuit proved unfortunate for Sir Thomas Harrington and the two Neville knights, who ran into a rearguard the next morning by Tarporley Bridge and were all captured, destined to spend the next nine months incarcerated in Chester Castle. First blood in the campaign thus went to York. All of his contingents, though widely disparate, succeeded in gaining their objective, destroying a Lancastrian army en route. For the Queen, this was both a tactical reverse and a strategic setback. She had previously summoned the Stanleys, Lord Thomas and his brother Sir William. The former was Salisbury's son-in-law and, despite protestations of loyalty, he avoided the muster. Sir William, less vacillating, threw his lot in with the Yorkists. With their available forces concentrated at Ludlow the Yorkists had successfully frustrated attempts to prevent a full muster. York was at the heart of his dominion, with his affinity in numbers and under arms, a notable victory under their collective belt. He could, perhaps, look forward to the outcome of any further stand-off with some degree of equilibrium. Yet if this was the case, he would have cause to regret his complacency.

York's manifesto was in the form of an apologia to Henry, excusing his and his fellowship's outwardly treasonable actions. The Yorkists were on very uncertain ground; however real the perceived threat, they had taken up arms in defiance of their sovereign and had made war on his appointed officers. Margaret riposted by offering a general amnesty, only excluding those who had had a hand in Lord Audley's destruction. As a war of words bickered, the Lancastrians assumed the tactical initiative, advancing northward towards Ludlow.

Ludford Bridge

Preparing for battle, the Yorkists, on 12 October, deployed in a strong defensive position by Ludford Bridge, their ordnance arrayed before the line. Their situation, in strategic terms, was less secure than their strongly fortified lines might imply. The York–Neville faction was still a minority. In the four years since First St Albans, York had not materially succeeded in widening his power base. Support from the magnates was not forthcoming and the deficiency was exacerbated when Buckingham, the moderate, came off the fence and sided with the King. Though York was strong in numbers, the only magnates beneath his banners were his sons Edward, Earl of March, and Edmund, Earl of Rutland, with Salisbury, Warwick and Lord

Clinton.[20] This imminent struggle would be no repeat of St Albans. The Lancastrian army was far stronger in terms of magnatial support and had the inestimable advantage of being led, at least in name, by the person of the anointed sovereign.

Taking up arms against the King was not something that the Yorkist affinity had necessarily bargained for. Despite a series of elaborate charades aimed at a contrary pretence, the commons quickly became aware that they were on the threshold of high treason.[21] Warwick appears to have given the Calais contingent, the cream of the army, bland assurances that such an eventuality would never arise. The men might respect the Earl, even like him, but he was not their lawful king. It was Andrew Trollope who decided the issue at Ludlow. It appears that the burden of his royal oath was too weighty a consideration. He and his detachment simply changed sides there and then, opening a massive breach in the Yorkist line, breaking down floodgates through which others were quick to stream. Despite a desultory cannonade, mere bravado, the game was up for York and the Nevilles. The day was lost before it had begun. On the pretext of returning to the castle, the leaders simply took to their heels, abandoning the rump of their affinity and conceding a bloodless victory to the Lancastrians.

This matter of oaths was one of great weight – once taken, an oath could not be lightly broken. This punctiliousness must seem at odds with an age of civil war, treachery and bloodshed, yet it was the oaths of loyalty which magnates and gentry had taken which now caused the Yorkists' seemingly inexpugnable position to unravel so swiftly. The ceremony of unction, as Professor Goodman points out, the anointing with holy oil, raised the Prince to a position whereby his rule received divine sanction. However weak he appeared thereafter, however manifest the shortcomings of his governance, the process could not be undone. It had, of course, been undone, in the cases of Edward II and Richard II, but these were regarded as aberrations, acts contrary to the natural order. The 'Rout' of Ludford was a disaster for the Yorkists, they suffered no losses, but their fellowship, all of their materiel, their lands and treasure were given away in an instant. The Duke even abandoned Duchess Cicely and his two youngest boys, George and Richard. Their flight was precipitate and chaotic. York and Rutland eventually gained the sanctuary of Ireland whilst Warwick, Salisbury and March fled toward the Channel and the refuge of Calais, still held by Fauconberg.

John Dinham, gave the fugitives shelter at his home by Newton Abbot, then paid for their safe passage.

Jean de Waurin has left a dramatic version of the Yorkist debacle at Ludlow:

> *Then the said Andrew Trollope secretly went away to all those of the Calais garrison and so exhorted them that they joined his party so that they all came together to the Earl of Warwick and told him that they did not wish to fight against their sovereign lord and incontinent turned from the other party without anybody being able to stop them.*[22]

Their lives might be safe, at least for the moment, but the Yorkists appeared to have lost everything else. Their forces were scattered, their estates forfeit, their fortunes impounded and, perhaps even more unfortunate, their integrity was destroyed. The victors of St Albans had run away like thieves in the night, fleeing from the face of their rightful sovereign. When, on 2 November, the exhausted, begrimed trio finally disembarked at Calais it must have seemed that their hopes were entirely dashed and their prospects in ruins. Queen Margaret had achieved a great deal. She had rebuilt the court party from the ashes of St Albans, had steadily increased her strength till the time was ripe and had carefully orchestrated a total collapse of the Yorkist faction. The blood shed in the streets of St Albans had produced a new generation of resolute retainers, sworn to vengeance, that most powerful of motivations, whom she had now led to a successful outcome. What, of course, she had failed to secure were the heads of the Yorkist leaders suitably posed on spikes. The wheel had indeed turned, but not, by any means, for the final time.

Notes

1 Gillingham, op. cit., p. 93.
2 RP v 284–5.
3 Lord Bonville had married his grandson and heir to a daughter of Salisbury.
4 Lander, op. cit., pp. 57–9.
5 Ibid., p. 59.
6 Ibid., p. 60.
7 Calais was to remain an English town for more than two centuries after its capture from France by Edward III, following an epic siege lasting nearly a year in 1346–7.

8 Calais was referred to as the 'brightest jewel in the English Crown'; it was the port of entry for a range of English raw materials: tin, lead, cloth and, above all, wool.

9 For an assessment of the Queen's character, see A. Weir, *Lancaster and York* (London 1995), pp. 112–30.

10 The livery badge of Edward of Lancaster, as Prince of Wales, was the swan and ostrich feathers.

11 A. Goodman, *The Wars of the Roses* (London 1981), pp. 35–6.

12 The office of Lord Privy Seal, or Keeper of the Privy Seal, may date back to the reign of King John. The holder was an important member of the Royal Household as the Privy (or private) Seal was personal to the monarch and accompanied the court on progress.

13 Durham, a County Palatine, had a unique history. Early Norman attempts to maintain control of fractious Northumbria were fraught with strife. In the late eleventh century, Bishop William St Carileph, was created bishop and also given the authority of an earl.

14 This attempt was led by Pierre de Breze, the energetic seneschal of Normandy, and a tough fighter.

15 Davies, p. 75.

16 Buckingham, though a moderate, was currently at odds with the avaricious Warwick in a property dispute, a bone of contention that cannot have inclined him toward the Yorkists.

17 The detachment Warwick had brought from Calais was commanded by the Master Porter of the place, the respected and highly experienced veteran, Andrew Trollope.

18 Fought in 1356, a great and signal victory of Edward, the Black Prince, in which he captured the King of France.

19 Haigh, op. cit., p. 20.

20 John, 5th Lord Clinton of Maxstoke (1410–1464).

21 Gillingham, op. cit., p. 105.

22 Waurin V, pp. 275–6.

Chapter 6

Northampton 10 July 1460 and Wakefield 30 December 1460

Thy father slew my father; therefore die.

William Shakespeare, 3 Henry VI, *I. iii. 47*

The Yorkists in Exile

Queen Margaret could be allowed a brief smile of triumph as the Yorkists crumbled at Ludford and their leaders fled like thieves in the night. She had fully restored the supremacy of the court party and driven her enemies into ignominious exile. This did not render her son's inheritance safe. York was ensconced amongst friends in Ireland. The Nevilles, with the Earl of March, were secure behind the walls of Calais. Clemency to those implicated if not fully committed to the Yorkist faction was called for. The Lancastrian Parliament which assembled at Coventry in November 1459 inevitably attainted the leading Yorkist peers and their more notable adherents. Lesser fry were dealt with more leniently, by fine or censure. York was well received in Ireland. On paper he was deprived of authority and Wiltshire appointed in his stead on 4 December – but this had little practical effect and the Duke enjoyed great personal popularity. The dilettante Wiltshire was unlikely to take up his appointment. Englishmen on the whole had no interest in service in Ireland, regarding the place as intractably savage, generally uncomfortable and totally unprofitable.

Calais was, of course, an entirely different proposition: Calais mattered, it mattered very much. It was England's great trading colony, the Pale, England's shop window. Had the Lancastrians been sharper they would have tried to seize the place by surprise after Warwick had left for England. As it was, Somerset fitted out a punitive expedition, following on the fugitive Yorkists' return. His force included, amongst his officers, Andrew Trollope – who could claim the loyalty of the remaining garrison; Lord Roos; and Audley's son, now created Lord Audley. Warwick was prepared for the assault; his defences were manned and ordnance primed. The Duke did manage to effect a landing in the Pale at Scales' Cliff from where he advanced to the walls of Guines, one of the vital ring of castles sealing the Pale. Here, by assuring the garrison their arrears of pay would be met, he was able to gain a lodgement. Those who, through contrary winds, were blown into the harbour at Calais, fared less well.

The Queen's government failed both in its efforts to support Somerset's toehold in the Pale and in its efforts to isolate Warwick. Attempts at embargo were ineffective and largely ignored by merchants and sea farers; the economic imperative invariably triumphed. The Earl had established an accord with the Burgundians and, as ever, his buccaneering won plaudits from the men of Kent, who responded with ample intelligence of the larger force now being assembled at Sandwich against him. In the creeping winter dawn of 15 January 1460, a Yorkist cutting out party under John Dinham,[1] almost a thousand strong, and with a posse of citizens from the town, made a lightning descent on Sandwich. The whole fleet, together with its astonished admiral, Earl Rivers,[2] his wife[3] and their son Sir Anthony Woodville, were taken and convoyed, in triumph, back to Calais. William Paston, writing in late January, confirmed the event and the subsequent treatment of the captured Woodvilles:

As for tidings, my Lord Ryvers [Rivers] was brought to Calais, and before the lords with eight score torches, and there my Lord of Salisbury rated him, calling him knave's son, that he should be so rude to call him and these other lords traitors, for they shall be found the king's true liege men, when he should be found a traitor etc.[4]

The November Parliament had not been asked for a subsidy, a fiscal detail overlooked in the flush of political triumph.[5] Whilst the Court, enfeebled by chronic cash shortages, sought to empower the Sheriff of Kent, Sir Baldwin Fulford, to scrape together a fresh expedition,[6] Warwick again seized the initiative, boldly sailing from Calais to Ireland to confer with his uncle. Having scooped up more prizes during his unopposed passage, the Earl reached his destination without any serious effort to prevent him. He remained for a full two months, proof of his confidence in Calais' defences. This development stirred deep unease in London, and rightly so – there can have been little on the Yorkist peer's agenda other than planning a successful descent on England. For Warwick, Ludford Bridge was both a setback and a salutory lesson. Of the Yorkists' intention, the 'what' was not difficult to fathom, more taxing was the 'how' and, critically, the 'when'. Even the first was by no means totally clear. To return and seize power through military action was obvious, but what was the nature of the power sought? Did York simply aim to create another unsatisfactory protectorate, where his position would be as assailable as before, or was there a more ambitious plan? Did the Duke now propose to seize the throne for himself and his heirs?

Somerset, immured at Guines, and unable to return due to Warwick's mastery of the Channel,[7] was equally embarrassed by chronic cash shortages, unable to pay the accrued wages of the garrison as he had promised. Audley and Humphrey Stafford of Southwick had attempted to land a dribble of reinforcements but the elements, again, had proved Yorkist in sympathy and they had drifted helplessly into the main harbour, to join the rapidly swelling 'bag' of captives. On 23 April, however, Somerset, who was nothing if not energetic, managed to scrape together a sufficient number of enthusiasts to mount an attack. Striking up the Boulogne Road, he was bested by the defenders at Newnham Bridge. The fortress was not seriously threatened.

It was not until May that Warwick set sail from Ireland, putting in motion events that could have led to another spectacular fight at sea though, in the encounter that was to follow, it was bluff and nerve which decided the day, rather than blood and iron. The court party had determined to intercept the Earl, and his old rival, Exeter, had amassed a respectable squadron for the task. This included the ships Fulford had acquired and a number of others, boasting, as a particular taunt, Warwick's former flagship *Grace Dieu*.[8] In all, he had some 14 keels. Exeter's squadron was a significant menace, the Yorkists sailed warily, the Earl sending a sleek caravel[9] flying ahead to scout the narrow waters of the Channel where the confined straits suited an ambush. The precaution proved sound, for Warwick's vessel detected an enemy presence. Further intelligence was gleaned from local fishermen, who, when questioned, confirmed the location and strength of the Lancastrian fleet.

The Earl, together with his sailing master, Lord Duras,[10] convened a council of war; the captains had faith in the Earl as a fighting admiral, they had the weather gauge, good intelligence – the masters all urged in favour of giving battle. Warwick required no further encouragement. He hoisted his colours and steered straight for Exeter's squadron. The Duke proved unequal to the challenge and scuttled into Dartmouth, leaving the Earl to sail on to Calais, to a hero's welcome – a bloodless victory under his belt. If this was disappointing for the stalled and frustrated Somerset, who looked vainly for sight of his own reinforcements mustering at Sandwich, then he was doubly discomfited when Dinham, with Sir John Wenlock[11] and Fauconberg, staged a repeat of his earlier spoiling raid. The Lancastrians, ably commanded by Osbert Mountfort and mustering some 400 bows and bills, were not caught totally unawares, and gave a good account of themselves before Mountfort, like so many of his comrades, was captured – 'went into the bag'. There was one crucial difference in tactics in this later, June 'descent': Fauconberg remained in occupation of Sandwich. The beachhead had been secured.

The Road to Northampton

Military preparations were complemented by vigorous propaganda. Warwick's stirring deeds at Calais and at sea had helped win hearts and minds in Kent. Exeter, as the King's admiral, had made a very poor showing. On 26 June Warwick led the main expedition from Calais, accompanied by his father, the Earl of March, together with the new Lord Audley, who had swapped allegiance. In numbers, the Earl's command was no greater than perhaps 2,000, though the men were mainly veterans and the commons of Kent were vociferous in support. The legitimacy of the invasion received a filip from the presence of the papal envoy, who found the Yorkists more congenial than their enemies.[12] Such was the degree of Bishop Coppini's partisan leanings, that, on 4 July, he wrote an open letter to the King:

> On coming to Calais, owing to recent events, I found almost everything in turmoil, and those nobles all ready to cross to England, declaring that they

could not wait any longer in the existing state of affairs. Nevertheless, after I had conferred with them and exhorted them to peace and obedience, they gave me a written pledge that they were disposed to devotion and obedience to your majesty.[13]

The Legate goes on to say that his presence with the Yorkists is purely occasioned by his desire to present himself as the honest broker. Such a boon to the Yorkist propaganda campaign was priceless, for what more telling evidence could there be of the virtue and justice of their cause than the apparent seal of the Holy Father himself? Thomas Bourchier, Archbishop of Canterbury, also joined the rebels, giving further and considerable weight to their manifesto. As the Yorkists advanced toward Canterbury, local Lancastrian commanders, with a keen eye for the weather vane, promptly defected.[14] The march through Kent was unopposed, a triumphal progress with a constant stream of recruits, some of whom, like Lord Cobham, were ancient comrades. In London the government experienced a thrill of near panic. The burgesses were anxious to retain a degree of neutrality whilst appearing to remain loyal to the Crown, insisting that they police the city and resisting an attempt by the Lancastrian Lord Scales[15] to act as a military governor.

Warwick cannily refused to be deterred by warnings of armed resistance and continued his inexorable advance, offering the city fathers an escape route by the assertion that he came only to correct failures in the administration, reformer rather than rebel. The burgesses were quick to grab the proffered lifeline and sent a party to confirm that the gates would be opened. A wiser, less belligerent man than Scales might have judged this as a propitious moment to withdraw, to retreat into the Lancastrian heart of the Midlands as the court intended. However he, with a number of diehards, barricaded themselves in the Tower[16] in the hope that their tenure of this great bastion would be a substantial thorn in the Yorkists flesh.

As June faded into July the Yorkists, on the first of the month, reached Southwark. A muster on St George's Field was swollen by the thousands who had joined the Earl's colours on the march through Kent. The commons of the south-east had amply demonstrated where their sympathies lay. On 2 July the Yorkists entered the city, with the host setting up camp by Smithfield. No time was wasted; the bishops, handily meeting in convocation, were canvassed for their support; the burgesses importuned for the supply of baggage wagons and the uplifting of the royal ordnance from Whitechapel. This was clearly intended to be deployed against Scales who was holding out in the Tower, though the instruction was tactfully phrased as being for the defence of the city. The Davies chronicle describes the scenes in London as the Yorkists addressed the assembled clergy:

> *Then was a convocation of the clergy holden at St Paul's in London, and thither came the said earls: And the Earl of Warwick there purposed, and recited before all the convocation, and innumerable people standing about, the causes of their coming in to this land; and misrule and mischieves thereof; and how with great violence they had been repelled and put from the king's presence, that they might not come to his highness for to excuse them of such false accusations as were laid against them.*[17]

Warwick skilfully drew the townsmen into the Yorkist web; the burgesses were persuaded to top up the war chest with a 'loan' of £1,000 and the besieged Lancastrians, holding on in the great fortress, were denied re-supply. More of the magnates, including Lords Saye, Abergavenny and Scrope of Bolton, Viscount Bourchier and the Duke of Norfolk, came in. On the 4th the van marched from the city, a commanded party was detached by Ware, as there was a rumour the King might be found at Ely. It is unlikely the city fathers regretted their leaving, medieval armies were rapacious and unpredictable guests, many of the burgesses would have heaved a corporate sigh of relief. Salisbury, Cobham and Wenlock were left to continue the blockade of Scales' garrison in the Tower.

Henry was not in flight, even though his Council was in some disarray. The Queen and Prince Edward were left in Coventry whilst the King with all his available power marched south as far as Northampton. He had tarried in order to give Northumberland, Clifford, the other northern lords and their affinities time to catch up; none of these, however, arrived in time for the battle about to be fought. The chronicle sources are unreliable in terms of the number of soldiery available to King Henry – perhaps 10,000 men at most. The vestiges of moderate opinion inclined toward some form of mediation but the hawks, including the bellicose Lord Egremont, favoured a further trial of arms. Warwick's prickers would soon have alerted him to the fact that the King was neither at Ely nor in flight and that he was, in fact, marching southwards from the Lancastrian territory in the Midlands with an army at his back. Fauconberg, leading the detachment toward Ely, was hastily recalled to complete the Yorkist muster at Dunstable, before the combined forced marched on toward Northampton. Any chance of serious talks had by now evaporated; even Buckingham, hitherto prominent amongst the doves, was in no mood for compromise with Warwick. Prior to the battle the Earl sent a delegation, led by the Bishop of Salisbury, to seek some ground for negotiation. He got short shrift:

> *The duke of Buckingham that stood beside the king, said unto them, 'Ye come not as bishops for to treat for peace, but as men of arms'; because they brought with them a notable company of men at arms. They answered and said, 'We come thus for surety of our persons, for they that be-eth about the king be-eth not our friends.' 'Forsooth', said the duke, 'The earl of Warwick shall not come to the king's presence, and if he come he shall die.'[18]*

The Battle of Northampton

As the royal army lacked a full muster of the northern men, the King's officers had wisely chosen a strong defensive position outwith the town walls. With the Nene at their backs they dug a moated ditch to cover their entire frontage, utilising a water passage to connect the defences to the river. This ditch or fosse was made even more formidable by planting lines of stakes. The defence, thus fully enclosed, is reminiscent of the Franch redoubt at Castillon that had proven too tough a nut for old Bull Talbot. This position formed a 'tea cosy' shape, with the ditch and palisade forming an elliptical front facing south-west and sealing the open flank of a natural bend in the river. Studding the palisade was an array of ordnance, sited to pour fire on an attacker making a frontal assault. Given the natural strength of the river barrier, no other approach was feasible; the King's officers must have felt their position impregnable. If so, they would have been quite wrong. Two rogue elements would combine to frustrate their plans: the weather, nature's caprice, combined with the more material caprice of men.

Within the fort, Buckingham commanded the left-hand division, the King's pavilion to his immediate left rear; Shrewsbury, Egremont, Sir Thomas Percy and John, Viscount Beaumont, held the centre whilst the right was taken by Sir Edmund Grey of Ruthyn. Though the chronicler has suggested the Yorkists could field 60,000, this is patently a wild exaggeration, though it may be safe to assume Warwick's forces outnumbered those of the King, as the latter were denied their full muster. To the right of the defensive redoubt the main road toward Northampton ran over the bridge across the Nene from Buckingham, whilst the Towcester road came in from the right, joining the main highway just south of the Nene crossing. Southwards again, branching to the left, ran the approach to Delapre Abbey,[19] the buildings of which stood some way in front of the Lancastrian left centre.

Rain fell in torrents on that wet morning, 12 July. This discommoded both sides, the Yorkists struggling to manoeuvre in the muck, whilst the downpour soaked much of the Lancastrians' powder to the extent that many of the guns would not fire. As Warwick marshalled his divisions in column, Fauconberg was leading the left, the Earl himself the centre, whilst the young Earl of March prepared to be blooded on the right, advised by the older John Mowbray, Duke of Norfolk. Whether the Duke was already afflicted by the complaint that would claim his life less than a year later is unclear. Between showers Warwick attempted further mediation but his envoys were turned away without an audience. The Earl had heralded that he would, at two in the afternoon, speak with the King in person or fall in the attempt.

> *Then on the Thursday the 10*[th] *July, the year of Our Lord 1460, at two hours after noon, the said earls of March and Warwick let cry through the field, that no man should lay hand upon the king ne on the common people, but only on the lords, knights and squires: then the trumpets blew up, and both hosts countered and fought together half an hour.*[20]

Deployed in their columnar formation, the Yorkists appeared poised to deliver their main blow against the Lancastrian left – that flank commanded by Grey of Ruthyn. They were thus advancing over relatively open ground between the abbey and the river. Even if the ordnance was spoiled the defenders still possessed bowstrings, and a fierce, clothyard storm greeted the attackers as they struggled to maintain cohesion over the sodden ground. It appeared that the palisade could be held, regardless of the failure of the guns. But it was at this point that Grey, by prior arrangement, took his men out of the fight. They simply stood aside and even helped the Yorkist van surmount the dyke! This understanding, negotiated between Warwick and the slippery Ruthyn, undermined the entire position and decided the day in a single stroke. The lines were breached, the Lancastrian left, secure in their livery of the black ragged staff, remained as indifferent spectators whilst their erstwhile enemies dealt with their erstwhile friends. From now on there was no real battle. The Yorkists simply rolled up the flank of their enemy. Warwick had no quarrel with the commons, who might expect full quarter. For the Lancastrian nobles no such clemency was forthcoming. Buckingham, with Egremont, Shrewsbury and Beaumont, formed a final ring around the King's tent and all fell in its defence.

> *The Duke of Buckingham, the Earl of Shrewsbury, the Lord Beaumont, the Lord Egremont were slain by the Kentishmen beside the king's tent, and many other knights and squires.*[21]

Though the toll amongst the gentry of the court faction had been high, the commons suffered relatively trifling loss, perhaps 300 or so;[22] most of whom perished not from wounds but by drowning as they struggled over the swollen Nene.[23] King Henry found himself once again in the hands of subjects who protested to the full their loyalty, whilst the blood of his magnates still gilded their swords. The disaster at Northampton robbed Scales' beleaguered garrison in the Tower of any further purpose, their numbers had been swollen by a horde of *bouches inutiles,* who squawked in fright at every alarm and consumed meagre provisions at a frightening rate. Salisbury had established a siege battery – 'laid great bombards on the further side of the Thames'[24] – and there was some desultory exchange of fire, though his main weapon was blockade. His son's victory proved an even more potent tool, however, with the Lancastrian army scattered; its leaders dead, there was no point in further defiance and Scales formally surrendered on 19 July, three days after King Henry was towed into the city by the victors. During the campaign Scales' garrison had been firing continuously and at random into the crowded streets of the city, though quite what such terror tactics were intended to achieve is unclear, as Davies relates:

> *When the earls and lords were gone to Northampton, they that were within the Tower cast wild fire into the city, and shot in small guns, and brend and hurt men and women and children in the streets.*[25]

Both Scales and Hungerford had negotiated terms and these were honoured. Warwick dragged a few unfortunates from the garrison before a drumhead tribunal, mainly adherents of the Exeter, and sent them to the gallows. The Londoners were no less belligerent and, though Scales escaped the axe, his barge was set upon by Thames boatmen and he was summarily killed, his mangled, nude remains being deposited unceremoniously in the porch of St Mary Overy at Southwark.

The Act of Accord

Warwick held the reins of power. He also controlled the person of Henry VI. His position was very similar to that of his uncle in the aftermath of First St Albans. The difficulties he faced were also not dissimilar: to control the person of the monarch did not suffice to make the puppeteer king. The Queen, her son and the Duke of Somerset were all still at large, the court party was damaged but not destroyed – those northern lords, whose fathers' blood lay heavy, were unaffected. What had changed in the Yorkists favour was that they commanded the sympathies of a much broader constituency of peers. Yet, as the Earl divined, this effect could be transient. Henry, however many times he might be bested in the field, was still king (we are reminded of a later rebel, the Earl of Manchester, summing up the situation in the era of the Civil War[26]). At this stage there was no suggestion that the Yorkists enjoyed any broad support from the magnates for, in the modern idiom, 'regime change'. Removing the existing monarch was contrary to God's Law, there was no dominant factional support for the notion of York or perhaps the Earl of March as a substitute. With his customary acuity, Warwick recognised the need for moderation. Before Ludford the Yorkist cause could only rally a quartet of peers, by now this support had more than quadrupled.

Walking a tightrope is never easy, and the depletion of the Calais garrison had been a calculated risk; Somerset was still holding Guines. In theory, the Duke posed a continuing threat, but the decision at Northampton had robbed him of prospects. He and Warwick parleyed on Newnham Bridge and Somerset felt constrained to surrender the castle in return for his liberty. He may also have given undertakings, as a condition of parole, that he would refrain from ever taking up arms against the Yorkist faction. He then withdrew into voluntary exile in France. In England matters were still finely balanced, the Yorkist grip on London and the south-east was secure but Lancastrian sentiment remained strong in the north. Warwick, returning from his successful detour to Calais, was circumspect; a flag waving progress through his estates in the Midlands and a suitably pious excursion to Walsingham followed.[27]

And what of the Duke of York? He had been no more than a spectator of his own triumphal campaign. If any of the peers had uncertainties as to his intentions these were quickly dispelled when he landed near Chester early in September. His mood had hardened since the days of his Protectorate; he came not to support the Crown but to seize it. His parade through the Marches and the West Midlands was akin to a royal progress, his host swelling daily. If the commons reacted with enthusiasm, there was alarm amongst the peers. They were simply not ready for this. His entry into London on 10 October resembled a gaudy pageant, 500 retainers, proclaimed by fanfares, the royal banners floating above, his sword borne upright after the style of the sovereign. His state entry into the Palace of Westminster could have been a finely judged piece of theatre that might have carried all before him but, in failing, appeared farcical. He marched directly up to the vacant throne and laid a proprietory hand on the cushion, allowing the gesture to linger long enough for, as he hoped, loud cheers of approbation to swell through the great hall. None came; the gesture fell flat. Tantalisingly, we have no knowledge of the previous talks between uncle and nephew. Clearly, it had been agreed that York would delay his return until the Lancastrians had been defeated in the field; whether the capacity in which he would reappear was discussed is uncertain. Abbot Whethamstede may have been a witness to these dramatic events in the palace of Westminster:

> While, however, he [York] was standing thus and turning his face to the people and while he was judging their applause, Master Thomas Bourchier, Archbishop of Canterbury, rose up and having exchanged greetings asked if he would come and see the king. He, as if stung in soul by this question repled shortly, 'I do not recall that I know anyone within the kingdom whom it would not befit to come sooner to me and see me rather than I should go and visit him.'[28]

What is certain is that York's ill-judged mummery only ended when the Archbishop of Canterbury tentatively stepped forward to enquire if the Duke might like to see the King, threatening to destroy the fragile web his nephew had so cleverly and assiduously spun. Despite his rebuff from Parliament York blundered on, breaking into the King's personal apartments and taking over. Abbot Whethamstede doubtless voiced the disgust of many at such high-handed vandalism:

> Having smashed the bolts and thrown open the doors, he lodged there for no little time more like a king than a duke. After such high-handed conduct

*on the part of the duke had been noised about amongst the vulgar and also
how he had made his entry in this way on the strength of his own unlawful
judgement and by no means as a result of considered and weighed resolve,
forthwith all estates and ranks, age, sex, order and condition began to mur-
mur vehemently against him.[29]*

Since the debacle at Ludlow, Warwick had been the mainspring of the Yorkist faction; his was the energy, the drive, the dash, the daring and the genius
that had transformed their fortunes. It was he who had held Calais and re-
peatedly humiliated the court party, he who had orchestrated and imple-
mented the skilful propaganda, organised and led the army which had, with
minimal fuss, transformed the political situation. He had achieved what the
older generation had failed to do – a wider constituency of peers who were
prepared to accept the Yorkists in de facto control of the throne. The Duke
had blundered, thereby threatening to undo all that had been won. For
Warwick this must indeed have been galling.

We cannot now discern what prompted the Duke into such folly; perhaps the years of patient service he had given, the genuine abuses he had
suffered, had finally convinced him that there was no other way. We do
know that a strained interview took place as York appropriated the royal
apartments. Salisbury had alerted his son to his uncle's demonstration and
Warwick, with March, hurried to confront him. The two earls were plainly
dismayed at this crass stupidity, and the volatile Neville controlled his passion with difficulty. The Duke, affecting indolence, made light of the matter, being supported by his younger son Rutland, an intervention which
earned him sharp rebuke from his brother. A factional split was not something the Yorkists could afford, there was nothing to be gained by falling
out over the spoils before the prize was won. Warwick had no option but
to bite his tongue and try to salvage what he could. As York had now
launched a full constitutional challenge, his claim which, in law was a
strong one, would have to be judged. Lawyers tussled over the central
dispute – that the seizure of the throne by Henry IV in 1399 was illegal and,
therefore, Henry VI as his descendant had no right to retain it. The crown
should pass to the next legitimate successor in title to Richard II – Richard,
Duke of York.

The magnates squirmed over their expressed allegiance to Henry. All of
them had sworn to support him – the House of Lancaster had held the
throne since 1399; he was the annointed King. Their lordships, even if they

had no particular love for King Henry VI, nonetheless could not bring them-selves to do away with him. The plain fact was that nobody wanted to make such a momentous decision, with all of the likely consequences. Parliament might be packed with Yorkist sympathisers but the Lancastrians could still command a broad constituency in the shires. Their lordships referred to the King's Bench, who neatly passed the poisoned chalice back, intimating that the matter was so weighty – touching as it did upon the instituton of the Crown – that it was above their authority and beyond their competence 'whereof they durst not enter into any communication thereof'.[30]

To dethrone Henry could lead to a renewal of the civil war. The Queen, her son and the rump of her faction were at liberty and undefeated in the field. Thus the constitutional settlement of 1460 was inevitably a compro-mise, a solution that tried to partly please both sides and, in the way of such things, succeeded in pleasing neither. By the provisions of the Act of Accord, passed on 24 October 1460, Henry, for the remainder of his life, would continue to occupy the throne. On his death the crown would pass to York and his heirs, who, in the meantime were to enjoy an annuity in the amount of £10,000. Had Henry been childless, this might just have suf-ficed, but of course he was not, and his defiant Queen would never acqui-esce to a settlement that disinherited her son. It was this Act which charged the failing batteries of the Queen's cause. After Northampton she had fetched up in temporary sanctuary in Harlech, narrowly escaping a Stanley ambush which relieved her of the modest treasure she retained. The Act of Accord, for any Lancastrian, offended against the natural laws of inheri-tance. It could be strongly argued that the statute, as it appeared, was noth-ing more than a form of usurpation, with the King in the grip of his enemies. The Queen was not without allies and, as the weeks of autumn passed, the threads of her cause began to reunite.

The Road to Wakefield

From Wales the Queen's trusted adherent Jasper Tudor pledged his sword. Somerset ended his brief exile and based himself at Corfe Castle from where he could stir mischief in the west. The Courtenays had experienced a change of heart and were willing to defect. In the north, tempestuous young men like Northumberland, Lord Roos and John Clifford were ready. The ring of discord quickly began to tighten. The borderers took up Neville lands; the westerners, in the closing days of November, galvanised by Somerset, were able to strike northward through the Cotswolds to Coventry, and then finally to rendezvous with the northerners at York. More Lancastrians were said to be mustering in the East Riding.

Despite the reverse at Northampton and the loss of the King's person, Queen Margaret, who had sailed to Scotland to canvass further aid, enjoyed considerable support. The northern kingdom was ruled by James II, 'James of the Fiery Face',[31] who had ascended the throne as a minor after the assassination of his Anglophile father James I at Perth in 1437. Such a powerful muster of enemies could not be ignored. On 9 December, a Yorkist army, led by York and Salisbury, with the former's son Edmund, Earl of Rutland, and the latter's, Sir Thomas Neville, marched north from London onto the dismal mire of the winter roads. Edward, Earl of March, was sent westwards into Wales with a smaller contingent to confront, or at least contain, the Tudors whilst Warwick held the capital.

> . . . and anon after the said Duke of York, the Earl of Rutland his son, and the Earl of Salisbury, a little before Christmas, with a few persons went in to the north also, for to repress the malice of the northern men the which loved not the said Duke of York ne the Earl of Salisbury.[32]

There was logic in this. It was the Earl who had the rapport with the peers, it was he who kept the King close and who could maintain a close watch on the south coast – he numbered the wardenship of the Cinque Ports amongst his offices. Warwick still contolled the reins of power; his brother George was Chancellor and Bouchier acted as Treasurer. The governor of the Isle of Wight, Geoffrey Gate, an adherent of the Earl, did good service when he captured Somerset's younger brother, Edmund Beaufort, a handy prize and useful pawn.

> She [the Queen] sent unto the Duke of Somerset, at that time being in Dorsetshire at the castle of Corfe, and for the Earl of Devonshire, and for Alexander Hody, and prayed them to come to her as hastily as they might, with their tenants as strong in their harness as men of war, for the Lord Roos, the Lord Clifford, the Baron of Greystock, the Lord Neville,[33] the Lord Latimer, were waiting upon the Duke of Exeter to meet with her at Hull.[34]

York was, as he marched north, embarking on a final miscalculation. His intelligence seems to have been lacking in so far as he failed to detect the weight of the opposition being mustered against him – the young lions of

Plate 1 Towton – view from behind the Lancastrian line, the field is just south of the track, to the left of the picture toward Towton Dale

(photograph by Adamskii Bespoke Photography)

Plate 2 Towton – the cross is venerable, mounted on a more modern obelisk, its exact origins are uncertain. It has been variously described as 'Lord Dacre's Cross' or part of a funerary monument associated with Lord Clifford. It stands just to the rear of the Lancastrian right wing

(photograph by Adamskii Bespoke Photography)

Plate 3 Hedgeley Moor – a view from the Lancastrian line towards the Yorkist approach march

(photograph by Adamskii Bespoke Photography)

Plate 4 Hedgeley Moor – '*Percy's Leap*', said to mark the spot where Sir Ralph Percy met his death

(photograph by Adamskii Bespoke Photography)

Plate 5 Tewkesbury Abbey – a view towards the Abbey, as would have greeted the fleeing Lancastrians, though likely very very less tranquil!

(photograph by Adamskii Bespoke Photography)

Plate 6 Tewkesbury – the battlefield plaque
(photograph by Adamskii Bespoke Photography)

Plate 7 Tewkesbury – Bloody Meadow, the evocative name applied to ground on the flood plain of the River Severn which witnessed such dire slaughter at the climax of the battle

(photograph by Adamskii Bespoke Photography)

Plate 8 Bosworth Field – looking towards King Richard's left flank

(photograph by Adamskii Bespoke Photography)

the Lancastrian cause, undefeated and spurred by vengeance. An intimation of what was to follow occurred when his column was ambushed by a commanded party under the energetic Trollope near Worksop and extricated itself only with difficulty and some loss. On 21 December the Yorkists reached what appeared to be a secure northern base, York's castle at Sandal on the southern outskirts of Wakefield.[35] In fact Sandal was more trap than refuge, for the Lancastrians had boxed the place in on three sides. Moreover, York may have been tricked by the assurances of Lord John Neville – one of the Cumbrian sept, the Earl of Westmorland's brother and Salisbury's uncle. He had intimated he would raise forces in the north-west to take on the Lancastrians at Pontefract, which Sandal was well placed to mask. York may have had some 6,000 men under his banners but, if he had placed faith in the blandishments of Lord Neville, he was to be sadly disillusioned:

> *Then the Lord Neville, brother to the Earl of Westmorland, under a false colour went to the said Duke of York, desiring a commission of him for to raise a people for to chastise the rebels of the country; and the duke it granted, deeming that he had be true and on his part. When he had his commission he raised to the number of 8,000 men, and brought them to the lords of the country; that is to say, the Earl of Northumberland, Lord Clifford and Duke of Somerset.[36]*

Ranged against York's slender forces were several enemy columns, all within easy striking distance. Somerest, with the Earl of Devon, lay to the north. Northumberland and his Marcher ruffians nearby. Exeter, supported by Trollope, was encamped across the line of the Calder to the south. To the south west, Wiltshire commanded a further contingent. The open ground spreading south of Sandal appeared bare of troops, but Clifford was lurking to the east, whilst Lord Roos had men in the woods to the north-east. The jaws of the trap were all in place and ready to be sprung. Active Lancastrian patrolling had prevented the quantity of supplies needed to sustain the Yorkist arrivals from reaching the castle. But Somerset had been careful not to show his full hand, and the Duke of York and his officers were negligent in their scouting, for some 18,000 of their enemies now virtually surrounded them.[37] Sandal was effectively under siege, Somerset maintaining an offence of invective to sting his enemy into precipitate action. York's best chance was to sit behind high walls and pray for early relief. This was well enough in theory but to feed his army in the depths of winter York needed to send out constant foragers, scouring the bleak northern landscape, through necessity ranging farther and farther afield as the area's meagre resources were relentlessly consumed.

The Battle

As the old year was ebbing, on 30 December, just such a foraging party was active north of Sandal Castle toward the River Calder and the town of Wakefield beyond. Fields laid bare, hedgerows limned with frost, a grey, silent land, dense woods black as crows. At a point just west of what was then Cock n'Bottle Lane, these foragers were engaged by a detachment of Somerset's men, the bulk of the Duke's forces being screened within the woods that masked the line of the river. The action, etched against the gaunt skeleton of drab winter trees and lowering skies, could easily be observed from the ramparts of the castle. At first, it seemed as if the two forces were evenly matched, then, from the east, also emerging from woodland, a further detachment.

These newcomers appeared to be in force and York might have been convinced this was Lord Neville, advancing to his aid. Seeing the potential to strike hard at Somerset and Courtenay's division, York marshalled his host and marched out in a northerly direction, along the line of the lane, to complete what they hoped would be the rout of a sizeable Lancastrian contingent. This was to be the Duke's final error. Most authorities agree the battle began in the manner described above; a definitive account of what happened next is more difficult to construct. Quite possibly York was deceived into believing Neville's men were there to assist his party rather than partake in its destruction. There may have been a further deception in that the wily Trollope had some of his command don Warwick's livery of the bear and ragged staff to lead the Yorkists further into the illusion that they were about to be relieved. This latter seems a ruse too far. Salisbury and York would have been aware if the Earl was marching to their aid. Whatever his understanding, York was soon disabused but, making the best of the situation, attacked the enemy line forming against him. Such a resolute onset discomfited Somerset and Neville, who swiftly began to give ground. Their line only stabilised when Northumberland came up.

The battle thus developed more by chance than design; Somerset had probably intended nothing more ambitious than beating up enemy foragers.

With York fully committed and the battlefront aligned on a north–south basis, his lack of intelligence harvested fatal consequences. Lord Roos was soon closing in on the Yorkist right, coming from the east. Exeter and Trollope were throwing on harness to filter in from the west and fall on the exposed left. York had taken with him his son Rutland and a number of other officers including his trusted lieutenant, Sir David Hall. Salisbury and Thomas Neville remained with a reserve in the castle. Assailed frontally and in flank, York could only hope to execute a fighting retreat back to the shelter of Sandal's walls, a distance of perhaps half a mile. Salisbury, plainly perceiving the danger, took the obvious decision to strip the ramparts of every available man and rush to his brother-in-law's aid. A brave and, in the circumstances, entirely rational step, though one that finally condemned the entire force.

Salisbury's reserve stiffened the Duke's embattled line, and the fight raged with merciless intensity. Despite the odds, the Yorkists were giving a good account of themselves, with no suggestion of a rout, even as the jaws of the trap closed around three sides. It was Lord Clifford who finally dealt the death blow. His division was encamped south and east of the village of Sandal Magna, and was thus the last Lancastrian force to arrive on the field, perfectly placed to cut the Yorkists off from their intended refuge behind the walls of the castle. The end was not inevitable; York may have placed Rutland in the keeping of the lad's tutor, Sir Robert Aspall, with an injunction to flee the stricken field. Tradition asserts that the Duke, who had ridden out onto the field, was unhorsed and suffered a near crippling wound to the knee. With a handful of his household retainers, he and those around him fought on until the end, their backs against a scattering of elms.[38] York remained, to the last, a valiant knight. Perhaps as many as three thousand Yorkists lay stiffening on the cold ground: Sir David Hall, Sir John and Sir Hugh Mortimer, Sir Thomas Neville, Sir Thomas Harrington and Sir Thomas Parr. Salisbury was captured by Trollope's billmen and hauled off to Pontefract:

> The Earl of Salisbury was taken alive, and led by the said Duke of Somerset to the castle of Pomfret [Pontefract], and for a great sum of money that he should have paid had grant of his life. But the common people of the country, which loved him not, took him out of the castle by violence and smote off his head.[39]

Wiltshire, whose fellowship had not engaged, took possession of Sandal Castle. It was Lord Clifford who captured the luckless Rutland by Wakefield Bridge, killing the 17-year-old Earl in cold blood. Having stripped the bodies of the slain, the victors seem to have thrown most of the corpses, already stiff in the great chill, into a ditch adjacent to the site of York's final stand. This would mark the point where the slaughter reached its bloody denouement and the press of fallen would lie thickest. Corpses would be strewn along the entire line of the Yorkist retreat. That night showers of snow are said to have fallen, spreading nature's cloak over the carnage. With the heads of their fallen adversaries impaled on spikes above Micklegate Bar in York, the Lancastrians could turn their full attention to the road south.

Notes

1 Lord Dinham (1443–1501) of Hemyock Castle, Hartland in Devon. He was variously High Sherrif of Devon and Treasurer of England.
2 Earl Rivers was the father of the future Queen, Elizabeth Woodville, and served both as Constable and Treasurer under Edward IV.
3 This was Jacquetta of Luxembourg, widow of John of Bedford.
4 PL i 506.
5 Gillingham, op. cit., p. 108.
6 Apparently, he had asserted this could be achieved for no greater outlay than 1,000 marks (a mark = 13s. 4d., say 67p); see Lander, op. cit., p. 71.
7 The Davies chronicle places Wiltshire, Scales (see note 15 below) and Hungerford in pro-Yorkist Newbury, throwing their weight about.
8 Gillingham, op. cit., p. 109.
9 A caravel was the classic sailing vessel of the Age of Exploration. It could be lateen- or square-rigged, fitted with an after castle, and typically disposed 80–100 tons in weight.
10 Gaillard de Durefort, a Gascon who later fought for Edward IV at Barnet.
11 Sir John, Lord Wenlock (c.1400–1471).
12 Coppini had been dispatched by Pius II to London in February 1459, to try to raise interest in a fresh crusade; see Lander, op. cit., p. 73.
13 Ibid., p. 73.
14 John Fogge, John Scott and Robert Horne; see Gillingham, op. cit., p. 111.
15 Thomas, Lord Scales (c.1400–1460).
16 Lords Hungerford, Lovell, de la Warr, de Vesci and the Earl of Kendal.
17 Davies, pp. 94–8.
18 Ibid.

19 Delapre Abbey, originally a Cluniac Convent, founded in 1145; several prisoners from the fight were held there with a number of casualties being buried in the churchyard.

20 Davies, pp. 94–8.

21 Ibid.

22 Haigh, op. cit., p. 33.

23 Sir William Lucy – this unfortunate knight arrived late for the fight; he was spotted by an enemy, who coveted Sir William's wife, and consequently murdered. The widow did, subsequently, wed the assassin! See Haigh, op. cit., p. 29.

24 Gillingham, op. cit., p. 117.

25 Davies, pp. 94–8.

26 The Earl of Manchester, a loyal Parliamentarian observed that should Parliament defeat the King one hundred times he would still be king, but a single decisive defeat would bring about a traitor's end for all of them!

27 The Shrine at Walsingham – between Norwich and King's Lynn – a very popular shrine to the Virgin.

28 Whethamstede, pp. 376–8.

29 Ibid.

30 See Gillingham, op. cit., p. 117.

31 James was so called as he was afflicted with a large birthmark which covered virtually the whole of one side of his face.

32 Davies, pp. 106–7.

33 John, Lord Neville, of the Westmorland branch, subsequently killed at Towton.

34 Gregory, pp. 208–10.

35 Sandal Castle, originally associated with the de Warennes. The castle began life as a twelfth-century motte and was rebuilt in stone during the thirteenth.

36 Davies, pp. 106–7.

37 Haigh, op. cit., p. 33.

38 Edward IV subsequently erected a wooden cross to mark the spot where his father had fallen; see Haigh, op. cit., p. 39.

39 Davies, pp. 106–7.

Chapter 7

Mortimer's Cross 2 February 1461; Second St Albans 17 February 1461

All the lords of the north they wrought by one assent,
For to destroy the south country they did all their entent.

Yorkist ballad

Mortimer's Cross

In early February 1461 a strange meteorological phenomenon occurred
in the winter's dawn – three suns blazoned from a cobalt sky. To the super-
stitious minds of medieval men, this was a very grave and significant
event.[1] Edward, Earl of March, had celebrated Christmas in the south-
west of England at Gloucester. His mission was to suppress tremors of
Lancastrian sentiment being felt in Wales. It was a matter of pacification,
as we might say today 'giving some stick'. Around the middle of January,
however, he received dire news from the north. His father, brother, uncle
and cousin were all dead at the hands of enemies, their severed heads food
for the crows in York. The shock of this calamity must have been severe,
especially for one still in his teens. But Edward, from the moment he was

pitched into the leadership role, demonstrated the charisma and genius necessary to revive the fortunes of his cause. Around him at this time was a corpus of close adherents, men such as the volatile Sir William Herbert and his brother Sir Richard, who would become key figures in the later polity of the 1460s. The young Lord Audley remained true to his Yorkist alliance and the army was bolstered by the support of other stalwarts such as Sir William Devereux, Lord Grey of Wilton, John Milewater and Humphrey Stafford.

With the knell of the older Yorkists still sounding, the obvious reaction was to return poste haste to London and link up with Warwick, to rebuild a viable field army with which to defend the city. More bad news followed: a Lancastrian force under Jasper Tudor, Earl of Pembroke[2] had unfurled its banners in Wales. The danger was obvious, Edward could not afford simply to turn away and ignore this fresh threat, nor could he permit these Welsh adherents to join their victorious comrades in Yorkshire.

Tudor had been reinforced by Wiltshire, who had raised a contingent of French and Breton mercenaries, stiffened with Irish galloglass.[3] Their combined forces, at this point, were marching toward Hereford. Edward did not hesitate. He swung his troops toward the town, marching upon Mortimer's Cross, some 17 miles north; here he was planning to inderdict the Lancastrians' line of advance. His forces were modest, perhaps a little over ten thousand, mainly Welsh raised by the Herberts, plus his own retainers. The road from Hereford to Wigmore (a Yorkist hold) ran more or less due north, veering slightly westwards. The waters of the River Lugg, swollen by winter rains, flowed roughly parallel on the eastern flank, before angling westwards north of the crossing with the Ludlow Road. The ground between the larger road and the river, east of the Y junction with the Leominster road, formed the Wig marsh. Edward deployed his army in the customary three battles: Walter Devereux on the left, Herbert the right and himself the centre. The Yorkists faced west with the Hereford road and, beyond that, the marsh and river behind them. They stood in a line running north/south, with the main body standing between the two road junctions. The Lancastrians had little choice but to accept the hazard of battle; their foes probably enjoyed greater numbers, perhaps by a couple of thousand – by no means disastrous odds. Wiltshire, with his mercenaries, confronted Devereux; Pembroke faced March; and old Owen Tudor took the Lancastrian right, opposite the Herbert brothers.

On the morning of 2 February, that strange meteorological phenome-non, the image of three suns or parhelion, greeted the Yorkist army: 'three suns in the firmament shining full clear'.[4] Many quailed, surely this was a bad omen. Rising to the challenge, Edward pronounced that this apparition represented the holy trinity and God thus favoured his cause. What followed, beginning about midday, after the armies had shuffled and jockeyed, was a rather confused affair, one with markedly different outcomes on each flank. It may have been Wiltshire's professionals who began a steady Lancastrian advance, bearing down in fine style upon the Devereux wing of the Yorkist army. Here, the superior élan and discipline of the free lances quickly began to tell. The Yorkist left was pushed inexorably backwards, across the line of the road, into the alluvial wetlands by the river, and here they broke beneath the hacking strokes of the hired bills. Panic is a pestilence – it spreads with astonishing speed, men, but a few moments before fighting with resolution, give way, casting aside weapons and harness. Now the slashing bills of the mercenaries hewed at the mass of fugitives. Many undoubtedly drowned in the spate or were hacked down as they floundered in the mire, the bloody spoor of battle staining the cold waters.

In the centre, matters had gone less well for the Lancastrians. As both sides came to contact, the ground was hotly contended and Edward could make no headway against Tudor's Welshmen. The young paladin was every-where, his great height[5] and marked prowess provided a ready inspiration for his men, who, yard by yard, began to gain the upper hand. The Earl of Pembroke fought a good fight but, with that same appalling suddenness, his line snapped and dissolved in precipitate rout, spilling westwards in con-fusion and beyond any prospect for a rally. Thus the Lancastrian left had triumphed and taken their enemy's ground but, in the centre, the situa-tion was reversed, the honours were virtually even. March had broken Pembroke's centre but his left was still on the field and undefeated. On the right the course of the battle had witnessed a rather curious twist. Owen Tudor had led his division on a wide-flanking movement to the right. This was a very curious manoeuvre indeed for, in so doing, he left the right flank of his son's brigade very much exposed and 'in the air'. Undeterred, Tudor took his men on a circular ramble toward Kingsland, south and east of the field. Herbert was not slow to profit from his opponent's folly and fell upon the Tudor's exposed left. Assailed with such resolution, in a most unfavourable position, the Lancastrian right simply gave way.

Wiltshire, commanding his steady mercenaries, appeared to be the final hope. His force was intact and buoyed by victory, but the Earl could not persuade them to engage with Edward's central division. These professionals could see the battle was lost and so discerned little incentive to expend further blood and sweat when their prospects for future wages had just vanished with Pembroke and his father. Despite Wiltshire's best efforts, his men would fight no more, and the Earl once again turned his thoughts toward escape. With his customary agility, Wiltshire succeeded in evading his foes, as did Pembroke. Owen Tudor was less fortunate: harried the long miles back toward Hereford, he, Sir John Throckmorton and a clutch of other officers were finally taken. The carnage and cull of senior Yorkists at Wakefield ensured that they would be unwise to expect clemency. Gregory puts the total Lancastrian dead at around 3,000; this seems on the high side. Wiltshire's mercenaries suffered trifling loss and the main blow fell against Pembroke. Even Owen Tudor's wing broke before any serious loss had mounted, though some would fall in the rout. Mortimer's Cross is, to an extent, neglected by the chroniclers, so our evidences for the course of the fight are meagre. Gregory, at least, does give an account:

> *Edward, Earl of March, the Duke of York's son and heir, had a gre [good] journey [battle] at Mortimer's Cross in Wales the second day of February next so following, and there he put to flight the Earl of Pembroke, the Earl of Wiltshire. And there he took and slew of knights and squires and of the [missing] to the number of 3,000 etc.*[6]

Gregory further relates a particular anecdote from the aftermath, concerning Owen Tudor who, right to the end, refused to believe that the defeat would cost him his head. In this, however, he was sadly deluded; mercy had perished in Yorkshire – along with Throckmorton and another eight Lancastrians he faced the block:

> *This Own Tudor was father unto the Earl of Pembroke, and had wedded Queen Katherine, King Harry the VI's mother, weening and trusting all away that he should not be headed till he saw the axe and the block, and when he was in his doublet he trusted on pardon and grace till the collar of his red velvet doublet was ripped off. Then he said 'That head shall lie on the stock that was wont to lie on Queen Katherine's lap', and put his heart and mind wholly unto God, and fully meekly took his death.*[7]

The Lancastrian March from the North

The disaster at Wakefield had robbed the Yorkist faction of their senior commanders and destroyed one of their field armies. It had confirmed the Lancastrian grip on the north and provided the court party with a clear-cut victory to redress the defeat at Northampton. One particular trump, however: the person of King Henry VI, was still in Yorkist hands.

Though her western adherents were beaten, Queen Margaret could count upon a very potent concentration of available forces in Yorkshire. With some Scottish hobilers she had crossed the border in the wake of her adherents' triumph and had rejoined the northern lords at York. The road to the south lay open and beckoning. For a largely rural population, living in villages and hamlets, the passage of armed men had nothing to recommend it, regardless of any nominal allegiance. Armies were rapacious, and the force Queen Margaret now proposed to lead south was a very large one. We cannot be sure of numbers but it is reasonable to suppose that it was at least 20,000 strong.[8] The northern lords, Northumberland and Clifford, with Somerset, Neville and Dacre would be leading many of their own affinity, Trollope his regulars from Calais. These men could be controlled, but the army would attract free lances from both sides of the border, those 'roaring northerners' (*Bobinantes Boreales*) whom their southern contemporaries so heartily despised.

It would have been remarkable if some excesses had not taken place, and undoubtedly these did occur, though whether such depredations were quite on the biblical scale as depicted by the shrill accounts of contemporary writers is less certain. This invasion from the north, likened to a whirlwind, or a plague of locusts 'covering the whole surface of the earth', would be terrifying enough to small communities for whom the passage of such great numbers was largely unprecedented. Many panicked and took to the roads, crowding the rutted mires of country lanes, spreading tales of atrocity, a tide of refugees who brought fear as a contagion in their wake. Without doubt, the northerners gave little thought to sparing the districts through which they passed. They were depicted by such chroniclers as Abbot Whethamstede and the monks of Croyland Abbey as leaving a belt of devastation thirty miles wide. In the Fens the monks hurried to hide their valuables and erect as many obstacles as they could to deter an attack. Happily, these precautions, sound as they must have seemed at the time, were not tested, for the host kept to the general line of the Great North Road. The Croyland Chronicle probably articulated the fears of the southerners, when the Prior, hysterical over the depredations wrought by these wild men from the north, wrote:

> *The duke [York] being thus removed from this world, the northmen, being sensible that the only impediment was now withdrawn, and that there was was no one now who would care to resist their inroads, again swept onwards like a whirlwind from the north, and in the impulse of their fury attempted to overrun the whole of England.*[9]

Actual details of particular horrors are remarkably lacking. Without doubt the northerners plundered as they went, as much through necessity as inclination. To the countrymen and townspeople this apocalyptic vision of a great northern invasion as murderously rapacious as Tamerlane, would have been terrifying enough. The Prior of Croyland waxed lyrical in his well-rehearsed outrage: 'When the priests and the other faithful of Christ in any way offered to make resistance, like so many abandoned wretches as they were, they cruelly slaughtered them in the very churches or church yards.'[10]

Certain locations, notably towns like Grantham and Stamford, the inhabitants of which were understood to be notably Yorkist in sentiment, were afforded special treatment. In these the army was allowed free rein as a reminder to citizens of the perils of false allegiance. Defeat at Wakefield had not robbed the Yorkists of their advantage in the ongoing propaganda war, and this grand chevauchee was a perfect gift. Warwick had, prior to Northampton, proved himself the very master of acquiring hearts and minds. The Lancastrians had no such skills, and the relentless, ruthless and unchecked advance of their army provided a perfect scoop. The Earl, from London, could broadcast and embellish the atrocity stories. The dispute between factions was a lesser issue than the north–south divide, which could be played up to the hilt.

When it comes to the action in the next major fight, the Second Battle of St Albans, we are fortunate that on that occasion two of the chroniclers were present as eye witnesses. Abbot Whethamstede was a spectator, understandably a rather nervous spectator, watching the drama unfold from the relative sanctuary of the abbey itself, whilst William Gregory marched beneath Warwick's banner. His account, therefore, has the urgency of the participant's view:

> *The lords in King Harry's party [he means here the Yorkists] pitched a field and fortified it full strong, and like unwise men brake their array and took*

*another, and ere that they were all sette a-buskyd [fully deployed] to battle
the queen's party was at hand with them in town of St. Albans, and then
all thing was to seek and out of order, for their prickers come not home to
bring no tiding how nigh that the queen was.[11]*

Warwick had not anticipated the disaster at Wakefield, he had now lost both
father and brother and it would be entirely reasonable if he was distracted.
The Earl, for all his many talents, was not necessarily at his best in a crisis.
He was wrongfooted by the Lancastrians' success and disconcerted by the
subsequent march south, though, skilled pamphleteer as he was, he was
swift to capitalise on and embellish tales of the northerners' excesses. Rather
more than a war of words was required to keep Queen Margaret's army
from battering at the gates of London. With the Earl of March fully occupied in the west it was up to Warwick to shore the Yorkist position. This
necessitated a blocking move north of the capital, and there were enough
London and Kentish adherents to form a respectable army, although not
one that could be expected to equal the northerners in terms of overall
numbers.

The Second Battle of St Albans

By 12 February the Earl of Warwick had marshalled his available forces and
advanced as far north as St Albans, the scene of his triumph six years earlier.
Now he would be fighting the sons of those lords whose blood had stained
the streets before. It is unlikely that so intelligent a man missed the potential for dramatic irony. Quite why he chose the town is not entirely clear. His
enemies were marching straight down the Great North Road, and having
taken up Grantham and Stamford, they now approached through Peterbor-
ough, Huntingdon and Royston. As Colonel Burne suggests, it must have
been the case that the Queen's army veered westwards and that, informed
by scouts, Warwick moved to conform. We know the Queen had reached
Dunstable by 16 February, which allowed the Earl four full days to prepare
his position.

To ensure he covered the north and north-west approaches, the Earl
established a line of some four miles in length, stretching from St Albans
on the left or westward flank, to the aptly named No Man's Land.
Warwick had divined that the Lancastrians would be moving in a

westerly direction, towards Harpenden. Here, they had to decide whether to mount their thrust toward London, down the St Albans road or that from Hatfield. By covering Barnard's Heath and Sandridge, he blocked both and wisely covered his exposed flanks at St Albans and No Man's Land.[12] This strategy was sound in theory, but meant the Yorkists were strung out along a wide frontage – in an era before wireless communication, this entailed substantial risks. Gregory describes, in some detail, the ingenious, elaborate but ultimately useless, fieldworks the Earl had installed to protect his line:

> *Also they had nets made of great cords of four fathom of length and of four foot broad, like unto a haye [rabbit net], and at every two knot there was a nail standing up right, that there could no man pass over it by likelihood but he should be hurt. Also they had pavysse [pavises – large wooden shields] bore as a door i-made with a staff folding up and down to set the pavysse where they liked, and loops with shooting windows to shoot out at, they standing behind the pavysse, and the pavysse as full of 3d [1½ p] nail after order as they might stand. And when their shot was spend and done they cast the pavysse before them, then there might be no man come unto them over the pavysse for the nails that stood upright, but if he would mischief himself.[13]*

Colonel Burne asserts that the flexibility of the Lancastrian tactics at this point suggested the personal direction of the Queen herself, though the experienced Andrew Trollope would certainly have been consulted. It is claimed that the northerners benefited from treachery within their enemies' ranks and that a certain Kentish captain, named Lovelace, provided full details of the Earl of Warwick's deployment. It is possible that the unfortunate Lovelace was chosen as a scapegoat to ascribe the Yorkist defeat to causes other than poor generalship. Whatever the source of this key intelligence, the Queen's army did not take the direct line from Harpenden but chose to move further westwards in a broad outflanking motion which Warwick's inertia and extended lines made possible. This was a bold stroke, one which entailed a fast, forced march as far as Dunstable, then on through the winter darkness, for the leading formations to arrive at St Albans by dawn on 17 February. This was boldness indeed for, strung out along the line of approach, the Lancastrians would have been at risk of a crushing attack on their exposed flank had Warwick's scouts been more diligent. The perils of a night march, in winter conditions, moving large bodies of men over unfamiliar terrain, were sufficient to deter even the most resolute of commanders. That this was carried out so efficiently was no mean feat.

The Earl of Warwick has been citicised for relying too heavily on his field works, and perhaps he surrendered the initiative too willingly. On the other hand, his position was an unenviable one: part of the Yorkist strength, including many veterans, had been extinguished at Wakefield, much of the remainder was in the field with Edward to the west and the Earl had not had time to weld his scratchbuilt force into an effective field army. By contrast, his enemies possessed greater numbers and an army that had been successfully welded in battle. A Yorkist outpost at Dunstable, some two hundred men under Sir Edward Poynings, was easily overrun and silenced by death or capture, before even being able to raise the alarm. The Lancastrian army followed the dead straight arrow of Watling Street to cover the dozen miles to St Albans, which the head of the column probably reached at around three in the morning,[14] though it was clearly light before they began to infiltrate the sleeping town. Such was the speed and sureness of the night march that the town was taken completely unawares. The timber gate or barrier, which guarded the point where the road crossed the ancient ditch, a natural blocking position, was undefended. The passage of such large numbers of heavily armed men could not long remain unnoticed. By the time the forward elements, led by Trollope, had penetrated as far as the centre, the startled defenders were under arms and stringing their longbows.

Despite being unprepared and outmatched, the Yorkist bowmen gave a good account of themselves. The attackers, crammed in the narrow street, could not make any headway and, as the clothyard shafts continued to find their mark, the Lancastrians recoiled. Their van withdrew in good order to regroup north of the River Ver by the old Roman settlement and St Michael's Church. The solution, as in the earlier fight, was to find some means to outflank the defenders whilst keeping their attention fixed on the main axis of attack. An opportunity arose when it was discovered that the passage over the ditch by Folly and Catherine Lanes was also neglected and unguarded. Whilst the remainder of the Lancastrian detachments were still coming up, passing by St Michael's, the van crept along Catherine Lane to bypass the defence and burst into St Peter's Street. For the Yorkists this was doubly serious, assailed from two sides and their line of retreat effectively severed. These Lancastrians, spilling into St Peter's Street were also exposed to a flank attack, launched by additional Yorkists, drawn from the main battle line.

It was at this point that the second battle of St Albans came to resemble a repeat of the first, but with roles reversed – it was the Yorkists who were now hemmed in the streets. The relatively main thoroughfare of St Peter's Street, the southern portion of which was held by the defenders, became the cockpit as both sides came to strokes. These Yorkists were chosen men and fought with panache. They contested every foot of ground, despite the odds, and were not dislodged until the fight had raged for several hours. It must have been near midday before the last of the defenders was cut down or driven off. John Whethamstede might well have feared for the townsfolk and the sanctuary of his abbey as the din of this savage prelude reverberated.

From the Yorkist prospect, this hard-fought respite could have provided the 'balcony' for a vigorous counter-attack against an enemy whose overall position was by no means entirely favourable. It is likely that the main line of defence ran along the crest of the shallow ridge now crowned by the Sandridge road (Colonel Burne considers whether this was the ground Warwick's forces occupied or whether they deployed by the old Celtic dyke at Beech Bottom[15]). Warwick used the time to prepare for the blow which must soon fall upon his left flank. This necessitated redeploying his men on the threatened left, drawing them from their positions in Beech Bottom and establishing a new line on the higher ground. At the same time the Earl had to attempt to reinforce this wing, moving detachments from his centre and right. Given the extended nature of his overall disposition and the difficulties of communications, this would be a most difficult exercise.

When complete, the new line had its right anchored in Beech Bottom, stretching over Barnard's Heath, in length just under a thousand yards.[16] The Lancastrians had secured the town but had not yet achieved any significant tactical advantage. The men were tired from the travail of their night march, and those who had fought would be in need of respite. They now faced another tough assault, the new Yorkist line, half a mile or so beyond St Peter's, in the town centre. Deprived of the inestimable advantage of surprise but confident in numbers and élan, the attackers advanced toward's Warwick's improvised left. A bitter melee developed in the winter's afternoon, the roar of battle spreading through the still calm of a quiet landscape. The contest was sharp and fierce, both sides locked in the tempest of slashing bills, and, for the moment, neither could gain the upper hand. Warwick's various anti-personnel devices certainly impeded the attackers, including the fearsome Trollope who later reported he had suffered injury from a caltrap. This had pierced one amoured sabaton and held him fast to the spot, obliging, as he recorded, his enemies to come to him; of these he boasted of killing no less than 15![17]

William Gregory, hotly engaged as a participant, observed that the great guns did little execution and the handgunners could not deliver effective volleys in the press. This was now very much a soldier's battle, a grim, unrelenting slogging match, where a man could only comprehend what was occurring in his immediate vicinity, blinded by sweat, increasingly parched even as snow began falling. The Yorkists here were commanded by Warwick's brother John, Lord Montagu, a brave and highly competent officer. It seemed as if the contest was locked in stalemate, but more and more Lancastrians were being flung into the fight. Warwick's promised reinforcements had still not come up. Where was the bulk of the Yorkist army which had not yet struck a blow whilst their comrades, but a short distance away, fought for their lives against lengthening odds? The Earl of Warwick was outflanked and now outmatched;[18] the tactical initiative had been snatched away and the weaknesses of his position were rapidly becoming obvious. Possibly the Earl experienced one of those peculiar crises of confidence that were wont to afflict him in moments of great stress, when his carefully prepared plans started to unravel.

It was perhaps this uncertainty that now communicated itself to his officers in the centre. He experienced distinct resistance to his pleas for them to advance – his was a raw, largely untrained army. It was the crisis point, and the delay, the need to bully and cajole the main body to march, proved fatal. By the time the rest had grudgingly conceded the need for an immediate advance, the van was overcome and in rout. As they advanced, the deluge engulfed them. An army in rout is a terrible sight – men, who have fought with valour, robbed of their manhoods, stampeding like terrified cattle, throwing aside their arms and harness. The road from Sandridge runs along the line of the Iron Age fosse and then climbs up toward the reverse slope of the Barnard's Hill ridge. Now there came this terrified mob of broken men; the flood spilling over the ground. For Warwick this spelled catastrophe. For a short spell the centre managed to hold a shaky line at the base of the incline, but the panic was now in their blood, sure as contagion and, very soon, despite the Earl's frantic efforts, his centre was pelting after the left.

Warwick was not yet ready to admit failure. His right wing, still to the rear, remained intact. If he could bring these fresh soldiers into the fight a total rout might yet be averted. It was at this point that Lovelace and his company broadcast their defection and quit the Yorkists to assume their new allegiance. This fresh blow was too much and robbed the Earl of any prospects. Later, a taint of faintheartedness would hang over his reputation on the field; his conduct on that day mitigates strongly against this. In spite of these shattering reverses he managed to weld sufficient men into a creditable rearguard, enough to form a stubborn line, along a stretch of higher ground 500 yards south of No Man's Land. This truncated remnant was still just adequate to see off a series of probing attacks and keep the ground, until winter's dusk offered the cloak of darkness. The Earl managed to rally perhaps 4,000 of his survivors and lead them off the stricken field and out of immediate danger. He probably left as many more dead on the bloody heath. The quiet rural lanes would be filled with the stiffening, naked corpses of the fallen, robbed of all dignity, surrounded by the litter of battle and the wreckage of their carefully wrought defences. The northerners had triumphed again. Gregory has left a succinct summary of the defeat:

> *And in the midst of the battle King Harry went unto his queen and forsook all his lords, and trust better to her party than unto his own lords. And then through great labour the Duke of Norfolk and the Earl of Warwick escaped away; the Bishop of Exeter, that time Chancellor of England, and brother unto the Earl of Warwick, the Lord Bourchier, with many other knights, squires and commons fled, and many men slain in both parties.*[19]

Warwick also contrived to lose the person of the King. Dragged in the wake of the Yorkist army, like an unwilling mascot, Henry had, once again, been a spectator as the battle for his crown raged around him. He is said to have spent most of the battle seated calmly beneath a spreading oak, in good spirits, much cheered by the sight of his oppressors' rout. So great was the confusion amongst his retreating enemies that Henry appears simply to have been overlooked, left unmolested and largely forgotten until being greeted by his own victorious adherents. Lord Montagu was amongst the haul of captives which included Henry's immediate custodians, Lord Bonville and Sir Thomas Kyrill. This pair had agreed to remain with their royal charge, to safeguard his person, and in return for this undertaking their lives would be spared. In this assurance, they were misled, not by any deliberate falsehood on the King's part for he no doubt intended that the promise be honoured.

Henry's word counted for little in so far as his own affinity was concerned. Both Bonville and Sir Thomas were summarily tried and executed – Queen Margaret allowed her 8-year-old son to act as 'judge' in these summary proceedings, so that he might learn the lessons of intemperate revenge. Had the Queen had entirely her own way, Lord Montagu would have joined these unfortunate knights in their appointment with the headsman. However, the Duke of Somerset, whose word carried far greater weight than that of the King, required the Neville's life to be spared because he was fully aware that his own brother was captive at Calais and the life of one man's sibling acted as surety for the other. That night Henry lodged within the abbey, where Abbot Whethamstede beseeched him to curtail the unchecked depredations of his northerners, who had stripped the town of provisions. Despite his voluble allegations of atrocity, this was the worst he could actually accuse them of, the inevitable consequence of armies in battle and on the march. Neither the abbey precincts nor the parish churches had been despoiled, which suggests the wild men were perhaps better behaved than hostile propaganda might suggest.

The Lancastrian Withdrawal to the North

This fresh disaster for the Yorkists was, in some ways, worse than Wakefield. Warwick had been defeated but a short march from the capital, the road to which now lay open, and the person of King Henry VI had been lost, returned to the bosom of his family and the victorious mass of his adherents. Final victory appeared to lie within Lancaster's grasp. The obvious move was to advance directly upon, and seize, the city whilst Warwick was reeling and Edward, from the west, not yet come up. Fearfully pragmatic, the burgesses indicated they were willing to bow to the inevitable, sending a team of representatives to negotiate the King's access. These included the dowager duchesses of Buckingham and Bedford; the former could obviously demand an audience by virtue of her husband's blood. The city fathers nervously required that their streets be spared the ravages unleashed on Stamford and Dunstable and that the Lancastrian lords rein in their abominable northerners. An Italian, Carlo Gigli, the London-based representative of one Michele Arnolfini, based in Bruges, wrote to his principal on 22 February, describing the nature of the negotiations which had taken place:

> *They [the envoys] returned on the 20th [of February] and reported that the king and queen had no mind to pillage the chief city and chamber of their realm, and so they promised; but at the same time they did not mean that they would not punish the evildoers. On the receipt of this reply by the magistrates a proclamation was issued that everyone should keep fast to his house and should live at peace, in order that the king and his forces might enter and behave peacefully.*[20]

Perhaps it was due to the newly liberated Henry's wish to secure goodwill but whatever the reason the army was indeed reined in, to the extent that the Lancastrians withdrew to Dunstable. This was a fatal error and one that, above all, was to herald ruin. Srategically, the only viable course, at this point, was for the victors to capitalise on their win and seize London, regardless of the finer feelings of the burgesses. To give Edward and Warwick a respite, to enable them to effect a juncture of their forces to draw breath and recover the initiative was cardinal folly. Strong, ruthless action was required; hearts and minds could wait for later. But in this the greatest test of their resolve, and their single, golden opportunity, the Lancastrians failed. Queen Margaret would be aware of the unenviable reputation of her light-fingered army, but this was not the time for a PR exercise, however badly needed. If the city fathers were understandably nervous, the populace appeared more resolute: Yorkist propaganda had bolstered continued support in the streets. As Carlo Gigli continued to relate, with the understandable nervousness of a businessman whose enterprise may, at any moment, be wrecked by an undisciplined mob of rampant soldiery:

> *But less than an hour later all the people ran to arms and reports circulated that York [the Duke was of course, already dead] with 60,000 Irish and March with 40,000 Welsh had hastened to the neighbourhood and would guard their place for them; and they said that the mayor must give them the keys of the gates. They called for a brewer as their leader, and that day this place was in an uproar, so that I was never more afraid than then that everything would be at hazard.*[21]

To placate their ire, the burgesses had ordered that provisions be sent out to the Lancastrian army, but the citizens, made of sterner stuff, hijacked the load and distributed these victuals through the tenements of the poor.[22] On 22 February Edward and Warwick, who had withdrawn westwards after the debacle at St Albans, joined forces at Burford in the Cotswolds.[23] On the 26th the pair made a joint triumphal entry into the city. It seemed as though it was the Yorkists who had scored the signal victory. The King's failure to act swiftly and consolidate his grip whilst the 'window of opportunity' remained ajar, was now bearing bitter dividends. The London chronicler Robert Fabyan described the strength of the welcome the joyful citizens afforded to the Earl of March: 'And upon the Thursday following th'Earls of March and of Warwick with a great power of men, but few of name, entered into the City of London, the which was of the citizens joyously received.'[24]

As Henry was reunited with his Queen and, nominally at least, restored to the command of his faction, the political dynamic was altered. York's taking off had cleared the stage for Edward, as his eldest son and heir, to lay claim to the throne. It was time to slough off any pretence that the Yorkists were striving to free King Henry from pernicious counsellors, and grasp the dynastic bull by the horns – England was ready for a new king. In the person of the 19-year-old Earl the Yorkists had the perfect candidate. Of great height, considerable good looks, affable in manner, irresistible to women and the very image of the martial hero. Edward was a complete contrast to the unwarlike Henry. If the Earl of Warwick had failed as a field commander, he had not lost his political acumen, nor had his vast energy and powerful charisma declined. Whilst young Edward stood by to claim his inheritance, the Earl manipulated and orchestrated the popular mood. The showman in Warwick excelled himself; in a flurry of spectacle Edward was presented as king. This performance was mainly aimed at the commons for, besides the Nevilles, his power base was alarmingly thin. Norfolk was with him and he had ecclesiastical support from Canterbury; Salisbury and Exeter was not lacking. Robert Fabyan described the performance:

> . . . and upon the Sunday following the said earl [March] caused to be mustered his people in St. John's Field, where unto that host were proclaimed and shewed certain artlicles and points that King Henry had offended in, whereupon it was demanded of the said people whether the said Henry were worthy ro reign as king any longer or no. Whereunto the people cried hugely and said, Nay, Nay. And after it was asked of them if they would have th'Earl of March for their king and they cried with one voice, Yes, Yea.[25]

Having abandoned any attempt on London, the Lancastrian host, like the ebbing tide, receded northwards, relinquishing the prospect of retaining any grip on the south (doubtless to the heartfelt relief of southerners). Without securing London it was simply not possible to retain such large forces in a land already stripped of provisions. To keep her army intact the Queen now had to retreat, to seek security in the Lancastrian heartlands of the north, where her supply lines were more certain and her affinity more numerous. In so doing Margaret surrendered the initiative, which her forces had successfully maintained since destroying York and Salisbury at Wakefield. The court party's position was by no means hopeless. Edward still had only the slimmest support from the magnates, as Robert Fabyan correctly observed when describing his entry into the city on 26 February, acclaimed by the commons but with few lords in attendance. Even Coppini, that most partisan of foreign observers, was cautious when he described these events to Duke Sforza in Milan, pointing out that the Yorkists, despite their defeats in the field, were ahead in the political stakes.[26]

The country was rife with uncertainty and rumours, some of these very extravagant indeed. Prospero di Camulio, the official Milanese ambassador, recounted that it was being said that Margaret had poisoned her husband, the King, and was replacing him with the Duke of Somerset![27] If Edward wanted to make his throne secure he had to eliminate the Lancastrian field army and, once again, secure King Henry. Edward of Lancaster was a further dynastic impediment who would have to be effectively corralled or removed. What was now proposed was indeed regime change – as ever a most perilous and momentous undertaking. It remained to be seen if Edward was equal to the challenge. With his keen diplomat's eye, di Camulio summed up the situation in correspondence, opining that the new King enjoyed favour, certainly in London:

As usual in common and great matters, opinions vary in accordance with men's passions. Those who support the claims of Edward and Warwick say that the chances in favour of Edward are great, both on account of the great lordship which he has in the island and in Ireland, and owing to the cruel wrongs done to him by the queen's side, as well as through Warwick and London, which is entirely inclined to side with the new king and Warwick, and as it is very rich and the most wealthy city of Christendom, this enormously increases the chances of the side it favours. To these must be added the

good opinion of the temper and moderation of Edward and Warwick.
Some, on the other hand, say that the queen is exceedingly prudent, and by
remaining on the defensive, as they say she is well content to do, she will
bring things into subjection and will tear to pieces these attacks of the people,
who, when they perceive that they are not on the road to peace, will easily be
induced to change sides.[28]

To give his crown any lustre of legitimacy, Edward needed an indication
of God's favour that even the unction could not, in these singular circumstances, afford – he needed the ultimate vindication of trial by battle.

Notes

1 A parhelion occurs when a pair of luminous spots appear at points of 22 degrees
  or more on both sides of the sun and at the same elevation, hence the appearance
  of three suns.

2 Owen Tudor of minor gentry stock, had begun his career at the court of Henry V.
  After the King's death he became clerk of Queen Katherine's wardrobe. In 1429
  they married in secret and their two sons were raised to the peerage, Edmund
  (the father of Henry VII) to the Earldom of Richmond, and Jasper, as Earl of
  Pembroke.

3 'Galloglass' were elite Hebridean mercenaries in the service of Irish magnates.

4 Edward is said to have adopted his famous banner of the 'Sunne in Splendour'
  from the inspiration of the parhelion.

5 Edward, from measurements conducted on his skeleton, was some 6ft. 4in. in
  height.

6 Gregory, p. 211.

7 Ibid., p. 211.

8 The Lancastrians numbered perhaps eight thousand in all; see Haigh, op. cit., p. 42.

9 Croyland, p. 531.

10 Ibid., p. 531.

11 Gregory, pp. 211–14.

12 Colonel Burne (following Mortimer Wheeler) observes that this ground had
   been fortified by the later Celtic invaders as a barrier against their predecessors;
   see Burne, *More Battlefields*, p. 84.

13 Gregory, pp. 211–14.

14 Burne, op. cit., p. 86.

15 Colonel Burne discusses the matter of whether Warwick had first selected the
   line of the ridge or made use of the possibilities of the old Celtic dyke and fosse,
   substantial traces of which survive in Beech Bottom. This would form a natural

obstacle in itself and is placed across the line of the road. The counter to this is that the line of the old works is not continuous, leaving the left flank very exposed; see Burne, *More Battlefields*, pp. 88–9.

16 Ibid., p. 86.
17 See Haigh, op. cit., p. 53.
18 Warwick was poorly served by his scouts; any proper reconnaissance would have uncovered the true nature of the Lancastrian deployment, but the work was undertaken so negligently that only one patrol apparently recorded a sighting and this, incorrectly, placed the northerners a safe nine miles distant! See Burne, op. cit., p. 90.
19 Gregory, pp. 211–14.
20 CSPM i. 49–50.
21 Ibid.
22 The citizens were led by Sir John Wenlock's cook – who may be presumed to have been Yorkist in sentiment!
23 Lander, op. cit., p. 89.
24 GCL pp. 194–6.
25 Ibid.
26 Ibid.
27 CSPM i. 58.
28 Ibid., i. 58–9.

Chapter 8

'Palmsunday Field' – Towton 29 March 1461

Let him fly that will,
I will tarry with him that will tarry with me.[1]

The northern party made them strong with spear and shield,
On Palmsunday afternoon they met us in the field,
Within an hour they were right fayne to flee, and eke to yield,
Twenty seven thousand The Rose killed in the field,
Blessed by the time that ever God spread that flower.[2]

The Approach to Contact

Having seized the initiative handed to him, Edward, after being acclaimed by a great gathering in St John's Fields, suitably orchestrated by Warwick, did not dally. John Mowbray, Duke of Norfolk was sent into the eastern counties to raise his affinity, whilst the Earl carried his mission into the Midlands. On 11 March, Fauconberg led the van northwards from London. The King, as we may now style him, with the main body, followed two days later. In Yorkshire, Somerset was making his dispositions to meet the onslaught: Northumberland, Clifford, Trollope, and Randolph, Lord Dacre of Gilsland, were under his command with a total force of perhaps 40,000 soldiers, a most formidable array, the largest to take the field thus far. The royal family was safely lodged in York, the severed heads and twisted faces of their former adversaries grinning down from Micklegate Bar.

The Duke of Somerset had his muster on the gentle plateau that swells between the villages of Towton and Saxton, tents and bothies crowding behind the formidable barrier of the River Aire. It can hardly have been a congenial billet, the bare upland cut by the icy winds of a lingering medieval winter. The King obliged, however, by moving with speed and decision. Once across the Trent he continued on the march north, even though Norfolk's division had not yet come up – bad roads and the Duke's rapidly failing health impeded their deployment. Safely across the Don, the Yorkists, by Friday, 27 March, were drawing close to Ferrybridge. The weather continued inclement but it was imperative to seize a bridgehead over the Aire. John Radcliffe, Lord Fitzwalter, attempted to take the crossing by a bold *coup de main*. His assault drove back the defenders, and though the bridge was slighted it was not completely destroyed; by the end of that wet, blustery Friday, the planks had been replaced and the Yorkists had gained a foothold on the farther bank. Seemingly secure on the northern side, the attackers were themselves vigorously assailed, in the pallid light of dawn, by a commanded party of their enemies, led by Clifford himself with 500 picked troops. Fitzwalter, together with Warwick's bastard brother Sir Richard Jenny, was cut down in the melee. Hall provides a vivid account of the fray:

> *The Lord Fitzwalter hearing the noise, suddenly rose out of his bed, and unarmed, with a poleaxe in his hand, thinking that it had been an affray amongst his men, came down to appease the same, but before he could say a word, or knew what the matter was, he was slain, and with him the bastard of Salisbury, brother to the Earl of Warwick, a valiant young gentleman, and of great audacity.[3]*

Gregory's Chronicle has Warwick himself in the thick of the fight, leading the rearguard, and wounded in the thigh by an arrow. The tactical success, however, rested with Clifford and by noon the Earl, with the battered survivors, was explaining the debacle to Edward at Pontefract. It is possible the Kingmaker (as he has since been dubbed) was distinctly 'wobbly' at this point, suffering one of those crises that beset him when confronted with the unexpected. This was probably the moment at which Hall accredits the Earl with making the histrionic gesture of killing his horse – to indicate there would

Figure 3: King Edward IV
(© National Portrait Gallery, London)

be no further retreat. This smacks of theatre, though Warwick knew well how to pull an audience. If his lieutenant did waver, the young monarch was made of sterner stuff. Edward's instinctive and sure grasp of tactics, presumably boosted by sage advice from the veteran Fauconberg, dictated an immediate riposte. Hall recounts the Earl's conduct in a suitably melodramatic passage:

> *When the Earl of Warwick was informed of this feat [the destruction of Fitzwalter by Clifford], he like a man desperate, mounted on his hackney, and came blowing to King Edward saying 'Sir I pray God have mercy on their souls, which in the beginning of your enterprise hath lost their lives, and because I see no success of the world, I remit the vengeance and punishment to God our creator and redeemer' and with that he alighted down and slew his horse with his sword, saying 'Let him fly that will, for surely I will tarry with him that will tarry with me' and he kissed the cross hilt of his sword.*[4]

Warwick was to return to Ferrybridge and pin Clifford to the crossing whilst Fauconberg led a strong flanking movement, bolstered by the support of fellow veterans Sir Richard Blount and the Kentishman, Robert Horne, splashing through the swollen but passable ford, four miles upstream at Castleford. Clifford was, in turn, surprised when the Yorkists descended on his right flank. He was disconcerted but not dismayed, leading his affinity, the 'Flower of Craven' as they were called, in a fighting withdrawal. Somerset's inertia, at this juncture, is hard to fathom – bad weather and poor communications played their part but it was clearly vital to deny the Yorkists passage of the Aire; his failure to reinforce Clifford is unexplained.

In Dinting Dale, the Westmorland men made their stand. Clifford fell to an archer when, it is said, he injudiciously removed his bevor to slake a raging thirst. Many of his fellowship died with him (the dead Lancastrian left a young heir, barely 7 years of age and who lived to fight against the Scots at Flodden

Figure 4:   Elizabeth Woodville

(© National Portrait Gallery, London)

over half a century later). Sir John Neville, brother to the Earl of Westmorland (who, according to Davies, was credited with misleading the Duke of York prior to the Battle of Wakefield) perished in the extended skirmish.

> *[Clifford's force] met with some that they looked not for, and were attraped before they were aware. For the Lord Clifford, either from heat or pain, put off his gorget, was suddenly hit by an arrow, as some say, without a head and was stricken in the throat, and incontinent rendered his spirit. And the Earl of Westmorland's brother and all his company almost were slain, at a place called Dintingdale, not far from Towton.[5]*

Andrew Boardman, in his excellent and definitive study of the battle, comments on the difficulties over these actions, lumped together as the 'Battle' for Ferrybridge. The fight has two distinct stages – an attack upon Fitzwalter's Yorkists, ostensibly guarding the secured crossing place, seen off with loss, then the second phase where Fauconberg completes the destruction of Clifford. The latter has not enjoyed a good press. A fearless fighter, he is known to history by the unfortunate epithet of 'The Butcher'; his affinity, the 'Flower of Craven', appear to have been something of an elite, infected by their Lord's uncompromising ardour.

Jean de Waurin gives a somewhat different view of the battle. He describes Edward, from Pontefract, dispatching John de la Pole, Duke of Suffolk, to scout the Lancastrians at Ferrybridge. This commanded party comes under attack and is duly reinforced so the fight develops as an encounter battle. With the position at a stalemate, Edward himself comes up to assess the prospects and, fearing the enemy must now be further reinforced, orders an immediate assault. The fight raged from noon until nearly dusk, some 3,000 casualties on both sides – a significant encounter in itself.[6]

The facts, as Andrew Boardman concludes, after a detailed analysis of the sources, are that the bridge was broken down by the retreating Lancastrians and left unguarded.[7] Fitzwalter's pioneer company seized the ruined crossing and repaired, at least in part, the damage. They in turn were taken unawares the next dawn by Clifford. After Warwick, learning of the reverse, had confirmed the loss to Edward, the King immediately moved strong forces to wrest back the contested crossing. What then ensued was a desperate and hard-fought encounter wherein Warwick and the King both fought in the melee, the former being wounded in the thigh by a chance arrow. Clifford, with the narrow ground in his favour, denied the attackers any advantage for several hours. Realising that his head-on assault was at risk of proving a costly failure, Edward ordered Fauconberg to mount his flank attack via Castleford. Clifford then attempted to disengage, retreating back to his own lines, but was overwhelmed by the Yorkists' mounted van.

A question arises as to whether Clifford was simply abandoned by his comrades who, depending upon the exact location of the Lancastrian encampment at this stage, may have had a grandstand view of his destruction, or whether his force was wholly out of view. It seems incredible that, whatever jealousies may have obtained between the headstrong Clifford and his fellow commanders, they would allow him to be decimated in front of their lines without raising a finger. The effect on morale may easily be imagined. It seems more likely that, in the fog of war, the danger to Clifford and 'the Flower of Craven' was not immediately obvious to their comrades, and that the rout was accomplished before a relief could be mounted. For the trapped Lancastrians, harried virtually to within sight of safety, this must have been a bitter conclusion. They had fought all day against great odds and held their ground with honour but now, as the freezing blanket of darkness arrived to cloak their retreat, the Yorkist prickers and mounted archers were swarming around them like vengeful hornets. We may assume the Flower of Craven sold their lives dearly, bunched around the body of their revered leader like housecarls of old.

With the way cleared, his enemies discomfited and motionless, Edward led the bulk of the army toward Castleford and the crossing there. By dusk on that day in a cold, northern spring, the Yorkists were safely over the last major obstacle between them and the Lancastrians; a major trial of arms was now imminent and unavoidable. Edward's prickers were as far forward as Saxton but the baggage was left behind at Ferrybridge, so the Yorkist army, as it straggled in tired columns, would be faced with a cold and hungry bivouac. One of the more contemporary accounts of the battle comes from the pen of Warwick's brother, George Neville, who wrote in the immediate aftermath to the papal legate, Francesco Coppini, Bishop of Terni:

> *The King, the valiant Duke of Norfolk, my brother aforesaid and my uncle, Lord Fauconberg, travelling by different routes, finally united with all their companies and armies near the country round York . . . Our adversaries had broken the bridge which was our way across, and were strongly posted on the other side, so that our men could only cross by a narrow way*

which they had made themselves after the bridge was broken. But our men forced a way by the sword, and many were slain on both sides. Finally the enemy took to flight, and very many of them were slain as they fled.[8]

Moving large bodies of foot over wet, miry ground, the lanes a nightmare of slime, would constitute an NCO's nightmare. Encumbered by harness and personal weapons, the weary men slithered, stumbled, plodded and cursed toward the higher ground, the keen edge of a biting wind freezing their sweat, tempers frayed, nerves taut and bellies empty. They finally stood on the rim of ground that would become legendary as England's bloodiest field; they could have been forgiven had the significance of the moment eluded them. Somerset had elected to fight south of York, with the Wharfe running behind and the Ouse flowing to the east. York, the northern capital, could not be easily given up, tantamount as this would be to an intimation of defeat. A further withdrawal over the harsh sweep of the North Yorkshire Moors and into the poorer districts of Durham or even Northumberland was out of the question, the land too bare to support so great a host.

Battle

Past Towton, the land rises gently to a low plateau, the climb barely perceptible except to the west where there is a marked decline into the Cock Burn. The valley below was more densely forested in the fifteenth century, a tangle of scrub, alder and birch, poorly drained. To the south-west, up beyond Bloody Meadow, the rise becomes more noticeable, still topped by a stand of timber named Castle Hill Wood. The swell is neatly bisected by a lateral depression, known as Towton Dale, which slopes into what was, at that time, a marshy gully in the west. The position generally accepted as that taken up by the Lancastrians on the day of the battle is spread along the crown of the ridge line, north of the dale, immediately to the south of the present monument. It was, therefore, necessary for the Yorkists to deploy on the higher ground lying to the south. It has, nonetheless, been suggested that Somerset's men might have advanced some 300 yards southwards, with Towton Dale in their rear. The Duke was certainly not blind to the potential for ambush offered by Castle Hill Wood and concealed a strong, commanded party beneath the trees, still bare and stark against the leaden skies.

It was now dawn on 29 March, Palmsunday. As sombre priests moved before the lines, men knelt to take a scrap of earth in their mouths. The imminence of mortality is a powerful incentive to piety, and no medieval soldier would draw before making due and proper obeisance. Waurin again provides a distinct view of the events which occurred in the run-up to the battle. The Chronicler asserts that it was only after the army had broken camp that the Yorkist scouts reported the enemy's advance:

> When the [King] and his lords were told that King Henry was nearby in
> the fields they rejoiced, for they wished for nothing more but to fight him.
> The [King] called for his captains and told them to put their men in for-
> mation and to take their positions before the enemy came to close. And so it
> was he organised his battles, and he sent some men to look around the area
> because they were only 4 miles from the enemy.[9]

As the Yorkists toiled up the slope from Saxton they would have been out of sight of their enemies deployed on the farther ridge.[10] Not until they had ascended to this lip of the plateau would they have glimpsed the formidable array that faced them. Even with the biting wind and driven flurries the strength of their opponents would have been immediately obvious. Now there was the bright panoply of war, the silken banners unfurled and harness gleaming, breaks in the sleet showing the massed rows of bills. It would have been a daunting sight, the most crowded field in England's long cata-logue. It was to be a battle, yet also it was a vendetta, a blood feud between the scions of the noble families on both sides of the dale. All had lost fathers, brothers, cousins and friends to the blood lust of the other. The rotting skulls of York, Salisbury and Rutland still fed the crows, the blood of St Albans and Northampton was still heavy on the minds of the Lancastrian lords. The commons took their cue from the magnates – many of lesser blood might also have left family dead on earlier fields.

Edward was in no hurry to unleash the offensive; his men were almost certainly outnumbered as Norfolk's division still lagged some distance behind. He himself seems to have taken station in the centre with Warwick whilst his uncle Fauconberg led the right. The Yorkist rearguard or left wing would comprise a substantial reserve and the cadre of mounted skirmishers. Facing them, Northumberland and the experienced Trollope had the Lancastrian right or van, Somerset and Lord Welles the main body, King Henry's banner flowing above with Exeter on the right. It is almost certain that Fauconberg's Yorkist van (the right) was the first division to sight the enemy, strongly posted to cover the deployment of the main battle and rear. Whether the advancing columns, as they marshalled into line, comprised companies of bows, bills and men-at-arms placed alternately or whether the archers stepped to the front as distinct missile troops is unclear. Andrew Boardman suggests the van was entirely comprised of a mass of bowmen and the subsequent fall of events would tend to support this view.[11]

As the hosts were marshalled into line, at about ten in the morning, a brisk shower of dense rain and sleet gusted over the field, chased by a strong southerly wind. This blew hail directly into the faces of the Lancastrians, obscuring their vision. Fauconberg, his veteran's eye quick to discern the possibilities, bade his bowmen advance and loose, shooting at extreme range but with the scurrying wind to lend wings to their flights. The shafts found their mark and the Lancastrians shot in reply, but they loosed into empty ground some 40 metres short, the Yorkist archers having now smartly stepped back. Capitalising on his success, the wily Fauconberg repeated the tactic, returning his adversaries shafts back into their own ranks. Hall describes Fauconberg's initiative:

> The Lord Fauconberg, which led the forward of King Edward's battle being a man of great policy and much experience in martial feats caused every archer under his standard to shoot one flight and then made them stand still. The northern men, feeling the shoot, but by reason of the snow, not perfectly viewing the distance between them and their enemies like hardy men shot their sheaf arrows as fast as they might, but all their shot was lost and their labour in vain for they came not near the southern men by 40 tailors yards.[12]

Such an exchange of missiles frequently dictated the outcome of the fight, for the losing side, that suffering the greatest loss, was left with no alternative but to advance to contact to avoid the storm, dreadful to endure. The shafts would deluge the Lancastrian ranks and whilst a man-at-arms in full plate might escape injury, the lesser protection worn by the commons would leave them horribly exposed. Men would be snatched from the ranks to writhe and shudder in the snow, their lifeblood spilling copiously onto the white, some riddled with shafts, stuck like porcupines through their bodies, limbs and faces. Fauconberg had the inestimable advantage of the wind but the shooting demanded a very high degree of skill; happily for Edward his archers were equal to the task.

A great shout of 'King Henry' burst from thousands of throats, rolling over the windswept ground, and the Lancastrians surged forward. The tramp of armoured men, slogging over the wet slush, drowned the keening of the wind, the great, rolling crash as the opposing ranks collided like breakers on the shore. The biggest and bloodiest fight in the history of these islands was now fully underway. It was probably sometime before noon. King Edward had pointedly sent his horse to the rear, showing he would stand the full hazard of battle with his retainers – and live or die accordingly. Such gestures were important, none of the young monarch's fellowship need doubt his seriousness: this was the battle for England. It would appear that the Lancastrian centre was the first division to engage. Northumberland, on the flank, lagged somewhat behind; quite why is uncertain, it is very possible his companies had suffered worst from Fauconberg's deluge. For the whole of their advance the attackers would still be subject to a hail of arrows, men marking targets more closely as the gap narrowed, the popping of handguns heralding their imminent approach. It seemed that Northumberland's blow must fall against the King's division, as Waurin confirms:

> *At that moment . . . [the King] saw the army of the Earl of Northumberland coming for battle carrying the banner of King Henry. [The King] rode his horse along his army where all the nobles were and told them how they had wanted to make him their king, and he reminded them that they were seeing the next heir to the throne which had been usurped by the Lancasters a long time ago. He suffered his troops and knights to help him now to recover his inheritance and they all assured him of their desire to help and said that if any wished not to fight they should go their own way.*[13]

As the Yorkist archers fell back, fierce fighting burst along the line, a murderous, hacking melee of bills, poleaxes and swords. In such combat the number of fatal casualties would be perhaps less than might be expected, the greatest loss of life occurred when one side dissolved in rout and became prey for the victors. Many would suffer wounds, cuts to the head, body and lower limbs; if a man fell he was lost, snuffed out by a flurry of blows. The noise would be terrific, a lunatic cacophony of grinding blades, shouts, exhortations, curses, and screams of injured and dying men. The mounds of dead which contemporary illustrators show piling on fields of battle would build up as the fight burned brightly in various sectors.[14] It would not be at all a tidy, neat, precise coming together of opposing lines. Knots of men would eddy and swirl as with the ebb and suck of the tide, temporarily disengaging as the ranks were thinned or disordered, the very press of dead forming a considerable barrier so that the living must fight on top of the heaps of slain, adding their blood and entrails to the score.

In the dense fog of battle, men would stand with comrades in their companies, telling who was friend and who was foe was no easy matter and there was no recourse to polite enquiry. Men might wear livery jackets, emblazoned with their lord's badge, but this would do little to avert confusion. The standards provided the main anchor and rally point as the melee pounded. Commanders would be able to exercise a diminishing level of control, the fight taking on its own momentum, the roar and fury of the red mist further obscured by the slanting showers that burst over the field as the afternoon wore on. If the Yorkists enjoyed the considerable morale advantage of having the inspiring persona of their youthful king on the field, they lacked numbers and, as the fight continued, this began to tell. The Lancastrians steadily gained ground, the landscape behind this slow attrition spewing a carpet of horrors, a banquet of unquiet death and mortal pain, the keening of the wounded whipped and eddied by the fitful wind. At one point Edward was saved by the swift action of a Welsh retainer Davyd ap Mathew. In recognition of this, and in addition to material reward, the King granted his saviour the honour of standard bearer and the insertion of 'Towton' into the family arms.

Somerset may have chosen this potentially crucial moment to spring his ambush from Castle Hill Wood, the attack falling on the left of the Yorkist line. Evidence for this is largely anecdotal, but the lie of the ground admirably suited such a tactic and the frequent snow showers would have acted as a further screen. If such an attack was successfully launched then the Yorkists would have found themselves, at this point, assailed on two flanks and would very likely have given ground. This would potentially have been fatal: just such a blow delivered from the flank, had contributed greatly to the Scottish victory at Otterburn in 1388. Quite possibly the Lancastrians had retained their mounts and charged as cavalry, adding to their enemies' discomfiture. The assault may well, as Andrew Boardman convincingly asserts, have been of sufficient weight to cause the entire line to alter its alignment, the left flank of the Yorkist army being pushed some way down the line of the present B1217.[15] Part of the army may even have routed, provoking a crisis for the young King and his senior officers. Waurin appears to support this possibility:

> When Lord Rivers, his son and six or seven thousand Welshmen led by An-
> drew Trollope, following the Duke of Somerset himself with seven thousand
> men, charged his cavalry who fled and were chased for about eleven miles.
> It seemed that Lord Rivers' troops had won a great battle, because they
> thought that the Earl of Northumberland had charged on the other side,
> unfortunately he had not done so and this became his tragic hour for he
> died that day. During this debacle many of [King Edward's] soldiers died
> and when he learned the truth of what had happened to his cavalry he was
> very sad as well as very annoyed.[16]

It may well have been the case that Lord Rivers (Edward's future father-in-law) and Trollope led the ambush party. The latter was a tried exponent of such handy surprises; once successful the attackers pelted off in pursuit of their enemies, so the effect of the advantage gained was thus diluted. One is reminded of Prince Edward's (Longshhanks') horsemen at Lewes in 1263 and Prince Rupert's squadrons at Naseby, nearly four centuries later. Andrew Boardman points out that Edward, a decade later at Tewkesbury, was very aware of the risk and potential of the woods on his flank;[17] this may have represented knowledge dearly bought. What appears certain is that, for some hours, the outcome hung very much in the balance, but with the advantage shifting inexorably to the more numerous Lancastrians. Edward may have been saved from a worse catastrophe by a possible failure of command in his enemies' ranks, with Northumberland advancing too slowly to capitalise on the success of the ambush party. Indeed, his division may have been forced to give ground, with the Earl himself, at this critical point, being struck down.

Lord Dacre was also amongst those who fell; like Clifford, overcome with thirst he removed his sallet, only to be transfixed by an arrow. No man encumbered by full or part harness can fight indefinitely without relief, quite the contrary, an armoured man, however fit, will tire after no more than a few moments of combat. Exhausted men have to be rotated and they need water; dehydration and heat – trapped within the carapace of steel – can be as debilitating as wounds. Dacre probably died in North Acres,[18] but despite this loss of a senior officer the juggernaut pressed on, forcing the Yorkists to give ground. As yet there was no rout but perhaps an intimation of panic; a tremour ran through the ranks.

The crisis was now at hand. All of the Yorkists' reserves, under Wenlock and Dinham, would have been long since committed, very likely the whole of Exeter's rearward division would be in the Lancastrian line. Once King Edward's men were pushed to the lip of the escarpment, disaster loomed. If the Lancastrians could maintain this steady pressure they would sweep their battered enemies from the field and win the day; the stakes could not have been higher. Edward, his Black Bull banner streaming in the wind, performed prodigies of valour, a paladin and inspiration to his bone-weary soldiers. George Neville, admittedly partisan, refers to the courage and leadership of not only the King, but of his brother and uncle.[19] Personal leadership was the vital element of medieval generalship – the magnate was always a knight, expected to find his place in the thick of the press and there to accomplish chivalric feats. Edward of York perfectly filled this role, his great height, commanding physique, skill at arms and personal courage formed the very stuff of legend.

Desperately ill, the exhausted Norfolk may have been at Pontefract on the evening of 28 March[20] (he was to die in November); despite this, he had his men on the move next morning. Following the old London road through Sherburn-in-Elmet, past the corpse-strewn field at Dinting Dale, where the stiffening remains of the fallen stayed frozen in the sack-like postures of death, his men began arriving on the field, deploying on their comrades' right flank at some point in the early afternoon. Such much-needed and fresh reinforcements were able to shore up the Yorkist line and provide a greater parity of numbers. Though Somerset may have sensed the victory slipping from his grasp there was no panic in the Lancastrian ranks, the Duke moved men to shore up the left whilst trying to maintain pressure on the centre and right.

For the moment there was stalemate, the slaughter continued into the wet afternoon, scudding clouds driven by the sharp-edged wind, a scattering of hail and snow, blinding the combatants and settling a pall over the rising mounds of dead and wounded. Nonetheless, the arrival of Norfolk's division may finally have been the decisive factor. When the fighting was of such long duration and the mettle of the parties so finely balanced, any fresh reinforcement at the crisis point must have a telling effect. Somerset was within an ace of winning the battle when his ambush party crashed against the Yorkist left. Dire as this was, the line was not completely fractured, nor was it rolled up in the classic manner. Most probably by a mix of Edward's generalship, shoring up the weakened front, and by the folly of those Lancastrians who succumbed to the lure of pursuit and plunder, the crisis was averted. Norfolk's reinforcement, less dramatic, may have achieved the greater tactical advantage.

Those struggling in the line would have little sense of events beyond their immediate periphery. Pouring with sweat in clammy harness, their vision restricted to the narrow opening of the visor, disorientated by a constant, relentless crescendo of noise, it would be impossible to gain a meaningful insight into the shifting fortunes of the armies. But the Yorkists had stopped retreating; it was now their turn to exert pressure, to build up the steady momentum of the advance, with new blood and untried muscle swelling their ranks. Pressure from Norfolk's fresh troops was causing Somerset's line to bend backwards in response, curving like a flexed bow, still, however, in good order. At some point in the long, blood-soaked afternoon, the Lancastrians began to give way. At first, a trickle from the rear, that swelled into a stream, then into an unstoppable river in spate. Once morale was gone, rout was inevitable, the collapse finally swift and terrifyingly sudden as the thinning ranks at the front found themselves deserted. Vergil's account, though it post-dates the battle by half a century, does suggest that the collapse, when it came, was swift:

> Thus did the fight continue more than 10 hours in equal balance, when at last King Henry [by whom he surely means Somerset] espied the forces of his foes increase, and his own somewhat yield, whom when by new exhortation he had compelled to press on more earnestly, he with a few horseman removing a little out of that place, expected the event of the fight, but behold, suddenly his soldiers gave the back, which when he saw this he fled also.[21]

It was by the rim of Towton Dale that the line finally fractured. A few hardy souls determined to form rally points around their banners and sell their lives as dearly as possible, but the rest joined the deluge. Many scrambled or slid down the slush-covered gradient toward the Cock River. Bloody Meadow became a vast killing field, panicking survivors fought each other to gain the narrow span of the bridge, swirling waters below swollen with the downpours. Exhausted men were dragged down by the weight of harness and sodden jacks; it is said the waters were so swollen with the tide of corpses that men could cross dry shod over the 'bridge of bodies'.[22] As men pelted through the narrow lanes of Towton and on to Tadcaster, they were harried and hacked by swirling knots of cavalry who carried the slaughter virtually to the gates of York.

That night the victors would camp on the field, numbed by exhaustion, beset by the icy keening of the wind, around them the moans of the wounded and dying, the surgeons busily at their trade, the stink of blood and ordure in their nostrils. On the field, those piles of stiffening bodies would shift and shudder as some desperately wounded wretch fought a last struggle for survival. For the defeated there were no comrades to lift them from the ground, no medical attention, however crude by our standards, just the cold and the blood-soaked ground. In the bitter dark the 'jackals' would come, the untouchables of medieval society, stripping the bodies of everything, picking over the carcasses of battle, their knives and clubs settling the final fate of many who still lingered.

Quite how many men died on the field and in the rout cannot be clearly ascertained. Polydore Vergil later assessed the total as 20,000. Hall gives a more precise but unsubstantiated figure of 36,776. The Paston correspondence mentions a toll of 28,000. Whatever the exact level of mortality, the butcher's bill was very high indeed, this was England's bloodiest day – before 1 July 1916 on the Somme. Of the total number of dead, the majority were Lancastrians: besides Clifford and Dacre, Northumberland died of wounds, and Lords Neville, Morley and Welles with the redoubtable Trollope fell on the field; Thomas Courtenay, Earl of Devon was taken and executed – Micklegate Bar was soon to host a whole new array of heads. The Yorkists had escaped with remarkably few gentry casualties, only Lord Fitzwalter and Robert Horne. George Neville summed up the day in his correspondence with Coppini:

That day [Palmsunday] there was a very great conflict, which began with the rising of the sun, and lasted until the tenth hour of the night, so great was the pertinacity and boldness of the men, who never heeded the possibility of a miserable death. Of the enemy who fled, great numbers were drowned in the river near the town of Tadcaster, eight miles from York, because they themselves had broken the bridge to cut our passage that way, so that none could pass, and a great part of the rest who got away who gathered in the said town and city, were slain and so many dead bodies were seen as to cover an area six miles long by three broad and about four furlongs. In this battle eleven lords of the enemy fell, including the Earl of Devon, the Earl of

Northumberland, Lord Clifford and Neville with some cavaliers; and from what we hear from persons worthy of confidence, some 28,000 persons perished on one side and the other.[23]

To avoid being thought too enthusiastic over the copious shedding of so much Christian blood, the Bishop concluded his missive with a suitable exclamation of (admittedly somewhat partisan) piety:

O miserable and luckless race and powerful people, would you have no spark of pity for our own blood, of which we have lost so much of fine quality by the civil war, even if you had no compassion for the French.[24]

If up to twenty thousand men died, then twice as many would have been wounded. Every dwelling, every cottage and bothy in the area would have been crammed with hacked and bleeding men, the roads for days – even weeks – after the fight jammed with walking wounded and men carried on carts. In a savage close-quarter fight, most of the combatants would expect to sustain some injury. Warwick, as has been noted, was struck in the thigh by an arrow. It was the Duke of Wellington who commented, on the field of Waterloo, that apart from a battle lost there was no sadder sight than a battle won. The grim field of Towton would have been a very dolorous sight indeed.

Notes

1 Attributed by Hall to the Earl of Warwick, prior to Towton and after the Yorkist reverse at Ferrybridge.
2 Rose of Rouen pp. 343–7.
3 Hall, pp. 254–5.
4 Ibid., p. 255 – the Earl had taken care to mount a hackney, far less valuable than his destrier; the melodrama would be equal but the cost more bearable!
5 Ibid., p. 255.
6 Waurin, pp. 237–8.
7 Andrew Boardman, *The Battle of Towton* (Stroud 1994), p. 64.
8 George Neville's correspondence to Coppini; quoted in Lander, op. cit., pp. 92–3.
9 Waurin, pp. 330–40.
10 Hall places the Yorkist camp around the village of Saxton and thus the army's advance would be concealed until they ascended the southern plateau, very roughly between the present B1217 to the west and the A162 to the east. Hall

appears to make it quite clear that the two hosts marshalled out of sight of each other and that it was only when the Yorkists attained the rim that each could perceive the other's array – see Boardman, op. cit., p. 108.

11 Boardman, op. cit., p. 104.

12 Hall, pp. 255–6.

13 Waurin, p. 340.

14 Many contemporary illustrations show the field piled with great masses of dead.

15 Boardman, op. cit., p. 132.

16 Waurin, p. 340.

17 Boardman, op. cit., p. 132.

18 Dacre is said to have been struck either in the throat or head whilst taking refreshment; a legend persists that he was sniped by a youthful archer who had hidden himself in a nearby bur oak or elderberry – see Boardman, op. cit., p. 133.

19 Cited in Boardman, op. cit., p. 1.

20 Norfolk was, as we are aware, a very sick man; his exact movements remain unclear. Boardman concludes, and this must be right, that the Duke was probably something in the order of a full day's march behind the main body of the Yorkist army during the march north; see Boardman, op. cit., pp. 77–8.

21 PV p. 111.

22 See Boardman, op. cit., pp. 80–2.

23 Neville's correspondence, quoted in Lander, op. cit., pp. 92–3.

24 Ibid.

Chapter 9

War in the North 1461–1463

The Act of Attainder, passed by Edward IV's victorious Parliament, attainted all of the northern lords who had fallen in the Battle of Towton: the Earl of Northumberland, Lords Clifford, Neville and Dacre. Many others from the region also found themselves dispossessed: Sir Humphrey Dacre, Sir Thomas Findern, Sir John Heron, Sir Henry Bellingham, Sir Robert Whittingham, Sir Ralph Randolf, Robert Bellingham of Westmorland, Thomas Stanley, John Smothing, Robert Bolling, Robert Hatecale, Richard Everingham, Richard Cokerell (these last five from York), Roger Wharton from Westmorland and Rauf Chernok from Lancashire. Of these attainted a number, including Bellingham, his brother, Randolf and Stanley, had been previously implicated in the disturbances of the early 1450s (though Stanley, at that time, had been of the Neville faction).[1]

The Lancastrians in Northumberland

In his correspondence to Coppini, George Neville had been at pains to stress the magnitude of the victory: 'The armies having been formed and marshalled separately, they set forth against the enemy and at length, on Palmsunday, near a town called Ferrybridge, about 16 miles from out city, our enemies were routed and broken in pieces.'[2] Though the Lancastrians had been grievously beaten, the Milanese ambassador to the court of

Charles VII, Prospero di Camulio, writing a mere four days after George Neville, sounded a shrewdly cautious note: 'Firstly, if the King and Queen of England with the other fugitives mentioned above are not taken, it seems certain that in time fresh disturbances will arise.'[3] This observation was to prove grimly prophetic as the focus of the war moved northward into Northumberland, where it was to fester for the next three years.

The county of Northumberland was a different region from North Yorkshire where the troubles of the preceding decade and the battles of that phase of the wars which occurred between 1459 and 1461 had been centred. There is, perhaps, a tendency amongst historians to point generally to the 'north' as though the land north of the Trent was a single region. This is, of course, not the case, nor was it so in the fifteenth century. The cultural, topographical and social fabric of the north embraced 'a kaleidoscope of overlapping regions and localities'.[4] Northumberland is the most northerly of English counties and shares a long border with Scotland; Northumbrians and Scots had been embroiled in endemic warfare, since the late thirteenth century.[5]

To the west Carlisle, with its great red sandstone Norman Keep, had been the gateway to the English west for centuries, defying every effort by the Scots. The city was a flourishing port in its own right, plying the busy routes to Ireland and Man. Naworth and Askerton Castles stood along the West March, the Scots' frequent choice of incursion route. A number of these fortifications were to prove significant in the struggles of 1461–64 but none more than the three great east coast fortresses of Alnwick, Bamburgh and Dunstanburgh. Of these, the first was a jewel of the Percies and much improved by them over several generations.[6] Bamburgh occupies a spur of the Whin Sill, rising 150 feet from the flat coastal plain. The ancient seat of the Northumbrian kings, it is said to be the 'Joyous Garde' of Arthurian legend.[7] Begun by Thomas, Earl of Lancaster, Dunstanburgh also occupies a dolerite outcrop, much rebuilt in the later fourteenth century by John of Gaunt, who held the wardenship in the 1380s.[8]

After receiving the dire news of her defeat at Towton, Queen Margaret fled north into Scotland with King Henry, her young son Edward of Lancaster and a scattering of survivors including Somerset, Roos, Exeter and Sir John Fortescue. Margaret might have shared the view that Northumberland was solidly Lancastrian in sentiment, following the lead of the Percies who, as it has been argued 'have the hearts of the north and always have had'.[9] Whilst the Earl of Northumberland found his hegemony challenged in Durham and North Yorkshire by the Nevilles, Salisbury and his affinity had little influence in the most northerly shire. On 22 April 1461, some three weeks after Towton, King Edward IV progressed northwards to Newcastle where on 1 May he attended the demise of James Butler, Earl of Wiltshire, whose happy knack of slipping unscathed from a number of tight spots had finally deserted him. With him was John Neville, Lord Montagu, who had previously been held captive in York. He had escaped the fate of the Yorkist lords taken at Wakefield when he himself was captured at Second St Albans. His brother Richard had Somerset's younger sibling Edmund incarcerated at Calais, so a form of quid pro quo had obtained. Having established his authority, however, the King soon tired of the north, pressing matters awaited him in London and he was pleased to delegate mopping up operations to the Nevilles.

James II, King of Scotland, had led a six-day chevauchee through the English borderland in 1456 and had attempted to retake Berwick in the following year. His interest in the dynastic struggle unfolding in England was largely opportunistic and he had petitioned Charles VII of France to launch an assault on the Calais Pale. When James heard of the Yorkist victory at Northampton and the capture of Henry VI, he sat down before Roxburgh, the last bastion of the former Pale. On 3 August, with his batteries sited, he was to be joined by his Queen, Marie de Guelders. The King ordered a cannonade to herald his consort but one of the great guns burst, a not infrequent peril, and James was fatally wounded when a fragment smashed his thigh.[10] His heir, now King James III, was only 8 years old and Scotland was again subject to the uncertainties of a Regency Council. This body quickly split into factions – the 'Old' lords led by Bishop Kennedy of St Andrews and the 'Young' who championed the widowed Queen. Margaret of Anjou was desperate for allies, to the extent that she would trade both Carlisle and Berwick. On 25 April, the keys of Berwick were handed over but the citizens of Carlisle would have no truck with Scots and grimly barred their gates, refusing the Queen's summons.

A joint Scots and Lancastrian expedition was dispatched to besiege the city, and the Yorkists perceived the threat sufficiently potent for Edward to bring forward the date of his coronation to 28 June, so he would be free to lead a march northwards. In the event this proved unnecessary as the resourceful Montagu, raising local forces, saw off the besiegers. Margaret had demonstrated not only the measure of her desperation but an epic disregard for the sentiment of the very northerners she sought to woo, to whom the Scots were a despised and frequent foe. Berwick-upon-Tweed was destined to remain in their hands until 1482 when it was retaken by Richard of Gloucester, at which point it had changed hands no less than 14 times![11]

There were further disturbances: the French were said to be about to descend on the Channel Islands, led by Queen Margaret's fervent admirer Pierre de Breze. With the death, however, on 22 July of Charles VII, the likelihood of French intermeddling diminished. The new sovereign had little time for the gallant de Breze who was effectively put out to grass.[12] Warwick won the loyalty of a Burgundian captain, the Seigneur de la Barde who, having succumbed to the Earl's charisma and the attractions of his pay chest, led a company of handgunners previously in the service of Duke Philip, joining the Yorkist ranks after the disaster at Wakefield.[13]

In England the spark of rebellion flared briefly in East Anglia and, more seriously, in Wales where, as in Northumberland, the Lancastrian lords still held several major castles. By the autumn the Welsh adherents had been bested in the field and their strongholds systematically reduced; by the end of the year only mighty Harlech still held out. Feeling themselves relatively secure in Northumberland, the Lancastrian lords, Dacre, Roos and Richemont Grey, launched a raid into Durham, advancing their banners as far as Brancepeth, with King Henry present in their train. True to his fresh allegiance, Lawrence Booth, the Prince Bishop, previously a staunch supporter, but now converted by the great victory at Towton into an equally enthusiastic Yorkist, mustered the county levies and saw them off:

> The problem here [the north] was a complicated one, Henry VI and his supporters were sheltered and aided by the Scots, and, to a lesser extent, by the French. The region itself was remote, difficult of access and dominated by the great fortresses.[14]

Alarums and Excursions

In July Warwick was appointed as Warden for both East and West Marches, ably assisted by his brother Montagu. The Nevilles continued mopping up until September, by which time Alnwick had surrendered and a garrison of 100 men-at-arms had been installed. In early October Dunstanburgh capitulated, the terms of surrender being negotiated by the Lancastrian castellan, Sir Ralph Percy. It might be presumed that the Yorkist triumph was complete, but for as long as the defeated court had a base in Scotland, the border would be troubled. Edward IV, painfully aware of the narrowness of his own affinity and his fragile grip on the sceptre, was prepared to be accommodating and overlook past affiliations, a bold if risky strategy, in contrast to Warwick's approach which was considerably more, and ruthlessly, pragmatic. The King was disposed to permit Sir Ralph to remain in charge at Dunstanburgh, a mistake, for the Percy soon reverted. Another Lancastrian, Sir William Tailboys, emerging from Scotland, swiftly recaptured Alnwick, whilst, in the west, Lord Dacre seized Naworth.[15]

Both Edward and his lieutenant perceived that a diplomatic offensive against the Scots, aimed at depriving the Lancastrians of their foothold in the northern kingdom, was the only sure means of establishing firm control over the English border Marches. Warwick thus held preliminary talks with Marie de Gueldres in April 1462, followed by a further meeting in July, but the Scottish Council, already divided, seemed determined to sit on the fence and wait upon events. In March Somerset and Lord Hungerford had returned empty handed from a begging mission to the French court. Undeterred, Margaret of Anjou borrowed £290 from the Regent and sailed from Kirkcudbright in April, prepared, as a measure of her desperation, to trade Calais as she had done Berwick.[16]

Whilst Warwick sought an accommodation with Marie de Gueldres his forces in Northumberland resumed the offensive; by July Montagu had compelled Dacre's surrender and regained Naworth, a vital bastion in the west. In the east Tailboys surrendered the keys of Alnwick to the Yorkist triumvirate of Lord Hastings, Sir John Howard and Sir Ralph Crey, whilst Bamburgh was taken by Sir William Tunstall:[17] 'The support and sympathy of the local population worked against what was regarded as a hostile government and enabled even small forces of active rebels to defy it for months on end.'[18] Detail on the surrender of Alnwick is somewhat confusing. Worcester is the only chronicler who mentions the event, whilst the Paston correspondence places Lord Hastings at Carlisle with Warwick in July, though this would not necessarily have prevented him from accepting the surrender. Equally, there is no reason to doubt the appointment of Tailboys as castellan; he remained a staunch Lancastrian until, diverted by greed, he misappropriated the funds placed in his care.[19]

The Paston Letters also place Sir William Tunstall at Bamburgh in the autumn of 1462; his brother, Sir Richard, sat in the opposite camp and had been in the castle that summer. The collapse of the defensive chain of great border holds and the lack of any material support from either France or Scotland appeared to sound the final knell for King Henry's faltering faction. Queen Margaret remained unbowed, however, and proved able still to fan the dying embers of her cause. On 25 October she made landfall, possibly, as Worcester asserts, at Bamburgh; the expedition was led by the faithful de Breze and comprised some 2,000 French mercenaries. The invaders marched inland to Alnwick which, being but poorly provisioned, promptly surrendered. Hungerford and de Breze's son were left in command. Somerset based himself at Bamburgh where, by the fortune of war, Sir William Tunstall was taken by his brother Richard; Dunstanburgh also changed hands. Though these achievements passed control of the border fortresses back into Queen Margaret's hands, there was no popular upsurge in favour of her house. Whether she intended simply to foment local anti-Yorkist sentiment or whether she was seeking, in the larger game, to open a bridgehead for Scottish intervention, remains unclear.[20]

What is certain is that, having secured these three key bastions she, with the bulk of her expeditionary force, immediately took ship, presumably heading for Scotland, to press there for significant intervention. Though she and de Breze did complete the sea passage, many of the ships were wrecked by adverse weather in the cold North Sea; men were scattered, stores and cash were lost. Some 400 French were stranded on the Northumbrian coast; foiled in an attempt to enter Bamburgh, they fell back towards Holy Island, firing what remained of their boats. Though they overawed the few defenders, they soon found themselves under determined assault from Yorkists led by the bastard of Ogle and 'One Maners, a squire'. Falling back and barricading the Priory, the French were soon obliged to seek terms.[21]

Though clearly wrongfooted by the Queen, Warwick soon recovered and had marched his forces into Northumberland by 30 October, with the King following on 3 November. Though he reached Durham by the 16th Edward was debilitated by a bout of measles which enfeebled him for the short, remaining span of the year.[22] Meanwhile, the Earl vigorously prosecuted siege operations against the northern castles. Establishing his forward command post at Warkworth, he entrusted the Duke of Norfolk with responsibility for supply and logistics through the port of Newcastle. The Earl of Kent was charged to reduce Alnwick, with Lord Scales, the Earl of Worcester and Sir Ralph Grey besieging Dunstanburgh; Montagu and Ogle leaguered Bamburgh. This was Warwick at his best, marshalling a war of attrition, free from the uncertainties and snap decisions necessary in open field. The Earl rode around his outposts on a daily basis, and the supply from Newcastle moved smoothly despite the onset of winter conditions and the desperate state of the roads.

The tactical initiative had swung the other way. From Bamburgh Somerset and the turncoat Percy looked out over the besiegers lines; Sir Richard Tunstall and Thomas Fyndern held Dunstanburgh. John Paston recorded that William Hasildene, Matilda Walsh and John Carter acted as purveyors for the Yorkists before Bamburgh, and the King's Pavilions were erected by William Hill, a servant of the Master of the Tents. Paston goes on to suggest that Warwick had mustered some 10,000 soldiers whilst Somerset had less than 300 defenders.[23] Thorough as these siege preparations had been, it would appear that the mere show of strength was sufficient to overawe the defenders: there was no bombardment, the great guns never progressed further than the dockside at Newcastle. Even the lighter field pieces were not deployed; these would have been turned against Scottish forces had any intervention occurred. There was a natural reluctance to reduce the vital border holds by gunfire, these, in normal circumstances, being vital for the defence of the northern shire and borderland. The prospect of campaigning throughout a miserable Northumbrian winter had scant appeal:

> *Tough, hardy and used to discomfort as they were, medieval soldiers had a deep distaste for winter campaigning . . . Henry V had forced his armies to maintain winter sieges in Northern France, but no one had yet attempted them in the even bleaker conditions of Northumbria in December.*[24]

On Christmas Eve the Lancastrian Lords negotiated the surrender of both Bamburgh and Dunstanburgh: for the abandonment of their allegiance to Henry VI both Somerset and Sir Ralph Percy were to be restored to their titles and property. Both swore fealty to Edward IV. This capitulation may reflect a loss of morale – neither fortress was yet seriously threatened, but there appeared little hope of relief and Somerset may possibly have been resentful of the Frenchman de Breze being given overall authority over his head. Edward, for his part, was prepared to exercise a fair measure of pragmatism, but the feud with the Beauforts ran deep, the blood of his father, brother, uncle and cousin, stained Somerset's hands.[25]

In the meantime, the remaining garrison at Alnwick maintained their continued defiance. They had cause for comfort as the indefatigable de Breze was leading a Scots relief force. Warwick was caught off-balance and appears to have been seized with that particular indecision which gripped him in moments of sudden crisis where his careful planning and rigid control of events was suddenly undone. He withdrew his forces before Alnwick with such indecent haste that the Scots were led into the belief that they were being lured into an ambush. This produced a near-farcical denouement as the Scots, in turn, speedily withdrew, leaving only a skeleton force, and the discomfited besiegers reoccupied the lines they had so recently abandoned.[26] The depleted garrison wasted no time in coming to terms, and Warwick appointed Sir John Ashley to command with Ralph Grey as deputy – a demotion the latter bitterly resented, believing the senior post should have been his. As was so often the case, this personal grudge would bear bitter fruit.[27]

By the end of 1462 the position appeared to have returned to that which had obtained in the summer, prior to Queen Margaret's return – but the Yorkist grip was flimsier than the tactical position would suggest. Percy was at heart a Lancastrian, and Grey was nursing his resentment. In the spring of 1463 Percy reverted, opening the gates of Bamburgh whilst Grey seized Alnwick by a coup de main:

> And within three or four months after that false knight and traitor, Sir Ralph Percy, by false treason, took the said Sir John Astley prisoner, and delivered him to Queen Margaret, and then delivered the castle to the Lord Hungerford and unto the Frenchmen accompanied with him.[28]

The Flight of Queen Margaret

Having neatly reversed the position in Northumberland, the Lancastrians now concentrated their efforts against Norham, that 'Queen of Border Fortresses' held by the Prince Bishop, and a prize which had, for decades, eluded the Scots. Frustrated by the loss of Alnwick, Bamburgh and now Dunstanburgh which Sir Ralph Percy had also gifted, Warwick was constrained to move swiftly and raise the siege of Norham, with Lord Montagu scattering Queen Margaret and her Marchers after a lightning advance. So swift and sure was this riposte that both she and King Henry were nearly taken. The Lancastrian garrisons made no attempt to interfere. In spite of this success, the Earl did not propose to sit down once again before the great walls of the coastal castles. He now preferred to bring further diplomatic pressure to bear on the Scots and thus cut off the Lancastrians' aid at source. Warwick could undoubtedly sense that enthusiasm for the House of Lancaster was waning; the Scots efforts at Carlisle and now Norham had been contemptuously repulsed. Henry, sensing the mood swing of his hosts, transferred his truncated court either to Alnwick or Bamburgh.[29]

Edward had, by now, obtained a further grant of taxation revenues from the English Parliament to be expended against the Scots (though the Commons approved the funds it was some time before the King came into possession of the cash). Warwick had, however, precipitated offensive action, with the support of the Archbishop of York, by launching a destructive chevauchee into the Lothians.[30] Margaret and de Breze were both presently engaged in the siege of Norham, and their forces were surprised and scattered by Montagu. After the debacle at Norham, Queen Margaret, fearful for her son's safety and accompanied by de Breze, took ship for Flanders where she proposed to solicit aid from Duke Philip. These wily Burgundians, the Duke and his son, the Count of Charolais (later famous as the mercurial Philip the Bold), were prepared to make encouraging noises, and Charles wrote reassuringly to Henry – immured within Bamburgh's stout walls (this correspondence was carried by a John Brown and William Baker, the latter one of Exeter's affinity). No practical assistance was, however, forthcoming.

Gregory[31] asserts that the Lancastrians sailed immediately from Sluys, having escaped from the trap at Norham, pursued, as the Chronicler avers, almost to the walls of Bamburgh. Margaret and her shrunken contingent, which included Exeter, Fortescue and the remaining Frenchmen, filled four 'balynggarys' (ballingers were large, sleek, double ended and oared galleys). Gregory also recounts that a French drummer boy refused to embark and waited calmly on the shore. This disenchanted youth demanded, vociferously, a place in Warwick's retinue and the Earl inclined to the request, the renegade doing good service for a number of years.[32]

Unmolested by either Warwick or his brother, King Henry maintained the facade of dominion over his tiny Northumbrian domain. In December

1463 he issued letters of protection to William Burgh, Constable of Prudhoe, seeking to consolidate his faction's grip in Tynedale, where Lancastrian sentiment remained viable. Early in the New Year he issued a charter to the burgesses of Edinburgh. The French ambassador, who attended this shadow court and whom the King used as a messenger to his wife in Burgundy, was Pierre Cousinot. Henry's proposed strategy comprised a tripartite alliance between himself, as titular King of England, the Count of Charolais and the Duke of Brittany. He pleaded with the great lords of France to work against any understanding that might be brokered between Edward and Louis. He begged aid from the Burgundians. He begged aid, particularly ordnance, from Rene of Anjou, his father-in-law. He entreated the Bretons to exploit unrest in Wales and join with the Earl of Pembroke.[33] Henry's main difficulty was lack of funds, and all of his entreaties included a request for cash. Deprived of parliamentary grants, destitute of lands and treasure, he had no fiscal base to fund aggressive action; his faction had no real leadership and the prospects for 1464 seemed bleak. The single rogue card was John Beaufort, Duke of Somerset, the erstwhile champion of Lancaster. His decision, taken in that spring, to revert to his hereditary allegiance, would spark the final, dramatic denouement of the campaigns in the north.

Notes

1 RP v 477–8.

2 CSPM pp. 61–2.

3 Ibid., pp. 74–7.

4 A. J. Pollard, 'Characteristics of the Fifteenth Century North' in *Government Religion and Society in Northern England 1000–1700* ed. C. Appleby and P. Dalton (England 1977), p. 131.

5 L. W. Hepple, *A History of Northumberland and Newcastle upon Tyne* (London 1976), pp. 14–15.

6 N. Pevsner and I. Richmond, 'Northumberland' in *The Buildings of England* (London 1992), pp. 135–6.

7 Pevsner and Richmond, op. cit., pp. 155–6.

8 Ibid., pp. 258–9.

9 D. Charlesworth, 'Northumberland in the Early Years of Edward IV' in *Archaeologia Aeliana* (4th Series 1953), p. 70.

10 M. Lynch, *Scotland: A New History* (London 1991), pp. 146–51.

11 R. Lomas, *Northumberland – County of Conflict* (East Lothian 1996), pp. 45–50.

12 P. Murray Kendall, *Warwick the Kingmaker* (New York 1957), p. 86.

13 Ibid., pp. 202–3.
14 Ross, op. cit., p. 56.
15 Gillingham, op. cit., pp. 140–1.
16 Scottish Exchequer Rolls vii Ramsay ii p. 290.
17 Gillingham, op. cit., p. 141.
18 Ross, op. cit., p. 60.
19 Worcester, p. 470.
20 Ibid., p. 480.
21 NCH vol. 1 p. 48.
22 Worcester, p. 480.
23 PL no. 464.
24 Ross, op. cit., pp. 62–3.
25 Gregory, p. 219.
26 Ibid., p. 219.
27 Ibid., p. 220.
28 Ibid., p. 221.
29 'The Year Book de Termino Paschae 4 Edward IV' in Priory of Hexham, Surtes Society p. cviii gives Alnwick as the location but NCH vol. 1 p. 46 claims Bamburgh – the latter seems more likely being on the coast and closer to Scotland.
30 Ross, op. cit., p. 65.
31 Gregory, p. 222.
32 Ibid.
33 NCH vol. 1 p. 46.

Chapter 10

Hedgeley Moor 25 April 1464
and Hexham 14 May 1464

enry Beaufort, his brother-in-law, Sir Henry Lewis and Sir Nicholas Latimer had all been attainted in 1461 and all three were in Dunstanburgh when the fortress was surrendered on 27 December 1462. In the circumstances they, with Sir Ralph Percy, were treated with extreme leniency. Percy was confirmed as castellan of both Dunstanburgh and Bamburgh; on 17 March in the following year he received a commission to accept the submission of other rebels. This clemency reflects an element of realpolitik – Percy was still a name that carried great weight in Northumberland; if Edward could secure their allegiance he effectively kicked away the greatest Lancastrian prop in the north. Somerset fared even better – he appears to have served with some distinction against his former associates, having all the charisma and fortitude of the Beauforts. King Edward made much of him, hunting with his former mortal foe, who even enjoyed the signal honour of acting as a Knight of the Bedchamber. The Duke received cash subsidies and the hefty annuity of 1,000 marks. Tournaments were mounted in his honour and the King personally intervened to save Somerset from certain death at the hands of an unruly mob in Northampton.[1]

The Road to Hedgeley Moor

Why then did the Duke defect and resume his former allegiance? He could, presumably, have accepted a safe conduct and withdrawn north of the border as other members of the Dunstanburgh garrison chose, though whether Warwick would allow the former commander-in-chief this option is uncertain. There is a suggestion that he had already approached the Earl some months beforehand to explore terms. On 10 March 1463, his attainder was reversed and yet, by December, he and Percy had both reverted. Hicks has asserted, probably correctly, that this was not due to hubris or an unwillingness to accept reality; Somerset was neither fool nor dreamer – he must have known the odds were long and that no second chances would be forthcoming. What occurred was, therefore, a crisis of conscience, the pull of his affinity – the oath given to Henry VI was too compelling and triumphed over expediency. The cause might be hopeless but honour outweighed the odds.[2]

Possibly both Percy and Somerset regarded their earlier compromise as nothing more than a necessary ruse to gain time whilst matters turned more favourably. Having said that, there were scant grounds in December 1463 for imagining the prospects for Henry VI were improving. The Duke and Sir Ralph were not alone, both Sir Henry Bellingham and Sir Humphrey Neville subsequently defected. Some commentators, particularly Ross, regard Edward's policy of 'hearts and minds' as naive and culpable, a political blunder.[3]

This may be too censorious. Edward had won the crown by the sword; his affinity amongst the magnates was narrow. To survive and establish a stable regime he needed, urgently, to broaden his platform of support. To achieve this it was clearly necessary to win over former opponents. Simply killing them was not, as recent history had showed, an effective policy. The blood spilled on the streets of St Albans had pooled into a legacy of hate and resentment that had led to the carnage of Towton. The effects of this titanic fight should not be underestimated – the Yorkists had won, but only by a whisker, it was a field that could have gone either way. No Prince would consider having to repeat such an epic campaign; the drain on blood and treasure was simply too great, the stakes too high. Edward had judged that suborning his former enemies not only brought new friends but demoralised the remaining diehards and, by the close of 1462, he could have been justified in thinking that the flames of resistance had guttered out.[4]

Edward's contemporaries certainly took the harsher view. Gregory, no friend to Somerset, observed that: 'the savynge of hys lyffe at that tyme cuasyd mony mannys dethys son aftyr, as ye shalle heyre'.[5] Hicks views Percy's defection as the more serious because of the power of his name in Northumberland, notwithstanding the fact that the King still held both Somerset's brother and Percy's nephew as hostages.[6] Edward's policy of conciliation was at best a gamble and one which, in these leading instances, clearly failed.[7] At the time it seemed a risk worth taking if the prize was a lasting peace; this was not achieved and the Lancastrian cause in the north was to enjoy a final, brief revival in the spring of 1464.[8]

Early in the year sporadic unrest erupted throughout the realm. In 15 counties, from Kent to Cornwall and as far north as Leicestershire, the disruption was sufficiently serious for the King to delay the state opening of Parliament. There is evidence from the contemporary record that Somerset might have, mistakenly, perceived King Henry to have received some fresh impetus and supply: 'herynge y King Henry was comynge into the lande with a newe strength'.[9] It is uncertain where these fresh troops were coming from and how they were to be paid – perhaps there was a hope the French might intervene or even the Scots. Somerset began his reversion by attempting to seize Newcastle, a considerable prize, being the Yorkists forward supply base. A number of his affinity formed an element of the garrison but the attempt did not succeed; Lord Scrope with some of the King's household knights frustrated the scheme. The rebel Duke was very nearly taken at Durham, where he was obliged to flee from his lodgings in no more than his nightshirt. Gregory reports that a number of his retainers were captured, together with their master's 'caskette and hys harneys [helmet and armour]'.[10] Others attempted to slip through the net and escape Newcastle; any who were caught suffered summary execution.

There is also some further doubt as to fugitive King Henry's whereabouts. The Year Book claims he was at Alnwick, though this may be incorrect, for the same source claims Margaret and de Breze were with him when we can, in fact, be certain that both were in Flanders at this time.[11] NCH still places his diminished court at lordly Bamburgh, and this seems more credible – Alnwick was nearer the Yorkists at Newcastle whilst Bamburgh had access to the sea.[12] Somerset may have proceeded directly to Henry or, equally possible, he may have made for Tynedale, where a crop of castles – Prudhoe, Hexham, Bywell and Langley – remained staunch. At some point, either in February or March, he was joined by his former comrades, Ralph Percy and Sir Humphrey Neville of Brancepeth, with their retainers. With the Duke's defection a new sense of urgency infuses the faltering cause of the House of Lancaster.

And urgency there was, for the Scots were showing willingness to treat with Warwick, who had detailed his brother Montagu to march north and provide safe passage through the uncertain reaches of the frontier for a team of Scottish negotiators. These talks were initially scheduled to take place at Newcastle on 6 March, but the increasing tempo of alarums caused the start to be delayed until 20 April and the venue shifted southward to calmer pastures. Edward, on 27 March, announced his intention to travel north and organise suitable escort for the delegation waiting at Norham.[13] The success of any such mission would be fatal to Lancastrian hopes, so Somerset was placed in a position where he was bound to take the field, with such forces as he could muster, and stake everything. Consequently, he dispatched a commanded body of foot, 'four score spears and bows too',[14] under Neville, to lay an ambush 'a little from Newcastle in a wood'.[15] Forewarned by scouts or spies, Montagu easily avoided the trap and chose a safer route into the city where he was reinforced by 'a great fellowship'.[16] He then set out to march northwards to the border.

Somerset's best chance now lay in forcing a decisive encounter, causing a defeat in the field that would leave the Scots immured and serve to show that the Lancastrians still had teeth. By mustering every spear he could find and stripping his handful of garrisons the Duke might, as Gregory suggests, have been able to muster 5,000.[17] This seems a very generous estimate notwithstanding the fact that he could count upon his own affinity with those of Percy, Neville, Bellingham, the turncoat Grey, Lords Hungerford and Roos. We have no note of the force Montagu was leading north but it would certainly have been the equal of anything his enemies could deploy. As the Yorkists marched north from Morpeth, the Lancastrians sallied from Alnwick, both sides probing with a screen of light horse or 'prickers'. Nine miles west of Alnwick Somerset drew up in battle order, blocking the way northwards to Norham.

Though the chronicles provide only scanty details of the battle which ensued, a careful perambulation of the ground which, save for the spread of cultivation, remains largely undisturbed, indicates that the fight took place on the shelf of rising ground just north of where Percy's Cross now stands.

This is the area between, to the south, the stand of timber known as Percy's Strip Wood and the monument ('Percy's Leap'). Here, the ground is roughly level, slightly undulating, rising toward the northern flank. In the spring of 1464 the land was not under the plough but was an expanse of open moor, largely devoid of trees. With the Lancastrians facing south, in front of Percy's Leap, the Yorkists most probably carried out their initial deployment on the line of the present woodland.

As they approached from the south, the main body of the Yorkists would have had no opportunity to view the strength of their enemy until they ascended the slight rise, which swells from the lower ground. The Lancastrians would not have wished to deploy to the south of the position suggested as this would be to lose the advantages that the field conferred. Haigh[18] shows the Yorkists drawn up somewhat to the south of this position and indicates that the Lancastrians advanced to contact over open ground. I think this unlikely. Yorkist morale was most probably higher and Montagu may have enjoyed greater strength – he was, by nature, a confident and aggressive commander. This is, however, conjectural as the chronicles remain frustratingly silent as to these initial dispositions, and the numbers certainly cannot be assessed with any degree of confidence.[19] Somerset may, like Warwick, have been prone to indecision at key moments (his failure to reinforce Clifford at Dintingdale stands as a clear example).[20]

It could be assumed that the fight commenced with the customary duel of arrows (though there is no evidence) and Yorkist supremacy was swiftly asserted. Before ever striking a blow, the whole of the Lancastrian left or rearward division, commanded by Hungerford and Roos, dissolved in total rout, leaving the centre under Somerset, Bellingham and Grey, together with the right or vaward, under Percy, horribly exposed. Montagu ordered the advance to contact.[21] Most probably the melee occurred in the vicinity of Percy's Leap, a short, savage and largely one-sided encounter. The Lancastrian centre soon joined their fellows on the left in flight, Somerset and his officers swept along, unable to stem the rot. Percy by now was virtually surrounded; fighting bravely, he sustained mortal wounds seeking to break the ring. An enigmatic legend lingers over his last moments – 'I have saved the bird in my bosom,' he is said to have uttered as his mount stumbled the dozen yards between two low outcrops. What was meant by this remains uncertain, perhaps he referred to his true loyalty to Lancaster – ironic then, from a man who had changed sides with such facility.[22]

Montagu's victory was complete and, though the chronicles give no hint of the losses, probably cheaply bought. Aside from Percy and those retainers around him who held their ground, most of the defeated escaped unscathed. Morale was clearly a major factor in the Lancastrian defeat. Despite his humiliation on the field, Somerset was able to rally many of the Lancastrians and retreat, in reasonably good order, into Tynedale, whilst Montagu was fully occupied with the diplomatic game: King Henry's kingdom had shrunk further but was not yet extinguished.[23]

With the Scots now in negotiations, and the French in talks (which had begun the previous autumn) at St Omer, the Lancastrians' diplomatic isolation was all but complete. As Northumberland was no longer viable as a bridgehead, there was little incentive for Somerset to disperse his forces in isolated garrisons; simply holding ground was pointless. With the Scots set to change horses, bargaining chips like Berwick and Norham had no further currency.[24] Henry's prospects appeared brighter in the west, for in March there were some fresh disturbances in Lancashire and Cheshire. Resistance flared briefly in Skipton in Craven, seat of the Cliffords who, with their local affinity, had bled so liberally for Lancaster. None of these alarms developed into a serious threat.[25] However, King Edward continued to feel insecure in the north and west; commissions of array were sent out to the Midlands and Yorkshire, no writs were issued in Northumberland, Cumberland, Westmorland, Lancashire or Cheshire.[26]

The Battle of Hexham

Both sides were short of cash. Edward had been granted subsidies to prosecute the war in the north; Norham had been relieved but, beyond that, little had been achieved bar Montagu's notable success in the field. Parliament's subsidies and a further grant from convocation had been gobbled up by existing commitments, particularly the garrison at Calais.[27] The Yorkist administration was surviving on loans and was substantially in the red. Raising taxes built resentment in all quarters, and this was exacerbated when there was no tangible gain. So vociferous was this dissatisfaction that the King felt constrained, in November 1463, to remit some £6,000 of the subsidy granted in the summer.[28] Somerset was under even greater pressure, he had no taxation revenue, no grants nor other subsidies, he was obliged to beg, borrow and steal. Even when monies could be scraped together, these could disappear through misappropriation. When captured, hiding in a coal-pit, after the final defeat at Hexham, Lord Tailboys was loaded with pilfered funds:

> *He hadde moch money with hym, both golde and sylvyr, that shulde hav gon unto King Harry; and yf it had come to Harry, lat kynge of Ingelonde, hyt wolde have causyd moche sore sorowe, for he had ordynyd harneys and ordenance i-nowe, but the men wolde not go one fote with hym tylle they had mony.*[29]

Henry now appears to have moved his lodgings to Bywell Castle, where he was in residence by the latter part of April. After the rout to come, the victors found left behind the King's helmet or 'bycoket' (a coroneted cap), 'richly garnysshed wt ij crownys, and his followers trapped wt blew velvet'[30] – evidence of a hurried departure. There was a suggestion that the Lancastrians might have been bolstered by 'a great power out of Scotlade';[31] more likely these were riders from Liddesdale and Teviotdale, drawn by the scent of booty. Bywell was not a significant castle and possessed no strategic value.[32] Both Tynedale and Redesdale were administered as 'Liberties' – franchises where the Crown sub-contracted the business of local government to franchisees, which led to a fair measure of autonomy. The Lancastrians still had a foothold in Tynedale,[33] holding Hexham, Prudhoe and possibly other centres.[34] How much local support the Lancastrian cause enjoyed is questionable. The northern lords, Percy, Dacre and Clifford had all bled freely, their affinities thinned and leaderless. Much had changed since the halcyon days of 1459–60; even then Queen Margaret had offered free quarter and plunder as incentives, now her cause was depleted by the disaster at Towton and three more years of attrition.[35]

There is no indication of how long King Henry remained at Bywell; in all probability he shifted westwards to Hexham, the fled deeper. It was likely that he was gone before the battle, and therefore the story of a precipitate flight from Bywell is almost certainly fanciful. Somerset would have been a fool to leave the King so exposed: Henry, however diminished, was his only trump. Montagu left Bywell undisturbed on his approach march – he would not have done so had he entertained any notion of Henry's presence there. Hexham was a larger castle and further west. In the fifteenth century the enceinte comprised the Moot Hall and Gaol, linked by a strong curtain wall.[36]

Montagu, by the end of the first week in May, had returned from York to Newcastle, and being aware, through scouts and agents, of Lancastrian activity in Tynedale, resolved to take the offensive. On this occasion he would not be hamstrung by diplomatic duties and could concentrate his considerable abilities toward achieving a decisive outcome. Thus, 'on xiii of May, my lorde Mountague toke his jornaye toward Hexham from Newcastelle'.[37]

Advancing with his forces strung along the north bank of the Tyne, Hexham was his immediate tactical objective, his strategy being to expunge the Lancastrian presence once and for all. Somerset would have been aware of this, and though some Tudor chroniclers assert King Henry was present on the field, this is clearly fanciful. Gregory avers he fled north back into Scotland but, as this was no longer safe, it is more probable that he slipped further into the west, to Lancashire. Montagu crossed the Tyne either at Bywell or Corbridge; only the line of the Devil's Water now stood between him and the Lancastrian base of Hexham.[38] Devil's Water follows a meandering course from the high ground of the county toward the Tyne. From Hexham the ground shelves markedly toward the crossing at Linnels Bridge, some two miles distant, then, on the south side, rises steeply in the direction of Slaley. The traditional site for the Battle of Hexham, challenged by Dorothy Charlesworth, lies south of the present B6306, on low ground by the banks of the stream and as featured on the OS 1:25000 map.

As the best contemporary source, the Year Book describes the actual field as '*un lieu appelle Livels sur le ewe Devyls*'.[39] Worcester says a hill one mile from Hexham.[40] Ramsay, who had visited the location or talked to someone who had, observes tellingly that '[the site] is a nice, sheltered camping ground . . . but a very bad battlefield'.[41] The Year Book, which also states the fight occurred on 15 May, merely points to Linnels as a general area. Worcester refers to a hill, suggesting, quite pointedly, rising ground, and Dorothy Charlesworth observes that the low ground is indeed most unsuitable.[42] It appears clear from a perambulation that the traditional assessment of where the battle took place is badly flawed. To the rear it is hemmed by the water and, to the front, by steeply rising ground which impedes visibility and inhibits manoeuvre, making a gift of the heights above to the attacker.

Later writers have accepted this view[43] without re-examining the topography and considering the implications. Charlesworth argues, compellingly, that whilst Somerset may have camped on the Levels he did not deploy for battle there; rather, on the morning of the 15th, he drew up his forces on the higher ground along the crest of Swallowship Hill. Had he not done so, Montagu could have outflanked him and gained Hexham from the ford over the Devil's Water directly below the hill. The chroniclers do not really give us any assistance here,[44] we are in the area of 'inherent military probability' as advanced by Colonel Burne. If, as Dorothy Charlesworth supposes, the defenders occupied the rise of Swallowship Hill, no such outflanking move would have been possible; with the stream circling the base, the crest of the hill commands all of the viable crossings. As the ground, on both elevations, drops quite sharply toward the Devil's Water, it would be possible for Somerset to refuse both flanks and channel the attacking Yorkists against his centre. It may therefore be that his line was curved to conform to the contours; Grey and Neville commanded on the left, Hungerford and Roos the right.

The Lancastrian left thus dominated the ford that lay below them, and that to the north by Earl's Bridge; from the right it was possible to cover Linnels and the more southerly ford by Newbiggin. This is conjecture, but the nature of the ground clearly favours Dr Charlesworth's view. This was the deployment which confronted Lord Montagu, who then made his own dispositions accordingly. Whilst he probably fielded more troops, with higher morale, both his flank commanders, Lords Greystoke and Willoughby, were former Lancastrians. The former, on the left, had fought at Second St Albans, where the latter, now on the right, had also served with him, losing his father Lord Welles in the wrack of Towton. Willoughby had made his peace with Edward at Gloucester in September 1461, and had done good service since.[45]

Whether this fight began with a duel of arrows is not recorded, the Yorkists may have advanced swiftly to contact and the melee was both swift and certain of outcome. Hungerford and Roos, on the Lancastrian right, were the first to give ground, and the line dissolved in a precipitate rout. Somerset may have tried to cling to the crest and rally but he was swept away in the confusion of panic; the fords were soon choked with fleeing men. With the brief fight over, only the business of pursuit remained.[46] Casualties in the combat were most likely very light; the chroniclers do not mention any knights killed on the field. More noble blood by far was spilt by the executioners in the killing spree which followed. Worcester argues that Montagu fielded 10,000 men against Somerset's 500[47] but no commander would accept battle against such odds. Perhaps the Duke could count on no more than 500 retainers of his own immediate affinity.

Conversely, Warkworth argues that the Lancastrians had 'gathered a great people in the north country' and that the Yorkists were outnumbered, having no more than 4,000.[48] Looking at the ground, the position on Swallowship Hill covers a front of around 1,000 yards; allowing one man per yard and a gap between divisions, a force of at least 4,000 would be needed to give substance to the deployment. For his part, Montagu would surely have been less enthusiastic to engage had his army not been equal to or greater than that of his opponent.

Unlike the immediate aftermath of his previous victory, Montagu was not encumbered by distractions and was fully able to harry the fleeing Lancastrians. Somerset, Hungerford and Roos were all taken, captured 'in a wood faste by'.[49] Henry Beaufort, 2nd Duke of Somerset, could not anticipate any further clemency; Montagu, like his brother, was not interested in reconciliation. It was now time for retribution and the Duke was executed the following day in Hexham; Hungerford and Roos were conveyed to Newcastle where they too faced the axe 'behedid at Newcastle'.[50]

Others, including Sir Philip Wentworth, Sir Edmund Fitzhugh, John Bryce, Thomas Hunt and a reiver called 'Black Iaquys' ('Black John' or 'Black Jack'), were given appointments with the headsman at either Hexham, or perhaps Middleham, 'after some writers'.[51] At least one captive, Sir Thomas Hussey, was executed at York (see Appendix 1).

The Siege of Bamburgh

Lancaster in the north was ruined; Somerset and the rebel lords hunted out, their retainers scattered. Humprey Neville managed to escape the hounds, like Beaufort his attainder had followed on from Towton but he, too, had been subsequently pardoned. He had previously escaped from the Tower, and possessed a genius for survival – with Sir Ralph Grey and the odd remnant he regained Bamburgh, where the reduced garrison maintained a show of defiance. The embezzling Lord Tailboys was also netted and his hoard provided a handy bonus for Montagu's soldiery: '... the sum of 3,000 mark. And the lord's meinie of Montagu were sore hurt and sick, and many of him men were slain before in the great journeys, but this money was departed among them, and was a very wholesome salve for them.'[52] Tailboys was killed at Newcastle on 20 July, the last of the crop of prisoners to face the axe.

Barely two weeks after Hexham, John Neville, Lord Montagu, before King and court at York and in the presence of both of his brothers, was elevated to the earldom of Northumberland. This was the high-water mark of his house, the zenith of the Nevilles. Whilst at his northern capital, Edward ratified the treaty with the Scots, concluded on 11 June, which secured a truce of 15 years' duration. Warwick, as the King's lieutenant was charged, once again, with the recovery of the three border fortresses. To assist in these operations Edward had assembled a formidable siege train, 'the great ordnance of England', the bombards 'Edward', 'Dijon', 'London', 'Newcastle' and 'Richard Bombartel'.[53] The sight of these great guns was sufficient to owerawe the shaken defenders at Alnwick, which capitulated on 23 June, followed, the following day, by Dunstanburgh. Bates, however, maintains that the latter was, in fact, stormed and that the governor, John Gosse, of Somerset's affinity, was taken and sent southwards to York to face his execution.[54]

Bates goes on to assert that Warwick maintained the feast of St John the Baptist at Dunstanburgh while Henry VI was still within the walls of Bamburgh. He further claims that Henry made good his escape with the aid of Sir Henry Bellingham.[55] NCH concurs and suggests Sir Thomas Philip, William Learmouth, Thomas Elwyk of Bamburgh, John Retford of Lincolnshire, all described as gentlemen, together with John Purcas of London, a yeoman, Philip Castelle of Pembroke, Archibald and Gilbert Ridley, from Langley, Gawen Lampleugh of Warkworth, also a gentleman, John Whynfell of Naworth, yeoman, and Alexander Bellingham from Burneside in Westmorland, were all in the King's reduced household during this episode.[56]

This is most certainly inaccurate. None of those mentioned appears to have fought at Hexham or, if so, definitely avoided capture. It is more likely that these individuals were in the King's service before the debacle on Devil's Water and fled westwards at the same time. Bates, with the NCH, suggests Sir Ralph Grey also escaped back to Bamburgh before the rout, rather than after.[57] Once again this seems unconvincing – Grey and his retainers would be needed on the field. Bamburgh was very much a last resort for a defeated captain who was all too aware that his duplicity excluded him from amnesty.

Though perhaps the greatest of the Northumbrian fortresses, Bamburgh was not built to withstand cannon, and the deployment of the royal train before the massive walls gave ample notice of deadly intent. The Earl of

Warwick dispatched his own and the King's herald, Chester, to formally demand the garrison's surrender. Quarter was offered to the commons but both Grey and Neville were excluded from any terms, 'as out of the King's grace without any redemption'. Grey, with nothing to lose, breathed defiance; he had 'clearly determined within himself to live or die in the castle'.[58] The heralds responded with a stern rejoinder and one can perhaps hear the words of the Earl of Warwick resonating through the chronicler's account (my emphasis):

> *The King, our most dread sovereign lord, specially desires to have this jewel whole and unbroken by artillery, particularly because it stands so close to his ancient enemies the Scots, and if you are the cause that great guns have to be fired against its walls, then it will cost you your head, and for every shot that has to be fired another head, down to the humblest person within the place.*[59]

Thus began the only siege bombardment of the Wars. The bombards 'Newcastle' and 'London' were emplaced, sighted, loaded and began firing, the crash of the report like the crack of doom, with a great sulphurous cloud of filthy smoke drifting over the embattled ramparts. Whole sections of masonry were blasted by roundshot and crashed into the sea.[60] A lighter gun, 'Dijon', fired into the chamber in which Sir Ralph Grey had established his HQ in the eastern gatehouse; he was injured and rendered insensible when one of these rounds brought down part of the roof.[61]

Humphrey Neville, ever the survivor, seized the moment of his ally's fall to seek terms, securing clemency for the garrison and, cleverly, for himself. The dazed Sir Ralph was tied to his horse and dragged as far as Doncaster to be tried by Sir John Tiptoft, Earl of Worcester and Constable of England. One of the indictments lodged against him was that he 'had withstood and made fences against the king's majesty, and his lieutenant, the worthy lord of Warwick, as appeareth by the strokes of the great guns in the king's walls of his castle of Bamburgh'.[62] Grey was executed on 10 July – the war in the north was, at last, over.

Notes

1 M. A. Hicks, 'Edward IV, the Duke of Somerset and Lancastrian Loyalism in the North', *Northern History* vol. xx, 1984, p. 24.

2 Ibid., p. 25.

3 C. Ross, *Edward IV* (London 1974), pp. 51–2.

4 Hicks, op. cit., p. 31.

5 Gregory, pp. 221–3.

6 Hicks, op. cit., p. 32.

7 Ibid., p. 33.

8 Ibid., p. 34.

9 Fabyan, p. 683.

10 Gregory, p. 224.

11 Year Book p. cviii.

12 Gillingham, op. cit., p. 180.

13 Gregory, p. 224.

14 Ibid., p. 224.

15 Ibid.

16 Ibid.

17 Ibid.

18 Haigh, op. cit., p. 80.

19 Gregory, p. 224.

20 Boardman, op. cit., p. 75.

21 Haigh, op. cit., p. 80.

22 G. Brenan, *The House of Percy* (England 1898), vol. 1, p. 93.

23 Gillingham, op. cit., p. 152.

24 Ross, *Edward IV*, p. 56.

25 Sir J. H. Ramsay, *Lancaster and York* (Oxford 1892), vol. II, p. 302.

26 PL no. 252.

27 Ramsay, op. cit., vol. II, p. 302.

28 Ross, *Edward IV*, p. 55.

29 Gregory, p. 226.

30 Fabyan, p. 654.

31 London Chronicles p. 178.

32 B. Long, *The Castles of Northumberland* (Newcastle upon Tyne 1967), p. 76.

33 Lomas, op. cit., p. 136.

34 Ibid., pp. 154–5.

35 Long, op. cit., p. 38.

36 Ibid.

37 Gregory, p. 224.

38 Charlesworth, op. cit., p. 62.

39 'A place called Levels on the Devil's Water'.

40 Worcester, p. 779.

41 Ramsay, op. cit., vol. II, p. 303.

42 Charlesworth, op. cit., p. 64.

43 Haigh, op. cit., p. 84.

44 Gregory, p. 224.

45 Ramsay, op. cit., vol. II, p. 303n.

46 Ibid., p. 303.

47 Worcester, p. 479.

48 Warkworth, p. 4.

49 Fabyan, p. 654.

50 London Chronicles p. 178.

51 Fabyan, p. 654.

52 Gregory, p. 219.

53 'Edward' is alter listed in an inventory of 1475: the Master of the Ordnance, John Sturgeon, handed into store at Calais, 'divers parcels of the King's ordnance and artillery including a bumbartell called "The Edward"'; see Blackmore, op. cit., p. 33.

54 C. J. Bates, *History of Northumberland* (London 1895), p. 202.

55 Ibid., p. 200.

56 NCH vol. 1 p. 47.

57 See Worcester, p. 280n – the assumption may be based on a misreading of the Latin text: 'Radulfus Gray fugit de Hexham ante bellum inceptum ad castrum Bamburghe et post bellum de Hexham multi ex parte Regis Henrici fugerunt in eodem castro'. It is more probable the chronicler is describing Grey's flight as the battle opened rather than beforehand.

58 NCH vol. 1 p. 48.

59 Warkworth, pp. 37–9.

60 NCH vol. 1 p. 48.

61 Warkworth, pp. 37–9.

62 NCH vol. 1 p. 49.

Chapter 11

The Overmighty Subject – Warwick the Kingmaker 1464–1469; the Battles of Edgecote (26 July 1469) and Empingham (12 March 1470)

O n 12 March 1470, at Empingham, just north of Stamford, King Edward IV confronted a large body of rebels, mainly drawn from Lincolnshire and the north. No magnate stood at their head. Rather they were led by Sir Robert Welles and others of the local gentry. What was telling about 'Losecote Field', as the skirmish at Empingham came to be known, more concerns those who were not there and yet whose liveries were plainly to be observed. These were the King's cousin Richard Neville, Earl of Warwick, and the King's brother George, Duke of Clarence. In the aftermath of the war in the north in 1464, it might have seemed inconceivable that the Yorkist faction could disintegrate into internecine conflict having finally, as it appeared, won the struggle quite comprehensively. Edward seemed completely secure. The old king was a captive, 'taken beside a house of religion on Lancashire, by the mean of a black monk of Abingdon, in a wood called Cletherwood, beside Bungerly Hippingstones',[1] his armies destroyed, his champions dead, the rump of his faction driven into impecunious exile. Where had it all gone wrong?

Richard Neville – 'Warwick the Kingmaker'

King and Earl had worked very closely together during the years 1461–64 and the royal affinity was narrow. Both Neville earldoms, those of Salisbury and Warwick were consolidated, and the Earl confirmed as the richest and most powerful of magnates. Lord Montagu was Earl of Northumberland, though the rump of the Percy affinity in Northumberland would continue to chafe. Despite this apparent hegemony, the north was by no means certain, no more so than Wales. The Yorkists had triumphed in the field but an alternative remained – Margaret of Anjou with her son, Edward of Lancaster, secure in France. As the boy grew to manhood he would increasingly be a talisman for a revived Lancastrian faction.

In this first portion of his reign Edward IV faced a difficult task, one which he embraced with energy. He was determined to avoid the weaknesses which had beset and belittled the previous administration. He championed the rule of law and, by 1468, had enacted measures to curb most forms of retaining. There is evidence, including his involvement in the bickering Paston–Howard feud, of the King making use of his Council as an executive body to deal with magnates who offended, rather than relying on the provisions of common law as before. Edward had energy, dynamism, charisma and his reputation as a great captain. His charisma and affable exterior cloaked a decisive and, when necessary, ruthless pragmatism. He was not a ruler to be trifled with, a facet that would become increasingly evident after his restoration in 1471.

Crown finances and the need to establish a proper fiscal footing were an early priority. During the 1460s the creditworthiness of the royal household was re-established. Spending was curtailed and brought into line with income – average outgoings of £11,000–£12,000 per annum were half those of the late 1440s. The era also witnessed the commencement of what has been dubbed 'The Yorkist Land Revenue Experiment' – intensive exploitation of Crown estates, aimed at maximising revenue. Lands managed by hard-nosed agents with an eye to profit; and a shift, in terms of day-to-day fiscal control, from exchequer toward the chamber. This path was by no means easy nor free from failure. It has been suggested that the disturbances of 1468–69 in part arose from the misuse of grants awarded to fund hostilities against France but which the King appropriated for his own purposes.

On 1 May 1464, before the final Lancastrian defeat in Northumberland, Edward had secretly and, in haste, married a widow, Elizabeth Woodville (see Figure 4, p. 119), who already had two sons by her late husband, an ardent supporter of Henry VI, who had died fighting for that sovereign's cause at Second St Albans.[2] The lady's father Richard Woodville, Earl Rivers, was a mere gentleman, one who had also served Henry VI, though her mother Jacquetta of Luxembourg, widow of John, Duke of Bedford, belonged to the very highest tier of European nobility. This was the same Rivers that the York-ist peers had upbraided at Calais, and Edward was plainly not unaware of the consequences of this sudden union and did not choose to reveal the fact until a subsequent Council meeting at Reading in September. Warwick had been pressing for a French marriage. The Earl was swayed by the flattery of Louis XI. The 'Universal Spider' knew the subtle arts of diplomacy. Edward had kept his new bride a secret for a full four months, so the Earl blundered on with diplomatic overtures, unaware that his plans were already thwarted.

In terms of patronage, the royal larder was embarrassingly bare. Lands stripped from defeated enemies after Towton had been distributed amongst the King's affinity – the Nevilles, Lord Hastings, Sir William Herbert and Humphrey Stafford. It is probably unlikely that Edward elevated his in-laws to form the basis for a separate affinity. There was no available bank of estates from which to draw. Marriage was the only currency remaining. So greedy did these importunate Woodvilles prove that they established a virtual stranglehold on the market in advantageous matches.[3] This proved a serious difficulty for the Earl of Warwick, who had unwed daughters of his own, and who had set his sights on marrying both to the King's brothers – Clarence and Richard, Duke of Gloucester. But this the King refused to sanction. He was obliged to the Nevilles, mindful of their invaluable support and the sac-rifices they had made, but tying both highly eligible brothers into the web of the Neville affinity was a step too far.

As an added insult, or what to Warwick appeared a slight, the King agreed the marriage of his niece, the Exeter heiress, to Thomas Grey (one of the Queen's sons by her first marriage). The Earl had intended this valuable catch should go to his own nephew, Montagu's son. Kings must always be wary of Kingmakers, and Edward could not afford to ignore the fact that the security of his throne rested, in no small measure, upon the continued support of the Nevilles. He knew his cousin well enough to appreciate the breadth of his ambition. He respected Warwick, would heed his advice, but would not be controlled. This went to the core of the Earl's increasing alienation; his vision of the Yorkist administration was his own. Edward had a strongly hedonistic streak and Warwick would be happy to see this indulged whilst he maintained important affairs of state. What he had failed to appreciate was the altered nature of his status as between a war and peace footing.

With the Woodvilles Edward made policy from necessity. The Queen's family were irrevocably bound to him. By marrying them off to every magnate who came onto the market, the King was extending his affinity, and every extension weakened the Neville monopoly. Edward had other friends besides: Sir William Herbert became Earl of Pembroke in 1468, taking on Jasper Tudor's Welsh possessions, again to the annoyance of Warwick, who saw his own hopes in Wales eclipsed. The Courtnenay Earldom of Devon passed, in the following year, to Humphrey Stafford. All of this was bitter gall to the Earl of Warwick. The Nevilles had been York's main prop, both his father and brother had perished in the cause. The Earl had laboured mightily on Edward's behalf, he and his brother Montagu had fought a long, hard and thankless campaign in the north. These were not the rewards he expected. Warwick had envisaged himself as the King's first minister, constantly at the young sovereign's side – the fount of power behind the throne.

Dislike was mutual; if Warwick despised these Woodville parvenus then they had no love for the haughty Earl, and drew both Herbert and Stafford within their swelling web.[4] Even if the prospect of a dynastic marriage had been squandered, Warwick was hopeful of a French alliance whilst the King inclined more toward Burgundy, England's former ally and the glittering court of Charles the Bold. The matter of foreign policy, therefore, became fundamental to Warwick's perception of his own standing and influence. If he could not be seen to direct foreign policy, then what real role did he have? Louis was prepared to go further than flattery. He viewed the prospect of a Burgundian alliance with understandable alarm and may have suggested to Warwick that France would sponsor a Lancastrian revival, with the Earl reversing his role. The Milanese ambassador, writing in May 1467, observed:

It is asserted that the Earl of Warwick will come here [France] and soon. His majesty will go to Rouen to meet him. There is a fresh report that

M. Charolais [Charles the Bold] has again opened secret negotiations to take King Edward's sister to wife, confirming once more the old league with the English. If this takes place, they have talked of treating with the Earl of Warwick to restore King Henry in England, and the ambassador of the old Queen of England is already here.[5]

Edward was not to be deflected, his instinct was to ally with Burgundy and leave open the possibility of renewing hostilities with France. A raft of treaties with the King's future brother-in-law followed and the accord was sealed by a marriage contract, Edward's sister Margaret became Duke Charles's third wife. This was not entirely achieved without Woodville influence – Earl Rivers might have risen from the ranks of county gentry but as we have seen, his wife, Elizabeth's mother, Jacquetta of Luxembourg, came from a very different drawer and could trace her illustrious line back to Charlemagne. The marriage, celebrated in 1468, was a massive affair, a showcase for the renewed amity with England; funded by the vast wealth of Burgundy. The Milanese, Giovanni Petro Panicharola, something of a gossip, wrote that the Duke, who was perhaps acquiring something less than a blushing virgin, had been:

informed of what more and more people know, to wit that his future consort in the past has been somewhat devoted to love affairs, indeed in the opinion of many she even has a son, he has issued a public edict and ordinance, that no one in his country, in the presence of his lordship or elsewhere in private or public shall be so bold as to make mention or speak of such a thing, under pain of being thrown into the river forthwith, when he is found in such error.[6]

The alliance had the added benefit of removing any possibility that the exiled Margaret of Anjou might receive funding from Burgundy. She had made efforts to draw out support as early as 1463, but Charles had no time for such lost causes. Two years later, in 1465, correspondence from the Milanese ambassador to France recorded that Margaret had made renewed entreaty to Louis XI. The pretext for intervention was that 'King Edward and the earl of Warwick have come to very great division and war together'.[7] This was clearly a propagandist exaggeration but may suggest that, even at this point, cracks in the relationship between monarch and subject were beginning to show.

For the Earl of Warwick this Burgundian marriage came as a double blow. Not only were his hopes of an understanding with France dashed, but the Woodvilles emerged as champions of the rival alliance. Humility was not a virtue the Earl would recognise; he was driven by hubris, by a supreme confidence in his own abilities, spurred by a humourless avarice. His reaction now was to sulk, to withdraw from court and pour scorn on the Burgundian alliance to any who would listen. Such a prickly temperament would always be susceptible to flatterers and no doubt many would be found within the Earl's affinity. This was indeed substantial; from his palatial base at Middleham, the Earl was effectively viceroy in the north – the old Percy rivalry was broken, and his brother Montagu was now Earl of Northumberland. The Nevilles controlled the border Marches, their power boosted by the shower of offices and sinecures the King had lavished on them. If Edward was no puppet, he was mindful of the good service given, and the blood shed, by the Nevilles.

Rumours arose that Warwick was seeking, through Louis XI, to effect some form of accord with the exiled Lancastrians. Sir William Herbert took prisoner a courier to the beleagured garrison of Harlech, who suggested, under question, that such was the case. Herbert, however, had no reason to love Warwick and it would seem far more likely that the Earl was concentrating his efforts on his current protégé, George Duke of Clarence. In 1467, the King's brother was 18, brilliant and gifted, with the same stature and looks. He was nonetheless fickle and unstable. For kings, having brothers is as potentially dangerous as being surrounded by over-mighty subjects. Clarence, until such time as the Woodville marriage produced male issue, was Edward's natural successor. If Warwick could not rule through the King, he might fare better with his mercurial brother. At what point these ideas began to take shape cannot be ascertained but Warwick was always careful to keep his finger firmly attuned to the popular pulse. A born propagandist, he entertained lavishly and dispensed largesse on an epic scale, though always with purpose. Clarence had no cause to love the Woodvilles, and the vast Warwick inheritance added great lustre to the lure of the Earl's eldest daughter, Isobel. Despite the King's opposition to the match, the Earl sent emissaries to Rome to argue for the necessary dispensation (the matter of consanguinity arose).

In the course of 1468, Edward was sufficiently secure to contemplate an invasion of France and the renewal of the Hundred Years War. Parliament and the Church granted funds, and an expeditionary force was being fitted out to aid the Bretons under Lord Mountjoy. Nonetheless, the prospects for armed intervention faded when Louis moved in September 1468, first to patch up his quarrel with the Bretons and then to make accommodating overtures to the Burgundians. Edward's plans were frustrated before a blow could be struck. This was most inconvenient, both Church and Commons had paid for a war and the best the King could now offer was some rather pointless posturing by the fleet, ostensibly to respond to a Lancastrian threat from Harfleur. Edward's efforts had consumed a great quantity of treasure with nothing tangible to show.

The Battle of Edgecote

Such failure sparked a wave of popular discontent – the taxpayers felt cheated, lawlessness appeared to be rife. All of this grousing was not, of course anything new; complaining is the taxpayers' right, and medieval Englishmen were no lovers of taxation. This time the rumblings of unrest swelled to danger level, particularly in the north, where two shadowy figures, Robin of Redesdale ('Robin-Mend-All')[8] and Robin of Holderness[9] emerged to provide focus for discontent. The principal manifesto of these apparently disparate rebels concerned, first the burden of taxation and second, in the case of Robin of Holderness, the issue that the rightful Percy heir should be installed as Earl of Northumberland, replacing Montagu.

To this, Neville responded with vigour, capturing Robin of Holderness and striking off his head at York. If the East Riding was pacified, the upland dales of Northumberland were not, and in June 1469 Robin of Redesdale appeared in Lancashire where he was able to continue his work of agitation. Edward sensed the threat but not its magnitude. By 18 June he was at Norwich, in the process of touring East Anglia, and he proceeded first to the shrine at Walsingham, then on to Fotheringay, where he spent an unhurried week with Queen Elizabeth. It was 5 July before he reached Stamford and five days later before he moved forward to Newark. During June and early July he made provision for a limited muster and summoned ordnance from the Tower, whilst issuing commands to both Pembroke and Devon to raise their local forces and bring these to him in the East Midlands. Such limited measures seemed more precautionary than urgent, and suggest a want of accurate intelligence on the King's part.

From Stamford he requested a company of archers be sent by the burgesses of Coventry. A few days later, the tone of this request had sharpened – as many men as possible were urgently required; the threat was suddenly imminent. Edward now fell back to Nottingham, for his scouts had finally brought news of the enemy, very disquieting news. Robin of Redesdale, no will o' the wisp outlaw, but a rebel general, in command of large forces, was on the march. Exactly how substantial were these numbers was unclear but it was evident that the King was considerably outnumbered. What was also becoming clear was that Robin had some very powerful backers: the Earl of Warwick, George Neville, the Archbishop of York (Chancellor until Edward dismissed him), and with them, none other than the King's own brother George, Duke of Clarence.

It would not be difficult to detect Warwick's guiding hand in the drafting of the rebel manifesto. The King was guilty of excluding those senior magnates whose counsels should prevail, in favour of a coterie of parvenus which included both Pembroke and Devon, together with Lord Audley, Earl Rivers and the other Woodvilles. The manifesto cited the inglorious reigns of Henry VI, Edward II and Richard II – all of whom had been deposed by force.[10] The officers of this rebel army included Sir William Conyers of Marske and his brother Sir John. Both were from Warwick's affinity, the latter steward of the lordship of Middleham. With them were Warwick's nephew Sir Henry Fitzhugh, and a cousin, Sir Henry Neville. The constitution of the rebel army thus exhibited a very distinct Neville bias. Edward was culpable in that he had not seen this coming. He now faced the strong possibility of an attack by superior forces whilst his own were either busy mustering or, as in the case of Pembroke and Devon, still too far distant to help. The pretext of recommissioning Warwick's ship the *Trinity* – refitted at Sandwich, and ready by the early part of June – had enabled the two Neville brothers and Clarence to perfect their plans. Flaunting the King's prohibition, the Earl proposed to marry his eldest daughter Isobel to the royal Duke. By the end of the month he had pre-empted the King's correspondence to the burghers of Coventry and requested them to place troops at his subsequent disposal.

Archbishop Bourchier proved amenable in the matter of granting a licence for the forthcoming wedding – this was to hand by 1 July and by the 6th the wedding party was sailing for Calais. The ceremony then took place, rather hurriedly, with George Neville officiating and John de Vere, Earl of

Oxford, another of Warwick's brothers-in-law, in attendance. This step, once taken, provided the signal for a full insurrection. The Nevilles now openly circulated copies of the rebel manifesto, adding their own endorsement. The muster was set for 16 July at Canterbury. As ever the Kentishmen flocked to Warwick's banners and, some four days after the initial muster, he was on the road to London with substantial forces at his command. Edward, meanwhile, remained stationary at Nottingham; his best hope lay in the contingents of Pembroke and Devon, hurrying now toward him. At the same time, the northern rebels were also on the move, avoiding contact with the King's command and looking to link with Warwick, cutting Edward off from his capital.

By 25 July the rebel army under Robin of Redesdale was set on a collision course with the combined forces of Pembroke and Devon. The latter's capability was significantly eroded by a petty dispute which arose over contested billeting arrangements. Both divisions were to camp at Edgecote but the marshals bickered over the scarce billets, and the senior officers allowed themselves to be drawn in. Both Herbert and Stafford were highly conscious of their honour and the latter seems to have rather flounced off, taking his archers with him, and they encamped nearer to Banbury. Pembroke's men were stationed with the River Cherwell guarding their exposed frontage; prickers brought news that rebel forces were in the field and that the morrow would witness a general engagement.

In the warm summer's dawn the northerners attempted to push across the river barrier and come to strokes with the Welshmen. It was now that the lack of missile troops began to tell. Pembroke's bills fought hard and well but, deprived of archers, suffered loss and finally had to give ground, conceding the crossing. Robin of Redesdale, perceiving his advantage, put in fresh attacks. The Welsh resisted manfully, their dogged courage being rewarded, sometime after midday, when elements of Devon's force at last began to come up. This might have been sufficient to stem the tide had the rebels not also received reinforcements. These were from the van of Warwick's army: a detachment of horse, led by trusted and experienced knights Sir William Parr and Sir Geoffrey Gate, and a professional captain, John Chapman.

These fresh arrivals put heart into the rebels and dismayed the King's men, who now thought the Nevilles were upon them in force. The exhausted Welsh simply gave way, their resolute companies dissolving in rout, sweeping Devon's latecomers from the field. Pembroke and his brother Sir Richard Herbert who had done valiant service that day and fought to the last, were both taken and promptly executed. Perhaps as many as 2,000 of their Welsh retainers lay around them.[11] Rebel losses are unrecorded but these cannot have been light. Sir William Conyers (probably 'Robin of Redesdale' himself) had fallen, and his brother Sir John had assumed the leadership. Devon, for the moment, escaped, though his nemesis was not long delayed. The King's position was now critical. He had been depending on his western affinity; their destruction left him completely exposed. Campaigns such as Mortimer's Cross and Towton had secured Edward's reputation as an effective and dynamic commander. By contrast, his performance in 1469 was woeful. Not only had he been outmanoeuvred and left impotent at Nottingham, whilst the decisive events occurred elsewhere, but he had stayed a spectator whilst his available forces were destroyed at Edgecote and his lieutenants eliminated. He also appears to have been surprised at the popular support for the rebels; thereafter, his customary clemency towards the commons was less assured.[12]

He remained ignorant of the disaster until he had quit Nottingham and marched as far south as Olney, still thinking to meet with the reinforcements under Pembroke and Devon at Northampton. By the time news of their destruction reached him it was too late. Morale amongst his own slender forces collapsed, and the men simply deserted, leaving the King isolated and obliged to surrender himself to George Neville. The Archbishop, rather ominously, appeared before his sovereign in full harness; Edward, the King, was now a captive of the Nevilles and the Kingmaker. Warwick, on paper, had achieved much. He had successfully mobilised his northern affinity and kept the King guessing, whilst binding the feckless Clarence through marriage. He had capitalised on support in the south-east to carry out a brilliant pincer movement, isolating Edward, decimating his available troops and ridding himself of a handful of rivals.

The Kingmaker was now in control, that was not in question, but what, exactly, did he control and what were his longer-term political objectives? He had no real support from the magnates, he controlled the person of the King but, as York had found out before him, rule by proxy simply did not work. Besides, Edward IV was not Henry VI; the Earl had had the better of him, but the game was far from over. Edward was still King; if Warwick had any notion of replacing him with Clarence, presumably by declaring that the King was a bastard, he showed no such intention. Indeed, he continued to treat his cousin with the deference due to his degree. Nonetheless, Edward remained a 'guest' of the Nevilles, first at Warwick Castle, then north at their great fortress of Middleham. Written nearly two decades after the events it describes, the account of the second Croyland Continuator provides a vivid record of the aftermath of Warwick's seeming triumph:

> *For the people, seeing their king detained as a prisoner, refused to take any notice of proclamations to this effect, until, having been entirely set at liberty, he had made his appearance in the city of York; after which the enemy were most valiantly routed by the said earl, and the king, seizing the opportunity, in the full enjoyment of his liberty came to London.*[13]

The uncertainty of the perceived interregnum prompted a rash of disturbances, private feuds and general lawlessness. Humphrey Neville of Brancepeth, from the Lancastrian branch, was stirring up fresh troubles in Northumberland. Warwick found he was unable to respond; he lacked any authority to act on behalf of the Crown. Men had flocked to his banner to remove unfit counsellors, not to replace the King; that task had been accomplished. The Nevilles no longer possessed a current manifesto. Blatant self-interest was no substitute, the Woodvilles were unpopular but many of the magnates owed their advancement to the King, the rest had grown used to the stability of his rule. The alternative of an over-mighty subject in charge of the realm purely for his own ends offered no attraction whatsoever.

The Battle of Empingham ('Losecote Field')

Edward's moment for action had come. By the middle of September the fetters of restraint had been slackened and the King was visible at both York and Pontefract. Warwick had failed to raise sufficient troops to deal with Humphrey Neville. Edward now did so, scotched the rebellion and supervised the ringleader's taking off at York on 29 September. Emboldened, he summoned his own affinity – Suffolk, Arundel, Northumberland and Essex, with Hastings and Mountjoy – to a northern council, after which he returned to London. Warwick had failed, and yet Edward made no overt moves against him. The experiences of the summer had been chastening. No sanctions were imposed on the Nevilles, Clarence and their ally Oxford; an outward show of amity was preserved. This notwithstanding, Warwick had the blood of the King's lieutenants, the Queen's father and brother on his hands. It was, in effect, a stalemate, one that could not continue indefinitely. The Duke of Gloucester picked up the various offices in Wales which the Earl had subsumed. Outwardly the Nevilles lost nothing by their treason. Sir John Paston wrote that: 'the king himself hath good language of the Lords of Clarence, of Warwick, and of my Lords of York [George Neville] and Oxford, saying they be his best friends . . . his household men have other languages'.[14]

There was one change and this required delicacy. John Neville had remained aloof from his brother's intrigues, secure, as he imagined, in his earldom of Northumberland. Edward was, however, being pressed to restore this great jewel to the Percy heir, a prisoner ever since the demise of the third Earl at Towton. Edward, if he appreciated the political necessity of restoring the Percy hegemony in Northumberland, wished, at all costs, to avoid alienating so true a servant as John Neville. Compensation, on a suitable scale, had to be found. Happily for Edward, the killing of Humphrey Stafford, who had not long survived the debacle at Edgecote, had created a vacancy. The revenues from Devon would be ample recompense for the loss of the Percy lands, and the pill was sweetened yet further when the King agreed to the union between Montagu's son George and his own eldest daughter Elizabeth. This brought the Neville Earl an additional prize when he was elevated to the dukedom of Bedford.

For Warwick too this appeared to augur well. The King had not outwardly objected to the union between Isobel and George, and now a Neville, his own nephew, the lad he had previously planned to marry to the Exeter heiress, was to scoop the King's daughter. The new Percy Earl of Northumberland, after his years of captivity, escaped from the margins and came fully into his inheritance on 1 March 1470. The Earl of Warwick was, nonetheless, too experienced to have any real doubts as to his future prospects; he was a marked man. The King, over the longer term, would not forget what had occurred in the summer of 1469. His wife would certainly never permit him to do so. She might smile outwardly at Warwick, but this was the very man who had, on no legal pretext whatsoever, murdered her father and brother. At some point, one side or the other would have to make the first move, and Richard Neville was not a patient man.

Richard, Lord Welles and Willoughby,[15] was a leading gentry figure from the south-east corner of flat and fertile Lincolnshire. He had been

active, or certainly implicated, in Conyers insurrection and, during the autumn and winter of 1469–70 fell into enmity with his neighbour Sir Thomas
Burgh of Gainsborough,[16] a member of the King's closest affinity. Welles, his
son Robert and a brace of his brothers-in-law, Sir Thomas de la Lande and
Sir Thomas Dymmock 'took up' Burgh's property. Edward chose to intervene on behalf of the victim who was, after all, a household knight and the
King's Master of Horse. The King summoned a muster at Grantham for
12 March 1470. This announcement sparked a contagion of rumours,
undoubtedly fanned by Welles and his affinity, that the pretext of relieving
Sir Thomas Burgh was but a cloak to hide a wider intent to exact recompense
from the county for its perceived support for Conyers' faction that previous
summer. To what extent Welles was acting as mouthpiece for a wider conspiracy is unclear, but we might discern the hand of the Earl of Warwick and
his new son-in-law.

By the beginning of 1470 Warwick was allegedly raising forces to swell
the King's muster from Warwickshire, whilst Welles and Dymmock, by now
certainly his creatures, sought and were granted pardon at Westminster.
Despite this apparent resolution of the local disturbance, Edward pursued his
warlike preparations, sending out commissions of array and drawing out his
great guns from the Tower. He delayed his departure from London just long
enough to have words with his brother Clarence, whose objective may have
been to hold the King back by bland assurances. The brothers met at their
dowager mother's London residence and the younger gave out that he was
merely en route to his estates and the arms of his wife in the west. With this,
Edward seemed content but, on quitting Baynard's Castle,[17] he joined
forces with Arundel, Hastings and Sir Henry Percy and began his northward
march. Clarence, however, ventured no further west than the Hospital of
St John's, Clerkenwell for a clandestine meeting with Welles[18] and others of
his and Warwick's affinity. He next rode north, also to join the Earl and spread
the pestilence of rebellion. The flames were already being fanned. Sir Robert
Welles, in his father's absence, had flaunted outright defiance of the King. His
manifesto, broadcast from every county pulpit on 4 March, suggested the royal
army was intent on laying waste Lincolnshire. The rebel muster was to take
place near Lincoln, at Ranby Hawe, on the following Tuesday.

By Wednesday the King, at Waltham Abbey, was aware of the scale of
the disturbances and the identity of the orchestrator. Dymmock and Lord
Welles were summoned for a more detailed interrogation. On Thursday, a

youthful messenger from Lord Cromwell at Tattershall Castle,[19] brought further intelligence that the insurgents numbers were being swelled by recruits from the northerly shires: fantastic totals, a hundred thousand and more, were mooted. Whilst these figures were wild exaggerations, there could be no denying that the threat was potent. Edward appeared to have a major fight on his hands. This time, however, he was ready.

> [W]hen he [Edward] was commen unto Waltham the 6th day of March, on the morrow after, the 7th day of March, there was brought unto him word that Robert Welles, calling himself great captain of the Commons of Lincolnshire, had do made proclamations in all the churches of that shire the Sunday the 4th day of March in the king's name, the duke [Clarence], earl [Warwick] and his own name, every man to come to Ranby Hawe upon Tuesday the 6th day of March, upon pain of death, to resist the king in coming down into the said shire.[20]

The King now received correspondence from his scheming brother, intimating that the Duke had judged it wiser to travel north and link up with his father-in-law, that both might come to his assistance. Whether the King bought this line or whether he was simply paying out the rope is not certain. He did, however, authorise both to raise forces in Warwickshire and Worcestershire. This does not necessarily imply he continued to trust either, their records argued strongly against such trust. More likely, he hoped now to draw all his enemies out into the open and 'see who blinked first'. Edward had a sizeable contingent of his affinity with him, trusted men and veterans, well furnished with ordnance. The King was the greatest captain of his day, undefeated in the field. He would not be caught napping again.

Lord Welles and Sir Thomas Dymmock were useful pawns. Under questioning, both had admitted to having a hand in the present unrest but failed to implicate either Warwick or Clarence. Sir Robert was advised that the price for his continued defiance, apart from the personal consequences of treason, would be the immediate execution of his father. At this point Welles was poised to rendezvous with the rebel magnates, already south of Grantham. Warwick needed the rebel muster to converge with his own around Leicester whilst also causing the Yorkshiremen to march south. With his, Clarence's and Welles' forces thus combined, he could confront the King. Sir Robert committed the cardinal error of turning away from his confederates, marching now toward Stamford, as though seeking battle.[21]

The king being at Huntingdon did the said Lord Welles to be examined, and Sir Thomas Dymoke and other severally, in which examination it was knowledged that in the Lord Welles all such counsels and conspirations were taken and made betwixt his son, the said Sir Thomas Dymoke, the commons and other; and that he and the said Sir Thomas Dymoke were privy and knowing of their communications, and they might have let it and did not, but very provokers and causers of the same, with other circumstances touching it. Whereupon the king gave him an injunction that he should send to his son, commanding him to leave his fellowship, and humbly submit him, or else they for their said treasons should have death, as they deserved.[22]

Monday 12 March, saw the King encamped around Stamford, his prickers thrown out before as a covering screen. This time the rebels would not get the better of him through faulty reconnaissance. Further assurances were received from Warwick and Clarence that, by that evening, they expected to make their billets in Leicester, prior to coming up to join him. He wrote back a letter of thanks:

Upon the Sunday the 6th day of March [should be the 11th], the king come to Fotheringay, where he had new knowledge that his rebels were passed Grantham towards him, but somewhat they began to change their way towards Leicester; which, as it was after clearly confessed, was done by the stirrings and messages sent from the Duke of Clarence and the Earl of Warwick unto the said late Sir Robert Welles and other petty captains, desiring them to have [been] by the Monday at Leicester, where they promised to have joined with them with 20,000 men, as it appeared after in effect and by several confessions of the said captains.[23]

An interesting tactical opportunity now presented itself. Welles, responding to fears for his family, had played into the King's hands. His army lay a bare five miles away, his confederates, at least for the moment, safely out of the way at Leicester:

Sir Robert Welles being onwards on his way towards Leicester, understanding his father life to be in jeopardy, by a message brought him from his father, knowing also that the king was that Sunday at night at Fotheringay, and deeming that he would now have passed Stamford the same Monday, not intending to make any submission ne beyng [nor bowing] in his fellowship, but disposing him to make his part good against the king, and traitorly to levy was against his highness, arredied him and his fellowship that day to have set upon the king in Stamford the Monday night, and so to have distressed him and his host, and so rescued his father life; and for that intent turned with his whole host out of Leicester way and took his way towards Stamford upon that same purpose.[24]

Should anyone in the ranks of the royal army remain in doubt as to the seriousness of the King's intentions, the spectacle of Welles and Dymmock being publicly executed in front of the assembled companies must have constituted a very sobering sight, their earlier pardons clearly overlooked:

[Edward] thought it not according with His honour ne surtied [suretyhood] that he should jeopardy his most royal person upon the same to leave the father [Lord Welles] and the said Sir Thomas Dymoke of live that such treason had conspired and wrought, as so it was thought to all the lords, noblemen and other that time being in his host; wherefore his highness in the field under his banner displayed commanded the said Lord Welles and Sir Thomas Dymoke to be executed.[25]

If the rebels, drawn up before the King's forces and treated to this sanguinary spectacle were equally in doubt as to the consequences of treason, this must have constituted a rude awakening, though it was they who now advanced to contact. After a brief cannonade, what, in a later age, might be described as 'a whiff of grapeshot', the two sides collided. The royal foot advanced steadily and in good order toward their less experienced adversaries who, shaken by the volleys, shivered and broke. The fight dissolved into a rout almost before it had begun. Casualties would, therefore, be light, particularly amongst the King's men; the rebels, harried from the field, would suffer far more. Losecote Field was fought and the most telling evidence, cast-off liveries, offered eloquent testimony of treason.

The Flight of the Conspirators

Edward's firm action, leading to decisive victory, had confounded the conspirators. One of the dead from the field, tellingly attired in the Duke's livery, had been carrying correspondence from Clarence to Sir Robert Welles, tangible proof of guilt. The King, returning to Stamford, could contemplate the extent of his deliverance. Through swift and ruthless action, the complete reverse of his sluggish conduct the previous year, he had thwarted a wider conspiracy. He now wrote again to his brother and cousin, bidding them disband their forces, the emergency being passed, and to report to him, accompanied only by their immediate retinues.

The game was up. Receiving the King's instructions, neither Warwick nor Clarence needed to entertain many doubts – at best total submission, followed by swingeing sanctions; at worst, the headsman's axe. Both were still at Coventry when the royal messenger, John Donne, reached them. In fact they had not proceeded to Leicester at all. Recruiting was slow, their efforts to stir up more trouble in the west spluttered fitfully and without effect, and the Midlands were no more enthusiastic. The pair made suitably compliant noises, intimating they would come in without delay and with scarcely more than a thousand retainers. However, as Donne pointed out to them on 15 March, the road to Burton upon Trent does not lead to Stamford.[26] The peers disingenuously advised that they merely needed to contact some of their outposts before hurrying to the royal presence:

> . . . the king supposing verily that they had been that Monday night at Leicester, as they afore so had written to his highness that they would have been. And it is to deem so they should have ben, or at least upon Tuesday, ne had be the king's victory on the Monday, and that they no such number of people as they looked after, which caused them to staker [waver] and tarry still at Coventry, where the said John Donne found them.[27]

Edward had already advanced to Grantham where the now captive Sir Robert Welles awaited; Sir Thomas de la Lande had already been taken in the earlier rout. Their evidence damned both Warwick and Clarence as instigators of the plot and, this time, there was clear intent to dethrone the King and place the crown upon his brother's head:

> And this plainly, their purpose was to destroy the king, and to have made the said duke king, as they, at the time that they should take their deaths, openly before the multitude of the king's host affirmed to be true.[28]

Fresh intelligence confirmed that the Yorkshire rebels, led by Scrope of Bolton and Sir John Conyers, staunch supporters of the House of Neville, were still under arms. Immediately Edward responded: John Neville, Lord Montagu now Duke of Bedford, was put in command of operations in the north, charged with snuffing out the conspiracy. At Grantham, the King's southern affinity was swelled by the arrival of Norfolk and Suffolk, Lord Mountjoy and

John Tiptoft, Earl of Worcester.[29] By 16 March the royal army had attained Newark, additional measures were taken to deal with the flutterings in the west, whilst correspondence shuttled back and forth between Edward and the two rebel peers. The pair intimated they were bent on complying with the royal summons and would attend upon the King at Retford. Mere tosh, of course, as they were hoping to salvage something from the wreck of their treachery by joining the northern affinity at Rotheram. Edward's replies were, in the circumstances, moderate. He promised clemency, though would not commit to a formal safe conduct: for Warwick and Clarence this undertaking must be unequivocal. The King riposted by staging another demonstration of the penalties for treason, at Doncaster this time: Robert Welles and Richard Warren became the doomed players in a very public display of the headsman's art.

To further weaken his opponents' position, Edward cannily offered a general amnesty, a route to escape that many were happy to take.[30] For Warwick and Clarence it must, by now, have been horribly clear that their plans were steadily and irrevocably unravelling. Even as they pressed northwards, the King was readying his army for a further trial of strength. By sunrise on Tuesday 20 March his divisions were under arms and marching in battle array. This time there would be no contact. When his prickers trotted into Rotheram they found the streets empty, both rebel lords fled and their northern affinity dissolved. Warwick and Clarence, with such retainers they had in hand, were galloping over the stark uplands of the Pennines to seek out Lord Stanley in the unlikely hope that he might, even yet, throw in with them. They were now more hunted fugitives than rebels under arms.

Edward moved rapidly northwards. By 22 March, his army was at York. On the 24th he issued a final warning to his brother and cousin. They had four days only remaining in which to submit – unconditional surrender, thereafter all offers of clemency were withdrawn.[31] Even before this ultimatum, he had taken the precaution of writing to Gerald Fitzgerald, 8th Earl of Kildare, leading magnate and Lord Deputy of Ireland, intimating that Clarence was deprived of office and was to be replaced by Worcester, whilst Lord Wenlock at Calais was apprised of Warwick's removal. Scrope and Conyers had clearly detected which way the wind was blowing and hurried to crave the King's mercy. Whilst this was forthcoming, Edward was very aware of just how dangerous the Neville domination of the north could be.

He had reinstated the Percy heir as 4th Earl, and John Neville appeared satisfied with the estates he had received as compensation. His loyalty in the recent crisis had proved unshakeable – Clarence had, after all, been trying to stir up resentment in the south-west amongst the rump of the Courtenay affinity – and he was rewarded with a marquisate.

Although Henry Percy came from solid Lancastrian stock, the emasculation of the family, as local rivals to the Nevilles, had proved dangerous. A monopoly of magnate influence, especially in so sensitive an area, was fertile ground for disaffection and a ready source of fighting men for whom a greater loyalty to the throne might not carry anything like so much pull as the local connection. In the north-west Stanley was not placed to offer the rebel peers any succour. The King's youngest brother Richard of Gloucester, still in his teens, was moving eastwards from Wales, bringing further Crown forces. Warwick and Clarence now fled to the south-west, relying on the Courtenay faction to assist in their escape, for flight was the only course left open to them. Edward had already dispatched officers bearing commissions to raise the western shires. He hurried his army in their wake, arriving at Exeter on 14 April. He would allow his enemies no respite.

The Earl, knowing the situation was hopeless, had resolved to quit the realm and take ship for Calais; with him went his countess and both daughters. Isobel, Clarence's wife was, by now, 'great with child'. Having raised additional forces in the west, the King now marched eastwards. By 25 April he was in Salisbury, concerned that his enemies might attempt a landing somewhere on the south coast. But Warwick, having sailed from Devon, was making for his old lair of Calais, pausing only to attempt an abortive cutting-out action against loyal ships in Southampton harbour. The new Earl Rivers, the Queen's brother Anthony, would have no difficulty in remembering that this was the very man who had slaughtered his father and brother and who, before that, had humiliated him at Sandwich. The attack was seen off with loss, and the fugitive Earl failed to secure his own favoured ship, the refitted *Trinity*.

If this was disheartening, Calais was worse. Wenlock was of Warwick's affinity but the garrison and the marshal, Lord Duras, were more inclined to remain loyal to the Crown. Consequently, the exiled Gascon ordered the guns run out. Warwick might have expected a salute from the massed ordnance – he did not anticipate whistling roundshot. Wenlock, as it appeared, was true to the King and received great largesse. In fact he was playing a careful double game, outwardly Edward's man but, in fact, faithful to his Neville allegiance, as noted by Philippe de Commynes, acting as Charles the Bold's envoy:

> *Wherefore he [Wenlock] advised him [Warwick], as the best thing he could do, to retire into France, and not to concern himself for Calais, for of that he would give him a fair account upon the first opportunity. He did his captain good service by giving him that counsel, but none at all to his king. Certainly no man ever showed such great loyalty as Lord Wenlock, considering the King of England had made him Governor in Chief of Calais, and the Duke of Burgundy settled a large pension upon him.*[32]

There was, in such circumstances, no question of the rebels' diminutive fleet being able to break in by force, and Duras had already requested aid from the Burgundians, should any be needed.[33] Charles the Bold was soon given cause to rue his hostility and even though an English fleet was already in the Channel, in hot pursuit, the Earl could not resist the temptation of a large Burgundian merchant convoy, with as many as 60 vessels. Warwick took them all as prizes and continued to sail toward the west, gobbling up other targets of opportunity as fast as they could be sighted. The choleric Charles, fuming at this insult, prepared a squadron in the haven of Sluys, site of Edward III's great naval victory in 1340. Lord Howard, commanding the English men o'war, came up with the rebel Earl, and a sharp fight ensued. The outcome was indecisive but the King's ships were at least able to relieve Warwick of some of his prizes.

With his treasury made good by the fruits of piracy, the Earl sailed into the French port of Honfleur, effectively offering his sword to Louis XI. The King of France was, of course, already providing sanctuary for Warwick's arch adversary Margaret of Anjou and he rather took fright at the notion he might become a target for retaliation both from England and Burgundy. Warwick had been comprehensively outmatched but he was not yet defeated. The Kingmaker had still to play his trump – the neglected and largely forgotten figure of Henry VI. The paladin of York, who had shed so much blood to win the throne for Edward, who had lost both father and brother to the vengeful Lancastrians, was poised to broker the most astounding alliance of his colourful career and, in so doing, plunge England back into the cycle of dynastic violence that would ruin both his own house and that of Lancaster.

Edward IV, for his part, knew full well the mettle of his enemy and that his crown would never sit easy whilst the Kingmaker was at large. His presence on the Continent, even without the great bastion of Calais, was cause for vigilance. It was some comfort that Warwick and Clarence had won very limited support from the magnates. Lord Stanley had flirted with their cause; Scrope had been more active but was easily cowed. Two of the Earl's brothers-in-law, John Talbot, Earl of Shrewsbury, and John de Vere, Earl of Oxford, had lent support; the latter had now also fled to France.

Those who had been actual leaders of the Lincolnshire rising had all been summarily dealt with. The ruthless manner of their taking off showed the King had imbibed lessons in realpolitik from his cousin; this was a different King from that which had been so easily outmanoeuvred the previous year. Those of the gentry who had been implicated, knights like Sir Geoffrey Gate (captured in the abortive attack on Southampton), would find themselves arraigned before John Tiptoft, Earl of Worcester, now appointed as Constable and whose penchant for refined brutality would garner widespread opprobrium.[34] Gate was fortunate in that he received clemency. Others did not. In all, slightly more than 50 men, mainly of the middling sort and primarily drawn from Warwick's affinity, shire gentry such as Sir Walter Wrottesley and Sir Edward Gray, were on the list. Though the Lincolnshire rebellion was over, peace was by no means yet assured.

Notes

1 Henry had been captured in July 1465 in Lancashire – Warkworth, p. 5. Harlech did not in fact finally capitulate until 14 August 1468.
2 Elizabeth refused to submit – allegedly as she might be too lowly for a royal wife, but she was above being the King's whore. The King was not accustomed to refusal; see Lander, op. cit., p. 105n.
3 An example was the union between the young John Woodville and the Dowager Duchess of Norfolk, who was approaching 80! From September 1464 to 1470, every English Earl in the market for a wife was accommodated from the Woodville supply of daughters.
4 A. Goodman, *The Wars of the Roses* (London 1981), p. 72.
5 CSPM i 117–18.
6 Lander, op. cit., p. 114.
7 Ibid., p. 109.
8 See Appendix 2.
9 Ibid.
10 Gillingham, op. cit., pp. 161–2.
11 Haigh, op. cit., p. 102.

12 Goodman, op. cit., p. 72.

13 Cited in Goodman, op. cit., p. 81.

14 Cited in Gillingham, op. cit., p. 166.

15 *c.* 1429–1469.

16 Sir Thomas (later 1st Lord Burgh) was the son of the elder Thomas Burgh, who married Elizabeth Percy in 1430, thereby acquiring the manor of Gainsborough; the present Old Hall was built by the son.

17 Baynard's Castle was originally an early medieval addition, studding the south west corner of London's ring of walls; it subsequently became a palatial residence. Now vanished, it is commemorated by Castle Baynard Street, south of Old Victoria Street. Part of the action of Shakespeare's *Richard III* takes place there.

18 The Prior of St Johns was Warwick's creature and had briefly acted as Chancellor during the Earl's ascendancy in 1469; see Gillingham, op. cit., p. 169.

19 Tattershall Castle, in Lincolnshire, a prime example of the castle as country house. Built by Ralph, Lord Cromwell (who had been Treasurer to Henry VI) in red brick and designed for comfort rather than defence, it is still intact and is currently in the care of the National Trust.

20 'The Chronicle of the Rebellion in Lincolnshire 1470' (ed. J. G. Nicholls), Camden Miscellany vol. 1, 1877, pp. 5–12.

21 Ibid.

22 Ibid.

23 Ibid.

24 Ibid.

25 Ibid.

26 Gillingham, op. cit., p. 172.

27 John Donne is best remembered for a remarkable triptych he commissioned from the artist Hans Memling and which shows Donne and his wife Elizabeth (Hastings' sister) being presented to the Virgin and Child by their saints Barbara and Catherine. This is now in the National Gallery, see Lander, op. cit., p. 122n.

28 'The Chronicle of the Rebellion in Lincolnshire' pp. 5–12.

29 Tiptoft enjoyed a singularly grim reputation for severity.

30 Sir William Parr was the grandfather of Henry VIII's last wife, Catherine Parr; he himself gained considerable influence in the household of Edward IV.

31 The fugitives were priced at a cash reward of £1,000 or lands with an annual income of £100.

32 Cited in Gillingham, op. cit., p. 177. All Wenlock could manage in the short term was a gift of wine to ease the suffering of Isobel, who was going through the agonies of childbirth, an added worry for her father. She survived but lost her baby.

33 Lander, op. cit., p. 124.

34 Warkworth records that Tiptoft caused the victims to be hanged drawn, quartered and beheaded, with his own added refinement of anally impaling the remains of the torsos and heads on the same timber spike; see Gillingham, op. cit., p. 176.

Chapter 12

The Road to Barnet
14 April 1471

Here is to know, that in the beginning of the month of October, the year of our Lord a 1470, the bishop of Winchester, by the assent of the Duke of Clarence and the Earl of Warwick, went to the Tower of London where King Henry was in prison by King Edward's commandment, and there took him from his keepers, which was not worshipfully arrayed as a prince, and not so cleanly kept as should seem such a prince; they had him out, and new arrayed him, and did to him great reverence, and brought him to the palace of Westminster, and so he was restored to the crown again.

Warkworth's Chronicle

The 'Re-adeption' of Henry VI

This remarkable and somewhat bizarre 'Re-adeption' of Henry VI was one of the most quixotic episodes in English political history and one which split the Yorkist affinity, saw Yorkists and Lancastrians fight side by side and ultimately sealed the ruin of the houses of Lancaster and Neville. When Warwick and Clarence had sought sanctuary in France, laden with prizes but with England and Burgundy both in hot pursuit, Louis XI had reacted with alarm. These renegade swashbucklers promised nothing but the prospect of the old alliance of France's enemies once again revived and under arms. Warwick, his cause ruined, had nothing to offer and, besides, Louis was already hosting the truncated rump of the Lancastrian court in the north-west of France at Angers on the Loire, ruled by a woman who would have named the Earl as her arch foe.

As ever, the King of France was not slow to spot an opportunity. He had no cause to love Duke Charles, and the reckoning with Burgundy was over-due. For the moment he made reassuring noises about suitable compensation for the Duke's numerous losses. It was true that any succour he offered the fugitive Yorkists would increase the risk of an Anglo-Burgundian alliance but, thanks to the Duke's marriage to Margaret of York, that was already a reality. If Louis could bring about a rapprochement between Margaret of Anjou and the Nevilles, their coalition might yet unseat Edward IV and replace him with the more compliant, infinitely less dangerous Henry VI. To English observers such an alliance seemed unthinkable after nearly two decades of bitter enmity and an ocean of blood. Louis had an undoubted liking for Warwick, and his influence with the Earl was strong, besides, the Nevilles were in no position to vacillate. Warwick would be aware that, if he was to strike, he must strike soon, whilst some resentment against the King still simmered and whilst his northern affinity, the fount of his power, remained intact. With Henry Percy back in control of his lands, the Neville hegemony was again fractured; Percy would incline toward the King, to whom he owed his return, rather than the old enemy.

Margaret of Anjou was summoned and, on 22 July, the Earl of Warwick bent his knee to the Queen who he had harried from the north in 1463 and who he would not have seen since the days of the Lancastrian court. Her son, then an infant, was now a teenager, one already schooled in revenge and who apparently talked of little else than cutting off rebel heads. The chief of those rebels now craved pardon from the lad's mother and begged forgiveness for the impressive catalogue of wrongs he had committed:

> *And so the queen, thus required by the king, as it is said, counselled also by the servants of the King of Sicily her father, after many treaties and meet-ings, pardoned th'Earl of Warwick, and so did her son also.*[1]

Warwick went further; he proposed a marriage alliance between Anne, his younger daughter, and Edward of Lancaster. He was made to grovel, to stay penitent on his knees whilst the Queen enjoyed her tirade, made to promise he would repeat this humiliation in public at Westminster after he, the Earl, had won back her husband's kingdom:

> *and so the queen perservered fifteen days ere she would anything intend to the said treaty of marriage, the which finally, by the mean and conduct of the King of France and the counsellors of the King of Sicily being at Angers, the said marriage was agreed and promised.*[2]

Nonetheless, three days later Anne and Edward entered into a formal betrothal in the sacred precincts of Angers Cathedral. It was altogether remarkable. When the Earl left Angers to pursue his plans, Anne was left behind, to all intents and purposes a hostage:

> *Item, that from thenceforth the said daughter to th'Earl of Warwick shall be put and remain in the hands and keeping of Queen Margaret, and also that the said marriage shall not be perfected to th'Earl of Warwick had been with an army over the sea into England, and that he had recovered the realm of England in the most party thereof.*[3]

The Earl of Warwick now had two sons-in-law, both of whom, interestingly, wished to become King of England: Edward of Lancaster by right of his father, and Clarence as a Yorkist replacement. For the Earl, the Duke was become something of an encumbrance; his usefulness had ended on Losecote Field and now Warwick had other fish to fry. If Clarence had any doubts as to his position, these would have been dispelled when he, like his father-in-law, swore fealty to his family's enemy and undertook to return those portions of the Duchy of Lancaster which his brother had settled on him. Much of his estate had, of course, been gained at the expense of attainted members of the faction he now sought to embrace.

During spring and summer the naval war escalated. Charles had been caught unawares by Warwick's initial buccaneering. His fleet was not ready to put to sea until June, when the Burgundian squadron, under Henrik van Borselen, teamed up with Howard's. The combined fleet was more than a match for the Earl and harried the Norman coast whilst maintaining its blockade of the Seine estuary. Prior to that, the Earl had continued to prey on Burgundian vessels and even mounted a cutting out action against the fleet moored in Sluys. With the resources available this blockade could not be maintained indefinitely. The Burgundians had scarcely been to sea before they withdrew to refit; hostile vessels belonging to the Hanse were spotted on the prowl down the English east coast and Howard experienced his own difficulties of supply. Warwick had anchored his and the French ships that Louis was providing, within the Norman ports, Barfleur and La Hogue. The Earl and his elder son-in-law established their headquarters at Valognes.

Howard's continuous spoiling raids on the coast had an effect, exacerbating the deteriorating relations with the local populace, who quickly tired of the excesses of drunken and unpaid soldiery. Money was a constant problem; to keep his forces intact Warwick needed cash which frequently meant more begging letters to Louis. The longer the blockade stayed in place and the longer offensive action was consequently delayed, the more desperate the exiles' position became. Margaret of Anjou inevitably had reservations about this new alliance. Above all, she would not hazard her precious son on any enterprise that entailed undue risk. In short, Warwick would have to win England first. Nonetheless, his hand was considerably strengthened. If he landed on the south-west coast, then the Welsh connection of Jasper Tudor could provide recruits and a safe haven. Both Shrewsbury and Lord Stanley made encouraging noises. The Neville affinity on the north would, as before, provide the catalyst.

George, Duke of Clarence, was the obvious weak link in the conspirators' chain. Should the Lancastrians regain power and unseat his brother, then of what value was he? Quite the reverse, he was a scion of the rival house. He was married to the Kingmaker's daughter but a second husband could doubtless be quite easily found. Edward, according to de Commynes,[4] sent 'a lady' to sound out his disaffected brother and try to turn him. He also replaced Wenlock in Calais with Howard and sent Worcester to command in Ireland, thus, as would be hoped, sealing up both 'back' doors to England.

In July, the pot began to bubble. Richard Salkeld[5] created disturbances in Cumberland whilst, in the east, Lord Fitzhugh[6] raised the Neville affinity. Quite possibly the Percy restoration had unseated a number of Neville sinecures and at least one of the disaffected, William Burgh, was of the Marquis of Montagu's affinity. Edward might have tamed the Neville faction in the north earlier in the year, but they were neither cowed nor vanquished. The threat was so serious that the King would have to raise a full muster. Percy, so recently restored, could not reasonably be expected to hold the north unaided. Warwick was thus wise in striking before any permanent shift of power in the region could occur. A rising there provided him with a ready-made northern army; this would achieve a further objective of draw-ing the royal muster away from the south and west.

None of this would have come as news to the King. Speed was of the essence. He had to move swiftly and decisively, smash or disperse the north-erners before the puppet master could strike elsewhere. This he achieved; a swift muster and swifter marching brought a royal army to Ripon by 16 August. The rebels melted away, but the King felt constrained to consoli-date his grip on the north before returning south. This was a difficult decision, to abandon the north was simply to invite the rebels to creep out and raise their banners again; equally, a prolonged sojourn would leave the south coast exposed. He needed, above all, to be sure of his lieutenants in the region, the recently restored Percy and Montagu – the former from a leading Lancastrian house, the latter the younger brother of the chief conspirator, recently deprived of an earldom. It was indeed a very fine balance. However, as the blockade was still effective, Edward would have felt he had some time in hand.

Warwick was becoming desperate. He had ordered his followers into their ships in late August but the men would not budge until they were paid. In terms of available cash resources the barrel was scraped dry, and yet more begging letters had to be sent off to the French court. The Earl's luck finally changed in early September, when gales damaged and dispersed the blockade ships. By the 9th his fleet had broken out from the Seine estuary into the Channel. The bid was on. Landfall, as expected, was on the coast of Devonshire; Tudor sallied into Wales, whilst the Earl of Warwick, with Clarence and Oxford, made for the north. Both Shrewsbury and Stanley joined their colours.

The force which mustered at Coventry was a substantial one. Edward's extended presence in the north had clearly weakened his position in the south and Warwick, as ever, had prepared the ground thoroughly. The royal muster was planned for Nottingham but the King placed great reliance on the northern army whose presence in the field he felt he could now count upon. The clarity of his judgement in relying so heavily on Montagu would be put to the test. On the other hand, it would have been difficult to find another magnate so well placed to assume the command. The Marquis was a tried-and-tested soldier whilst Percy, by contrast, was not; he had re-mained steadfast during the previous two attempts, though at that time still secure in his earldom of Northumberland.

The King was at Doncaster when he received the worst of tidings – Montagu had, in fact, defected and had opted to throw in with his brother:

> *wherefore he gave knowledge to his people that he would hold with the Earl of Warwick, his brother, and take King Edward if he might, and all tho that would hold with him. But anon one of the host went out from the fellowship, and told King Edward all manner of thing, and bade him avoid, for he was not strong enough to give battle to Marquess Montagu.*[7]

The strategic position was immediately and catastrophically transformed. Prior to this, Edward had intended to complete his muster at Nottingham and seek battle with the rebels at the earliest opportunity. Now he faced being caught between two Neville armies. The affinities of his younger brother Gloucester, Earl Rivers, Hastings, Worcester, Howard and Lord Saye were neither sufficient nor yet concentrated. Montagu had shown his brother's flair for timing, leaving the King no respite to plan an effective riposte. For Edward it was Ludford Bridge all over again and no recourse other than immediate and ignominious flight abroad. Escape was hurried, edged by desperation, the royal fugitives riding through the early autumn evening, bitter gall of defeat stinging their nostrils, away from Doncaster and into the east as far as possible from the closing jaws of the Neville trap. The King, had he had the oportunity to ponder, must have marvelled at this change of fortune. Scarcely six months before it had been Warwick and Clarence who were the hares and he, with the household men around him, the hounds.

The party would have pushed their tired mounts to the limit across the flat expanse of Lincolnshire to the long strand of the east coast, before a tricky and perilous passage in small boats over the treacherous, sucking flood of the Wash, to King's Lynn. Earl Rivers was not without influence in this far corner of East Anglia and succeeded in chartering a trio of vessels. On 2 October, the escapees hoisted sail for Burgundy, their only refuge. Even in the Channel they were not safe, no English ship pursued them, but a prowling pack of Hanse craft gave chase in earnest, to the very gates of Burgundy. At Alkmaar, Edward's luck finally shifted when, with the Germans virtually upon them and the tide contrary, the King's colour was recognised by Duke Charles's local governor, Louis of Bruges, Lord Gruthuyse, a former envoy with good remembrance of the dispossessed king.[8] Edward and his exhausted band received sanctuary in their saviour's comfortable townhouse at The Hague. So hurried had been the flight, after so swift a collapse, that the weary exiles were obliged to make good the costs of their charter by handing over personal effects and valuables. Not only was Edward no longer in power, he was penniless.

With the realm now firmly in the grasp of the King's enemies, he appeared to have lost all. On 2 November, Queen Elizabeth, in sanctuary at Westminster to where she had fled on the collapse of the Yorkist regime, gave birth to a son, the future Edward V. The King had been blessed with a boy, a son and heir; all that the lad needed now was a kingdom to inherit. Whilst the fugitive King was still on the seas his cousin, the Earl of Warwick, rode in triumph into London on 6 October, with the Duke of Clarence, the Earl of Shrewsbury and Lord Stanley in his train. It was on that day that the magnates attended Henry VI at his shabby lodging in the Tower and announced to the distinctly unregal figure that his throne was now restored to him, given back by the man who had contributed so much to its removal. Here was Warwick's difficulty: against the charismatic figure of Edward, still young, dynamic and proven, he had to resurrect the largely forgotten and distinctly unprepossessing figure of Henry VI. Warwick was, in effect, embarking on a further protectorate, and the available precedents were not encouraging.

Warwick's vaulting hubris had split the Yorkist affinity. Was he to rule, or was Margaret of Anjou expecting to hold the reins? Her faction included Edmund Beaufort, the blood of whose father and brother still garnished the Earl's fresh laurels, John Courtenay and Henry Holand, Duke of Exeter.[9] Warwick had little available capital from which to reinforce the status of his own affinity. Prospects for the Lancastrians now looked better than at any time for the best part of the last decade. Henry need no longer be their champion – Margaret had a young and imposing son, who would guarantee the succession. In the longer term the outlook for Warwick appeared a good deal less rosy than might have seemed the case in the warm afterglow of a bloodless win. His enmity with the Lancastrian magnates ran too deep, he had too much blood on his hands to secure a safe retirement. Warwick's difficulties were compounded by the fact that he was now relying on a mix of moderate or uncommitted Yorkists and returning Lancastrians, the former having grown rich, in many cases, on the forfeited estates of the latter. This was ticklish; Warwick could not favour one for risk of offending the other.

Matters in England had now taken on an added, European dimension. Louis XI had brokered the accord with Margaret of Anjou, and had supported and supplied Warwick to win England away from the Burgundian alliance and to bind the new administration into a raft of obligations with France. As recompense, he expected not only amity but a proactive military involvement, his first strategic objective being the recovery of those towns in the Somme basin, such as Amiens and St Quentin, presently occupied by Burgundy. For once the Universal Spider overplayed his hand; blatant hostility towards Charles the Bold convinced the Burgundians they could not hope for an accommodation with Warwick's regime. Charles had initially been entirely pragmatic. Edward was his brother-in-law but the marriage alliance had been entered into to bind England against France. That need still remained, the change of regime notwithstanding. The Duke was as ready to do business with the Earl as he had been with the King but Louis' rattling of the sabre after 3 December 1470 made it quite clear that Warwick was bound, as he had always inclined, to France. On 12 February 1471, England too declared war on Burgundy – this proved a blunder of the first magnitude.

Until that point Charles had ignored his exiled brother-in-law, denying him audience. His presence an unnecessary embarrassment, Edward received neither aid nor encouragement, their previous and vigorous co-operation against Warwick's treason and piracy overlooked; yesterday's man was without friends. Louis' warmongering immeasurably improved Edward's prospects. Charles was too canny to make a move in public, but Edward's empty war chest was suddenly heavier by £20,000, ships were found, a naval base on Walcheren established, and loans made available. Franco-Burgundian rivalry proved the cornerstone of Edward's salvation. He now also made overtures of amity to the mighty Hanseatic League, with which England had been on very poor terms since 1468. In recognition of this new accord, the Hanse sent a further 14 ships to swell his growing fleet.

Warwick had committed a strategic error in supporting Louis. Margaret of Anjou was still in France, reluctant to hazard the priceless jewel of the Lancastrian heir until she knew that England was safe. The breach with Burgundy gave Edward the window he needed – and he was not the man to squander such an opportunity. Like the Earl before him, the King knew he must strike quickly, before Englishmen became too accustomed to renewed Lancastrian rule. Besides, the Earl's position remained precarious. Two of the props of his administration were his eldest son-in-law and Percy, Earl of Northumberland. Clarence was uncertain: the Lancastrian accord, cemented by sister-in-law Anne's marriage, had left him very much in the cold. Henry Percy owed nothing to the Nevilles and all to the King; two generations before him had died fighting for the House of Lancaster. Percy was required to ally with Montagu, whose main grievance was the loss of Northumberland. This Henry Percy was cut from a different cloth to his forbears, not for him the mad rush into the heart of the press, he was wary and circumspect, knowing all too well the pain of forfeiture.

The Campaign of Barnet

In the course of the winter of 1470–1, and knowing from spies that, following Louis' declaration of war in December, the Burgundians were lending covert aid to Edward, Warwick began to plan his defences. His hand had lain lightly upon the rump of Edward's faction. The single exception had been the hated Worcester, taken in Huntingdonshire. Oxford supervised his trial on 15 October, followed by an appointment with the headsman.[10] The Duke of Norfolk and Archbishop Bourchier were both confined. These measures apart, Warwick trod very warily; he needed friends not more enemies. Montagu, from Pontefract, guarded the north; Oxford and Lord Scrope patrolled the eastern shires; Jasper Tudor was active in Wales, with Clarence in the west. Warwick had given command of the Channel squadron to his cousin the Bastard of Fauconberg, a swashbuckler after his own heart.

Edward set sail for England, from the port of Flushing, on 11 March 1471. It was his turn, again, to win the throne, the very sceptre he had taken in 1461, lost briefly in 1469, clung to the following spring, and lost that autumn. He had three dozen ships in line behind his own flag on the *Anthony* and, besides the exiles fled from England with him, he commanded some 1,500 free lances, retained by Burgundian coin. The King had intended to make for the rump of Norfolk, where he hoped to find friends; Cromer was raised the next day. Friends were few, Norfolk was in gaol and, as Edward's scouts, Sir Robert Chamberlain and Sir Gilbert Bedingham discovered, the coast was alive with defenders. With no haven here, the decision was taken to raise anchor and sail northwards up the east coast.

If this initial rebuff was discouraging, worse was to follow. Fickle winds arose and scattered the Yorkist fleet; at dawn on 14 March, Edward found himself alone off the Humber estuary. If the King can be excused of sloth and overconfidence on occasions, he was also capable of resolute action and daring. Undeterred by the paucity of men he had in hand, he came ashore

Plate 9   Bosworth Field – the well; allegedly marking the spot where the King fell

(photograph by Adamskii Bespoke Photography)

Plate 10 Bosworth – the view from Ambion Hill and from where Richard III, last Plantagenet King and last regnant monarch to die on the field of battle, prepared to charge

(photograph by Adamskii Bespoke Photography)

Plate 11 Middleham – the 'Windsor of the North' and home to some of the most powerful lords of the era: Salisbury, Warwick and Gloucester

(photograph by Adamskii Bespoke Photography)

Plate 12   Middleham – a favourite residence of Richard III and kernel of his affinity; the Tudors allowed the place to fall into decay

(photograph by Adamskii Bespoke Photography)

Plate 13 Dunstanburgh – 'the Fortress of Earl Thomas', a hold of the Dukes of Lancaster on the Northumbrian shore and, like Alnwick and Bamburgh, an important fortress in defence against the Scots, hence the Yorkists reluctance to batter the walls with their ordnance

(photograph by Adamskii Bespoke Photography)

Plate 14 Alnwick – the barbican; proud seat of the Percies, symbol of their power as 'Princes in the North', and a key bastion during the war in the north 1461–64

(photograph by Adamskii Bespoke Photography)

Plate 15 Bamburgh – ancient seat of the kings of Northumbria, possibly the 'Joyous Garde' of Mallory and certainly bombarded by Warwick in 1464. The Earl swore he would strike the head off one defender for every shot he was obliged to expend against the walls

(photograph by Adamskii Bespoke Photography)

Plate 16 York Micklegate Bar – this portal was garnished with the heads of slain Yorkist and Lancastrian leaders before and after the Battle of Towton

(photograph by Adamskii Bespoke Photography)

together with Hastings, and established a command post in the village of Kilnsea. Prickers fanned out to discover how the land now lay in Yorkshire and the north. Crucial to the King's hopes was the attitude of Henry Percy. Boldness was rewarded when Gloucester, with several companies, came in, the young Duke had reached the haven of Welwick; Earl Rivers was safe at Paull. Within the next 24 hours, all of the scattered elements were reunited; a march inland could now begin.

Warwick's precautions had, as ever, been thorough, and a large detachment of local levies under Sir John Westerdale, the vicar of Keyningham and Martin de la See, blocked the way. The odds were unfortunate and Edward could not afford to waste men and materiel in a petty skirmish, so he disingenuously claimed he had not come to oppose Henry VI but merely to assert his hereditary rights as Duke of York. This was a handy face-saver for the locals (possibly sweetened by an additional cash incentive). Involved, perhaps peripherally, in these negotiations, was Robert Hilliard the younger, 'Robin of Holderness' whose Percy connection may have been discreetly working in Edward's favour.

> *And, upon this opinion, the people of the country, which in great number, and in divers places, were gathered, and in harness ready to resist him in challenging of the realm and the crown, were disposed to content them self, and in no wise [ways] to annoy him, ne his fellowship, they affirming that to such intent were [they] comen, and none other.*[11]

Beverley proved sympathetic, but Hull was firmly barred and bolted, with a Lancastrian garrison standing to arms. The Yorkists bypassed the city and marched directly toward York. On 20 March, Edward was beneath the ramparts but his welcome was little more cheering. The 'Arrivall' records that, as the army approached York, Thomas Conyers, the recorder and the first civic worthy to ride out, poured pessimistic scorn on the King's prospects. But Edward refused to be put off and met two more of the burgesses, Robert Clifford and Richard Burgh, who proved somewhat more upbeat. Conyers returned for more discouragement but the King and his immediate retinue were led through the gates by Clifford and Burgh to meet the assembled dignatories.

Again, Edward played his dynastic trump, averring that he sought his hereditary right and nothing more. Thus reassured, the guard permitted him and little more than a dozen retainers to stay in the city, on condition the rest remained outside. On the 21st the march resumed, this time toward the family seat of doleful memory, Sandal Castle. Over a decade had passed since the defeat there, and the King must have reflected on the fickle fortunes that had attended his cause since. If he had advanced thus far without a fight, then there was some comfort but little more. Hardly a single recruit had come in and Montagu was scarcely ten miles away, at Pontefract. If Percy was secretly sympathetic, he was keeping the sentiment to himself. Nonetheless, inaction may, on occasions, by itself do good service. If Northumberland did not provide overt support, he offered no hindrance and he might, as with Hilliard, permit his affinity to lean in Edward's direction. Montagu could not take his eyes sufficiently from Percy to concentrate against the tiny Yorkist force; had he been fully able to do so then the King would simply have been overwhelmed. As it was, Doncaster was reached during the course of the third week in March without a bow or bill being raised against him.

Doncaster proved the key; the key that unlocked the dam, for it was here that Sir William Dudley came in. At Nottingham the host was further swelled by the affinities of such tried veterans as Sir William Parr and Sir James Harrington, who brought in over 500 between them. At Nottingham, there was news of the Lancastrians: Oxford, a highly competent captain, with Exeter and Lord Beaumont, was massing forces at Newark. Edward now showed his true mettle, pushing boldness to the limit, and marched against them. The old magic still worked, and even Oxford lost sufficient nerve to fall back before the far smaller force of invaders. Warwick, too, was on the march, recruiting in the shire the name of which he bore. By 25 March the King, regardless, was pressing on south, breaching the symbolic line of the Trent to attain Leicester, where his numbers were again augmented. Courage is a great motivator. Sir William Norris led in 3,000 bills of Hastings' affinity; now Edward had the full makings of an army.

> *At Leicester came to the king right-a-fair fellowship of folks, to the number of three thousand men, well abled for the wars, such as were verily to be trusted, as those that would utterly impart with him at best and worst in his quarrel, with all their force and might and do him their true service.*[12]

The Earl of Warwick now experienced quite the reverse. His flimsy alliance with the rump of the old court faction began to come apart at the seams. Edmund Beaufort and Sir John Courtenay marched not northwards but west toward Devon where Margaret of Anjou was expected. They simply forgot about the old King in whose name they fought, leaving him in the care of George Neville. This was a signal boon to Edward – that his foes should thus split, before a blow had been struck. Had the old Lancastrians stayed with Warwick and kept their affinities in his train, then Edward would still have been in serious difficulties. As it was, they had effectively withdrawn from the present contest. Warwick, with the forces at his disposal, bottled himself in Coventry, staying put behind the stout walls, awaiting the fellowships of Montagu and Clarence. The former could be relied upon, but not necessarily the latter. The Duke had been slow to move from Burford and, by 2 April, had advanced no further than Banbury, scarcely more than a few miles from the Earl of Warwick at Coventry but not, by any means, united with him. Matters had now reached a most interesting pass. Montagu was on the march south from Pontefract, leaving Percy, apparently immobile, in his rear. Edward was approaching confrontation with the Earl at Coventry whilst the King's brother lurked nearby. Clarence had need of reflection:

> And in especial, he considered well, that himself was had in great suspicion, despite, distain, and hatred, with all the lords, noblemen, and other, that were adherents and full partakers with Henry, the Usurper, Margaret his wife, and his son Edward, called Prince.[13]

The day of 3 April 1471 was to prove very important – in the course of the morning, on the Banbury road, Edward IV was reconciled with his erring younger brother, who now threw in with him, abandoning his father-in-law. This was not a sudden change of heart, for numerous intermediaries, including his mother, sisters (the Duchesses of Exeter, Suffolk and Burgundy), Hastings and Archbishop Bourchier, had been at work on the mercurial Duke. His defection left a gaping hole in Warwick's recruitment, some 4,000 soldiers were instantly added to Edward's score, and, at the same time, kicked away one of the props of his administration. Clarence had already written to the Earl advising it would be best to sit tight till he, Clarence, came up. Warwick, the arch user, was thus deceived and found the now combined Yorkist army arrayed before the walls of Coventry, with Edward in full harness, the very ideal of chivalry, daring him to battle. It was stalemate. The King's cause, so flimsy in March, had swelled mightily; Warwick would not be tempted, at least not until he was reinforced by Montagu. Deserted by his Lancastrian confederates, now abandoned by

Clarence, he found himself outflanked and impotent, for Edward now had the road to London clear before him.

> *The king, with his bretheren, this considering, and that in no wise he could provoke him [Warwick] to come out of the town, ne thinking it behoveful to assail, ne to tarry for the a-sieging thereof; as well for avoidance of great slaughters that should thereby ensure, and for that it was thought more expedient to them to draw towards London, and there, with help of God, and th'assistance of his true lords, lovers and servants, which were there, in those parts, in great number; knowing also, that his principal adversary, Henry, with many of his partakers [allies], were at London.[14]*

This was probably not what the city fathers necessarily wished to hear. The streets of the capital were awash with rumours and both King and Earl were bombarding the burgesses with orders. That Margaret of Anjou might also be expected any day added yet another level of uncertainty. John Stockton, the Lord Mayor, collapsed under the pressure. George Neville, abetted by the ageing Lord Sudeley[15], paraded Henry VI through the throng, as though the sight of this poor, bewildered man, led like a shabby dancing bear, would reassure any. In PR terms this ill-judged carnival proved detrimental. Marching by way of Daventry, Dunstable and St Albans, Edward IV reached the city on 11 April and, having thanked God from St Paul's, immediately directed his attention to pressing wordly matters. Henry VI, deserted by Lancastrians and Yorkists alike, was tamely handed over by Archbishop Neville, whose survival instincts were functioning as well as ever. The wretched man seemed relieved to be returning to captivity in the Tower whilst Edward, once again king, hurried to Westminster to greet his wife and the infant son he'd not yet seen.

Philip de Commynes offered his view on the King's return to his capital. He regarded three factors as important: the rump of his affinity within, the debts he owed to the mercantile class, who could ill afford to abandon their security, and the liberal showering of sexual favours on ladies of influence!

> *As I have been since informed, there were three things especially which contributed to his reception into London. The first was, the persons who were in the sanctuaries, and the birth of a young prince, of whom the queen was there brought to bed. The next was, the great debts which he owed in the town, which obliged all the tradesmen who were his creditors to appear for*

him. The third was, that the ladies of quality, and such citizens' wives with
whom he had formerly intrigued, forced their husbands and relations to
declare themselves on his side.[16]

As ever, the possession of London proved the key. A surge of supporters now
rallied to Edward: Sir John Howard, Sir Ralph Hastings and Lord Cromwell
all came in. Friday 12 April was Good Friday and brought news that
Warwick, bolstered by his brother's fellowship, was marching south and
was already at St Albans. Though his army numbered many Yorkists, the
Lancastrians had not all defected – both Oxford and Exeter remained with
their affinities. Edward did not hesitate; on Saturday his army debouched
from the capital, heading north on a collision course toward Barnet. It was
time for a reckoning. For both King and Earl this was to be the defining
moment in their long relationship and the greatest test of their ability to lead
men. In this, which was to be a trial of arms, Edward had no contemporary
equal, with his imposing presence and matchless prowess. Nonetheless,
Warwick had commanded numerous armies in the field and enjoyed some
success. His fellowship was strong and he counted experienced soldiers, such
as his brother Montagu and Oxford amongst his captains. Edward had, on
his side, both brothers, Clarence and the young Gloucester, each untried in
battle, together with old hands such as Hastings and Rivers:

> *but the king, well advertised of this evil and malicious purpose, did great*
> *diligence to recounter him, ere he [Warwick] might come near to the city*
> *[London], as far from it as he goodly might; and therefore, with a great*
> *army, he departed out of the city of London towards him, upon the Satur-*
> *day, Easter's even, the 13th day of April. And so he took in his company to*
> *the field, King Henry; and so, that afternoon, he rode to Barnet, ten miles*
> *out of London.[17]*

The Battle

Both men had crossed their respective Rubicons, for that evening the
prickers of each side bickered in the environs of Barnet and none need
doubt that a general engagement would follow the next day. As light thick-
ened, Edward's scouts pushed their foes away from the village. Barnet was
the obvious vantage for both armies, rising ground that dominated the
north road, looking in both directions. Though the fading day precluded

a detailed observation, Edward guessed that his cousin would try to push south and clear the shallow ridge. Accordingly he deployed about half a mile north of the town, Hastings taking the left, the King, with Clarence fast to him, the centre, and young Gloucester the right. This manoeuvre was carried out under the cloak of gathering night, whilst, to the north, the Lancastrians were attempting something very similar. That confusion should arise is scarcely to be wondered at.

A cross ridge runs from Barnet to Wrotham Park, which lies to the south of High Stone, by the joining of the Hatfield and old St Albans roads. The Lancastrian line, once marshalled, spilled perhaps a thousand yards over each side of the road. Unknown to both sides, the right flank of Edward's army overlapped the Earl's left and vice versa. Warwick, who enjoyed a marked superiority of numbers by perhaps as many as half,[18] deployed cautiously: Montagu, his best captain, led the centre; Exeter the left and Oxford the right. The Earl maintained a substantial reserve to the rear of his brother's division. Both the Marquis's position and that of the Earl of Exeter were masked by a hedge, which ran in a westerly direction. This same hedge continued on the east flank across Hadley Green, 150 yards or so north of the church.

The gap between the hosts was not very great. Sounds and smells carried through the chill spring night. Men might fancy they heard the voices of old comrades, for not only was this fight a civil war, it was largely one of the Yorkist fellowship against itself. Men who might have stood shoulder to shoulder at Mortimer's Cross, Towton or Hexham, now prepared to kill each other on the following day. This eve of battle is a dangerous time, even for the seasoned; it is when fears begin to crowd. Warwick, who will have been as prone to these as any, was possessed of a greater weight of ordnance.[19] He ordered the guns be charged and discharged through the hours of darkness; 'harassing fire' as it would now be termed. A tactical innovation but wasted as, in the darkness. His gunners failed to appreciate just how close their targets were and consequently overshot, the balls striking harmlessly behind the Yorkist lines. Neither side would, in consequence, gain much repose.

Dawn, on 14 April 1471 – Easter Monday – crept slowly, a pale light shining weakly through a thick, enveloping mist; the fog of war would be further obfuscated by nature's inconvenient caprice. Edward was staking much on superior leadership. He knew from Coventry that he possessed the psychological ascendancy, therefore he resolved upon an immediate offensive. The King would lead on foot, as was his custom, to share the hazard with his men. Across the intervening ground, the two armies were hidden by the fog and the rising countours. The Earl of Warwick also sent his horse to the rear; today he, too, would fight dismounted.[20]

> *On the morrow, betimes, the king, understanding that the day approached near, betwixt four and five of the clock, notwithstanding there was a great mist and letted the sight of either other, yet he committed his cause and quarel to Almighty God, advanced banners, did blow up trumpets, and set upon them.[21]*

Unlike Edward, the Earl commanded a force made up of both Yorkists and Lancastrians, a volatile and unstable mix. Either disparate element might be quick to detect the taint of treachery, the very scent of which could lead to their undoing. As the trumpets of the King's army blared, sounding the attack, both sides employed their great guns and brought bows to bear. Such was the confusion of the mist that neither achieved signal effect. As the Yorkists advanced to contact, Oxford immediately became aware of his advantage – that he effectively outflanked Hastings. The Earl was too good a soldier to waste such a gift. He threw his division forward, lapping beyond their enemies' flank, so as to come upon them partly from the rear, and quickly rolled up the line, driving Hastings' wing, virtually in rout, back toward Barnet. For the Yorkists this was a most inauspicious beginning. However, on their right, matters were proceeding rather more encouragingly, for that which had aided Oxford also facilitated Gloucester, in reverse, and it was now Exeter, on the Lancastrian left, who came under pressure.

Warwick immediately sent a portion of his mobile reserve to shore up Exeter's wing; the combatants lurched in a kind of lethal pirouette, pivoting on the Lancastrian right, centres locked around the triangular apex of the three roads, Exeter's wing echeloning backwards towards the ground now known as Dead Man's Bottom. For the moment, the overall tactical position had stabilised; Hastings' flank was gone, Oxford in pursuit, Edward locked with Montagu and Gloucester with the reinforced Exeter. The battle hung in the balance; so far the Lancastrians were doing rather better overall, but the day was not yet won nor lost.

This was the soldier's battle, the melee, when red mist compounded fog and smoke from the guns; when the steam of armoured men rose like a cloud; when the stink of sweat and wool and leather and of men's entrails spilled on the heath, clogging the senses; when the heaving, cursing, screaming mass surged back and forth, like the roaring of the waves. Bills lunged and hacked, aiming to pull a harnessed man to the ground, hooking behind the knee, when the savage downward thrust would finish the job. A man with an ancient title and a spread of acres, fluent in language and verse, falls to a village half-wit. Swords and polearms contested, swift dagger thrusts, the crushing swing of a mace. Knots of combatants swirling in the fog, harnesses bloodied and mired, blood in torrents, the heaped ground garnished with severed limbs, mounds of the fallen.

Oxford's victory had been complete. Hastings' men were routed, spilling through the lanes of Barnet, some pelting back into London to spread the dire news that King Edward was defeated. The Lancastrians gave chase, their commander desperately trying to restore some kind of cohesion, but the lure of plunder proved too compelling. On the field, the Yorkists continued to hold their own, more than that, to the extent that Warwick felt constrained to commit his final reserve. Yet it seemed the day might still be his, for presently he received word that Oxford had rallied many of his fellowship and was marching them, in good order, back toward the fight. Oxford's contingent was mounted, now moving north and east from Barnet. The fog persisted, and it was this with the shift in the line of battle which was to save Edward and, in the same stroke, destroy the Nevilles. One of the most telling ironies of the whole period of the wars was that Oxford's blow, his horse thundering through the mist, fell not upon the Yorkists but upon the flank of Montagu's division, his own side. In the fog of battle the star and stream emblem of the Earl of Oxford could easily be mistaken for the King's famed sun in splendour. As the horse charged, the northern archers let loose.

'Treason' – blazon of doom, the cry spread through all ranks, swifter than any pestilence. For Warwick, his army an unsteady federation of former enemies, this was the very worst that could happen and at the very moment when victory seemed assured. Edward, master of battle, sensed his chance, felt that check in the enemy's impetus. With great exhortations, he pressed his weary soldiers into fresh attacks, gathering his household men for a charge upon Montagu's banner: '. . . he manly vigorously and valiantly assailed them, in the midst and strongest of their battle, where he with great violence beat and bore down afore him all who stood in his way'.[22]

The Lancastrian officers were distracted: Oxford, the Marquis and Warwick, each trying to bolster his division, confusion their ruin. Against them now strode the King, in all his martial fury – the man who the Nevilles had grown up with, who Warwick had followed to victory at Towton, whose peerless prowess on the field they knew of old; truly the very Sun in Splendour, an English Achilles. In what was probably his finest hour, Edward proved unstoppable. The Earl of Warwick, as he frantically clung to his failing advantage, heard that Exeter was down,[23] then Montagu. The Lancastrian line collapsed, that moment every commander dreaded, when the knife-edge of morale faltered and men who had fought steadfastly for hours suddenly gave way to panic. The rout swelled instantly from a trickle to a torrent then to a flood, the whole of the Earl's army giving way, the field lost in a span of barest moments.

Perhaps as many as two thousand Lancastrians died, either in the fight or rout, Dead Man's Bottom allegedly deriving its name from the weight of slaughter which occurred there. The Yorkists lost far less, though the day was not cheaply bought, with perhaps half as many casualties as their defeated enemy.[24] Once he knew victory was his, Edward is said to have given orders that Warwick was to be spared, even sending off a commanded party of household men to the rescue. These arrived, however, too late. The Kingmaker had fought his last battle. For once, his horse was far to the rear by Wrotham Wood and we may, like Paul Murray Kendall, picture the 44-year-old earl, exhausted and dragged by the weight of his harness, attempting to run the gauntlet. Long before he reached the saddle, he was overtaken by jubilant Yorkists, brought to ground and his astonishing career ended by the classic thrust of a rondel dagger, driven through the eye into that remarkable brain. It was thus, anonymous in the pile of dead, stripped and stiffening, that he was found. The Battle of Barnet was over.

Notes

1 John Stow, the sixteenth-century London antiquarian, saved a number of early sources; the details of this meeting are provided by an anonymous fragment, quoted in Lander, op. cit., pp. 125–7.
2 Ibid.
3 Ibid.
4 Gillingham, op. cit., p. 181.
5 Richard Salkeld, of an ancient Cumberland line, had previously been keeper of Carlisle Castle.

6 At this time Fitzhugh of Ravensworth controlled, through wardship, the resources of both the Lovell and Latimer estates. He would also be able to sweep up
  the rump of the Tyne and Redesdale men who'd followed Robin of Redesdale
  (see Appendix 2).

7 Warkworth, pp. 10–13.

8 Louis of Bruges was one of the very few foreigners, only three in number who
  became English peers during the course of the fifteenth century. He was created
  Earl of Winchester by a grateful Edward in 1472; see Goodman, op. cit., p. 86.

9 Exeter, abandoned by his Yorkist wife, had been in dire straits whilst in continental exile, reduced to penury and even to begging.

10 It was fitting that Oxford should deal with the reviled Worcester as his father and
  brother had both been the Constable's victims in 1462.

11 'The Historie of the Arrivall of Edward IV in England and the Final Recouverye
  of his Kingdomes from Henry VI' ('The Arrivall') is our best source for these
  events, probably written by a member of the King's Household and eyewitness
  to at least some of the events.

12 'The Arrivall', pp. 2–15.

13 Ibid.

14 Ibid.

15 Ralph Boteler, Lord Sudeley of Sudeley Castle in Gloucestershire, was a veteran
  of the French wars of Henry V.

16 Quoted in Lander, op. cit., p. 135.

17 'The Arrivall' pp. 2–15.

18 Burne, op. cit., p. 109, suggests that the King commanded 10,000 men, Warwick
  perhaps half as many again. 'The Arrivall' only allows Edward 9,000 men. I tend to
  think the latter is probably correct but that the Lancastrians perhaps did not
  number more than 12,000 as Clarence had defected and magnates such as Beaufort and Courtenay were absent.

19 Burne, *Battlefields*, p. 109.

20 Montagu had, before battle was joined, expressed concern over the army's poor
  morale. It was at his urging that Warwick, usually circumspect with his personal
  safety, pointedly sent his horse to the rear; see Haigh, op. cit., p. 123.

21 'The Arrivall' pp. 2–15.

22 Ibid.

23 Exeter, though wounded, was not in fact dead. He survived the rout and recovered from his injuries, to spend a further four years in the Tower. Of the Lancastrian peers only the Nevilles lost their lives on the field. Oxford, both of his
  brothers who fought with him, and Lord Beaumont succeeded in winning clear
  and riding into exile north of the border. On the Yorkist side, Lords Saye,
  Cromwell, Sir William Blount and Sir Humphrey Bourchier all died.

24 Haigh, op. cit., p. 123.

Chapter 13

Tewkesbury 4 May 1471

In the days following the Yorkist victory at Barnet, curious Londoners could view the stiffening corpses of Richard Neville, Earl of Warwick, and his brother John, Marquis Montagu, displayed at St Paul's. The two men, in the prime of life, were laid out in rough coffins, naked, save what was necessary for decency, their wounds stark against livid flesh, as still as marble effigies. This was the Kingmaker's last public appearance. After the show the King, magnanimous, allowed them burial in the family vault at Bisham Abbey.[1] Perhaps after all, the bond still remained too strong to permit the normal mutilation attendant on a traitor's death.

The Campaign of Tewkesbury

Edward had no illusions that his troubles were yet at an end. Contrary winds had delayed Margaret of Anjou's expedition at Honfleur; the elements worked in the Yorkists favour, preventing a junction with Warwick's forces which could easily have proved decisive. On the day of Barnet, the Queen made landfall at Weymouth and a further trial of arms became inevitable. Sir John Paston had fought in Oxford's division and wrote to his mother after the fight, giving news of his own survival and giving also an impression of the fevered state of the capital, in those uncertain days of April 1471:

> Mother, *I commend myself to you and let you know, blessed be God, my brother John is alive and well, and in no danger of dying. Nevertheless he is badly hurt by an arrow in his right arm below the elbow, and I have sent a surgeon to him, who has dressed the wound; and he tells me that he hopes he will be healed within a very short time, John Mylsent is dead. God have mercy on his soul; Wiliam Mylsent is alive and all his other servants seem to have escaped.*[2]

In these extraordinary times, it was small wonder that people should sense a hint of divine judgement in the air. The changes in authority were bewildering and constant. Henry VI, who had been King, then deposed and largely forgotten, had been King again, but was now again deposed. His Queen Margaret of Anjou, with her son Edward of Lancaster, had come into the West Country to attempt a further restoration. So, Edward, who had lost his throne to Warwick temporarily in 1469, won it back, held it, then lost it again in 1470 and now, after a major trial of arms, had recovered the sceptre once more, must yet again fight to hold it. Margaret had, upon landing, proceeded to Cerne Abbey to confer with her lieutenants Somerset and Courtenay, whose defection has so weakened Warwick's army. She had every right to be concerned, for, if she failed, her son's life, the most precious jewel of Lancaster, stood at risk; and if Edward fell, his House fell with him. Somerset was bullish as to her prospects of raising fresh forces, despite the loss of Warwick's army.[3]

Jasper Tudor believed his Welsh connections still held good, and there was hope of support from Lancashire and Cheshire. Edward had disbanded a proportion of the army, which had fought so well for him at Barnet but, by 19 April, he had established his command post at Windsor and was garnering fresh supplies of men and material. Margaret, having decided the die was cast, proved equally active, carrying her recruiting banner through the far west, aiming at Exeter. She hoped to raise the nucleus of her army there, before veering north and west to seek out Pembroke's Welsh fellowship though, cleverly, she sent out fighting patrols due eastwards, to convey an impression that she might be headed straight for London. The threat to the Yorkist regime, nothwithstanding the elimination of Warwick, remained potent.

By the last day of April both sides were moving toward contact. Edward, knowing he must strike swiftly to contain the threat, had moved up through Abingdon to Cirencester. He must seek to scotch the snake before the contagion of rebellion could spread from the west. Margaret, meanwhile, had gained Bath, but a general engagement, at this time, was not advisable. Her forces were still too thin to confront those of the King, besides, this Yorkist had a formidable reputation already. He had defeated Pembroke at Mortimer's Cross, Somerset's brother at Towton, dispersed a rebel army at Empingham, and dealt with Warwick and Montagu.

On the first day of May the Queen turned toward Bristol, her intention being to seize a quantity of ordnance kept there – the King's army being much better furnished with guns. She met with no resistance, possibly quite the reverse, but Edward was closing the gap; by dusk his army was at Malmesbury. This diversion, on Margaret's part, was a considerable risk, for she needed to cross the Severn as quickly as possible to avoid being cut off. The nearest crossing was at Gloucester, and Edward was quickly narrowing the gap. Margaret was not seeking battle. She would not do so until her forces could be swelled by the Welsh. To beat the King she had, for the moment, to avoid contact.

It is possible that Lancastrian scouts had not done their job thoroughly, and that the Queen did not, on 1 May, appreciate just how close the hounds were. By the 2nd she knew better and embarked on a dash for Gloucester and the Severn crossing. The easiest route was through Berkeley, but this veered toward Malmesbury and she had no reason to doubt the watchfulness of the King's prickers, who were doing good service. Cunningly, she devised a stratagem to lure the Yorkists from the scent. The Lancastrian van was sent toward the high ground of Sodbury Hill, the southerly spur of the Cotswold Hills and the obvious ground if one were proposing to contest Bristol which was, after all, the second city of the realm.[4] The King's provosts, hurrying to seek billets in Sodbury, found themselves suddenly, and most unexpectedly, in the hands of their enemies. This misfortune completed the lure; the main body of Queen Margaret's host passed to the west of the town and marched directly for Berkeley. It was noon by the time Edward came up to Sodbury, expecting to fight that day, only to discover that the Lancastrian van was now a retiring rearguard and he had been thoroughly humbugged.

Whilst the King's prickers frantically scoured the ground for their vanished enemies, Edward fretted and Margaret made the most of the hiatus to put as much ground between them as possible. By that evening, after a forced march of 23 miles on a warm spring day, the footsore Lancastrians reached Berkeley, having gained a 12-mile lead over their opponents, still impotently astride Sodbury Hill. A further march of 14 miles would bring them safely to Gloucester. Sometime after midnight on 3 May, the Queen led her weary column once more onto its line of march. When, later that morning, possibly as dawn was breaking in the east, on what promised to be another hot and wearying day, the King's scouts brought him definite news of his enemy's whereabouts. He had been outwitted, but the game was far from finished. A hurried council of war was summoned – was the Queen aiming for Gloucester or possibly heading upstream to Tewkesbury?[5] Swiftly, as the army prepared to march on, at perhaps around 5.00 a.m., a galloper was sent off toward Gloucester to bid the governor to deny the enemy the river crossing at all costs and assure him that relief was at hand. With this sound precaution, the King had to next decide whether to follow his enemy over the flat alluvial plain or stick to the higher ground on the Cotsworld ridge. Deployed in column of divisions, the army began its hot and exhausting march.

Queen Margaret had done well. She had outmanoeuvred the greatest captain of the day and brought her army to the gates of Gloucester. But here, her luck changed. The Yorkist governor, Sir Richard Beauchamp, proved resolute. The gates were barred and the town's defences commanded the bridge, the vital bridge that spanned the Severn and spelt deliverance for the weary army. Edward's messenger had fulfilled his task. True, she could take the place at the point of the sword but time, as Beauchamp knew, was on his side, not hers. Margaret could not risk being attacked by Yorkist reinforcements coming up as her men struggled to gain the walls. There was simply no choice. The footsore companies must trudge the extra ten, hot and exhausting miles to Tewkesbury.

> [U]pon the Friday to about ten of the clock they were comen afore Gloucester; where their intent was utterly denied them by Richard Beauchamp, and other of the king's servants that, for that cause, the king had sent thither. Notwithstanding, many of the inhabitants of that town were greatly disposed towards them, as they had certain knowledge. Of this demeaning they took right great displeasure, and made great menaces, and pretended as though they would have assaulted the town, and won it upon them, but, as well those that kept the town as the said enemies that so pretended, knew well, that the king with a mighty puissance was near to them.[6]

It is a tribute to the Queen and her officers, that this raw and largely un-trained army should march 24 miles in a bare 15 hours and, despite the re-buff at Gloucester, still attain Tewkesbury by late afternoon, around 4 p.m.[7] The ferry at the lower Lode, one mile south-west of the settlement, was not defended but proved far from ideal as a crossing place. It would require too much time for the whole army to get over, with the attendant peril that the Yorkists would be upon them while the troops were divided between banks. There was no alternative but to establish a defensive perimeter on a gentle ridge that swelled just to the south of the town. Edward was in hot pursuit, anxious to come to grips and prevent the crossing, anxious also to make up for the deficiencies of the previous day. As the author of 'The Arrivall' records, the day grew hot and airless, the uplands bare of running water, by which the encumbered troops might refresh themselves and slake the thirst that gripped them. Food was equally in short supply – the men had only their bare rations to sustain them. Both armies had with them an artillery train and it was these monsters, the great guns, which dictated the pace. Each gun needed a team of oxen to draw it, and pioneers to level the way ahead as best they could, whilst sweating gun captains and matrosses (gunners' mates) heaved and cursed their iron charges over bad ground on worse roads.

It was at Prinknash that the host moved off the ancient upland track, the Portway, and, passing through Birdlip, entered Cheltenham – perhaps an hour after the Lancastrians had reached Tewkesbury. Their enemies were now only five miles away but the army, in 24 hours, had toiled over 31 miles of difficult ground. Neither side was fit to fight, but Edward was deter-mined the foe would not slip through the net a second time. So, after a much needed halt to rest and consume such victuals as could be doled out, the march, in the cool night, was resumed. A further halt was ordered at Tredington; Tewkesbury was scarcely three miles away. None of the parched and weary men could doubt that the fruit of all their labours, nearly 60 miles of hard marching in three days,[8] would be a battle at first light.

The Battle of Tewkesbury

The campaign of Tewkesbury was in many ways more complex than that of Barnet; the marches were more extended and detailed, the ground, in some ways less certain, but the objectives of both sides remained crystal clear. The

Lancastrians needed to get safely across the broad reaches of the Severn whilst the Yorkists had to prevent them. Despite Queen Margaret's best and sustained efforts, strenuous marches and clever ruses, a battle on the east bank of the river could not be avoided. 'The Arrivall' contends that the Queen's officers had chosen their ground well:

> *Upon the morrow following, Saturday the 4th day of May, [the king] apparelled himself, and all his host set in good array; ordained three wards [divisions]; displayed his banners; did blow up the trumpets; committed his cause and quarrel to Almighty God, to our most blessed lady his mother, Virgin Mary, the glorious martyr Saint George, and all the saints; and advanced directly upon his enemies; approaching to their field, which was strongly in a marvellously strong ground pight [placed], full difficult to be assailed.*[9]

Two roads led to the town of Tewkesbury: looking from the east, the left hand way came from Gloucester, along which the Lancastrians had come, whilst that on the right, from Cheltenham, was the passage followed by the Yorkists. A narrow cross-lane, like the bar of a capital 'A', linked the two, a mile or so south of the town, between Gupshill Manor and the site of Bloody Meadow. On the swell of rising ground north of the lane, parallel to it, the Lancastrians were deployed. Colonel Burne, in his assessment of the ground, finds that the terrain is less enclosed than the chronicler suggests, even allowing for subsequent clearance and drainage. Queen Margaret had delegated tactical command of her army to Somerset, the most experienced of her commanders and he had, in the circumstances, chosen his ground well, given that the need to fight had largely been forced upon him. Southwards from Tewkesbury the land rises to a level plateau with an open, cultivated area, known as the Gastons. To the south-west, as the ridge declines, a stream runs over the Bloody Meadow and into the Avon, north of its confluence with the mighty Severn.[10] Southwards and to the east is another low ridge, with Stonehouse Farm now located on the crown. A further slight emminence, wooded at the time, and called the Park, lies south of the stream.

Our understanding of the ground is hampered by the fact that the modern road cuts diagonally across the field, passing by the right flank of the Lancastrian centre. Somerset placed his divisions between two watercourses, his left by Swillgate Brook and the right resting on Coln Brook. The total frontage is some 700 yards, which would allow the comfortable deployment of a force perhaps 5,000 strong.[11] The scrub and timber, hedges and mires which may have hindered the Yorkist advance were the main impediment to the attackers. There appears to be no suggestion that the defenders had the time, or indeed the energy, after their fatiguing marches, to construct field works or dig ditches.

Somerset himself took the right of the line; command of the centre was entrusted to Edward of Lancaster – the Prince, now aged 17, had been bred to hate the Yorkist faction and thirst for their blood. Today he would have his chance, advised by the veterans Lord Wenlock and Sir John Langstruther, Prior of St John. This choice of Wenlock was somewhat ironic. He was a former adherent of Warwick, his nominee at Calais, who had fought for the Yorkists at Towton – and reflected the dangerous fusion of diehard Lancastrians and turncoat Yorkists. On the left, John Courtenay, titular Earl of Devon, commanded. His brigade stood to the left of the Cheltenham road, deployed between the highway and the stream.

Such ordnance as the army possessed was placed between the foot divisions in the usual way. In the strong morning light, Queen Margaret and her son, neither of whom had been in England for eight years, rode solemnly along the line to cheer the men. Whether the Queen's poor English was sufficient to permit a rousing address is unclear,[12] but her son was the grandson of Henry V, who, whilst still very young, had had his own baptism of fire, at Shrewsbury, over 60 years earlier. It remained to be seen if this Edward could emulate his illustrious forbear. They were not kept waiting long. Edward was anxious to engage and his army came from the Cheltenham road in the calm of first light, the tramp of thousands of harnessed men echoing through the narrow lanes. The Yorkists crossed the Swilgate Brook at Tredington, beginning to echelon to the left, pivoting on the present location of Stonehouse Farm. Edward, with his officers, will have been well to the fore. This ground afforded a good view of the enemy line and confirmed the strength of their disposition.

As the army deployed from column into line the King replaced Hastings, who had led the van until this point, with his brother Gloucester. This was not an exercise in favouritism, the left would face Somerset's right and the circumstances thus demanded a proven officer in command. Hastings was a trusted adherent who, in terms of loyalty, had never faltered. His performance at Barnet had, however, been desultory, even allowing for the serious disadvantage of being outflanked at the outset. Peter Hammond takes the view that Edward felt his energetic younger brother was simply more capable. With the van, on the left, facing Somerset, and Gloucester's extreme flank protected to a degree by the Coln Brook, the remaining two divisions deployed to their right. The lane, cutting across from the two larger roads, lay to their front and the King took command in the centre, keeping Clarence, as ever, by his side whilst Hastings, his flank resting on the stream, now had the right, opposite Devon.

As the two forces stood, fully arrayed and some 400 yards apart, silk banners and burnished plate brilliant in the morning light, the engagement began with an artillery duel. In this the Yorkists had the greater weight of shot and must have gained an early advantage, the fearful crack of the great guns reverberating, vast clouds of vile sulphurous smoke drifting over the field. It is unlikely that skipping roundshot caused many casualties on either side, but the battering would prove a frightful test of nerve. The science of gunnery, especially on the field, was relatively new, but whilst the guns might not yet have acquired their full killing power and dominance, the effect of bombardment, especially on raw troops, would still be considerable.

To simply stand and 'take it' requires discipline together with high morale, and these can swiftly be eroded by the nerve-shattering roar of the cannon. A Devon ploughman, dragged only recently from the field, was not accustomed to such vast noise, such hellish flame and smoke, as though the very doors of the inferno were opening before him. He was not prepared for the wicked skipping of the iron shot, turning files into mangled screaming bundles of ruined flesh and shattered bones, not prepared to have his comrade's brains liberally splashed over him. Both sides were at extreme range but an archery duel does seem to have taken place; very likely the bowmen stepped forward to shoot, though, again, it is probable that neither side suffered particularly heavy loss as a result:

> *Netheless the king's ordnance was so conveniently laid afore them, and his vaward so sore oppressed them, with shot of arrows, that they gave them right-a-sharp shower. Also they did again-ward to them, both with shot or arrows and guns, whereof netheless they ne had not so great plenty as had the king.*[13]

Even if the actual loss was trifling, Somerset would be keenly aware that his men could not endure this torment for long. We have no inkling as to the duration of the cannonade but it was probably of a fairly short span, perhaps ten or fifteen minutes at the very most. Then the Duke launched his attack. The plan was sophisticated and bold: he could perceive that Gloucester's left flank, even with the burn flowing by, was unsupported; he had also spotted the potential of the small rise which stood 500 yards further west, just to the east of the Gloucester road. It would, given the lie of the land, be possible for him to move a significant body of men, unseen by his enemy, over to this heavily wooded hillock, and position them for an attack on the exposed flank of the Yorkist line.

The Duke's line of advance would be effectively hidden by the stands of timber; a screen of troops would be left in the line, both to complete the illusion and to support the attack. At the same time, Wenlock would advance the centre and thus pin the enemy line whilst Somerset's attack rolled up the flank. As the guns belched smoke, Somerset led his commanded party on a march to the west, crossing the T-junction where the lane met the Gloucester road, swinging westwards and approaching the hillock, fully screened by the rise. They were able to move undetected to the easterly flank of the eminence:

> *In the front of their [the Lancastrians'] field were so evil lanes, and deep dykes, so many hedges, trees and bushes, that it was right hard to approach them near, and come to hands: but Edmund, called Duke of Somerset, having that day the vaward, whether it were for that he and his fellowship were sore annoyed in the place where they were, as well with guns-shot, as with shot of arrows, which they ne would nor durst abide, or else, of great heart and courage, knightly and manly advanced himself with his fellowship, somewhat aside-hand the king's vaward, and, by certain paths and ways therefore afore purveyed, and to the king's party unknown, he departed out of the field, passed a lane [the Gloucester road], and came into a fair place or close, even afore the king where he was embattled and, from the hill that was in that one of the closes, he set right fiercely upon th'end of the king's battle [my emphasis].[14]*

King Edward had not been completely blind to the potential of the high ground west of the hillock – the Park – and he had detached two companies of billmen from the centre. It is likely that this commanded party, chosen men, would have taken station on the southern edge of the wooded hillock so that, as Somerset completed his deployment, they were poised to assail his exposed right flank! It was a very singular situation. As the Lancastrian

division surged forward against Gloucester's flank, they achieved an immediate advantage, imperilling the Duke's entire position. Gloucester, despite
his youth, displayed a genius for command, swinging his men around to
form a front facing their attackers. A stout hedge, at the base of the hill,
provided a valuable barrier behind which the Duke's men could re-form
their lines relatively unmolested. As this manoeuvre was taking place the
remaining two divisions of the King's army began a leftwards movement to
close the gap otherwise created by Gloucester's shift.

As the position stabilised, melee beginning in earnest, the Yorkist detachment flung themselves against Somerset's exposed flank and rear. The full
element of surprise, upon which Somerset was counting, had not been
achieved, though the blow placed Gloucester in difficulties, only partially
relieved by the unexpected pressure from the Yorkist-commanded party.
Now, if Wenlock launched his attack from the front, the day could still end
well for the Red Rose. No attack came, Wenlock stayed supine as the tide
began, quite rapidly, to turn against Somerset's division. The Yorkists had
steadied and Gloucester could be reinforced without hindrance. This must
have been galling for Somerset; his plan was sound but depended on timing
and on the full co-operation of his officers. As it was, the battle was being
fought piecemeal, surprise and momentum gone, his men, themselves attacked and soon very much on the defensive.

> *The king, full manly, set forth even upon them, entered and won the dyke,
> and hedge upon them, into the close, and with great violence, put them up
> towards the hill and, so also, the king's vaward, being in the rule of the
> Duke of Gloucester.*[15]

The crisis point for the Yorkists came and went. Wenlock's inactivity decided the action; Gloucester's men began to exert pressure on Somerset's
isolated attackers who, unsupported and discomfited, refused to stand,
breaking rearwards, back the way they'd come, or scrambling for refuge in
the Park. The rout was hotly pursued by the victors who, in the aptly named
Bloody Meadow, took a fearful toll of their beaten adversaries. The ground
toward the Avon was soon choked with the detritus of battle: abandoned
arms and harness with a garnish of corpses.

> *[F]or the said spears of the king's party, seeing no likeliness of any bushment
> in the said wood-corner, seeing also good opportunity t'employ themselves*

*well, came and brake on, all at once, upon the Duke of Somerset, and his
vaward, aside-hand, unadvised, whereof they, seeing the king gave them
enough to do afore them, were greatly dismayed and abashed, and so took
them to flight into the park, and into the meadow that was near, and into
lanes and dykes, where they best hoped to escape the danger: of whom, nethe-
less, many were distressed, taken and slain.*[16]

Somerset, probably mounted, survived – survived to confront the unfortunate Wenlock. The taint of treachery hung heavy in the air again. Wenlock
was a former Yorkist, his inactivity could have been due to the fog of
war, uncertainty, faintheartedness – or outright betrayal. The Duke clearly
thought the latter, for he intemperately dashed out his subordinate's brains!
Whilst his rage may be understood, the effect on the shaken morale of the
Lancastrian remnant can be imagined; under pressure from the Yorkist centre and right, they simply gave way, rout, contagious as always, spread
unchecked. As the dam burst, a tide of fugitives spilled towards Tewkesbury,
and the previous scenes enacted in Bloody Meadow were repeated:

*In the winning of the field such as abode hand-strokes were slain inconti-
nent; Edward, called Prince was taken, fleeing to the town wards, and
slain, in the field.*[17]

For the House of Lancaster this moment spelt the doom of all hopes for,
amongst the bloodied bundles clothing the stricken field, were the mortal
remains of Edward of Lancaster.[18] The Prince had had his test, his baptism
of fire, the chance to wrest back his father's crown, and had failed. For Margaret of Anjou this would be the most telling blow, her spirit finally crushed
by the loss of her cherished son, sacrificed on the altar of ambition. Lancastrian survivors, including Somerset, fled to the Abbey, where they sought to
claim sanctuary. Prince Edward and the luckless Wenlock were already dead,
as was John Courtenay and Sir John Beaufort.[19] The battered survivors in
the Abbey were presently joined by King Edward IV, who came in not for
sanctuary, but to give thanks to God for his victory and, in a mood of mag-
nanimity, pardoned his surviving enemies skulking there. In law, however,
it transpired the Abbey did not have the requisite legal status, and the
fugitives suddenly found their pardons worthless. On 6 May they were
tried by Gloucester as Constable, and Norfolk as Marshal, inevitably being
convicted of high treason. Edmund Beaufort, Duke of Somerset, Sir John

Langstrother, Sir Hugh Courtenay and Sir Gervase Clifton, along with several others, next took their final journey to the block. Some, such as Sir John Fortescue,[20] Sir Thomas Ormonde and Sir Henry Roos, were more fortunate and received clemency. The Tewkesbury campaign was ended.

Margaret of Anjou, who had been the mainspring of the Lancastrian cause for so long, was taken the next day and conveyed to captivity in the Tower, almost an empty gesture for she was utterly broken. Later she was moved to less uncomfortable confinement at Wallingford Castle under the more sympathetic care of the Duchess of Suffolk.[21] Edward had added to his considerable laurels with yet another stunning victory and had dealt most effectively with the Lancastrian threat: Somerset and Edward of Lancaster were dead, Queen Margaret a captive, her army destroyed. Yet the King's labours were not yet at an end – the fine balance of the English polity had been disturbed by continual ripples of dissent, and now there was talk of more trouble brewing in the north. Having seen the convicted traitors dealt with in the confines of the Market Square in Tewkesbury, Edward, on 7 May, set off northwards.

It was en route to Worcester that the King had received the news that Queen Margaret was taken, and with her Anne Neville, her daughter-in-law – now a widow. By 11 May, the royal army had reached Coventry; commissions were sent out to raise further forces to confront any northern rebels. The latter, however, proved to be in fairly short supply. The old Neville affinity was ground down, and Percy remained steadfastly loyal; the rising was no more than a scattering of isolated disturbances and most hastened to seek the King's peace. Northumberland himself went to Coventry on 13 May, with no more than a few household knights in his train – a clear indication that the north was held in check. Edward was satisfied.

The Bastard of Fauconberg

Matters in the south, particularly in London itself, were less satisfactory. The author of these troubles was Thomas Neville, the Bastard of Fauconberg, cousin to both Edward and Warwick. He had been an adherent of the Neville faction, commanding the Channel squadron with the same buccaneering elan as his illustrious cousin. His command had not been distinguished by any tactical successes but he landed in Kent with several companies drawn from the Calais garrison, on or around 2 May, bringing with him a brace of stout Neville adherents – Sir Geoffrey Gate and Sir George Brook. Kent, as before, seemed ripe for mischief, and his fellowship soon swelled to perhaps a couple of thousand; the Mayor of Canterbury, Nicholas Faunt, proved sympathetic.[22]

From Sittingbourne, he sent correspondence to the burgesses in London, demanding free passage for his army, but promising that the men of his host would behave and pay for all they took. The city fathers were swift to reply, denying the request, affirming their loyalty to King Edward and expressing disbelief at Fauconberg's assurances of good behaviour.[23] They pointed out that the rebels were effectively without a cause – Warwick, Montagu, Edward of Lancaster and Edmund Beaufort were dead. This letter finished with the helpful suggestion that the Bastard would do best to seek terms from the King. Fauconberg was unlucky in that the City was held by a posse of staunch Yorkists, both Earl Rivers and the Earl of Essex were present, each with a strong fellowship, and the Tower was stuffed with men and ordnance. The Mayor, John Stokton, and Recorder, Thomas Urswick, both inclined to the King's faction and the burgesses generally dreaded the notion of an army of freebooters loose in the streets. Apart from the lure of easy spoil, the only asset to be had from London was the person of Henry VI as a talisman to ignite fresh risings.

These strong sentiments failed to deter Fauconberg who, on 12 May, began a series of assaults upon the city both by land and from his ships, which had sailed up the Thames. A timber outwork, or barrier, at the southern end of London Bridge, was torched, as were various commercial premises by St Katherine's, on the north bank. These were no more than probes, intended to sniff the extent of opposition. But the burgesses had been thorough – the Thames was lined with palisades, studded with ordnance. London would prove a very tough nut indeed. On the 13th the Bastard led his fellowship westwards, along the south bank to Kingston. A crossing here would have exposed the city to an escalade through the northern suburbs, but Rivers had several boats stuffed with troops, keeping station with the rebel forces, ready to bar any passage. Time was not on Fauconberg's side: Edward was on his way and the royal army could be relied upon to deal swiftly with so inferior a force, even if the men could be brought to stand. It is possible that Rivers pointed out these salient facts to Fauconberg in the course of a parley on Kingston Bridge.[24] If so, the ploy worked – even though Edward's arrival was less imminent than the Earl may have suggested. The Bastard could not afford to have his small force caught between a superior force and a hostile city, and so withdrew.

He was not yet done though; his army was encamped between Lambeth and Southwark in St George's Fields, and he proceeded to attempt the city by storm. This was a thoroughly considered plan, putting in simultaneous attacks at a number of points to force the defenders into spreading their resources thin. A battery from the ships was entrenched to bombard the city and provide covering fire for infantry assaults on London Bridge. The Bastard's ships ferried commanded parties to the north bank where they laid on at the Aldgate and Bishopsgate. These attackers were reinforced by a substantive force from Essex, drawn perhaps by the lure of sack. At all the danger points, citizens, bolstered with men-at-arms from the affinities of both Rivers and Essex, hastened to resist the attackers. The Mayor and burgesses commanded companies of chosen men, who dashed from danger point to danger point, shoring up the defence. The attacks were pressed home with great resolution, and the barrier at the Aldgate fell; houses were set on fire, clouds of smoke adding to the din and confusion. John Warkworth described the scene

> wherefore the Bastard loosed his guns into the city, and brent at Aldgate and at London Bridge; for the which brenning, the commons to London were sore wroth, and greatly moved against them: for and they had not brent, the commons of the city would have let them in, maugre [liking/pleasure] of the Lord Scales' [Earl Rivers'] head, the mayor and all his brother.[25]

The crisis came here, at Aldgate. Even with the barrier lost and in flames the stout portcullis held, but the defenders were shaken and ripples of panic could be felt. The local alderman, Robert Basset, reinforced by the Recorder, Urswick, took the bold decision to raise the portcullis and mount a sally. The Londoners, in stiff fighting, pushed the attackers back towards St Botolph's Church, then, as the contest hung in the balance, Rivers, choosing his moment, launched a flank attack with his household men, issuing from the Tower postern. The rebels were seen off with loss. This deliverance at Aldgate provided the signal for a general counter-attack. Essex led the charge at Bishopsgate – the city's gunners had bested Fauconberg's captains with concentrated counter battery fire. The beleaguered defenders on the Bridge, driven from the southern end, where more than a dozen houses were set ablaze, held the attackers off with more, well-sited ordnance. Everywhere these counter-attacks were pressed home with great resolve. The rebels, already flaky, deprived of covering fire, gave ground and finally fled, routing some five miles to Blackwall whilst numbers were cut down as they ran, or scrambled for safety aboard their ships.

More accustomed to counting houses and guild halls than the melee, the burgesses had done good service, though the opportune presence of Rivers' and Essex's men in the city, giving a professional edge to the defence, had significantly helped to tip the balance. Though beaten, with his survivors clinging to the north bank being withdrawn by the ships, Fauconberg did not yet fully concede defeat. His battered army, lighter by several hundred casualties, fell back to Blackheath for a few days. The ships, however, were withdrawn to Sandwich, and the Bastard, with only his professional retainers from the Calais garrison, soon followed, leaving the rump of his army leaderless and abandoned.

On 21 May King Edward entered London in triumph, whilst the rebels at Blackheath melted away. The Mayor, the Recorder, John Crosby, a sheriff and nine aldermen received knighthoods for their sterling work in holding the city. In the King's train were both royal dukes, those of Norfolk, Suffolk and Buckingham, a swathe of earls, including Percy, a cluster of lords and their retinues – marching with burnished arms, proud banners displayed – and, riding captive in a carriage, Margaret of Anjou. It was akin to a Roman triumph, culminating in a service at St Paul's. Gloucester, energetic as ever, next led the van towards Kent to settle matters with Fauconberg. The Bastard had undoubtedly opened negotiations for his surrender after his repulse. On 26 May, after the bulk of the royal army marched in the wake of Gloucester's division, Fauconberg formally submitted, surrendering his still impressive fleet of nearly fifty assorted vessels.[26] As the Bastard was bending his knee, the King was at Canterbury, opening an enquiry into the recent troubles. Nicholas Faunt paid for his adherence with his life, as did numerous others throughout the troublesome county. Several of the Essex men who had joined in the attack on Aldgate ended their careers with severed heads displayed above the gate they had failed to storm. Canterbury and Sandwich suffered civic penalties. Those not hanged by the neck were, in the parlance of the day, hanged by the purse – swingeing fines were levied on the disaffected.[27]

Warkworth gives us a succinct account of the King's actions in Kent:

And after that, the king and all his host rode into Kent to Canterbury, where many of the country that were at Blackheath with the Bastard, were arrested and brought before him; and there was hanged, drawn and quartered, one Fuant of Canterbury, that was loving to the Earl of Warwick; which entreated the Bastard for to depart from his host; and many divers men of the country were hanged and put to death.[28]

By the end of May, the King had sufficient leisure to write to his brother-in-law, Charles the Bold, and his former host, Louis of Bruges, informing them of his great victories. The Burgundians ordered bonfires and other celebrations to witness the Yorkist deliverance. Though England was safe, Calais remained uncertain and the garrison did not formally submit until July – Hastings was sent out as governor, with Howard as his deputy; that they carried funds to make good the perennial accrued salaries guaranteed a heartfelt welcome.

When, on 21 May, the King had recovered London, there was one detail outstanding, one final task needed to complete the destruction of the House of Lancaster. That night Henry, late King of England, was finally put down. 'The Arrivall' ascribes his death to natural causes, and perhaps the poor man had sufficient cause to wish himself dead. It is probable that Gloucester supervised the act, even if, contrary to what Shakespeare would have us believe, he did not bear the knife himself. Richard was Constable of England, such a chore was his responsibility – but the instruction could only have come from the King. This was not vindictiveness, merely housekeeping; with his son dead and his wife captive, he was just a loose end. Warwick's 'Re-adeption' and Margaret's efforts had doomed him as surely as the executioner's blade.

And the same night that King Edward came to London, King Herry, being inward in prison in the Tower of London, was put to death, the 2st day of May, on a Tuesday night, between eleven and twelve of the clock, being then at the Tower the Duke of Gloucester, brother to King Edward, and many other; and on the morrow he was chested [placed in a coffin] and brought to St. Paul's, and his face was open that every man might see him; and in his lying he bled on the pament there.[29]

Gloucester's involvement became more direct in the telling. Warkworth, no friend to the House of York, merely states that he was present in the Tower at the time the old king is supposed to have been killed. By the time we come to Sir Thomas More's account, Richard is the murderer. The sources roughly seem to agree that the time of death was late evening on 21 May, sometime before midnight; this is the date and time given by Warkworth, though 'The Arrivall' differs somewhat.[30]

On the following morning the dead body of Henry VI was carried to St Paul's with suitable ceremony. It remained there for the next 24 hours, with the face of the corpse exposed. This sufficed to show that the old king was dead and that, presumably, his death was due to natural causes. A funeral service was held in Black Friars on the 23rd, then the remains were further conveyed, again with due solemnity, by barge to Chertsey for interment. Edward did not stint on the expense, nearly £100 (a substantial sum in those days) was spent on the ceremonies. Henry was a failed ruler but a king nonetheless, and one who had ruled for as long as most people had been alive. With Henry interred, the final shroud could be drawn over the House of Lancaster. It was now, and for a second time, the Yorkist Age.

Notes

1 Bisham Abbey: This was founded as a community property by the Templars, and taken over by Edward II when the Order was suppressed. For a time, in the Scottish wars, the captive queen of Robert the Bruce was housed there. Acquired by the 1st Earl of Salisbury in 1337, it became the final resting place for his successors.

2 PL 169–170.

3 Edmund Beaufort had served with Charles of Burgundy during the campaign and Battle of Montlhery (Pierre de Breze was amongst the casualties on the French side).

4 Burne, op. cit., p. 119.

5 The Severn could be successfully crossed in three places: by the bridge at Gloucester which was, however, dominated by the city's defences; by the ferry a mile or so south of Tewkesbury, which was undefended, but some 10 miles further north; or, further north still by another 6 miles, the crossing at Upton on Severn.

6 'The Arrivall' pp. 18–30.

7 Beauchamp in fact made a sally against the Lancastrian rearguard and, in the skirmish that followed, captured several of their guns: see Burne, op. cit., p. 124.

8 Both sides had marched some 59 miles, for a tally of the relevant distances, see Burne, *Battlefields*, p. 125 (table).

9 'The Arrivall' pp. 19–30.

10 The name Severn is said to derive from that of an unfortunate Germanic princess, Savren, who was ritually drowned in the waters following a defeat.

11 As to numbers; it is likely the Lancastrians could field some 5,000–6,000 men, the Yorkists rather less; see P. W. Hammond, *The Battles of Barnet and Tewkesbury*

(New York 1990), p. 95: each division of the respective armies would contain 1,500–1,800 soldiers allowing for a tactical reserve.

12 Tradition asserts that the Queen watched the battle from Tewkesbury Abbey; see Hammond, op. cit., p. 94.

13 'The Arrivall' pp. 18–30.

14 Ibid.

15 Ibid.

16 Ibid.

17 Ibid.

18 Edward of Lancaster was most probably slain on the field or in the rout. Correspondence from Clarence to Henry Vernon, dated 6 May, refers to the Duke's brother-in-law being 'slayn in playn bataill'. A note from the Milanese ambassador, of 2 June, says the Prince was taken and killed. For a full discussion, see Hammond, op. cit., Appendix 2, p. 123.

19 He was Somerset's brother-in-law.

20 Sir John Fortescue had been Chief Justice under Henry VI and had borne exile with Queen Margaret. He was eventually pardoned; see Hammond, op. cit., p. 101.

21 'The Arrivall' pp. 18–30.

22 A former adherent of the Earl of Warwick.

23 Hammond, op. cit., p. 105.

24 Ibid., p. 107.

25 Warkworth, pp. 19–22.

26 The Bastard of Fauconberg controlled the rump of Warwick's navy, an asset that could not be left in such dangerous hands. His accommodation with the King was short-lived; whether either side intended a lasting accord is perhaps doubtful. In September he, with another illegitimate brother, William Neville, was fomenting trouble in the north, or so it was expedient to accuse them. On 28 September 1471 the Bastard was executed and his severed head spiked on the top of London Bridge, facing Kent, a suitable irony; see Hammond, op. cit., pp. 112–13.

27 The Commissioners appointed to conduct the enquiry into the matter of the Essex, Kent and Surrey rebels were Lord Dinham and Sir John Fogge. The Commission was chaired jointly by the Earl of Essex and Sir William Bourchier. The men of Essex seem to have fared worst, paying heavier fines; see Hammond, op. cit., p. 115.

28 Warkworth, pp. 19–22.

29 Ibid.

30 The death of Henry VI has been controversial both as to its exact timing and also the extent of Gloucester's involvement. Though Warkworth is supported by the GCL in asserting that the old king was killed on the 21st, some sources suggest the following day; this discrepancy may simply have arisen from the time, late in the evening, when the deed is said to have been done: see Hammond, op. cit., Appendix 3, p. 127.

Chapter 14

'This Sunne of York': the Yorkist Age 1471–1483

Now is the winter of our discontent
Made glorious summer by this sun of York;
And all the clouds that lour'd upon our house
In the deep bosom of the ocean buried.

William Shakespeare, *Richard* III, *I. i. 1–4.*

With his foes dead or scattered Edward IV entered upon a second, more secure, tenure, *'beau prince entre les beaux du monde'* as he was described by the observant Burgundian, Philippe de Commynes. His reputation as a great captain was assured by the brilliance of his victories at Barnet and Tewkesbury. The Woodville marriage had at least provided England with a queen of assured beauty and style, one who could wield ostentation as an instrument of policy. Such show was not mere vanity – Edward had witnessed the contempt directed at the shabbiness of his predecessor' court. He had youthful vigour, considerable good looks, charm and the inestimable advantage of knightly renown. This Yorkist looked like a true king of England; his court glowed with the assurance of style, the glitter of abundance.

The King's Rule

Edward, now freed of the millstone of the Nevilles, which had clouded the earlier part of his reign, was able to consolidate his grip on power. To do this he needed to heal old wounds, to bury the conflicts of the past and reunify the English polity behind the throne. In the three years after 1472 some 30 attainders were reversed,[1] even that inveterate schemer and arch Lancastrian, John Morton was rehabilitated.[2] George Neville, slipperiest of the brothers, had survived, bent his knee and retained his position as Archbishop of York, though, quite soon, he fell foul of the King and found himself behind bars at Calais. His vast haul of loot and accumulated riches was put under the hammer and raised the considerable windfall of £20,000.

The view that the court was dominated by the Woodville faction has now been challenged by various writers, such as Christine Carpenter (perhaps not the most recent writer but still persuasive),[3] who perceive that the King was firmly in control, using his family connection, as had previous monarchs (such as Edward III), to extend his influence. The magnates who came to control large swathes of territory, like Thomas, Lord Grey of Groby, Edward's stepson, later Marquis of Dorset, Hastings and Gloucester, were firmly under the royal thumb, and those, like Clarence, who transgressed, were dealt with decisively. A king who would not flinch from executing his own brother was not one to be trifled with. Edward was affable and out-wardly easy-going but this facade hid an iron resolve. The proliferation of local rivalries, such as the Percy–Neville feud which had so disturbed the peace in the previous reign, was curbed. Though Edward could be fierce when the need arose, he was careful to favour conciliation over brute force; though the Woodvilles did well, their advancement was an extension of the royal estate and influence.

Clarence and Gloucester

Edward had two surviving brothers – Gloucester, the younger, unswerv-ingly loyal, and George, Duke of Clarence, the turncoat elder, who would need a careful eye. Royal dukes were a problem, close enough to the Crown to be dangerous, always in the shadow of an elder brother who bore the sceptre, and prone through influence or ambition to mischief. As suc-cessors in title to the Kingmaker, each having married one of the dead Earl's daughters, they soon fell to squabbling. The Croyland chronicler took a tabloid interest in the dispute:

> *In fact, these three brothers, the king and the two dukes were possessed of such surpassing talents, that, if they had been able to live without dissentions, such a threefold cord could never have been broken without the utmost difficulty.*[4]

For Gloucester and Clarence, each was a rebuke to the potential of the other. Clarence was loud and rash, his younger brother calmer and more subtle, undoubtedly the cleverer of the two. In form they were also completely different. George had the stature and looks of the Neville side and their genius for manipulating the commons; Richard was smaller in stature, dark and reserved, physically more akin to his father. They both had claims to the vast Neville inheritance, through right of their wives. Clarence, despite his recent treasons, saw himself as the sole beneficiary entitled to the Warwick inheritance and he did not take kindly to the notion of sharing the spoils with Richard. He appointed himself as Anne's guardian and rejected his brother's suit. Gloucester appealed to the King, who decided in his favour – it was clearly not desirable that George should maintain control of so vast an estate.

Thwarted, Clarence now blandly denied any knowledge of Anne's whereabouts. After all, if she was not his ward, he was not responsible for her. The unfortunate young woman, a continuing pawn in the game that had already seen her widowed once, was located, disguised as a domestic in the house of one of the Duke's affinity, and escorted by Richard to temporary sanctuary. The King signalled his favour toward his younger brother by transferring to him a whole parcel of estates, wrested by attainder from the defeated Lancastrian magnates. This largesse displeased and further alienated George and led to the protracted dispute in Council.

Richard's biographer avers that Gloucester lacked his brother's ready charm and eloquence, though this inference cannot be implied from the chronicler's account, which rather presents a view that the pair were evenly matched. The feud simmered until Edward finally cajoled or demanded a resolution. The deal was straightforward: Clarence would accept the fact of Richard's marriage to Anne but would not be alienated from any portion of the Kingmaker's estate other than those lands already in Gloucester's keeping – essentially Middleham and various other manors in Yorkshire.

Richard relinquished any claim on the remainder of the Warwick inheritance, surrendered his office of great Chamberlain and consented to George assuming the earldoms of Warwick and Salisbury. On paper, Clarence appeared to have come off remarkably well, but there was careful policy in Gloucester's apparent humility. By accepting so modest a settlement, he appeared to by marrying for love rather than avarice, yet the gains he made were important in cementing his position in the north, where his considerable energies were to be focused, and confirmed him as the Kingmaker's natural successor north of the Trent. Clarence, though outwardly extending his estates, did not establish himself so fully as his younger brother.

King Edward had learnt from the mistakes of the Lancastrian court and understood how quickly the burden of taxation could erode his popularity. He heeded fully Parliament's expectation that the King should be able to manage his Household directly from his own revenues, without having to cast a part of his burden onto the public purse. The essence of his fiscal policy, therefore, was to so structure his own finances that the Household would become self-financing – a policy he affirmed before MPs as early as January 1468. After having come so close to losing his throne, through 1469–71, he did not, upon recovering his authority, deviate from this stated intent. Rigorous control of the Exchequer became a hallmark of the reign. Royal estates were properly and profitably administered, customs revenue burgeoned and the canny use of every legal means squeezed the last advantage out of feudal rights. Nor did the King, unlike his more fastidiously chivalric contemporaries, ignore the lures of trade. His long association with the mercantile classes provided a base for both networking and entrepreneurship. In this Edward proved to be adept, cashing in on the prevailing boom through a series of lucrative commercial ventures: 'like a private individual living by trade', as the Croyland Continuator rather sourly notes.

One Lancastrian lord who remained at large was the mercurial but experienced John de Vere, Earl of Oxford, who in 1473 staged a major raid on the south-west. He seized the key bastion of St Michael's Mount which, as Warkworth asserted, was 'a strong place and a mighty, and cannot be got if it be well victualled with a few men to keep it; for twenty men may keep it against all the world'.[5] Oxford used the fortress as a base for fomenting discord in Cornwell. Sir John Bodrugan, the County Sheriff, was instructed to lay siege to the place – no easy matter – and he proved insufficiently resolute, so the King gave his commission to Richard Fortescue, an appointment that discountenanced the Sheriff. Fortescue acted with greater vigour, skirmishing with the defenders who, nonetheless, could not be dislodged. Edward and his Council were working on more clandestine measures, offering pardons and bribes to Oxford's fellowship, many of whom were seduced to the extent that the defence was substantially depleted; on 15 February the Earl capitulated.

The French Expedition of 1475

Edward was considering the merits of a new French adventure – the defeat of Bull Talbot at Castillon had not necessarily finally convinced Englishmen that it was time to lay down the cudgels,[6] besides, what better vehicle than a foreign war for diverting the martial energies of restless magnates. With the final embers of Warwick's perfidy and Lancastrian hopes stamped out, peace on the Marches, good relations with Brittany and the usual Burgundian prompting, the time seemed ripe. The matter of a French expedition seems to have been in Edward's mind from at least 1472, for in November of that year Parliament granted the King a subsidy in the amount of ten per cent of income tax (this was for the specific purpose of raising 10,000 archers). This would have equipped a sizeable force but the cash proved easier to amass on paper than in reality – the parliamentary rolls disclose a rather seedy picture of corruption which frustrated the royal effort. Humiliated, the King was obliged to make full use of his web of commercial contacts to beg or borrow sufficient funds from which to prosecute the war. He relied heavily on the Mayor and Aldermen of London, arranging interviews with each and, working the royal charm to the full, extracted donations. The Aldermen acted as Edward's agents with the guilds and tradesmen, spreading the network to persuade each to subscribe according to his means.

Both Gloucester and Clarence entered into indentures to supply the King with men-at-arms and archers. Politically the decision was a popular one; the economic costs, inevitably, were high but Edward was a proven captain of the first rank. Calais still remained the gateway for operations in northern France, and Englishmen were glad to concentrate their energies against a foreign foe – a welcome shift from the debilitating stresses of civil strife. By 4 July the King, with his royal siblings, had reached Calais; even de Commynes, now acting as Louis XI's advisor, observed that the English host was both numerous and well disciplined, a formidable threat.[7] Two days after their arrival, on 6 July, the royal brothers were greeted by their sister, consort to Charles the Bold of Burgundy.[8] Her mercurial husband proved less reliable – his army, such as he had mustered, had been diverted to the siege of Neuss and he did not appear before the English Pale until 14 July, and then only with a small affinity. Despite the Duke's habitual bluster, there seemed very little prospect of any serious support from the Burgundians.

Edward advanced his host to St Quentin, which was to be readily surrendered by the Count of St Pol, passing as he did over the field of Agincourt. The King was under no illusions about the temperament of his adversary Louis XI, however the 'Universal Spider', was far too canny to commit any such tactical blunder. As the English army approached their destination they were greeted by a hail of roundshot. The Count of St Pol had rethought his allegiance, a change of heart prompted no doubt by the approach of a powerful French host: King Louis was on the march. It seemed as though a major engagement in the field might follow, but Louis was in no hurry to furnish the King of England with another Crécy to add to his laurels; he preferred scorched earth and subtle diplomacy. With the Burgundians conspicuously absent, it would be difficult for the English to exploit their limited success, and Edward judged the time had come for parley.

Having summoned his war council, both royal dukes, with those of Norfolk, Suffolk and the Marquess of Dorset, together with the Earls of Northumberland, Pembroke and Rivers, Lords Hastings, Stanley and Howard, the motion to commence negotiations was endorsed. Gloucester was the lone voice of opposition. Whether he craved the chance for glory or, as his biographer Paul Murray Kendall suggests, he was anxious to ensure the taxpayers got their money's worth, remains unclear. Edward had, however, made up his mind and he was undoubtedly correct, seizing the moment to wring such rewards as a relieved Louis might be disposed to offer. When the emissaries met on August 15 not far from Amiens, terms were cordially agreed. Louis was indeed prepared to pay heavily to have the English quit his kingdom. A seven-years truce would be supported by commercial arrangements; a premium of 75,000 gold crowns was payable immediately and an annuity of 50,000 thereafter. The Princess Elizabeth would wed the Dauphin, and both monarchs entered into a pact to assist each other in suppressing domestic rebels. This seemed to represent a remarkably good return on the English taxpayers' investment. Charles of Burgundy, who flew into a predictable tantrum and stormed off, was left in the cold.

The disagreement between Edward and his youngest sibling over the matter of the accommodation with France apparently produced no lasting rift between the brothers. The incident does tend to give the lie to a view of Richard of Gloucester as a ruthless and cynical opportunist. His dissent seems to have been motivated by conviction and a desire to do the right thing by England. Louis, his antennae as finely tuned as ever, must have been aware of these mutterings and delved yet further into his capacious purse to buy new friends amongst the English Council – Hastings was a signal beneficiary of the French King's politic largesse, as were numerous other magnates. Gloucester was not to be seduced, and though he behaved punctiliously, would not unbend.

Richard was no doubt expressing what many in England would be feeling – the expedition had produced no victory in the field, no laurels to Edward's crown. It had resolved itself into a purely fiscal transaction, where expediency triumphed over chivalry. The Croyland Chronicler records widespread mutterings as the army, unblooded, returned home, accompanied by a spate of petty disturbances. These the King suppressed with ruthless efficiency. The chronicler was of the view that only this prompt and draconian action averted a far worse backlash:

> However, if this prudent prince had not manfully put an end to this commencement of mischief, the number of people complaining of the unfair management of the resources of the kingdom, in consequence of such quantities of treasure being abstracted from the coffers of each and uselessly consumed, would have increased to such a degree that no one could have said whose head, among the king's advisers, was in safety; and the more especially those, who, induced by friendship for the French king, or by his presents, had persuaded the king to make peace in manner previously mentioned.[9]

The Fall of Clarence

In the event the foray against Louis XI, whilst it garnered no laurels, paid a handsome dividend by the terms of the Treaty of Picquigny, whilst the Anglophile James III of Scotland agreed to a further extension of the prevailing Anglo-Scottish truce for the unpredented span of 45 years.

'False, fleeting, perjur'd Clarence' – the Duke has been tarnished by Shakespeare's unflattering portrayal. He was physically imposing like his older brother, but doomed to live in the shadow of that greatness, tarnished by his perfidy with Warwick. He was proud, ambitious, eloquent and affable when it suited – but otherwise mercurial and untrustworthy. On 22 December 1476 Duchess Isabel died, leaving Clarence an eligible widower – and Charles the Bold had a daughter Mary, heiress to the dazzling fortune of Burgundy. Mary was not Margaret of York's daughter but from the Duke's previous (second) wife Isabella de Bourbon. Her quixotic father, after the collapse of the Anglo-Burgundian entente in 1475, had been pursuing an unsuccessful campaign against the Swiss, finally losing his army and his life in January 1477.[10] This was dire news, for it offered Louis the very pretext he had been seeking to procure the reversion of Burgundy to France.

For England this was most alarming. Burgundy was the market for English wool, tied by long association and dynastic alliance, the very presence of such a powerful ally and considerable threat served to guarantee France's willingness to stick to the terms of the recent treaty. Edward was inclined to take a cautious stance, opening talks with both sides, sending reassurance to his sister and niece whilst still dealing with Louis. Duchess Margaret was prepared to have her brother wed her step-daughter: for the Duke this was a dazzling prospect, he would be free of his brother's shadow, ruler of the wealthiest court in Europe, the splendours of which outshone those of its feudal superior. No prize was more worthy of winning, but the King was not prepared to acquiesce.

A former servant of the dead Duchess Isabel, the unfortunate Ankarette Twynyho, was arrested by Clarence's henchmen and condemned by a rigged court of conspiring to poison her employer. No due process, nor appeal, unduly lengthened the proceedings, and the wretched woman was hanged for her alleged crime. The Duke appeared to be giving a message that his wife's death was the work of the Woodvilles. Next, it was the Duke's turn to be on the receiving end: one of his household, an Oxford clerk named Thomas Burdett, was implicated in another, allegedly diabolical, plot and he two was hanged – stridently protesting his innocence.

If this was a warning, Clarence refused to take notice, blustering in the King's presence and spreading treasonable rumours. This was serious: Clarence was alleging his brother's bastardy, implying his marriage to the Queen bigamous, and inciting discord throughout his wide estates. Louis XI, always happy to stir the pot whenever opportunity offered, added his fat to the fire by suggesting Clarence's ambitions in Burgundy were but a stepping-stone to Edward's throne. For the King there was only one solution – his troublesome brother must be confined to the Tower. Gloucester had wisely remained aloof on his northern estates, careful to ensure no taint of his brother's arch-folly should stick to him. Richard hurried south for the Christmas festivities in 1477 and made a show of begging Edward to show clemency toward their brother. Nonetheless, Clarence was formally arraigned on 16 January 1478, with the King as principal accuser and the Duke an embittered defendant, 'For not a single person uttered a word against the duke, except the king; not one individual made answer to the king, except the duke.'[11]

Clarence was condemned by his own violence and rashness. On February 7, Buckingham, as President of the court, handed down the inevitable judgement and equally inevitable sentence. Eleven days later, the Duke was quietly killed in the Tower.[12] Gloucester did not appear to profit greatly from his brother's demise, at least not in material terms. His own young son, edward of Middleham, was elevated to the earldom of Salisbury and he retrieved the office of Great Chamberlain. The great earldom of Warwick was held in trust for the Duke's heir, and the King took responsibility for the welfare of his niece.

Gloucester, the North and Scotland

Whether Gloucester was, in any way, implicated in his brother's fall, as Shakespeare would have us believe, remains, like so much about Richard's life and motives, an enigma. Clarence was quite capable of pitching headlong into his own ruin; relations with his fellow royal duke had never been particularly cordial. The relationship between the King and his surviving brother appeared to function extremely well. Richard enjoyed significant autonomy in the north, though he was far from being a free prince. As Christine Carpenter points out: 'Gloucester's northern hegemony was less an independent fief than a regional command subordinated to Edward's authority.' In practical terms Gloucester's control maintained the border in a more peaceable condition than hitherto and prevented large-scale disturbances between the regional magnates; outwardly cordial relations were maintained with Percy and the Raby Nevilles (never great friends to their Middleham cousins). The Stanley–Harrington dispute festered, but was eventually resolved by joint intervention from Gloucester and the King.

In terms of his private life, Edward IV was a good deal less circumspect. Whilst the Queen might appear to rule the court she did not enjoy a monopoly of the royal bed, quite the reverse. Edward was dangerously attractive to women, and addicted to pleasures of the flesh. Lord Hastings was his boon companion and procurer, a role that scarcely endeared him to Elizabeth. Most celebrated of the royal mistresses was Elizabeth (Jane) Shore, a woman of middle rank,[13] whose affections, on the King's death, were transferred to Hastings – a matter which further deepened the rift between his lordship and the Marquis of Dorset, who was equally enamoured of the lady.

The King of England was not alone in being burdened with ambitious and ruthless siblings. James III of Scotland had a brace of 'Clarences' of his own, in the persons of two younger brothers, the earls of Albany and Mar. Unlike his English counterpart, the King of Scots did not possess a formidable military reputation, quite the opposite.

James's sexual preferences may be questionable but his contemporaries were certainly prepared to believe the worst. His passion for advancing low-born favourites, selected from the ranks of artists and musicians, merely fuelled speculation and unrest. If James failed to achieve the chivalric mould, his brother Albany was far more assiduous. It was said that he: 'lowit nothing so weill as abill men and good horse and maid gret cost and expenssis thairon; for he was wondrous liberall in all thingis pertening to his honour'.[14]

Like Clarence, Albany fully understood the value of manly show, but nonetheless heartily abused his office as Lieutenant of the Borders. His ambitions clearly reached further and he may have been in treasonable correspondence with his English counterpart prior to 1479. In that year both he and his brother Mar were arrested. The Duke had conspired to foment discord on a truce day,[15] (not necessarily a difficult matter), and several men had been slain in the subsequent fracas. Mar was further suspected of involvement in necromancy and the black arts, though this may have been mere propaganda. In the event any such leanings did him little good for he expired whilst still in captivity; suspicion of foul play inevitably clung to the King's favourites. Albany preferred not to take chances and contrived to escape from gaol the following year,[16] finding the climate in France more congenial. Louis was disposed to make much of the royal renegade, arranging an advantageous match and providing a comfortable if bleak exile.

Edward IV, however, was inclined to be more receptive. The idea of a puppet King of Scots clearly had its attractions, but Louis was already seeking to broker a rapprochement between James and his erring brother, anxious to keep the Scots on side should Anglo-Burgundian moves constitute a renewed threat to France. Still very much the Anglophile, James tried to steer the middle course, offering the hand of his sister as a consort for Earl Rivers. The offer liked not and Edward responded with demands; Berwick to be returned, the lurking Douglas to be re-habilitated and restored, James' son (the future James IV), to be educated in England and the inevitable matter of English overlordship.

James answered bluster with force. His counter-demands included the abandonment of any further co-operation with Burgundy and he sent Angus into Northumberland to underline his point with flame and sword, in the time-honoured fashion of the borders. Bamburgh was set on fire on 5 August 1480 and there were some minor, single ship actions off the North Sea coast. The Papal Nuncio stepped in to arbitrate – his perennial mission to raise enthusiasm for a crusade. Both sides were willing to accept a return to the stated truce but Albany remained, skulking like a cancerous growth, only waiting on his chance.

Gloucester was, of course, charged with the defence of Northern England; to all intents and purposes his province extended from the Trent to the Tweed. He occupied his late father-in-law's castles at Middleham[17] and Sheriff Hutton[18] and held a vast array of sinecures including Constable of England and Lord Admiral.

This Duke, prior to Edward's death, remains the model younger brother, loyal, competent, brave and industrious. His popularity in the north was very considerable, amounting, in centres such as York and Carlisle, almost to veneration, as the astute Italian observer Dominic Mancini noted:

He came very rarely to court. He kept himself within his own lands and set out to acquire the loyalty of his people through favours and justice. The good reputation of his private life and public activities powerfully attracted the esteem of strangers. Such was his renown in warfare, that whenever a difficult and dangerous policy had to be undertaken, it would be entrusted to his direction and his generalship. By these arts Richard acquired the favour of the people, and avoided the jealousy of the queen, from who he lived far separated.[19]

With the Scots riding into Northumberland in the spring of 1480, Richard was formally appointed as Lieutenant-General in the North during May. He accepted his office with typical energy, strengthening and victualling the border holds. In September, following the taking up of Bamburgh, he launched a counter-strike across the Tweed to prove such assaults would not pass without retaliation. Edward had already determined, with the full support of Council, that the Scots required a more lasting lesson, and a major expedition was planned for spring 1481. Gloucester used the winter months to good effect, carrying out necessary repairs to Carlisle's walls and attending to the maintenance of other key bastions. Then, having undertaken a census of those Marchers able to do service, the Duke set about recruiting in earnest. Money, as ever, was the main difficulty. A contract army was expensive; some funds might be raised through loans or grants but, inevitably, the burden fell on the taxpayer. Not forgetting his special relationship with York, Richard procured the City's exemption in recognition of its previous contributions, thus making political gain out of financial necessity!

Campaigning began with naval operations, directed by the competent Lord Howard but, despite this energetic beginning, the land campaign of 1481 remained a still-born thing. The King's obesity and possibly weakening constitution prevented him from taking the field. Local initiatives were left to Gloucester's discretion and he relied on a policy of aggressive patrolling. September witnessed a sudden alarm, when it seemed the Scots might cross the frontier in force, but in the event no major incursion occurred – Richard had already retired to York, believing the season over. Appraised of the risk, however, he and Percy, working in competent unison, raised sufficient forces and manned the line, though the threat proved illusory. Gloucester seized the moment to commence the fulfilment of what must have been a long-cherished ambition – the recovery of Berwick upon Tweed from the Scots. Now that the proposed campaign of 1482 had a clear objective, the autumn and winter were to be utilised as a breathing space to begin establishing siege lines and to ensure English superiority at sea; a naval blockade would be essential if the town's investment was to be complete. Richard conferred with his brother at Nottingham as the lines were being dug, and the King, accepting that his health prevented active participation, passed him the baton of command.

In the spring in 1482, when the last of winter's tentacles had finally receded, Gloucester took the field; beginning with a chevauchee into the west and taking Dumfries. By June he was again in the south, conferring with the King and his guest, the exiled Duke of Albany. Whether Edward ever entertained any serious hopes of Albany's prospects of supplanting his brother is uncertain. At worst his participation could provide a focus for the swelling tide of discontent among the magnates within Scotland itself. By 20 July Gloucester had again taken the field. His army, said to number 20,000,[20] was soon encamped before the much embattled walls of Berwick. This was a summons to war that even the peaceable James III could not ignore, especially as his turncoat brother rode as his enemies' mascot. After a stirring address to the Scottish Parliament, when he undertook to uphold the proud patriotism of his forbears, the King marshalled his host on the Burgh Muir of Edinburgh and set out for the borders by way of Lauderdale. On paper the available forces were impressive, well furnished with ordnance, but James had made the monumental blunder of taking with him his entire pack of sycophants. Douglas, boldest of the Scottish magnates, culled the lot at Lauder, but the Scots advanced no further.

Gloucester was not prepared simply to wait at Berwick and attend upon the Scots' convenience. Leaving Lord Stanley with sufficient reserves to man the siege lines, he marshalled the bulk of the army and advanced into Lothian. Angus, having sated his thirst for action by slaughtering the royal catamites, found he had less enthusiasm for a confrontation with Richard and retreated. The English harried as far as Haddington, and finally occupied Edinburgh. This was no mere chevauchee – the Duke was out to present Albany as a credible alternative; strict discipline and a rein on random pillage were maintained. On 2 August, Douglas sued for terms. James was their prisoner, Albany the rogue card; there was little to be gained from a trial of strength with superior English forces.

Albany acted as honest broker and Richard felt sufficiently satisfied to quit the Scottish capital and return to the siege. By the time he did so Stanley had gained the town and only the castle itself remained defiant. On 12 August the Duke dubbed a batch of newly created knights and paid off sections of his army. With no hope of relief the castellan was in an impossible position and capitulated two days later. Berwick was returned to England, changing hands for the fourteenth time since 1296; a considerable achievement nonetheless and the reward for a model campaign. As a bonus, the viper Albany was lodged in the very bosom of the Scottish polity. There is some suggestion that Gloucester was not without his critics, and the mere recovery of a border hold, however important, was perceived as a poor return for the outlay of so much treasure. As the Croyland Chronicler rather sourly concludes:

> *Ths trifling gain, or perhaps more accurately loss (for the maintenance of Berwick costs 10,000 marks a year) diminished the substance of the King and the Kingdom by more that £100,000 at the time. King Edward was grieved at the frivolous expenditure of so much money although the capture of Berwick alleviated his grief for a time.*[21]

When the English Parliament met, MPs had no hesitation in showering rewards upon the Duke of Gloucester. In this final year of his failing brother's reign, he was very much the man of the hour, his loyalty unquestioned and with a dozen years of diligent and successful service to his credit. His office of Warden of the English West March was confirmed and transformed into a hereditary title bringing with it the governorship of Carlisle, Bewcastle, and the Nicholforest and the shrievality of Cumberland;[22] control of virtually the entire Crown estates in the county. And, there was more – a subsidy of 10,000 marks was awarded to fund the creation, or rather re-creation of an English Pale in south-west Scotland, to comprise Liddesdale, Eskdale, Annandale, Wauchopedale and Clydesdale. This was the dowry Albany was to pay for English arms supporting his bid for the throne, an arrangement which he was no longer able to complete. Edward effectively assigned his expectations granted by the terms of the Fotheringay Treaty to his brother. It was all very impressive on paper but the proof would be in the winning.

History, however, had other ideas and was to cast a far greater lure. In April Edward IV contracted pneumonia, and died on the 9th of that month. The exact cause of his death remains obscure – gluttony and excessive consumption of alcohol had taken their toll of his once magnificent physique; he had become obese. It may be, as Professor Ross suggests in his *Edward IV*, that these factors contributed to a stroke or perhaps a series of strokes; this would at least explain the King's decreasing capability over the last months of his reign. The Croyland writer recalled the King's final days:

> *Neither worn out with old age not yet seized with any known kind of malady, the cure of which would not have appeared easy in the case of a person of more humble rank, [the King] took to his bed. This happened about the feast of Easter; and on the ninth day of April, he rendered up his spirit to his Creator, at his palace of Westminster.*[23]

From loyal subject to ruthless usurper, the transformation of Richard of Gloucester was now at hand. That England would once again plunge into a further, dark period of uncertainty, political murder and civil discord, albeit on a minor scale, would, as Professor Pollard points out, have surprised the majority of citizens. Edward IV appeared to have been a most successful ruler. Whilst the King lived, his division of localised power worked well, but on his death it failed to ensure a smooth transition of power to his minor heir. The very centralisation of regal power worked against such a smooth transition. Of course Edward could not have forseen dying at such a young age. Nonetheless, the main cause of the crisis of 1483 lay in the character and ambition of Richard, Duke of Gloucester, soon to become King Richard III.

Notes

1 Lander, op. cit., pp. 68–9.
2 Dr John Morton (1420–1500), Bishop of Ely and a Yorkist who, nonetheless, detested Richard III and was favoured by Henry VII, rising to the see of Canterbury.
3 Carpenter, op. cit., pp. 182–9.
4 Ibid., pp. 150–1.
5 Ibid., p. 151.
6 D. J Sadler, *Border Fury* (London 2004), p. 385.
7 Lander, op. cit., p. 155.
8 Charles the Bold of Burgundy, a mercurial adventurer, whose early intervention against Louis XI produced the mistaken conviction that Charles was an outstanding general.
9 Lander, op. cit., p. 160.
10 Charles the Bold finally met his demise at the Battle of Morat on 22 June 1476.
11 Lander, op. cit., pp. 164–5.
12 Legend, perpetuated by Shakespeare, has it that Clarence was drowned in a butt of Malmsey wine. Whilst this cannot be verified it may, nonetheless, be true.
13 Jane Shore, (née Lambert, 1445–1527), born into a well-to-do mercantile family, both beautiful and well educated, variously enjoying the favours of the King, Dorset and Hastings.
14 Sadler, *Border Fury*, p. 387.
15 A truce day was an occasion when the wardens of both kingdoms met to hear matters brought by alleged victims from both sides.
16 For details of Albany's dramatic and violent escape; see Sadler, op. cit., p. 387.

17 Middleham Castle: a twelfth-century stone keep; enlarged by the Nevilles with the addition of three ranges of domestic buildings, by the fifteenth century the castle complex had become palatial. It was here that Richard had spent much of his youth.

18 Sheriff Hutton Castle: another Neville hold, near Easingwold, originally built by the de Bulmers, it eventually passed to Henry VII and formed part of the Crown estate.

19 Murray Kendall, op. cit., p. 150.

20 Sadler, op. cit., p. 394.

21 Ibid., p. 397.

22 Shrievality – the office of High Sheriff of the county.

23 Cited in Lander, op. cit., p. 168.

Chapter 15

'Under the Hog' – Richard III and Bosworth 22 August 1485

The cat, the rat and Lovell our dog, rulen all England, under an hog.
Contemporary doggerel 1484

The Usurpation

The question of why Richard of Gloucester seized the throne in the spring of 1483 is one which has exercised his many determined admirers and his equally vehement detractors ever since. Much of what has been written about this, the final Plantagenet King and the last regnant English monarch to fall on the field of battle, has been influenced by the Tudor historians, whose view was partisan, and by Shakespeare's portrayal, equally unflattering. There is nothing to show that Richard coveted his brother's throne, though it is plain he did not lack ambition. He worked assiduously to build up his northern base. He was not frightened to disagree with Edward's policy when, as before Amiens, he believed such policy to be wrong. In that instance, as with much of his work in the north, he seemed to have been motivated by a desire to do right by the taxpayer. He does not appear cynical or avaricious. Was he perhaps a man like his father, whom he resembled – the loyal public servant driven by the excesses of others to stake his own claim? His position, as the surviving royal brother, changed on Edward's death. Prior to this point he was the loyal sibling, shunning the Woodville court and eschewing dangerous politics. With the King dead, and a minor on the throne, he became both an opportunity for some and a threat to others. To the Queen, with his impeccable chivalric credentials, his record of good service and untainted by the corruption of the greedy arriviste, he posed a threat – the one key magnate who, in accordance with the terms of the King's will, would act as head of the Regency Council, sidelining her own detested brood. To others, anxious to see these rapacious parvenus get their comeuppance, he was the obvious paladin.

Had he been content, had he deemed it safe, to remain simply as Protector and fade into the background as the King matured, then history's view

Figure 5: King Richard III
(© National Portrait Gallery, London)

might have been very different. Hubris undoubtedly payed a part – he had proved himself valorous and competent in his brother's shadow, perhaps he felt compelled to move toward the light; if so, then he was scarcely unique. The crime which has damned Gloucester's name and, whilst never finally proven, was certainly laid at his door during his reign, was that of murdering his nephews. Taking the lives of innocent children was regarded as an atrocity, even in an age where violence was commonplace. As Professor Pollard points out, it does not actually matter whether the King was guilty or not:

> *It was widely believed before the end of 1483 that they [the Princes] had met their deaths; political realignment took place specifically on that assumption. Richard III was held responsible by his contemporaries not just for the deposition of a rightful child king but also for his and his brother's subsequent deaths. The condemnation made it all the harder, although not impossible, for him to succeed.[1]*

It was Lord Hastings, no friend to the Queen, who informed Richard, still, in mid April 1483 isolated in the north, that the King was dead. Richard would be familiar with the terms of his late brother's will whereby he was appointed as Lord Protector during the minority of Edward V. Richard cannot have given any inkling of treasonable intent during the reign – he was being preferred to any of the Queen's clamouring kin. On paper he was the ideal choice. For Gloucester, the first questions he must have asked himself was how secure was his office and what level of real control could he exercise over a strong-willed twelve-year-old surrounded by the hostile chorus of his Woodville blood.

A keen observer of these times was the papal envoy Dominic Mancini, who was in England early in 1483. His report was written for Angelo Cato, Archbishop of Vienne by the end of the year, and he is certainly not biased in Richard's favour:

> *In this meeting [Council] the problem of the government during the royal minority was referred to the consideration of the barons. Two opinions were propounded. One was that the Duke of Gloucester should govern, because Edward in his will [this has not survived but the statement rings true] had so directed, and because by law the government ought to devolve on him. But this was the losing resolution; the winning was that the government should be carried on by many persons among whom the duke, so far from being excluded, should be accounted the chief . . . All who favoured the queen's family voted for this proposal.[2]*

What was agreed was that the young king should be brought to London for his coronation, planned for 4 May. The lad was presently at Ludlow in the care of his other uncle, Earl Rivers.

Hastings was at odds with the Woodvilles because they appeared strong: they had physical possession of the Prince; they controlled the Tower, stuffed with the dead King's treasure and his impressive ordnance; and their voices rang loudest in the Council.[3] Alerted by Hastings, Richard wrote a suitably worded letter to the councillors:

> *He [Richard] had been loyal to his brother Edward, at home and abroad, in peace and war, and should be, if only permitted, equally loyal to his brother's son, and to all his brother's issue, even female . . . He asked the councillors to take his deserts into consideration, when disposing of the government, to which he was entitled by law, and his brother's ordinance.*[4]

Thus encouraged, the Duke's partisans became more vociferous and created a rift whereby the Woodville faction sought to hasten the coronation whilst the Ricardian element wished to delay any such important decisions until the Duke himself was present. Dorset, according to Mancini, replied haughtily, opining that the Woodvilles had sufficient gravitas as to have no need to attend upon Gloucester's convenience. His disillusionment, nearer at hand than he could have imagined, must have come as a great surprise. We have to be wary of taking Mancini's view as accepted – the Italian was an acute observer but removed from the actual circles of power. Whether there was any degree of bad feeling between Richard and the Woodvilles is by no means clear. The death of a reigning monarch, with a minor as successor, was a time of uncertainty. The Yorkist line was barely two decades old. Richard's large estate, as Christine Carpenter points out, was vulnerable, being amassed through grant rather than by birth. The resentment of the Woodvilles seems to emanate from Hastings and the late King's Household men, including the Howards.

Hastings now used his own influence to try to limit the size of the escort that would accompany the young King from Ludlow to London. The ostensible reason would be to preserve the rule of law – an over-large escort would smack of a coup, and Edward V had no need of force. Hastings backed up his argument with the threat to decamp to Calais, his appointment since 1471, and from where he could prove a very sharp thorn indeed. The Woodvilles, unsuspecting, concurred; the King would travel with a retinue that did not exceed 2,000 men at arms. This appeared more than enough. In what seemed their hour of triumph the Woodvilles had over-looked Henry Stafford, Duke of Buckingham, one of their previous victims, forced into a marriage alliance at an early age:

> *Buckingham, since he was of the highest nobility, was disposed to sympathise with another noble; more especially because he had his own reasons for detesting the queen's kin: for, when he was younger, he had been forced to marry the queen's sister, whom he scorned to wed on account of her humble origin.*[5]

Buckingham was a vain, shallow character but imbued with driving ambition and gifted with a genius for oratory. He made a bad and vindictive enemy. He fastened upon Gloucester as his obvious ally in a crusade to unseat his arriviste in-laws. The pair met at Northampton on 29 April as Richard travelled south with the King's escort some 14 miles further down the Great North Road at Stony Stratford.

The view of Buckingham as a kind of evil genius may not be entirely removed from the truth. The destruction of the Woodvilles offered a shin-ing panorama of influence in Wales and the North Midlands. If Richard had not been plotting a coup during all the years he had acted as the faithful ser-vant then his actions in 1483 were prompted by opportunism or panic. Buckingham would be just the eloquent insinuator necessary to feed on the fear, and stoke the fire, of chance. Having agreed their joint strategy, both dukes had written to the boy king at Ludlow, enquiring as to his travel arrangements so that they might attend him on his journey and pay their re-spects, allegedly that their retinues might join with his to boost the specta-cle as the royal cavalcade entered London. The King and his uncle saw nothing sinister in this proposal, indeed why should they – Richard of Gloucester was the Crown's chief and most distinguished officer, with an unblemished record of public service.

Oblivious to the jaws of the trap that were closing about them, Rivers and Sir Richard Grey, the Queen's son by her former marriage, turned back toward Northampton to welcome the Protector. The pair, unsuspecting, enjoyed a cordial dinner with the two Dukes but, in the morning, as the wine fumes cleared, they found themselves under arrest, isolated from the King's party, of which Gloucester had now simply taken charge. In this single, bold move the Woodville's were checkmated. The royal escort put up no resistance – was the Duke not Lord Protector? Besides, Gloucester and

Buckingham had plenty of hard-faced northerners to back them up; Sir Thomas Vaughan and several lesser figures were added to the haul.

> *But when the Lord Ryvers understood the gates closed and the ways on every side beset, neither his servants nor humself suffered to go out, perceiving well so great a thing without his knowledge not begun for naught, comparing this manner present with last night's cheer, in so few hours so great a change marvellously misliked.*[6]

If Edward V was surprised by this turn of events, then his confusion is entirely understandable. The two dukes adopted a suitably rehearsed approach:

> *Wherefore they [Gloucester and Buckingham] reached the young king ignorant of the arrest and deprived of his soldiers, and immediately saluted him as their sovereign. Then they exhibited a mournful countenance, while expressing profound grief at the death of the king's father whose demise they imputed to his ministers as being such that they had but little regard for his honour, since they were accounted the companions and servants of his vices, and had ruined his health.*[7]

It was a coup in all but name, the Woodvilles ousted at a single bloodless stroke. If this was improvisation rather than careful planning, then it was nonetheless masterly. The Queen gathered her remaining children, including the young Duke of York, and fled to sanctuary at Westminster – though her flight was not so hasty as to prevent her from dragging a portion of the royal coffers with her from the Tower. Any outward show of amity quickly evaporated. The Protector, with his confederate Buckingham and 500 broadswords, rode into the capital on 4 May, the date set for his nephew's coronation. His manifesto was simple – he, Gloucester, the loyal and honest sibling, the late King's Lieutenant in the north, had rescued the young king from the clutches of a gang of ruthless adventurers, a quantity of 'captured' arms was paraded, evidence of the Woodvilles' evil intent.

So unblemished was the Duke's record of public service that no discordant voices were heard. Five hundred men was not an army but these were the big-boned, tough riders from the northern Marches and Warwick's former estates, an alien and frightening breed. It would have been a brave and somewhat foolhardy man who dared speak up – besides, the Woodvilles had no friends, their ruthless greed had deprived them of any allies other than themselves. Although Rivers and Grey were safe, the Earl's younger brother, Edward, still controlled the fleet, riding in the Downs. To contain this hostile squadron Richard moved swiftly to garrison the south coast and, using bribery, attempted to win the ships from their admiral. The crews of two large Genoese vessels, the main props, were quickly seduced – they overpowered the guards Woodville had placed aboard and defected. This crack became a fissure and the fleet disintegrated. The Protector now controlled, King, Council, capital and garrisons. His conduct thus far does not smack of opportunism, rather it suggests a high degree of careful planning and finely honed instincts. Hastings and Buckingham played their parts but, as both would discover, Richard could manage perfectly well without either.

Until this point Richard could be said to have acted within his remit as Protector. A new date, 22 June, was set for the coronation. Precisely when he decided to cross his personal Rubicon, the moment at which he resolved to seize the crown, cannot be identified; indeed, we cannot divine if this had always been the intention or whether it simply followed on from crushing the Woodvilles. From early in June 1483 we can detect signs that 'something' is brewing. Letters were sent out to the burgesses of York asking for soldiers. Hinting at Woodville plots, additional correspondence also borne by Sir Richard Ratcliffe and addressed to Lord Neville merely requested urgent, armed support. A muster was planned for the 18th at Pontefract. Northumberland was to command and the army then to march south.[8] Whilst the host did not in fact immediately proceed from Pontefract, what was certain was that Richard was building up his military strength either for a perceived trial of arms or a massive show of force. Another correspondent, Simon Stallworth, writing on 21 June, seems to have been in no doubt that the Protector intended to cram the capital with his armed affinity 'to what intent I know not but to keep the peace'.[9]

An even more sinister turn of events occurred on 13 June[10] in the course of a Council meeting. Hastings, Thomas Rotheram, Archbishop of York and Morton were all arrested as they sat. This was no accident of timing – Gloucester had directed the members to two separate venues so that he could isolate his targets. The wretched Hastings, Gloucester's erstwhile ally, was dragged outside and beheaded without further ceremony and with no semblance of a trial. This was political murder of the most brutal sort. Mancini adds the ironic comment that Hastings, having survived his Woodville enemies, fell at the hand of one he had always called a friend.

Inevitably there has been a great deal of debate as to why Richard turned on his former ally and why he had to be silenced so swiftly. It has been suggested that he was plotting with the Queen, still in sanctuary at Westminster, a most unlikely alliance but one perhaps forged because Hastings had become aware of Richard's true intent – a far darker purpose than he had ever personally intended. More likely, Hastings opposed the use of force to remove the young Duke of York from his mother's care. It was one thing to control the person of the young king, to keep him separate from his Woodville kin, at least until he was crowned, but the need to hold both brothers hinted at something rather different.

Hastings' sudden and savage demise effectively removed any threat of opposition from within the Council. By killing him Richard neutralised any influence which, even as a mere captive, he might still have had with the all-important Calais garrison. There is a chilling certainty over the whole business which suggests some element of careful preparation. To what extent Richard was acting under the malign influence of Buckingham cannot be ascertained; to contemporaries the sudden shift from loyal subordinate to ruthless usurper was bewildering. Three days later Westminster was surrounded by a ring of steel and the Queen bullied into surrendering her youngest son to the care of his uncle; no other choice was left open to her. The ostensible reasoning was that the King could not be crowned without his royal brother in attendance, and that the Duke of York should be entrusted into the care of the Archbishop of Canterbury, Cardinal Bourchier, with impeccable Yorkist credentials.

If the wretched woman had any doubt as to the alternative, the armoured hedge around the precincts provided eloquent testimony. It is perhaps not easy to feel sympathy for Elizabeth Woodville but a mother's anguish, surrendering her precious lamb to the hungry wolf which has already taken another, can easily be imagined and must excite our pity. It must have been a heartbreaking parting. Elizabeth was enough of a realist to know that both boys now stood in peril of their young lives; innocence was no talisman. From this point on, the atmosphere in London became electric, like the slow, static calm before a summer storm. Richard and Buckingham were in absolute control; if the Protector's intentions were not public, rumours abounded. The rule of law was steadily being supplanted by the rule of force. Richard had his hosts poised in the north, and squads of soldiery patrolled the streets. The Marquis of Dorset, having learnt from the fate of his late rival, took to his heels and fled to sanctuary. Despite the best efforts of Richard's henchmen, he slipped the net – perhaps there were those who were now prepared to wish even a Woodville well. What was obvious was that Edward V would not be crowned on 22 June.

In that very week the Reverend Dr Ralph Shaa preached a carefully rehearsed sermon in St Paul's. The text contained a startling revelation that the marriage of the late King to Elizabeth Woodville was bigamous and therefore void, the issue thus mere bastards. The sermon concluded with a plea to Richard, as the only true claimant, to ascend the throne.[11] As Pollard has written:

> *A powerful lobby has long maintained that Edward V was reluctantly but rightly prevented from becoming king because of the shocking revalation of his illegitimacy. The renewal of civil war, by implication, thus resulted from the refusal of some to accept the truth.[12]*

This would be the conclusion Richard would have wished his contemporaries to reach. The case, as we might expect, was expertly constructed but was never tested by the Prerogative Court of Canterbury, or by any impartial enquiry. If Edward was betrothed to Eleanor Butler, thus voiding the subsequent marriage to Elizabeth Woodville, the verdict might lie in the 'not proven' option. The emergence of so profound a revelation at such a point is altogether too convenient for the usurper's case, and the claims of hagiographers that Richard therefore had no choice but to act must be viewed with extreme caution. Even the most sympathetic examination of Richard's conduct reveals a degree of ruthlessness and a cavalier disdain for due process. From the instant of his brother's demise, Richard of Gloucester, like Shakespeare's Prince Hal, becomes a different man, one in whose nature, probity and devotion to duty simply do not feature. On 25 June, Rivers, Grey and Vaughan faced the headsman at Pontefract. After a seemly pause for consideration, Richard had decided the path of duty lay in accepting Dr Shaa's offer – the date for his coronation was set as 6 July. The Croyland Continuator gives a succinct account which clearly expresses the view that Richard and Buckingham had made long and careful preparation:

> *From this day [the date the younger sibling was removed from sanctuary], these dukes acted no longer in secret, but openly manifested their intentions. For, having summoned armed men, in fearful and unheard of numbers,*

from the north, Wales and all other parts then subject to them, the said pro-
tector Richard assumed the government of the kingdom, with the title of
king, on the twentieth day of the aforesaid month of June; and on the same
day, at the great Hall at Westminster, obtruded himself into the marble
chair. The colour for his act of usurpation.[13]

For the faithful, there were rewards. Richard suffered from the Yorkist deficiency of having a very narrow affinity and one which had a distinctly northern bias. On 28 June Howard was invested as Duke of Norfolk, his heir
elevated to the earldom of Surrey. Viscount Lovell replaced Rivers as Chief
Butler and Hastings as Chancellor, and received other plums, and Sir
Robert Brackenbury was awarded a number of the late Chancellor's
sinecures, including the job of Constable of the Tower. The Council began
to take on a northerly aspect. In addition to Lovell and Brackenbury, Lord
Scrope of Bolton, Sir Richard Ratcliffe,[14] Sir James Tyrrell[15] and Sir Richard
Fitzhugh[16] were all offered places. Both Northumberland and Thomas Lord
Stanley[17] had been previously appointed. Lord Dinham, a southerner, proved
an exception; he was elevated from deputy to captain of Calais and received
the stewardship of the Duchy of Cornwall.

A northern takeover was inevitably resented by the citizens of London
and by southerners generally. That these strong men from distant, northern
shires were now in control was continually evidenced by the bodies of
armed Marchers still on the streets. Whilst the Council was still markedly
Yorkist it did present a subtle shift toward a particular grouping, but
Richard had upset the factional applecart in that he had disinherited the
Yorkist heir, thus prompting a further split. Robbed of power, with the
Queen torn from her children, even the despised Woodvilles took on
stature. Richard's throne was thus secured, but very far from being secure:
already rumours were circulating that the princes had been murdered.[18]

On 26 June, at Baynard's Castle, the Lords and Commons submitted a
formal petition inviting Richard to assume the throne. Preparations for his
coronation were swiftly put into effect, swiftly enough to raise a presumption that such a splendid event may have been in the planning for some time
previously. The ceremony was attended by a suitable display of pomp and a
gratifying array of magnates, Norfolk and Buckingham being much in evidence, as were the Earls of Northumberland, Kent and Lincoln, together
with Lord Stanley and his formidable wife, the mother of Henry Tudor,

Margaret Beaufort. The new King and Queen were resplendent in their attire, and for sheer showmanship the event could not be faulted. If anyone thought of the hapless children immured within the Tower but a short distance away, they took care to keep such thoughts to themselves.

Buckingham's Rebellion

One man who was seemingly dissatisfied with the rewards doled out to him following the coronation was Henry Stafford, Duke of Buckingham. Precisely what caused the fatal rift between the Duke and the King is not known. Buckingham was no Warwick; he was eloquent and voluble, subtle and vindictive, but lacked the Kingmaker's steel core. John Morton, the Bishop of Ely, was under house arrest, confined since the fateful Council meeting on 13 June. He was kept in comfortable confinement within Buckingham's household and it may be, as has been suggested, that it was the subtle churchman who turned the fickle magnate. An important link was the formidable person of Margaret Beaufort – she was the likely conduit through which Buckingham communicated with the exiled Henry Tudor. The lady was also an intimate of Queen Elizabeth and was able to pass freely into the heavily guarded sanctuary at Westminster (though this was so corralled by the King's men it was more like a gaol). Buckingham, as confirmed by his subsequent attainder, was certainly in touch with Tudor before the end of September. The Duke was playing a very dangerous game, he of all people would have been aware of the fate awaiting the King's enemies.

The problem of taking on the Woodvilles was that there were so many of them. Richard's failure to capture Dorset was a serious blow. By the high summer of 1483 the Marquis felt sufficiently emboldened to emerge from hiding and join another surviving brother, the Bishop of Salisbury, in planning a counter-strike. Richard, for all his apparent success, had much to fear, and these were new enemies, men from within the Yorkist faction but who remained loyal to the line of Edward IV. Dorset could count upon knights such as Sir Richard Haute and John Guildford, already within the wider Woodville affinity, but also upon a host of figures from the late King's household – loyal Yorkists but who had found themselves displaced by this new northern clique.

If Henry Tudor had, thus far, rated only as a rank outsider, an exile of little account, the usurpation brought about a significant shift. Lancaster had no other heir and, with support from the Woodvilles, he might attract a following amongst disaffected Yorkists. There were few who believed that the Princes were still alive at this point. The Queen had daughters of marriageable age – an alliance with Tudor would regenerate and unite opposition to Richard. Until this point Henry had lived in unconsidered and obscure exile, presiding over a rump of defeated Lancastrians which included his uncle, Jasper Tudor. Though Richard had seen off the potential menace posed by Edward Woodville's fleet, the two vessels that had stayed loyal, *Trinity* and *Falcon*, together with their admiral, threw in with him. Immediately, therefore, there was a budding recognition that exiled Lancastrians and anti-Ricardian Yorkists might find common cause.

In the high summer of 1483, this swell of rancour was disjointed and largely unfocused, arising in Kent, the Home Counties and the west. Prominent amongst these potential rebels were the dead king's brother-in-law Sir Thomas St Leger, Sir John Fogge, Sir John Cheyne, George Brown, William Norris, William Stonor, William Berkeley, Giles Daubeney and Peter Courtenay, Bishop of Exeter, all of whom had been of the late King's affinity. The Courtenays were active in their kinsman's camp; the present head of the clan was thirsting after recovery of the lost earldom. What is significant amongst this stirring are signs of active co-operation between old Yorkists and old Lancastrians, and, ultimately, the emergence of a serious contender in the person of Henry Tudor.

Richard's finely tuned antennae picked up traces of these murmurings. The King had to be aware that the northern bias would cause resentment, and whatever fate had befallen the Princes, he could not fail to be aware of the wave of popular outrage their disappearance had sparked. At this point, however, he clearly had no doubts concerning Buckingham, who was placed in charge of the commissioners appointed to investigate these ripples of discord. Whether the Duke was the kingpin in a finely wrought plan – a series of concerted risings, or whether these were simply reactions, cannot be ascertained. Maidstone, Newbury, Salisbury and Exeter were all designated as flashpoints for the rebel musters. Tudor, funded by Brittany, would launch an amphibious landing somewhere on the south coast whilst Buckingham would raise his standard in Wales then march south to support the rest. The plan was that the King, faced with so many assaults from varying quarters, would be unable to concentrate his forces effectively against any single rising.

Exactly what degree of co-ordination between the varying rebel contingents existed is unclear. There is a suggestion that the Kentishmen were on the move prior to 18 October, the 'official' start date which Crown officers later assigned to events, although this may smack more of bureaucratic convenience than actual military activity. Evidence from the Paston correspondence would suggest disturbances in Kent were in the offing at least a week sooner, and the King appears already, at that point, to have been aware of his former ally's hand in the affair. If the Duke was counting on support from the magnates for his treasonable activities, he would be sorely disappointed. He may have had hopes of Lord Stanley but, as Henry Tudor would later discover, his step-father was exceedingly circumspect in his dealings, and, certainly in the autumn of 1483, remained outwardly loyal to Richard.[19] The risings were centred in the south and supported only by certain gentry and the commons, there was, as yet, no widespread discontent.

Richard reacted with his customary zeal, ordering a general muster at Leicester for the 21st. Four days later he announced an amnesty for any of the commons who might be having second thoughts. As for the leaders, each had a price fixed to his head, neatly graded in accordance with his perceived worth.[20] To contain Buckingham in Wales the King could offer the lure of his wide acres, a chance to despoil. This was very appealing; the Vaughans, led by Thomas, son of Sir Roger, mounted watch on the westward routes from Brecon while Humphrey Stafford did likewise in the east, mounting guard and breaking the bridges. The King's decisiveness was matched by the fury of autumnal rains that flooded the valleys and corralled Buckingham in his dismal march along the swollen banks of the Wye. Before his soaking followers had advanced as far as Hereford, the Duke's nerve broke and he stole away to seek refuge in the home of a supposed adherent, Ralph Bannister of Lacon Hall by Wem. Bannister promptly betrayed him to the County Sheriff of Shropshire, an act which earned the turncoat a share of the condemned man's dismembered estates. The rebellion in Wales was over almost before it had begun and without a blow being struck. Any concerted plan which may have existed was unravelling at a very rapid rate.

The King was solidly supported by the Howards; Norfolk garrisoned the capital whilst Stanley and Percy kept the north in check. The revolt spluttered out in disarray, rebels melting away as the royal army marched into the south-west. Buckingham's career was brought to a close by the headsman's axe at Salisbury on 2 November. Richard had no more mercy for his brother-in-law Sir Thomas St Leger. Henry Tudor had made landfall perhaps by Plymouth but, seeing how matters stood, he wisely weighed anchor, hoisted sails and returned to Brittany.[21] The rebellion was over and King Richard had surmounted the first serious threat to his authority. If the King had cut off the main head of the rebellion, most of the leaders, including Dorset, escaped to swell the ranks of the exiles. A rash of attainders followed, with the spoils again favouring the northerners. Sir Marmaduke Constable netted the dead Duke's lordship of Tonbridge and Penshurst in Kent. Brackenbury was given life tenure of the shrievality of the same county. Sir Robert Percy appointed as sheriff of both Essex and Hertfordshire; Scrope of Bolton headed the commissioners detailed to attend to matters in the westerly counties.

Thus the northerners appeared firmly in the ascendant. Such largesse, with its very strong regional bias, helped consolidate the King's grip on the north. It cemented the loyalty of his affinity but it did nothing to lessen the southerners' resentment – that could only fester and grow. The 'Great Chronicle of London' describes the general antipathy to this plague of northerners:

> In these days [second half of 1484] were chief rulers about the king, the Lord Lovell, and two gentlemen being named Mr. Ratclyff and Mr. Catesby of the which persons was mad a seditious rhyme and fastened upon the cross in Cheap and other places of the city whereof the sentence was as followeth, 'The cat, the rat and Lovell our dog, rulen all England, under an hog.' This was to mean that the forenamed three persons as the Lord Lovell and the other two that is to mean Catesby and Ratclyff ruled this land under the king which bare a white boar for his cognisance.[22]

The alleged creators of this doggerel, two fellows named Turberville and Collingbourne, were both tried for their sedition, and the former, on being convicted, suffered the full ghastly rigour of a traitor's death. In fact, of the three men lampooned, only Ratcliffe was a true northerner – the rhyme is more a skit on the king's inner clique. One consequence of the near bloodless rout of the southern rebels was the addition of survivors to Tudor's meagre band of adherents: Dorset, Bishop Peter and Edward Courtenay, Sir John Cheyney, Sir William Berkeley and Sir Giles Daubeney. The able Dr Morton fled to Flanders but the rest pitched up in Brittany. Henry's swelling affinity included both diehard Yorkists and convinced Lancastrians, a significant realignment of men whose driving motivation was a desire to be rid of the Yorkist Richard. The possibility of a Woodville marriage was thus an appealing one, and in the great cathedral of Rennes on 25 December 1483, Henry undertook to wed Elizabeth of York once he had secured her father's crown. All that now remained was the winning of it.

Once he had taken the throne, Richard had no need of his vast holdings on the Marches. A more aggressive ruler than James III might have sought to gain advantage from the relative insecurity of the new King's position, to make an attempt either on Berwick or at least Dunbar. But James was equally unsure of his position, his relationship with the magnates forever clouded by the debacle at Lauder, and Richard, with Buckingham's attempt firmly crushed, was inclined toward bullishness. The Scottish king's request for an eight-month truce was reduced to two. As the Duke of Brittany had shown himself disposed to assist the Welshman Henry Tudor in his attempt to throw in with Buckingham. The Bretons now felt the weight of Richard's anger.

English privateers, hungry for prizes, found little need to be too punctilious in distinguishing between Breton vessels and those from France or Scotland: a prize, after all, was still a prize. By the start of 1484 Richard was contemplating the renewal of hostilities with Scotland on land. Matters were transformed in April when the King's only son, the sickly Edward of Middleham, died leaving Richard without an heir. Grief and the more pressing threats from exiles abroad proved potent sources of distraction. Plans for a campaign on the borders were shelved and an extension of the truce, until that autumn, was agreed. War at sea nonetheless continued and the English fought a successful fleet action off Scarborough. This and their failure to recover Dunbar, prompted the Scots to seek terms and talks got under way at Nottingham on 7 September. Richard took personal charge of the negotiations with the Scottish commissioners, and the terms of a further truce to endure for three years were hammered out. To broker a lasting accord Prince James was now to be betrothed to Anne de la Pole, the King of England's niece and sister of the Earl of Lincoln, Richard's most likely heir since the death of Edward of Middleham. The thorny question of the English occupation of Dunbar and Berwick remained unresolved, possession proving the more powerful argument; Dunbar could provide the same anchor to an English Pale as Guines across the Channel, and would not lightly be given up.

Few kings of England since the days of Longshanks possessed such a detailed knowledge of the workings of justice on the border Marches as

Richard III. Though nominally West March Warden, the King delegated most of his duties to Lord Dacre as deputy and proxy. Under the terms of this new agreement the wings of wardens on both sides of the line were clipped, any who was found to have fomented discord faced attainder (this may have been an attempt to forestall any such large-scale unrest as Albany had sponsored in 1479). The Council of the North, Richard's creation, effectively took over the functions of wardens' courts, and the usual bills would be heard at twice-yearly joint meetings. Whilst Henry Percy, 4th Earl of Northumberland, was confirmed in his offices of East March Warden and Governor of Berwick, his commission, which expired on 8 December, does not appear to have been renewed. The very existence of the Council of the North served to undermine Percy hegemony, and, though he had always enjoyed cordial relations with the Earl, Richard was ever mindful of the overmighty subject.

Henry Tudor

It was time now to take seriously the threat of this Welsh upstart, living in apparent security at the court of Duke Francis of Brittany. The Bretons were highly vulnerable at sea, the Duke possessed a fleet but Richard could command the greater navy, and Breton ships became sure prizes for English masters. Francis had other, even more pressing concerns – he had no male heir and the French Crown would be unlikely to forgo the chance of recovering the duchy once he died. Louis' death in August and the accession of a minor provided a respite, but England was the main hope if Bretons wanted to maintain their quasi-independence from France.

The presence of Henry Tudor on Breton soil was thus a distinct embarrassment, and doubly so after Richard and Francis came to a more amicable accord in the late spring of 1484, an agreement whereby the King of England offered the Duke a brigade of longbows should the duchy be threatened. Henry, acute as he was, would soon divine that the wind was shifting and that he was Francis' trump. Tudor chroniclers relate an exciting tale of Henry's breathless escape from the Breton court, one bound ahead of pursuit. It was Morton, in Flanders, who got wind of the conspiracy, orchestrated by Pierre Landois, Breton Treasurer and the man holding the reins of government during the course of an illness which had afflicted the Duke, whereby the exiled Lancastrian was to be sold on to Richard III.

There may be some dramatic licence in this, but by that autumn Henry was re-established at the French court, his welcome fuelled by that residual dislike the Universal Spider had developed for Richard in the face of the latter's hostility in 1475. The increasingly Yorkist complexion of the diminutive exiled court received a distinct leavening when John de Vere, Earl of Oxford, held captive in Hammes since the failure of his raid on St Michael's Mount, managed to engineer his escape. Oxford was accompanied by a further brace of Yorkists, John Fortescue and James Blount. The Earl was an experienced and constant soldier – he provided Henry with a commander of note. The Tudor tide was rising. With these defections Richard's grip on the vital bastion of Calais suddenly appeared a great deal less firm. As ever, the King's response was energetic: Sir James Tyrrell was sent to take over Guines. At the end of the year, Lord Dinham laid siege to Hammes which eventually capitulated on terms. Dinham himself was replaced in the spring by John of Gloucester, the King's bastard.[23]

In March 1485, it was Anne's turn to follow her son Edward of Middleham to the grave. Her death was made uglier by a rash of rumours that the King had used poison and now, perversely, sought the hand of his niece Elizabeth. Rumour alleged he had become infatuated with her after he had reached a pragmatic understanding of sorts with his sister-in-law enabling her, together with her surviving children, to leave sanctuary.

The Croyland Continuator comments on the King's need for ready cash and the unscrupulous means used to fill the depleted royal coffers. The chronicler casts a sour glance at the false jollity of the court that December and gives voice to the rumours regarding his infatuation with his niece:

> [D]uring this feast of the Nativity, far too much attention was given to dancing and gaiety, and vain changes of apparel presented to Queen Anne and the Lady Elizabeth, the eldest daughter of the late king, being of similar colour and shape; a thing that caused the people to murmur and the nobles and prelates greatly to wonder thereat; while it was said by many that the king was bent, either on the anticipated death of the queen taking place, or else, by means of a divorce, for which he supposed he had quite sufficient grounds, on contracting a marriage with the said Elizabeth.[24]

Continuing this theme, the chronicler records the onset of the Queen's terminal illness, which occurred very shortly thereafter, the assertion being that the King planned to marry his niece, partly to forestall Tudor and partly so that he might beget an heir. Richard is accused of shunning his wife's bed during the course of this unexplained malady, though, of course, it may be that the complaint was contagious! In any event, he was obliged to issue a disclaimer, averring that he had no intention of seeking the hand of the Princess Elizabeth. This was sound policy, for the rumours were becoming uglier and he could not afford to offend his friends in the north by giving credence to any suggestion that he had done away with his wife who was, after all, a Neville.

Richard, during the summer months of 1484, had established his strategic base at Nottingham, where he was well placed to react to a threat from any point of the compass. His treasury still held the residue of his brother's pecuniary legacy and he had honours in hand, garnered from the earlier attainders, with which to win friends. As time went by, these resources would be quickly gobbled up by the costs of maintaining so strong a defence. The Welshman too, was not without financial difficulties, his potential patrons in France being diverted by political uncertainty there. As summer waned and winter approached, the conflict bickered in a propaganda war. Richard, on 7 December, denounced his adversary as a ruthless adventurer in league with the ancient and despised foe. This was given an edge when commissions of array were sent out the following day and, on the 18th, a full return of the military capacity of the realm was demanded.

For the King a contest with this new pretender would serve a double purpose: if successful, his throne would be secure, both physically and spiritually; if God granted victory. Richard would be vindicated – trial by combat offered salvation and an affirmation of legitimacy. Michael Jones, in his *Bosworth 1485: the Psychology of a Battle*, suggests that Richard may have been inspired by the parallel between his fortunes and those of Isabella of Castile who had overcome doubts as to the validity of her accession by trouncing her enemies at the Battle of Toro in 1476. This is conjecture, of course, not necessarily fanciful but without an evidential base. Henry Tudor was able to oblige – an English accord with Brittany had alarmed the French sufficiently to persuade them to provide funding for an expedition. In spring 1485, the Welshman moved his base to Rouen and began the work of assembling a modest squadron. Such moves could scarcely pass undetected – the King's spies had confirmed his fears of an invasion sometime during the summer, the English fleet was made ready to intercept, with George Neville appointed to command. The trustworthy Viscount Lovell took charge of coastal defences at Southampton, further propagandist blasts were loosed, and the shire levies put into order. By April Richard had returned to his command post at Nottingham. It was now simply a matter of waiting.

For Henry, Wales had to offer the most attractive landfall. Jasper Tudor had influence there, Sir William Stanley had a Marcher role, and Wales offered the prospect of attaining the Stanley lands in Shropshire and Cheshire. An advance through the Principality would take some time to counter and would give adherents the necessary time to come in. Henry was certainly in touch with the Stanleys, from whom he most likely received some intimation of support. Another target for covert diplomacy was the equally inscrutable Henry Percy, 4th Earl of Northumberland, Richard's principal ally in the north. If he could be suborned, or even neutralised, the pretender's task became that much less insurmountable. Time was a luxury neither side possessed. The cost of maintaining all-round defence was crippling Richard's over-taxed treasury; Henry understood the need for decisive action before his uncertain coalition dissolved – already the cracks were showing with the unreliable Dorset exhibiting fractious tendencies.

The Campaign

It was in high summer that Henry Tudor launched his bid – slender forces carried by a scratchbuilt French squadron, under the flag of Guillaume de Gasenove. The Welshman commanded perhaps 500 English exiles and three times as many Norman mercenaries led by Philibert de Chandee. Tudor was aiming for a landfall on the South Wales coast. His trumps were his own Welsh blood and the promise of help from local magnates such as Sir Gilbert Talbot[25] and Sir John Savage[26] with the hope of others, Rhys ap Thomas[27] and the Stanleys,[28] joining the colours after a successful landing. On 1 August the tiny fleet weighed anchor, and six days later, as a brilliant summer sun was dipping into the west, made landfall at Milford Haven. The whole business was an immense gamble. Henry Tudor brought very few soldiers. He was untried in war and was pitting himself against an entrenched opponent, a proven captain with the resources of all England at his call. Time was thus of the essence. The invader needed to gauge and marshal support before King Richard could strike.

That first evening, Henry took Dale Castle located just over Dale Point. There was no fight as such and the next day he marched the 10 miles to Haverfordwest. Such decisiveness was needed if Henry was to garner the supporters he was so counting on. Within three days he had moved on to Llanbadarn. There was a moment of concern at Cardigan, where the rebels believed themselves at risk from imminent attack by crown forces under Sir Walter Herbert. No such assault took place, but if that was comfort, the lack of recruits proved quite the reverse. Nothing could have been more galling for the Tudor than to see precious time slipping by whilst his tiny army languished in Wales. Without strong local support he could not guarantee the continued willingness of his mercenary corps. The free lances would be careful to weigh the odds and, if these defected, his diminutive rump could hope for nothing beyond escape. If this attempt failed then there was little prospect of another. On the 12th, however, matters took a distinct turn for the better when Rhys ap Thomas and his affinity came in at Newton.[29]

With these reinforcements, still modest in scale, Henry marched on toward Shrewsbury, evey step westwards taking him closer to an inevitable confrontation. Even with his Welsh allies, the pretender could not hope to contest Richard. But on the 15th at Newport Sir Gilbert Talbot, Shrewsbury's uncle, brought a further 500. The news from the Stanleys was far more equivocal. When the rebels entered Shrewsbury, Henry found both cash and assurances – but not a single billman wearing their eagle's claw livery. Lord Stanley, his stepfather, would move when the time was ripe. He had withdrawn from court, but his heir Lord Strange remained a 'guest' of the King, a hostage in all but name, and Stanley, with a father's anxious eye, knew the host to be ruthless. The Stanleys exercised considerable sway in the north-west and possessed strong Yorkist credentials. In the inter-magnate brawling of the 1470s they had sought, by force of arms, to dispossess the Harringtons of Hornby Castle in North Lancashire, the latter having, ironically, been weakened by their losses in fighting for York at Wakefield. Richard had intervened on their behalf, conduct not likely to endear him to the circumspect Stanleys.

In June Richard had moved his headquarters back to Nottingham, an eminently sensible choice, the great fortress standing at the heart of his realm, facilitating deployment in whatever direction events might dictate. Knowing that the pretender was on the seas, the King ordered his Great Seal be sent to him; as soon as news of the landing was confirmed he ordered a general muster at Leicester. It has been suggested that Richard moved less speedily than a rapid response would require. He might have expected the Stanleys to guard the western approaches, though he clearly had doubts as to Lord Stanley's loyalty. Equally, there was a case for allowing the rebels to land and move inland – even if, as was the case, they picked up some reinforcements, they would be no match for the royal army, and the further they marched from the sea, the more complete their ruin in defeat. For Richard, like Isabella of Castile before him, this was to be the definitive test. If his kingship was robust enough to destroy Henry Tudor, then the crown would sit more lightly; trial by battle was vindication, God's judgement.

It is unlikely that the King intended the invaders to advance unchecked as far as Shrewsbury. Herbert had failed to intercept, Rhys ap Thomas had played the turncoat and the Stanleys generally were conspicuous by their absence. Lord Stanley now sought to avoid the muster at Leicester by feigning illness, the sweating sickness, 'crafty sick'. Lord Strange's situation took a turn for the worse, not entirely to be unexpected. He was put to the question and blurted out that his uncle, Sir William, was in treasonable communication with Sir John Savage, a known Tudor sympathiser (and probably mouthpiece for the Stanleys). The young man probably offered these admissions to divert attention from his father. As it was, he wrote, doubtless with persuasion, a strong letter to his parent urging him to reconsider his proposed absence from the royal muster.

By this time Sir William Stanley had at least committed himself to entering into face-to-face talks with his brother's stepson. The meeting took place at Stafford on 17 August, though the bulk of Sir William's adherents were left encamped at Stone, carefully distanced from the rebel banners. Henry was clearly offered encouragement for, the following day, he continued his advance into an enthusiastic Lichfield where, it is said, the townsmen discharged ordnance to greet his arrival. Nonetheless, the Stanley affinity outwardly stayed aloof. Lord Stanley vacated the town prior to Henry's approach – his position was, to say the least, finely balanced. He could have no doubts as to the fate awaiting his son if Richard was given evidence of treachery. As it was, he avoided direct contact with his wife's son, but kept his forces moving on a parallel course eastwards. In so doing he might appear to be on his way to the King's muster at Leicester.

Richard, if he appreciated the faintheartedness of some of his officers, found enthusiasm for the royal cause rather more lukewarm than he had perhaps anticipated. The Duke of Norfolk had written to Sir John Paston, begging him to come:

Wherfor, I pray yow that ye meet with me at Bery, for, be the grace of God, I purposse to lye at Bery as upon Tewsday nyght, and that ye brynge with yow

seche company of tall men as ye may goodly make at my cost and charge, be
seyd that ye have promysyd the Kyng; and I pray yow ordeyne them jakets of
my levery, and I shall contente yow at your metyng with me.

Yower lover etc.[30]

But the knight stayed away. Sir Richard Brackenbury, at Stoney Stratford,
found that Sir Thomas Bourchier and Walter Hungerford, believed to be
waverers, had turned into defectors. Northumberland at least appeared loyal –
his northerners arrived at Leicester, yet the Earl had somehow overlooked
the need to inform the fiercely loyal citizens of York, keen to muster, where
their King's army was to be found. The scent of treachery was in the air. If
Richard was prone to what would now be termed paranoia, then this was
not without foundation. It was also on 17 August that the King rode to
Leicester. Three days later his enemy reached Tamworth. Beyond the town,
in the deepening dusk, the Tudor somehow became separated from the
bulk of his modest army and remained so until the following dawn, having
passed what must have been a vexing and disturbing night – a brush with
Yorkist patrols could have spelt disaster.

At Atherstone, he received a welcome reinforcement from Sir John Savage and had a further parley with his will o' the wisp allies, the Stanleys,
both brothers now in attendance. Sir Thomas and Sir William continued to
prevaricate. They had large forces in the field but would still not commit,
for young Lord Strange this would be a sure sentence of death. For Lord
Stanley, his son's presence as a hostage in the royal train, whilst undoubtedly
of major concern, was the perfect excuse for staying firmly on the fence.
Henry was too canny to have any illusions about the Stanleys, they remained opportunists. His real support was still dangerously thin.

Nonetheless, the die was cast. Henry had crossed the Rubicon and there
could be no going back. If he was deficient in experience, he was not bereft
of firm resolve. Richard, being apprised of the invader's recent moves,
marched out of Leicester on the 21st, proceeding, in the heat-laden dust of
summer, through Peckleton and Kirkby Mallory to Sutton Cheney. Henry
now hastened to conform, the combined affinities of the two Stanley brothers marching on a parallel but apparently separate course. Thus it was three
rather than two armies which were now converging. By dusk on the 21st
the main protagonists were encamped a bare four miles apart. Henry had
pitched his tents at Whitemoors whilst Richard had, almost certainly, already determined that the rise of Ambion Hill which lay roughly between

them, formed the ground upon which he would fight. For both men, one thing was not in doubt – the next day, 22 August, would decide their individual destinies and determine the fate of England.

The Battle of Bosworth

The Battle of Bosworth is one of the most important encounters in British history. It is to be regretted that the contemporary writers have left us with such a meagre outline. The Croyland Continuator provides some insights, but the fullest account comes later, from Polydore Vergil. Whilst not strictly contemporary, he had the inestimable advantage of being able to glean testimony from some of those who fought on the field, particularly the Earl of Oxford. A number of writers, most recently Michael Jones in 2002, have expressed doubts as to the battle's true location – a fascinating and worthy debate but beyond the scope of their current work.

Ambion Hill[31] is a spur, some 400 feet in height, which juts in a south-westerly direction rising from a gentle swell to quite a marked decline, the crest some 700 yards across. Richard would approach from the east, from Sutton Cheyney, which itself sits on the back of a shallow ridge. Though the ground was devoid of cultivation or woodland, difficulties of space meant it would not be possible to fully deploy either army along the ridge itself; supporting forces would be echeloned toward the rear, hampering a rapid movement of reserves. Nonetheless, it was a strong and commanding eminence, the left girded by a bog (now forested). The lower road to Sutton Cheyney circled the base.[32] Richard, with typical dash, seized the initiative, his greater experience at marshalling the host much in evidence, accepting the risk of advancing in column to maintain momentum. Norfolk led the van, the King the centre, with Northumberland bringing up the rear. Legend insists that the King paused to consult with his officers by the ancient burial, since called 'Dickon's Nook', which stands just north of the village by the fork in the road.

There are suggestions that he treated his army to a rousing address, but more likely he gave a simple exhortation. Some tantalising fragments suggest he hinted toward a confession of the murder of his nephews and that he should rather be judged by his actions since attaining the throne than the taking of it. But there is no certainty as to this. It would be very tempting to imagine the King seeking some form of atonement and that his 'crimes', as Shakespeare would have us believe, weighed heavily on his conscience.

Vergil, whom we may presume to have had the benefit of eyewitness testimony, described the scene:

> *It is reported that King Richard had that night a terrible dream; for he thought in his sleep that he saw horrible images as it were of evil spirits haunting evidently about him, as it were before his eyes, and they would not let him rest.*[33]

Henry too was on the march. If he lacked Richard's experience he possessed a considerable military asset in John de Vere, Earl of Oxford, but his prickers were less able and the rebels' advance from their camp at Whitemoors brought them up against the formidable obstacle of the marsh. This necessitated a sharp turn to the north for the van, a dangerous move with one flank fully exposed to Norfolk's men crowning the ridge above. This alignment necessitated a leftward shuffle for some 300 paces, time enough for Norfolk to advance to contact had he deemed the moment opportune. The Duke, doubtless to the Tudor's relief, did not elect to move, preferring to retain the considerable advantage offered by the rising ground. The rebels now deployed to conform, Oxford and the mercenary de Chandee taking the exposed van. Henry himself commanded the centre, drawn up behind with two smaller brigades, Savage on the left and Talbot to the right.

Bizarrely, and uniquely in the military history of the period, the third 'shadow' army of the Stanleys split, Sir William to the north and Sir Thomas to the south, watching both sides but aligned with neither. Those men standing beneath Sir William's banner must particularly have caused Richard great unease: they were only a few hundred yards' distant from his exposed right. A flank attack would be potentially catastrophic, whilst Lord Stanley, though effectively isolated from the royal left by the marsh, could swiftly advance to shore-up the rebel right. It was a very singular and worrying position. Richard, on the one hand, held the high ground and appeared to dominate his foes arrayed before the royal van, but if those treacherous Stanleys played him false, and this surely had to be their intention, then their intervention could decide the day.

In terms of numbers, the best estimate we have for the King's army suggests that Norfolk, with the van, commanded 1,200 archers and 200 horse; the King 1,000 bills and twice as many pikes; Northumberland 2,000 foot and, perhaps, 1,500 light horse on the flanks – a total of almost 8,000.[34] Tudor undoubtedly led far fewer men, but the two Stanley contingents combined, were they to be committed, would have boosted his army to near parity. If the Stanleys were worrying the King, their deployment offered little comfort for the pretender. The royal army had the higher ground and greater weight of numbers. Henry had begged Sir William Stanley to come up, but received yet another equivocal response. It was clear to both generals that the spectators would remain just that until it looked as though the day was decided – and then advance to join the victors. For the Stanleys themselves this procrastination was dangerous; no king ever likes a king-maker and neither Richard nor Henry would ever repose trust in such fair-weather allies. If the King gained the victory, retribution was certain.

As the sun strengthened and rose in the summer sky, a dazzling display of banners fluttered proudly against the perfect blue – the red, fire-breathing Tudor dragon, the White Boar of Richard III, Percy's Lion – light reflected from polished harness, shining through clouds of risen dust and the steam of men and horses. The guns unlimbered, businesslike while captains fussed and sighted, matrosses unloading powder and shot, the smell of battle, of sweat, of leather and waste and oil on mail. A seeming infinity of waiting, hosts in line, guns charged, air then rent by the crack of ordnance, belching filthy smoke and sending roundshot skipping, archers straining at the draw. The Battle of Bosworth opened with a conventional archery duel, which appears to have been inconclusive as neither side was so stung as to force the advance to contact. In the event, both moved forward together, the clash coming on the lower slopes as bill strained and thrust against bill, both vanguards fully engaged.

This contest probably spanned an hour or more – a soldier's battle of heaving, sweating, intense combat; a melee of crashing steel; the screams of wounded and dying; dry grass slippery with blood, faeces and entrails. At some point, whilst this conflict raged, the two Stanley contingents, hovering like prowling jackels, began to narrow the gap, yet still not joining the fight. To Henry this must have been galling: his men were outnumbered and if the battle continued then the attrition of his lesser forces would alone be sufficient to grant Richard the victory. Despite the odds, Oxford and his French mercenaries gave a good account of themselves, generally gaining the upper hand. Both generals fed in fresh men from the main body to stiffen their respective lines. The Duke of Norfolk, taking station in the thick of the fight to rally his men, became a casualty:

There was a marsh betwixt both hosts, which Henry of purpose left on the right hand, that it might serve his men instead of a fortress, by the doing thereof also he left the sun upon his back; but when the king saw th'enemies passed the marsh, he commanded his soldiers to give charge upon them. They making suddenly great shouts assaulted th'enemy first with arrows, who were nothing faint unto the fight but began also to shoot fiercely; but when they came to handstrokes the matter was then dealt with blades.[35]

What exactly happened next is subject to debate. The generally held view is that Henry Tudor decided on directing a personal appeal to Sir William Stanley, whose fresh troops were now so tantalisingly close. The Welshman's frustration can well be imagined, his cause in imminent peril of extinction whilst his supposed allies took their ease nearby. Such a move is certainly understandable and arguably would not have weakened his position overall as Oxford was directing the fight. Equally, it could be suggested that for any commanding general to quit the fray at so critical a juncture was grossly negligent. Richard III, from his vantage, watched this tiny mounted group, the pretender's banner waving defiance, ride off toward Stanley. Seizing the opportunity, Richard now led his household knights in a downhill scramble to intercept and destroy. This may be considered bold, even brilliant, to seize the moment to cut off the monster's head – but it was also rash, for as his cavalry thundered down the slope Stanley could immediately perceive Tudor's peril. He could no longer continue to sit on the fence; the moment of crisis was developing in front of his very eyes. He had to act; if Henry Tudor fell, the Stanleys were fallen too. Sir William knew Richard well enough, there would be no second chances, no hiding place.

The last Plantagenet King, at the head of his knights, smashed into the ranks of his opponent. There could be little doubt as to the outcome. Henry's standard bearer, Sir William Brandon fell, possibly to Richard's lance. None of the battles in the conflict had, so far, been decided by cavalry action alone; Richard had seized the initiative but at great risk – once committed to the charge, the horse were removed from the cover of the foot, exposed should impetus be checked. And it was. For Stanley, the moment of decision was at hand – Sir William sounded the advance and his entire force now engulfed the King's Household, their horses blown, momentum gone. Rarely can the fortune of war have altered so swiftly. Richard died bravely, wielding his war hammer to lethal effect until he was unhorsed, overpowered and cut down:[36] 'King Richard alone was killed fighting manfully in the thickest press of his enemies.'[37]

Whether Plantagenet and Tudor came to hand-strokes is perhaps less certain than Vergil asserts, though the tableau makes a fine dramatic flourish. Stanley's attack was certainly put in none too soon. An alternative version also persists, however. This insists that the Stanleys moved, in concert, to converge on the flanks of the royal army, showing their true colours as the clash between the two vanguards reached its height. If the beleaguered van and any residual units in the centre were thus assailed on both flanks, disaster was certain. Northumberland would not respond, his rearguard remaining supine, scarce further forward than Dickon's Nook. Richard, therefore, directed his charge not to the right in the hope of catching Tudor but to the left against the traitor Lord Stanley. Orders had been given to dispose of Lord Strange, but these, like the order to Northumberland to advance, were not carried out.

By attacking Stanley, Richard might have hoped to stabilise the field and prevent a rout; victory on the flank would surely be sufficient to persuade Percy to come up. It was a desperate gamble but, in the circumstances, the only throw left. Little wonder that Richard hurtled to his death, yelling 'treason, treason' before his horse became enmired and he fought his last fight on foot. 'Richard's Well', allegedly marking the spot where the King died and which sits within the present confines of the wood, was consolidated in the early nineteenth century by a Dr Parr, when the stone structure was constructed. Legend asserts that it was Thomas, Lord Stanley, who discovered the gold coronet, struck from the dead King's helmet, rolled beneath a hawthorn bush, and that it was he who placed this battered but potent symbol on his stepson's head. This denouement was said to have been enacted on the eminence now known as Crown Hill, where Henry had taken station after the tide of battle ebbed.

The King's death was a signal for the total collapse of the royal army. With no king to fight for, no general to lead, flight remained the only option. The Stanley intervention (whichever version is believed) had proved decisive. Perhaps as many as three thousand men lay dead on the field, mainly from the King's army. Besides Richard, late King of England, the Duke of Norfolk, Sir Robert Brackenbury, Lord Ferrers, Sir Richard Ratcliffe and Sir Gervase Clifton had also fallen. Viscount Lovell, Sir Humphrey and Sir Thomas Stafford managed to escape. Thomas Howard, Earl of Surrey, also escaped but surrendered soon after (it would be some time before the future victor of Flodden was to be fully rehabilitated). William Catesby was less fortunate, captured on the day of the fight, he was dispatched the next.

The citizens of York, recorded in the minutes of the city council, provided their late King with perhaps his most eulogistic obituary:

> *Wer assembled in the counsaill chamber, where and when it was shewed by diverse persones and especially by John Sponer send unto the feld of Redemore [Bosworth] to bring tidinges frome the same to the citie that king Richard late mercifully reigning upon us was thrugh grete treason of the duc of Northfolk and many other that turned agenst hyme, with many other lordes and nobilles of this north parties was piteously slane and murdred to the grete hevynesse of this citie.*[38]

Notes

1 Pollard, *Wars of the Roses*, p. 71.
2 Mancini, pp. 85–91.
3 Hastings' particular foe was Thomas, Marquis of Dorset, the Queen's son by her first marriage; they had quarrelled over the affections of Jane Shore.
4 Mancini, pp. 85–91.
5 P. Hammond and A. E. Sutton, *Richard III: The Road to Bosworth Field* (London 1985), p. 95.
6 Mancini, pp. 42–3.
7 Mancini, as quoted in Hammond and Sutton, op. cit., p. 96.
8 Gillingham, op. cit., p. 221.
9 Ibid., p. 221.
10 Ibid., p. 222n.
11 It was alleged that Edward IV, prior to his infatuation with Elizabeth Gray (née Woodville), had been betrothed to an Eleanor Butler and that this was a binding arrangement which rendered void his subsequent marriage to Elizabeth and made their issue bastards. Clarence's issue were debarred through his attainder, leaving Richard as the only true heir. It was, of course, remarkably convenient for Richard's cause that these facts emerged in such a timely manner.
12 Pollard, *Wars of the Roses*, p. 72.
13 Croyland Continuator pp. 566–7.
14 Sir Richard Ratcliffe was of Cumbrian gentry stock, married to a daughter of Scrope of Bolton; he was appointed as Sheriff of Westmorland in 1483 and quickly rose to be a loyal advisor to the King. He was a beneficiary of a number of the subsequent attainders.
15 Sir James Tyrrell (*c*.1445–1502), a knight of Suffolk. He married a daughter of Sir John Arundel of Cornwall; originally of the Duke of Suffolk's affiliation he served Richard in France in 1475 and then later in the Scottish War. He enjoyed high office but avoided both Bosworth and the subsequent attainders, surviving

until finally executed for treason by Henry VII. He is credited, by Sir Thomas More, with being the murderer of the princes.

16 The Fitzhugh family of Ravensworth in County Durham were part of the old Neville affinity.

17 Thomas, Lord Stanley, 1st Earl of Derby (c.1435–1504). The Stanleys were leading magnates from the north-west; Thomas was, in 1485, married to Henry Tudor's formidable mother, Margaret Beaufort.

18 The question of the Princes in the Tower is covered in Appendix 3.

19 Stanley received his wife's previously confiscated estates as his reward.

20 The senior ringleaders, Buckingham, Dorset and the two bishops, were priced at a reward of either £1,000 or lands worth £100 per annum, whilst lesser fry, the gentry, were valued at £500 or lands worth £40 a year.

21 Gillingham, op. cit., pp. 230–1.

22 GCL p. 236.

23 John of Gloucester was a minor, so the King was, in effect, taking Calais under his personal control.

24 Croyland Continuator pp. 571–3.

25 Sir Gilbert Talbot (1452–1517) was of the powerful Talbot family; he served as High Sheriff of Salop under Richard III but defected to Henry Tudor.

26 Sir John Savage (c.1432–1495) was a son-in-law of Stanley.

27 Rhys ap Thomas had been a supporter of Richard III though the family, who held the extensive Dinefwr estates, were traditionally of Lancastrian affiliation.

28 Sir William Stanley held the office of Lord Chamberlain of North Wales.

29 Thomas had been offered the Lieutenancy of Wales as an inducement.

30 PL vol. 3 p. 320.

31 Ambion or Ambien Hill derives from the Old English Ann Beame – 'one tree'. For a discussion on possible alternative locations; see M. K. Jones, *Bosworth 1485; Psychology of a Battle* (Stroud 2002), pp. 148–50.

32 The field has been much altered by the planting of the wood which now covers the site of the marsh and by the unfortunate proximity of the railway line that runs along the base of the rise.

33 PV (E) pp. 220–7.

34 Burne, *Battlefields*, p. 139.

35 PV (E) pp. 220–7.

36 The traditional view that Richard charged on the right against Tudor is challenged by the assertion that he in fact descended on the left against Lord Stanley; see Haigh, op. cit., p. 162.

37 PV (E) pp. 220–7.

38 *York House Books* transcribed by D. Atreed (Stroud 1991) 2/4 f. 169b.

Chapter 16

Stoke Field 16 June 1487

There was not one left to piss against the wall.
Sir Thomas Craig

Henry VII

Craig's pithy observation concerning the Plantaganet line is broadly correct, though, as Professor Pollard points out, the extinction was due, in no small part, to the assiduous elimination of likely competitors by the first two Tudor rulers. Some families had poured out their blood in torrents, the Percies being a case in point – the second and third earls died in battle as did Lord Egremont and several younger sons, yet the line was not extinguished. The 4th Earl remained a powerful figure and the traditional Percy hegemony in Northumberland continued largely as before. Many magnate families suffered through loss and forfeiture, of course, and even though many attainders were later reversed, the wars proved the ruin of some. Nonetheless, it cannot be said that the overall rate of attrition amongst the landed classes was markedly higher during this period than at other times.[1]

If the magnates were not substantially diminished, it may be that the power of the Crown did not swell so mightily after 1487. Henry VII is credited with establishing strong and centralist government but, whilst the first Tudor monarch's considerable abilities need not be in doubt, this trend was one that can be traced back to the reign of his father-in-law, Edward IV. The whole business of attainder proved useful to both, the reversal of forfeiture and the lure of confiscated estates were powerful means of building and controlling a royal affinity. Yet Henry's position was different from that of his predecessors. The fact that he was an outsider, an opportunist without an established faction, could be construed as a weakness – but he made it a virtue. Those who had followed him were a mix of old Lancastrians (such as Pembroke and Oxford) and disaffected Yorkists (Stanley and Dorset), with a motley of chancers. For a number of these, those who had been exiled, the recovery of their estates was sufficient reward; there was no need to create additional lordships. Some, like Sir William Stanley and Dorset, proved to be liabilities, but they were contained or dealt with. The political calm was not fractured. Henry enjoyed the considerable advantage of having replaced a King who, at least in the south, was largely unpopular. He could hold himself out as the architect of a Yorkist restoration – with the Stanleys favoured, the ruling elite of Edward IV's reign were effectively restored to predominance. Happily for Henry there was no Kingmaker on the scene to have to contend with.[2]

Royal control is perceived as having been inexorably and ruthlessly extended. The new King used his magnates as officers in his administration, but their overall influence in his Council diminished, and those who transgressed found themselves being sharply pulled to heel. Henry understood the power of wealth, he saw stability in being a richer man than his magnates. No Kingmaker would boast, even 'in his cups', that he owned greater estate than his sovereign. His was a significant achievement. He brought three decades of internecine strife to a close and re-established the authority of the Crown, which had, hitherto, been steadily eroded. He is seen as having curtailed the power of the magnates, asserted the rule of law, restored the Crown's finances and established his position as the unchallenged head of a centralised and efficient royal bureaucracy.

Recent writers, such as Christine Carpenter, have identified a particular difficulty in dealing with the reign of Henry VII, what she attributes to 'different historiographical traditions' – the interface between Tudor and Medieval historians. Traditionally 1485 has been identified as a pivotal year, introducing a great change – government of the realm becoming much more a 'king-centred' approach. In fact change was likely a good deal more gradual and Henry's reign did not necessarily witness, as some claim, a shift in power away

Figure 6: King Henry VII

(© National Portrait Gallery, London)

from the magnates to a class of advisers drawn more from the bourgeoisie.[3] An early priority was to gain control of Clarence's heir Edward, Earl of Warwick, and Robert Willougby[4] was dispatched in the immediate aftermath of Bosworth to bring the teenage lad, who lacked full capacity, within the greater security of the Tower. Henry was the titular heir to Lancaster, there being no other claimants, and he could also claim to represent the rump of Yorkist interest, disenfranchised by Richard III. There was a satisfying dearth of competitors. Percy was briefly imprisoned but, by the end of 1485 had been set at liberty and restored to his offices including the March wardenry, a post Lord Strange had briefly occupied in the interim.

Rebellion, when it flared, broke out in the north where Lovell and Humphrey Stafford sought to raise fresh mischief. Both men had sought sanctuary at Colchester after the wrack of Bosworth; both had been attainted but, by the spring of 1486 the former was active in Yorkshire and the latter in Worcestershire. The affair was largely still-born; many men had lost the appetite for conspiracy, most of Richard's northen affinity had accepted Henry's win and had no wish to incur the new King's wrath. At Lincoln when news of the disturbances reached him, Henry continued northwards, correctly gauging that the business would not merit a full muster and that his household knights and retainers would be sufficient for the task. From York, on 23 April, Jasper Tudor, elevated to the dukedom of Bedford, led a force to confront the rebels, and the canny offer to pardon those who laid down their arms prompted a rash of defections. Lovell's following disintegrated. He took temporary refuge with Sir Thomas Broughton[5] who, with Sir John Huddleston,[6] briefly kept the flame flickering in Cumberland. Lovell managed to give the hounds the slip and made good his escape to Flanders. Henry now turned south and west to stamp out the embers of Stafford's attempt. Sir Humphrey and his brother, Sir Thomas, again sought sanctuary, this time at Culham, by Abingdon. Their rebellion had raised no more followers than Lovell's aborted attempt in the north, their faltering cause sustained by a poor mix of rumour and pious hopes. Henry had, however, had quite enough of Humphrey Stafford and, as the royal judges were later to find, the normal rules of sanctuary did not obtain in cases of high treason. Stafford lost his head, though Sir Thomas and the other, lesser malefactors were treated with leniency.

Lambert Simnel

If men were losing their taste for armed conflict, factionalism, as Polydore Vergil later highlighted, once ingrained becomes a difficult trend to reverse. Richard Simons, a priest at Oxford, certainly seems to have thought so when he attempted to pass off one of his protégés as the young Earl of Warwick. This wretched and innocent youth had been the focus of Lovell and Stafford's abortive rising, and the magic of the name created a handy focus for any mutterings of discontent. What is remarkable is how so many influential people found it expedient to believe him, as Vergil relates:

> At Oxford, where he devoted himself to scholarship, he brought up a certain youth who was called Lambert Simnel. He first taught he boy courtly manners, so that if ever he should pretend the lad to be of royal descent (as he had planned to do) people would the more readily believe it and have absolute trust in the bold deceit.[7]

Henry had deemed it wise to parade the captive Earl, so-called, through the streets of the capital on 17 February 1486, to show that he had the young man safe and that, contrary to rumour, he had not been done to death in the Tower. Despite the patent implausibility of his claim, there were those who found it convenient to accept Father Simons' protégé as the real Earl of Warwick. Chief amongst these was John de la Pole, Earl of Lincoln, who had been the most likely heir to Richard III after the death of Edward of Middleham. He had submitted, readily enough, to Henry Tudor in 1485 and appeared to have had no interest in the pretensions of Lambert Simnel until after February 1487. At this point he defected to Flanders where he made common cause with Richard III's sister, his own aunt, the dowager Duchess of Burgundy.[8] In Ireland there was also disaffection, as Henry had refused to confirm Gerald Fitzgerald, 8th Earl of Kildare[9] in his office of Lord Deputy of Ireland. Simons had taken the boy Simnel across the Irish Sea, where he found willing listeners:

> *Having secured their trust, he decribed to them how he had saved from death the Duke of Clarence's son, and how he had brought him to that land, where (so he had heard) the name and family of King Edward were always cherished. The story was readily believed by the nobles and was soon communicated to others.[10]*

Margaret Plantagenet, ever since the death of her husband, Charles the Bold, had continued to wield great influence in Flanders. Her late brother George had been her particular favourite, and the chance to strike a blow at this Welsh usurper and perhaps place her nephew on the throne, was not one to be readily cast aside: 'She [Margaret] pursued Henry with insatiable hatred and with fiery wrath never desisted from employing every scheme which might harm him as a representative of a hostile faction.'[11]

With Lovell on hand in Flanders to stir the pot, this unlikely coalition posed a significant threat to Henry's throne and he, by the time April came around, had begun setting watchers along the coasts of East Anglia, Essex and the south-east. This was entirely logical as this coastline would offer the most opportunities to an invader launching his fleet from Burgundy. In this, Lincoln successfully humbugged the King by doing the unexpected. He and Lovell had sailed for Ireland instead and reached Dublin on 5 May. To give their cause a suitably sharpened edge, Margaret had met the cost of contracting 2,000 tough German professionals under a famous captain, Martin Schwarz:

> *Meanwhile John earl of Lincoln and Francis Lovell, having received from Margaret an army of about two thousand Germans, whose commander was that most martial man Martin Schwarz, crossed over to Ireland and in the city of Dublin crowned as king the lad Lambert.[12]*

On 24 May the rebels mounted a propaganda campaign by ostentatiously crowning the carpenter's son in Christ Church, Dublin and proclaiming him now to be Edward VI of England. A sham of course, but this did not mean the threat was anything other than real. The forces which the rebels could command would be greater than those which had accompanied Henry in his bid two years beforehand. Circumspect as ever, Henry took the precaution of confining the mercurial Dorset, to whom temptatation might prove too great a lure. He also undertook a timely pilgrimage to Walsingham, the royal presence serving as a reminder to the Duke of Suffolk. By the end of April, like Richard III before him, he had established his headquarters in the Midlands, using Coventry and Kenilworth as his major bases.

The Campaign

On 4 June the rebels landed in the north-west, at Peil Island near Furness on the coast of Lancashire.[13] Their total force might have been as great as 9,000.[14] Lincoln would have judged that the north-west and across the hills, Yorkshire and Richmondshire, might offer fertile ground for recruiting from the rump of the old Neville–Gloucester affinity. In this he was to be sadly disappointed. On the first night the army camped by Ulverston, where Sir Thomas Broughton swelled their ranks with his Cumbrians. Their marches next took them through Carnforth, where further disaffected elements of local gentry, Harringtons and Middletons, joined their colours. Later at Sedburgh, other gentlemen – Alexander Appleby of Carlisle, Nicholas Musgrave of Brackenthwaite, together with Clement Skelton of Bowness – also declared.

From Lancashire the invaders initially made for York, capital of the north, marching over the bare, upland sweep of the Pennines, but the city fathers were less than enthusiastic. True, they had been fervent partisans of Richard III, but the Tudor had exerted the lightest of touches and had conferred further honours upon the city. Northumberland had already written to the townsmen warning of his intention to reinforce the city within the span of four days. This tipped the balance and the burgesses replied to Lincoln's summons, which he had issued in the name of 'Edward VI' with aggression. They would refuse entry and man the walls should he resort to force. Spurned by the citizens of York, Lincoln during 9–11 June, swerved southwards toward Tadcaster. This was sound planning – to fritter away precious time trying to leaguer York would have been pointless. Besides, recruiting in Yorkshire was sluggish and sparse. Both Scrope of Bolton and of Masham were sympathetic but would not yet commit. Whilst encamped on Bramham Moor[15] the rebels' ranks were finally swelled by some local adherents: Sir Edmund Hastings of Pickering Lythe and Sir Robert Percy of Scotton.

Son of the notorious 'Butcher', Sir Henry Clifford had spent his youth in hiding and had just managed to claw back his family estates. Keen to demonstrate his commitment to the regime, he had led two companies of his generation's 'Flower of Craven' to reinforce York. Emboldened by the rebels' reluctance to attack the city, he trailed them to Bramham Moor, found them gone and, on 11 June, made camp by Tadcaster. Lincoln, sensing the opportunity for a classic descent and 'beating up' enemy quarters, struck that night and put Clifford to flight, capturing his equipment. Bolstered by this small but stylish success, the rebels continued their southerly passage through Castleford (12 June) toward Rotheram (13th), along the length of Ryknild Street[16] and in the direction of Newark. Passing the Trent would be no easy matter. The castle and bridge were defended by a royal garrison, and Lord Scales with a body of horse was already hanging on their flanks. They halted and drew breath at Southwell.

Henry, having established his headquarters at Kenilworth, did not march out until news of the invasion reached him, some five days after the rebels made landfall. Collecting such forces as could be raised locally, the royal army marched upon Coventry, then toward Leicester (a hard slog of 25 miles), and on to Loughborough. The King was probably still unsure as to whether the blow would fall from east or west of the Pennines but at Loughborough he received clear intimation that the threat now lay in the east and he continued his march toward Nottingham. The army, having run into difficulties of transport and billeting, had failed to make much headway during either of the two days following their departure from Loughborough. At Nottingham, however, the Stanleys came in, led by Lord Strange (Lord Stanley had been elevated to the earldom of Derby). This was the young man who had survived

Bosworth, under the shadow of the axe, now with some 6,000 bows and bills beneath his banner. At this point, the evening of Thursday 14 June, the rival forces were barely a dozen miles apart. Some captured scouts or spies were strung up from an ash tree, at the southern edge of the river crossing.[17]

In the north Clifford, doubtless still smarting from his earlier discomfiture, had joined forces with Northumberland. The Percy had mustered several thousand of his northerners and intended to shadow the rebels on their southward march. However, no sooner had the Northumbrians quit York than, two days later, both John, Lord Scrope of Bolton and Sir Thomas of Masham suddenly, and with a substantial following, appeared and demanded the city gates be opened immediately in the name of 'Edward VI'. The Mayor and burgesses held their nerve and demurred; the townsmen then saw off an attempt to force entry through Bootham Bar. Messengers were sent post haste after the Earl, acquainting him with York's peril. Immediately upon receiving this news, he turned his men around and force marched them north again, only to find the rebels had melted away in the interim. This may simply have resulted from a failure of nerve on their part. Alternatively, to give the Scropes more credit for guile, it may have been a carefully wrought ruse intended to create precisely this effect, drawing the northern royalists away from the rebel rear and leaving Lincoln free to deal with the King's army on more equal terms.

The Battle

The ground that now lay between the two main armies was dominated by the course of the Trent, a wide and full river obstacle, some 150 yards across where it flows between Nottingham and Newark; the ford at Fiskerton is some 4 miles south of the latter. The valley is broad and level, with a range of low ridges that swell gently from the alluvial plain. One of these runs south-west from the town of Stoke, at no point rising higher than 150 feet. This ridge is bisected by another which branches to the east about half a mile from the town and finally sinks into the valley floor after perhaps a mile and a half. The terrain was free of woodland and enclosure.[18]

At a council of war on the evening of 14 June, the King's officers had pressed for an immediate advance toward the rebel army with the aim of bringing on a contest.[19] The royal army had been swelled by a number of fresh contingents; John Morton, who had finally attained the archbishopric of Canterbury, contributed forces as did the Bishop of Winchester, the Earls of Devon, Shrewsbury and redoubtable Oxford were all present. Other veterans of Bosworth, including Sir John Cheyney, also donned harness in the King's cause.[20] Progress on Friday 15th, however, was still slow. The King heard Mass in Nottingham, whilst the marshals were struggling to establish order. Only 7 miles were covered that spring day, and the host encamped on the south bank of the river by Radcliffe. Next morning, a fine Saturday, the march resumed, this time with the army deployed in battle formation, with the van, under Oxford, to the fore. By nine in the morning, with the sun well up, they approached the line of the ridge described above and, arrayed along the crest, stood the rebel army.

The Earl of Lincoln had taken his army over the Trent late on the previous day, splashing through the ford at Fiskerton and planting his colours on the low ridge that dominates the crossing. Michael Bennett has calculated that the river was perhaps no more than 50 yards wide at this point and, in the early summer, perhaps only a couple of feet deep. When, the following morning, the Earl drew up his forces, these were facing away from Stoke and Newark, his prickers having informed him of the location of the royal encampment at Radcliffe. The King would have to therefore continue his advance along the Fossway, and the rebels were ideally placed if they intended to fight. And indeed Lincoln did wish for battle. His efforts at gathering local recruits on his march south had failed to produce significant numbers. With support for his cause no better than lukewarm, he needed to strike a speedy and decisive blow:

> *This field was the sorer foughten by reason that forenamed Martin Schwartz was deceived, for when he took this voyage upon him he was comforted and promised by th'Earl of Lincoln, that great strength of this land after their landing would have resorted unto the said earl. But when he was far entered and saw no such resort, then he knew well he was deceived.[21]*

The rebels' position was a strong one. With their right anchored on the highest point, the Burham Furlong, secured by the line of the river, that flank was secure. The high ground then ran eastwards toward the left which most likely rested on the line of the Stoke–Elston Road. Colonel Burne gives the rebels a frontage of some 1,800 yards, their deployment slightly convex toward the centre, conforming to the ground. This conformity with the terrain did imply the line was not straddling the Fossway head on, but rather inclined away to the left, so the whole was at an angle to the road. The attacker would therefore have to alter his deployment accordingly.

Although Lincoln had failed to win large numbers of recruits and, apart from Lovell and Thomas Fitzgerald, had no magnates standing alongside him, he was, nevertheless, supported by a leavening of gentry: Sir Thomas Broughton, Sir James Harrington, William Kay, William Hammond, Richard Harleston, Sir Henry Bodrugan, Sir John Beaumont, Alexander Appleby, Nicholas Musgrave, Clement Skelton and Thomas David. The English and Germans would be well harnessed; the Irish, however, would be lightly armed and mainly without armour. Lincoln, Lovell and Fitzgerald had little or no battlefield experience; doubtless all three deferred to Schwarz. His mercenaries, equipped with pike and halberd, would be well drilled in the latest continental tactics, in total contrast to the Irish. Bennett surmises, and I concur, that the army was thus drawn up in a wedge-shaped phalanx with the various bodies interspersed to provide some element of cohesion and add weight and momentum to the attack.[22]

The available evidence (and it has to be stressed that accounts of the battle are sparse) confirms that substantial gaps had opened up between the divisions of the royal army and that Oxford, with the van, was dangerously exposed. This suggests both poor intelligence and weak generalship on Henry's part. He should certainly have been aware of the rebel's proximity and their deployment. Oxford, hardened veteran that he was, should not have been left so isolated in the very face of the enemy. It does seem clear that the royal army suffered from rank indiscipline and that the job of the marshals that morning was particularly taxing. If Oxford, leading the van, commanded the more experienced and better-harnessed men and was not constrained to wait for stragglers, or left cursing impotently as ill-trained levies milled in confusion, then it is possible to see how such a gap might open. The accounts also speak of reinforcements being fed piecemeal into the fight, and companies going straight into the melee as they came up.

Oxford, it should be remembered, was no beginner; he was a skilled and experienced practitioner of the art of war. His division was substantial, perhaps 6,000 strong out of a total force perhaps as large as 15,000,[23] and comprising the cream of the royal forces, bolstered by the affinities of Sir Gilbert Talbot, Earl of Shrewsbury, Viscount Lisle and Sir Edward Grey. On his flanks he had the mounted contingents of, on the left, Sir John Savage and, on the right, Lord Scales, It may be that he had accepted the gamble of outstripping the rest but was confident he had sufficient resources available to deal with the rebels. If this was a calculated risk, then it was a bold one. The main body was under the command of Henry's uncle, the veteran Duke of Bedford, militarily undistinguished, most probably Oxford simply required him to feed regular reinforcements into the fight. Both senior commanders, Lincoln and the King, may have treated their followers to a rousing address. The rebels would certainly have needed a confidence booster, the numbers of their enemies all too apparent.

Schwarz may have begun the fight by ordering his crossbowmen and handgunners to shoot. No sooner had they discharged their pieces than the archers of Oxford's division made their reply. At once the disparity in the missile arm became obvious. The longbows bit deeply into the exposed Irishmen, causing heavy losses. For Lincoln there was only one recourse: an immediate advance to contact. The rebels surged down the gentle slope, smashing against the hedge of the royal van, the crash of armies resonating. The wild Irish, full of Celtic fury, but devoid of harness, suffered from the royalist arrow storm, but others of the van, dismayed by numbers, gave ground or even turned tail, crying that all was lost. This was the very crisis of the battle, and a lesser commander might have given way, but Oxford had faced these odds before, he knew how to handle his men, how to keep them to their colours in the brutal slogging match that turned the dry tussocks red. Accounts state that the carnage continued for a full three hours, and this evidences the notion that the battle was both long and hard fought.

Lincoln's best, indeed only, chance was to break Oxford before he could be reinforced, letting the panicked survivors flee back toward their comrades in the centre and allowing the contagion of fear to complete his victory. But the van did not break; some ran, most stood, held on in the desperate scrum of slashing bills and frenzied hacking. Gradually, as more and more royalist infantry reached the field, the attack began to run out of steam. The royalist line held then began to push, driving the rebels, now on the defensive, back toward the crest of the ridge. Likely the rot began with the Irish, their fire dampened and their numbers much depleted. They wavered then broke, streaming back over the reverse slope toward the river crossing. By this time completely isolated, Schwarz and his mercenaries sold their lives dearly. The ground now called the Red Gutter, which runs north of the Burham Furlong, became the scene, as the name implies, of the greatest slaughter. Many others drowned in their precipitate flight across the Trent.

Lincoln died fighting, Fitzgerald had most probably already fallen, Schwarz and Broughton, too, were amongst the casualties. Lovell, despite rumours of his bizarre death, escaped to Scotland.[24] Lambert Simnel and his Svengali priest were captured by a Northumbrian, Robert Bellingham.[25] It is said that some 4,000 rebels fell in the fight and subsequent rout, though this seems a rather high figure.[26] More were hanged by the King at Lincoln, and perhaps several hundred royalists died – the majority from Oxford's division:

> *[I]t was only then, when the battle was over, that it was fully apparent how rash had been the spirit inspiring the enemy soldiers: for their leaders John Earl of Lincoln, Francis Lord Lovell, Thomas Broughton and the most bold Martin Schwartz and the Irish captain Thomas Geraldine [Fitzgerald] were slain in that place.[27]*

Henry Tudor's crown, however, was safe.

Henry had arrived on the field in time to plant his banner on the Burham Furlong (where the monument now stands). He had wished to see Lincoln taken alive and is said to have been angered by the news of his death. The vanquished Earl was probably the better commander; Henry's organisation and scouting throughout the campaign had left much to be desired. It is ironic that the man who won two of England's most decisive encounters fought within a couple of years of each other was, in reality, no soldier (though he went on to win another confrontation at Blackheath in 1497). His victory was complete, and the King marched his army, or that portion of it which was not immediately paid off, back to Kenilworth. If Lincoln had failed to gather recruits in Yorkshire there was, nevertheless, evidence that his welcome had not been as hostile as the king would have wished. Consequently, Henry came north again and in August made a suitable show of royal authority in York, Durham and Newcastle, returning south by way of Richmond, Ripon and Pontefract.

Those who might earlier have wavered now flocked to affirm their loyalty or seek forgiveness. Henry was not seeking retribution, though both Scropes were temporarily incarcerated and only released on licence afterwards. His fresh triumph at Stoke did not imply that Henry could in any way relax his vigilance. He had in fact fought his last major battle and, in reality, the Wars of the Roses were now finally ended. In the summer of 1487, however, this was far from obvious, and the King would be glancing over his shoulder for the remainder of his life and reign.

When, two years later, early in 1489, Parliament voted an additional subsidy of £100,000 to fund renewal of the French war, serious riots ensued, and Henry Percy, 4th Earl of Northumberland became a casualty, not falling honourably in battle like his forbears, but miserably, as a hated tax-gatherer – a fitting end perhaps. The captive Earl of Warwick remained a beacon for discontent; plots emerged in 1489 and again the following year.

In 1491, a young Flemish adventurer, Perkin Warbeck, announced that he was, in fact, none other than Richard, Duke of York, younger of the two Princes in the Tower. Despite the improbability, Warbeck became the focus of a serious threat. He was supported by Margaret of Burgundy, who had learnt nothing from the Lambert Simnel fiasco and, in 1496, by an opportunist James IV of Scotland. Even after the pretender had been seen off, discredited and obliged to submit, plots and rumours of plots abounded. In November 1499, Henry, who had shown admirable restraint, finally felt constrained to send Perkin Warbeck and the hapless Warwick to the block. Only Edmund de la Pole, Lincoln's younger brother and a nephew of Edward IV, remained as a fitful pretender, penniless, itinerant and without serious support. Perhaps the crowning achievement of Henry's reign was that, on his death in 1509, Henry VIII ascended seamlessly to the throne.

The wheel had finally ceased spinning.

Notes

1 Very few noble lines were, in fact, extinguished; many more suffered loss through attainder. However, reversal was equally common – some 64 per cent of all those attainted between 1453 and 1504, as much as 84 per cent of the magnates, were finally restored; see Pollard, *Wars of the Roses*, p. 96.

2 Henry dealt sharply with instances of magnates' excess; Dorset, whom he never trusted, was imprisoned during the Lambert Simnel affair and later, in 1492, heavily fined and stripped of many of his estates; see Pollard, op. cit., p. 101 and Carpenter, op. cit., pp. 221–2.

3 Even Oxford was heavily fined when he transgressed as were Devon and the 5th Earl of Northumberland. Sir William Stanley, that most devious scion of his clan, overstepped the mark and finally went to the block; see Pollard, op. cit., p. 101 and Carpenter, op. cit., p. 221.

4 Of the line of Willoughby de Eresby, clients of the Earl of Oxford in Suffolk. This Sir Robert was of Broke, Wiltshire, elevated to Lord Willoughby in 1489 and Steward of the Royal Household.

5 He was later killed at Stoke.

6 The family is commemorated in the Huddleston Chapel in Holy Trinity Church, by Millom Castle, which houses a fine effigy of Richard Huddleston (d. 1494).

7 PV (H) pp. 10–27.

8 Lincoln's mother, Elizabeth, was one of the sisters of Edward IV.

9 Sir Gerald Gearoid Mor Fitzgerald, 8th Earl of Kildare (d. 1513) was an important and colourful figure in Irish politics of the late fifteenth century.

10 PV (H) pp. 10–27.

11 Ibid.

12 Ibid.

13 This landfall was not accidental; Sir Thomas Broughton had both estates and influence in the area.

14 Burne, *More Battlefields*, p. 150.

15 It was here that the 1st Earl of Northumberland, together with Lord Bardolph, fell in 1408.

16 Ryknild Street was probably an old Roman road; the line was first mapped by a local cartographer, John Warburton, in 1720.

17 Burne, op. cit., p. 151.

18 Ibid., p. 152. Burne records that two windmills, now vanished, existed in the fifteenth century and that one, called the Rampire, which crowned the ridge just to the west of the Fossway, was said to have been built on the site of Lincoln's camp.

19 The sources for the battle diverge sharply in their accounts. Vergil's account, which was followed by the later Tudor writers, appears to conflict with the contemporary version, that of the anonymous herald or pursuivant (junior officer of arms), who was almost certainly an eyewitness; see 'The Herald's Report' *c.* 1488–90, Cotton MS, Julius B. XII, fos. 27d–29d, amending J. Leland, 'Collectanea', vol. IV (ed. T. Hearne) Oxford 1774, pp. 212–15.

20 Sir John Cheyney gained a baronetcy, and the King dubbed a further 13 bannerets and 52 knights; see M. Bennett, *Lambert Simnel and the Battle of Stoke* (Gloucester 1993), p. 95.

21 GCL p. 241, and see also Bennett, *Lambert Simnel*, p. 91.

22 Irish and Anglo-Irish armies of this time would include elite household warriors, the Galloglas ("Galloglaich") and the much more lightly armoured infantry or kerns; see Bennett, op. cit., p. 94.

23 Haigh, op. cit., p. 176 and Bennett, *Lambert Simnel*, p. 95.

24 A skeleton was discovered many years later, walled up within the vault of Minster Lovell, said to represent his mortal remains.

25 Haigh, op. cit., p. 179.

26 Burne, *More Battlefields*, p. 159, and Bennett, *Lambert Simnel*, p. 99.

27 PV (H) p. 26. Lambert Simnel was put to work as a scullion and turnspit in the royal kitchens, though he subsequently prospered in service and rose to become trainer of the King's hawks.

The Military Legacy

A fter more than a generation of intermittent strife we must ask, What was the military legacy of the conflict overall? It produced a number of set piece battles, some like Towton on the epic scale, others, for instance Hexham or Hedgeley, much smaller, shorter and comparatively bloodless. We see the influence of the latter stages of the French wars in the construction of field fortifications such as those thrown up by the Lancastrians before Northampton in 1460. Battles were frequently bloody as losers in a civil war have no cash value: personal, family and dynastic feuds are brought to a sanguinary denouement.

During this period, the armourer's art reached its full and glorious flowering, with the gothic harness of the time achieving aesthetic and functional excellence. Conversely, the growing impact of hand-held firearms would soon render plate armour redundant. The battles themselves tended to be fought along traditional lines, with opposing forces facing each other in linear formation, divided into three conventional divisions or battles. There were some innovations: the use of fieldworks at Northampton, and the Earl of Warwick's measures before Second St Albans show marks of ingenuity – neither, however, was successful. The Lancastrian flank march prior to Warwick's defeat is also a notable example of some enlightened tactical thinking – possibly the professional captain, Andrew Trollope, was the author. Archery was a feature of most encounters and here the formidable missile power of the English longbow was turned in upon Englishmen, an element which greatly increased the level of casualties.

By the standards of later conflicts, the effects of the wars were relatively modest in terms of disruption to the socio-economic fabric. Some magnate families suffered great loss but life in town and shire generally was not significantly affected. Much has been made of the depredations of the great Lancastrian army moving south in 1461 but these may have been exaggerated (though abuses of the civilian population certainly did occur). During the latter half of the fifteenth century England was experiencing a strong measure of prosperity, with gentry families building fine 'castles' that were mere sham in terms of defence – more country house than fortress. Besides, an age was fast approaching when the gunner's art would ensure that castle-builders were constrained to return to their drawing boards.

Siege artillery played little role as there were few sieges during the course of the conflict. Harlech and St Michael's Mount are two notable exceptions, as are the operations between 1461 and 1464 against the Northumbrian castles – Bamburgh earning the unenviable distinction of being the only fortress to suffer bombardment. Field guns were employed in a number of fights: Northampton, Barnet, Tewkesbury and Bosworth – though their deployment did not, in any of these instances, have a marked effect on the outcome.

Wars in England were followed by others in Europe, such as the 'Great Wars' between Valois and Habsburg in France, where the predominance of chivalry was challenged by the development of mass armies, of mercenary Swiss pikemen, and by the increasing firepower of the musket. The Wars of the Roses thus stand on the rim of the era of medieval warfare on the brink of the age of pike and shot. Englishmen, clinging to their established weapons and tactical formations, were at risk of becoming anachronistic and, in the following century, major tactical innovation would develop elsewhere.

Glossary

Advowson   The lord's right to appoint an incumbent to a living.

Affinity   A magnate's following, comprising not just his own *vassals* or tenants but his friends and allies.

Annuity   The grant of a pension for life, payable in annual instalments, usually granted by the Crown or magnate.

Appenage   The lands of one of royal blood, with co-existent legal rights and privileges.

Arbalest   A type of crossbow where tension was achieved by mechanical means.

Attainder   Statutory deprivation of one found guilty of treason, forfeiture of all estates, rights and privileges. In the context of the Wars of the Roses, the inevitable consequence of failure or defeat. The Act of Attainder was passed by Parliament, and did not require a conviction of treason from the courts.

Banneret   A knight who was entitled to carry his own banner, conferred status over more junior knights, likely to be given a command in battle.

Bevor   A section of plate armour, worn with the *sallet* form of helmet to provide protection to the neck and lower face.

Bill   A pole arm, a deadly fusion of agricultural implement and spear, with a curved axe-type blade, a spike for thrusting and a hook on the reverse: a formidable weapon in trained hands.

Bombard   A heavy siege gun of the fifteenth century, irregular in calibre but throwing a massive ball, perhaps up to 60 lbs in weight.

Bond   An agreement or contract, confirmed by the pledge of cash as a recognisance – a surety for the act to be performed or for the refraining from an act, obviously forfeit should the contracting party default on the terms of the bond.

Caltrap   An anti-personnel and anti-equine device.

Captain   The officer responsible for a particular place or location but whose authority was limited to his charge.

Chamber The fiscal aspect or operation of the Royal Household; the management of the royal accounts as distinguished from the Exchequer, then as now the finances of the state as a whole.

Chancery The executive and administrative function of the Crown.

Chevauchee A large-scale foray aimed at laying waste the territory of an enemy, to belittle the foe and perhaps force him to accept battle.

Clothyard shaft A longbow arrow.

Commission of Oyer and Terminer From the French, literally to 'hear and determine', the commissioners were Crown appointees charged to examine and investigate acts of treason, felonies (serious offences) and misdemeanours (lesser offences) committed in a particular county or locality.

Constable The official in charge of a magnate's tenantry who might exercise his office within the lord's residence or with his soldiery in the field.

Crenellation The form of battlements on a castle's parapet, 'licence to crenellate' being required before a castle could be constructed.

Demesne A lord or magnate's personal holdings, those occupied and managed by him as opposed to being parcelled out to a tenant or tenants.

Destrier A warhorse, much prized and of considerable value.

Enceinte The circuit of the walls of a defended castle or town.

Feudalism The system of government and landholding introduced into England by William I: a feudal pyramid, whereby land was parcelled out to the tenants-in-chief, together with rights attaching to the land, in return for a complex raft of obligations, inherent amongst which was military service for defined periods and duration. The system prevailed all the way down the social scale from sub-tenants to the unfree agrarian poor or villains. 'Bastard Feudalism' is a difficult concept, championed by Stubbs in the nineteenth century but revised by MacFarlane subsequently – it embodies the notion of service being undertaken for cash payment rather than as part of a wider obligation.

Fiefdom A parcel of land, usually substantial, containing a number of *manors* with rights attached.

Fosse A defensive ditch.

Galloglass Elite Hebridean mercenaries in the service of Irish magnates.

Glaive A form of polearm.

Gorget A section of plate armour designed to protect the neck area.

Hagbut An early form of hand-held firearm.

Halberd A form of polearm with a broad axe blade.

Hand and a Half Sword The knightly sword of the fifteenth century, often known as a 'bastard sword' – a long, tapering double-edged blade, could be used either for the thrust or the cut.

Hanseatic League (or Hanse)   A trading federation of northern European and Baltic states which remained powerful from the thirteenth to the seventeenth centuries.

Harness   Full plate armour.

Hobiler or hobilar   Lightly mounted cavalry or mounted infantry, associated with the light horse of the Anglo-Scottish border.

Indenture   A form of legally binding agreement, the engrossment of which was, upon completion, cut into two halves along an indentation. An 'employee' or retainer could be contracted into service by means of an indenture.

Jack   A form of protective doublet. Stuffed with rags and generally sleeveless, worn by the commons; a more sophisticated form was the brigandine which had metal plates sewn between the facing and lining so that only the rivet heads, in decorative patterns, showed through the fabric covering.

Kern   An Irish mercenary footsoldier.

Kettle hat   A form of metal headgear worn by men-at-arms, with a wide protective brim, similar in appearance to the British helmets ('tin hats') of both world wars.

Lance   A tactical unit built around a knight's following, and which could therefore vary in size.

Leaguer   A siege or blockade.

Livery   The distinctive coat ('livery coat') worn by the lord's retainers, bearing his badge, thus the expression 'livery and maintenance' – the retainer is clothed and fed by his employer in return, in effect, for wearing his private uniform (and assuming his private quarrels). The Battle of Empingham or 'Losecote Field' refers to the haste with which the panicked rebels cast off the incriminating livery coats of their erstwhile paymasters, Warwick and Clarence.

Mainprise   A form of surety or bond.

Manor   A form of landholding, a knightly estate usually comprising the residence of the gentleman, a village or villages, woods, fields, mill(s), wine presses, church etc.

March   A frontier territory, administered by a warden, 'Marcher' lords were those who held lands along the Anglo-Scottish or Welsh borders.

Matross   A soldier who assisted gunners in loading, firing and sponging the guns.

Mesnie [meinie] Knight   One of a lord's household knights, i.e. of his domain or *demesne*.

Palatinate   Lands held by a count palatine, who enjoyed exclusive jurisdiction and extensive, quasi-regal privileges. The Bishops of Durham had the secular office of Counts Palatine for Durham and North Durham (Norhamshire in North Northumberland).

Poleaxe   A polearm, favoured by the gentry for close quarter combat: an axe blade, spear head and a hammer for battering an armoured opponent.

Pricker   A mounted scout and skirmisher, essentially light cavalry.

Quillon   The crossguard between the swordblade and hilt.

Re-adeption   The term used to describe the unique occurrence where the old King, Henry VI, was returned to the throne and the new King, Edward IV, was deposed.

Rondell dagger   A fifteenth-century, long-bladed knife, carried by all classes; could be used as a weapon or implement.

Sallet   A fifteenth-century helmet with a swept neckguard and often fitted with a fixed or moveable visor, worn above the *bevor*.

Slighting   Damaging or destroying defences, rendering them ineffective.

Tenants-in-chief   Magnates who held their lands directly from the Crown, rather than from a superior lord (these were known as sub-tenants).

Trunnion   The axis on which a cannon pivots.

Vassal   One who holds his land from his feudal superior on terms which involve an obligation of service as a condition of the tenancy.

Vedette   A mounted sentry, stationed some distance from camp.

Vintenar   A breed of NCO in charge of a platoon of 20 men.

Wapentake   A Norse term, literally 'the brandishing of spears in a popular assembly', long established even by 1086 (Domesday). The expression has the same meaning as the Saxon 'Hundred' and refers to main area sub-divisions within a given county.

Appendix 1

Executions Following the Battle of Hexham

❦

Gregory lists the following as having been executed at Hexham, the day after the battle: The Duke of Somerset, Edmund Fysche, Edmon Bradschawe, Wate Hunt and 'Black Jakys'. At Newcastle on 17 May: Lords Hungerford and Roos, Sir Thomas Fyndorne, Barnarde de la Mare and Nicholas Massam. At Middleham on 18 May: Sir Philip Wentworth, Wyllam Penyngton, warde de Copclyffe (Topcliff), Olyver Wentworthe, Wylliam Spyller, John Senyer and Thomas Haute were executed. At York on 26 May: Sir Thomas Hoosy, Thomas Gosse, Robert Myrfyn, John Butler, Robert Wattys (porter to King Henry VI), Thomas Fenwyke, Robert Cockefelde, William Bryce, Wylliam Dawson, John Chapman, John Edyrbeke, Rycharde Taverner, John Russelle and Robert Conqueror.

'The Short English Chronicle' agrees that the same list of executions took place at Hexham and at Newcastle on 17 May. Thomas Haute is described as a servant of Queen Margaret. The condemned at York are given as: Sir Thomas Hull, John Marfyn (another of the Queen's servants), John Butler, John Gosse (carver to the Duke of Somerset), Roger Water (described as a porter to King Henry and may, therefore, be presumed to be the same person as Gregory's Robert Wattys), Henry Docfford, William Dawson, William Pryce, Thomas Hegge, Thomas Fenwyck and John Champyon. Sir Ralph Grey, executed on 10 July could be said to have been the last casualty of the Lancastrian collapse in Northumberland.

Appendix 2

Who were Robin of Redesdale
and Robin of Holderness?

The *nom de guerre* of Robin of Redesdale has long been identified with Sir William Conyers and/or his brother Sir John. The Conyers family, from Richmondshire, were stars in the Neville firmament. This identification, championed by such eminent figures as Charles Ross has, nonetheless, been challenged – most recently by Ralph Robson.[1] He identifies the name with Robert Tailbois, the son and heir of the attainted Lord William Tailbois, the alleged Lancastrian embezzler, who was executed after the rout at Hexham.[2] The family was originally from Lincolnshire, where they maintained a strong connection, but their Northumbrian estates were grouped in Redesdale; they and their friends the Herons suffered in the attainders of 1464, with the Ogles being prime beneficiaries.

A connection has been made between the Robin of Redesdale of 1496/1470 and the alleged outlaw who sheltered Margaret of Anjou and her son in Hexhamshire in 1463. I have previously discounted this story as either romanticised or a confusion with events further north, by Norham. Philip Haigh refers to a possible incident at Hexham in 1462. All authorities appear to agree that the character in this affair is not the same person as the later Robin – the outlaw in question, if indeed he existed, may be the Black Jack or Jackie executed after the battle in 1464.

Ralph Robson makes the point that a person of the fifteenth century, when assuming a name such as this, would most probably retain his own Christian name, which argues against both the Conyers brothers. Robert Tailbois, certainly had cause for disaffection, and was descended from the first Robert de Umfraville, who had, from time to time, styled himself 'Rob o' Redesdale'. Robert was married to the daughter of Sir John Heron of Chipchase, who like his son-in-law had suffered attainder. The Tynedale and Redesdale riders had been active in the campaigns of Wakefield, Second St Albans, Towton, and the war in the north; these hardy dalesmen, inured to war, had the reputation of being the 'enforcers' of the Lancastrian host – their experience would undoubtedly have qualified them most admirably for this role!

Robert Tailbois was also related to Lord Welles, the instigator of the Lincolnshire troubles in 1470. The Tailbois manors of Kestaven and Lindsey had gone to Sir Thomas Burgh. This is all purely anecdotal of course but, during Edward IV's exile from September 1470 to June 1471, Robert Tailbois was appointed as a commissioner for the defence of the eastern seaboard; his was a high appointment, his fellow commissioners included Clarence, Oxford and Montagu. None of this proves he was the real Robin, of course, and he did not subsequently lose by his Neville affiliation. The attainder was reversed in 1472 by Edward IV and, thereafter, Robert held a succession of important posts in Lincolnshire, spanning the next decade. He also recovered his lands in Northumberland, as did his in-laws, the Herons of Chipchase.[3]

It is significant that both Robin of Redesdale and Robin of Holderness championed the cause of the Percies. This would be an embarrassment for Warwick as it impacted on his brother John, Lord Montagu, who was also Earl of Northumberland. There is a suggestion that Montagu did confront the Redesdale riders and put them to flight but, knowing his brother's hand in the business, then simply averted his eyes. Robin of Holderness was a different matter.

Tradition asserts that this Robin was in fact a member of the local gentry, Robert Hilliard, son of Robert Hilliard of Winestead, a staunch Lancastrain of the Percy affinity who had led a Holderness contingent at Towton.[4] Though captured, he suffered neither death nor attainder but became a JP in Holderness. The cause of the disturbance was an orchestration of a long-held grievance concerning a local tax of thrives of corn, due to the governors of St Leonard's Hospital in York. Warwick had previously examined the matter and decided in favour of the hospital.[5]

It is, however, unclear as to whether this purely localised matter was then linked to the more volatile question of the Percy heir. If so, it placed Warwick in a quandary and most accounts agree that Montagu, as Earl of Northumberland, moved swiftly to deal with the rebels. An armed confrontation occurred before the very walls of York, the rioters were easily dispersed and their leader, Robin of Holderness captured and promptly beheaded on the city pavement below Walmgate Bar, with his severed head later garnishing the gate itself.

This appears straightforward, yet there are telling inconsistencies in that Robert Hilliard, allegedly killed in 1470, inherited his father's property on the latter's death in 1489! After the collapse of the Warwick–Clarence conspiracy in March, Edward, at York, accepted the surrenders of Sir John Conyers, Lord Scrope and Robert Hilliard. It appears evident that Robert thus survived the affair of Robin of Holderness, which must thus imply that he was never involved, or that there were two Robins or, possibly, that Montagu fabricated the entire incident to demonstrate his loyalty and the head above Walmgate Bar was that of some luckless scapegoat or handy felon. Robert Hilliard the Younger, if further proof was needed, was made a Knight banneret by the 4th Earl of Northumberland at the siege of Berwick, during Gloucester's subsequent tenure. This does, as Philip Haigh points out, raise the possibility that Montagu was playing a clever double game throughout.

Notes

1 R. Robson, *The Rise and Fall of the English Highland Clans* (Edinburgh 1989), pp. 60–3.
2 Tailbois, discovered hiding in a coal mine, was said to have had some £3,000 worth of funds on his person, a very substantial sum.
3 Both branches of the Heron family, Herons of Chipchase and Ford were rehabilitated and continued to be active in border affairs for the next hundred years, John Heron, the Bastard of Ford, was a particularly colourful and notorious swashbuckler who, nonetheless, did good service on Flodden Field in 1513.
4 At about this time the cockerel device was added to the family arms, this may have been a reference to the Cock Beck; see Haigh, op. cit., p. 191.
5 Ibid., p. 190.

Appendix 3

The Princes in the Tower

Richard III remains an enigmatic and controversial figure, the arch villain of More and Shakespeare, one hand always on his dagger, haunted by the bloody memories of his many crimes. No single incident raises the tempers of the pro and anti Richard factions more than the probable fate of his nephews, Edward v and his brother Richard, Duke of York – the Princes in the Tower.

That the King was a ruthless usurper who dealt murderously with his opponents cannot really be doubted. Political murders were by no means uncommon in the fifteenth century, and such pragmatism probably raised very few eyebrows. Rivers, Grey, Vaughan and Hastings were all 'players' in the robust school of contemporary politics, their taking off, whilst arbitrary and without legal sanction, would have been forgotten had Richard reigned long and well. The alleged killing of innocent children was another matter, a base crime which offended God and nature. The man who as uncle and protector should have barred the door to any murderer, at best, if he did not bear the dagger himself, left the door conveniently ajar.

Contemporary opinion certainly considered the King to be guilty. In January 1484, Gaillaume de Rochefort, the French Chancellor, issued a public accusation of the double homicide.[1] No denial was ever issued and, guilty or not, the accusation clung to Richard, as though the stink of blood could never be expunged. The crime or alleged crime defined his brief kingship and haunted him to the grave and beyond: the clamour has endured for five centuries since.

Various efforts, by means of reconstructed 'trials', have been staged to exonerate the King and indeed no tangible evidence of his guilt has ever surfaced. To the extent that proof of criminality demands, quite rightly, that the accused's guilt be proven beyond reasonable doubt, no court could ever convict; were the matter to be heard in Scotland a verdict of 'not proven' might be entered.

If the Woodvilles were now able to bring a civil action against Richard III for damages arising from the alleged deaths of the Princes then they might well be successful. All of the attempts to exonerate Richard fall foul of the proviso that, if the King did not commit the alleged murders, then who did? Richard possessed means, motive and opportunity. He controlled the persons of the Princes, access to the Tower and the personnel involved. This afforded both means and opportunity. As for motive – the King possessed this in abundance. His regime could never sit safe with his nephews alive. Killing them was the only alternative and indeed some suggest that the foul deed was done the very night following the removal of the younger boy from Westminster Abbey.[2]

Richard may well have agonised over the necessity for the act – killing the two boys does not necessarily make him a monster. If the alternative was a likely renewal of civil war, then which was the lesser evil? To murder two innocents or see thousands perish on the field? Perhaps it was this which haunted the King during his short reign, the burden of guilt. To take innocent lives, the lives of children was as abhorrent then as now, no amount of realpolitik could wash away the guilt. Like Macbeth, the King was doomed to continue with the reek of blood forever filling his nostrils.

Sir Thomas More has provided the classic version of the death of the two boys, though even he admits to some confusion in the accounts from the time:

> *For Sir James Tyrell devised that they should be murdered in their beds. To the execution whereof, he appointed Miles Forest, one of the four that kept them, a fellow fleshed in murder before-time. To him he joined one John Dighton, his own horse keeper, a big, broad, square, strong knave. Then, all the others being removed from them, this Miles Forest and John Dighton, about midnight (the silly [innocent] children lying in their beds) came into*

the chamber and suddenly lapped them up among the clothes, so bewrapped them and entangled them, keeping down by force the feather bed and pillows hard unto their mouths, that within a while, smothred and stifled, their breath failing, they gave up to God their innocent souls into the joys of heaven, leaving to the tormentors their bodies dead in the bed. Which after that the wretches perceived, first by the struggling with the pains of death, and after long lying still, to be thoroughly dead; they laid their bodies naked out upon the bed, and fetched Sir James to see them. Which, upon the sight of them, caused those murderers to bury them at the stair foot, meetly deep in the ground, under a great heap of stones.[3]

More's account has been generally accepted as broadly accurate; it has the ring of high drama and the sheer, callous brutality of the crime has not been ameliorated by the passage of time. The evidence, however, is open to question. More avers that Tyrell, facing death for treason in 1502, confessed to lighten his soul ahead of the axe. No other contemporary account, however, refers to any such confession, nor has any copy of such been found. Such a revelation would be a gift to Henry VII and it seems inconceivable that he would fail to capitalise. More may have relied on an earlier source, John Molinet, writing around 1500. He states that the Princes were done to death during the summer of 1483 and their remains interred within the Tower. More suggests late July or August. Certainly it would seem that rumours circulating in London at the time opined this was the case; the contemporary commentators seem *ad idem* that Richard did away with his nephews. If he had decided to murder the boys, then there was little point in delaying execution of the deed – the longer they remained alive, the greater the threat their continued existence posed.

Polydore Vergil and the author of 'The Great Chronicle of London', both writing in 1502, give summer 1483 as the time of the killings.[4] Mancini reports that, whilst he was still in London in early July 1483, the lads were kept within the inner room and seen less and less frequently; occasionally they were observed behind barred windows or at play in the garden. By the autumn, they were seen no more. Murmurings of concern probably began as early as June. The Croyland Continuator observes that rumours of their fate were current by September. The King's contemporaries seem to be in no doubt that his was the guilty hand.

De Commynes, in his memoirs penned *c.*1500, suggests three possible scenarios:

- Richard killed them before his coronation.
- He killed them after it.
- It was Buckingham who organised the murders.

In pointing a finger at the Duke, De Commynes was not alone, several of the contemporary sources hint at his guilt, either in terms of complicity or instigation.[5] The weight of evidence may appear compelling but it is entirely circumstantial, there is not a single shred of tangible proof that indicates the King may have murdered his nephews; they simply disappear from history.

Events took a singular turn nearly two centuries later when, in 1674, workmen busy in the tower, discovered two skeletons, buried some ten feet down beneath a staircase leading to the chapel in the White Tower. Immediately there was obvious speculation that these were the mortal remains of the murdered boys. More did describe their initial resting place in uncannily similar terms, though, of course, he refers to them as having been subsequently re-interred elsewhere. Despite the obvious implications, other human remains have been found in the Tower and its environs, at least one of which dates from the Iron Age. The remains were placed in a funerary urn within the Henry VII Chapel in Westminster Abbey.

In 1933 the bones were subjected to a forensic examination. This was undertaken by a panel of contemporary experts, including Lawrence Tanner, the Archivist of Westminster Abbey, Professor William Wright, an anatomist, and George Northcroft, President of the Dental Association. The experts concluded that these were indeed the mortal remains of the Princes, being those of two boys, with the development of the bones being consistent with the age gap between the Princes. Later commentators have criticised the work as being imperfect in so far as the panel set out to prove these bones were those of the boys and that there was no attempt to confirm their gender. The debate, therefore, continues to rage but the bones, by themselves, are largely irrelevant – whether or not these belong to the Princes proves nothing either way concerning their uncle's guilt.

If Richard was not the killer of his nephews, then who was the guilty party? If we discount Buckingham, we are rather embarrassed by a lack of candidates. There is some suggestion that the Duke balked at the idea and that his unwillingness caused a rift with the King. Perhaps even the un-scrupulous Buckingham found the idea of the death of innocents a step too far. The one obvious choice would be Henry VII, assuming the boys were alive at the date of Richard's death at Bosworth. Neither monarch instigated any enquiry as to the fate of the Princes. In the Act of Attainder passed by Parliament in the autumn of 1485, Henry vaguely accused his dead rival of, *inter alia*, the 'shedding of innocent blood'; this is rather oblique and it would seem to be that Henry himself was unable to determine exactly what had happened. If Richard was, as we assume, culpable, he hid his tracks very well indeed.

Notes

1 This may have been based on information or rumour supplied by Dominic Mancini; see Lander, op. cit., p. 181.
2 Ibid.
3 Lander, op. cit., p. 184.
4 A. J. Pollard, *Richard III and the Princes in the Tower* (Gloucester 1991), pp. 114–39.
5 A fragment amongst the Ashmolean MS in the Bodleian Library also implicated Buckingham. The fragment uses the expression 'vise' – implying that the King acted either on his confederate's advice or possibly by his device. In the event, the Duke could not have acted without the King's sanction; accusing Buckingham does not, in any way, serve to absolve Richard.

Bibliography

Primary sources

Adam of Usk, 'Chronicon Adae de Usk' (ed. E. M. Thompson) London 1904.

'John Benet's Chronicle for the years 1400 to 1462' (ed. G. L. Hariss and M. A. Harriss) Camden Miscellany vol. 24 London 1972.

'Bishop Percy's Folio Manuscript' (ed. F. J. Furnivall and H. W. Hales) vol. 3 London 1868.

'Brut Chronicle' (ed. F. W. D. Brie) 2 vols. 1906–08.

'Calendar of Documents Relating to Scotland' (ed. J. Bain) vol. 4 1357–1509 London 1888.

'Calendar of Fine Rolls: Edward IV; Edward V; Richard III, 1471–1485' London HMSO 1961.

'Calendar of Patent Rolls, Edward IV 1467–1477, Edward IV, Edward V, Richard III, 1476–1485' London 1899–1901.

'Calendar of State Papers and Manuscripts existing in the Archives and Collections of Milan' (ed. and trans. A. B. Hinds) 1912.

G. Chastellain, 'Chronique des derniers Ducs de Bourgogne' in *Panthéon Littéraire* vol. 4 Paris (n.d.).

'A Chronicle of London from 1089 – to 1485' (ed. H. Nicholas and E. Tyrell) London 1827.

'Chronicles of London' (ed. C. L. Kingsford) Oxford 1905.

'Chronicle of the Rebellion in Lincolnshire 1470' (ed. J. G. Nicholls), Camden Miscellany vol. 1 1847.

Phillippe de Commynes, 'The Memoirs of the Reign of Louis XI 1461–1483' (trans. M. Jones) 1972.

The Cotton MS in the British Library.

'Croyland Abbey Chronicle' (ed. H. T. Riley) 1854.

'The Croyland Chronicle Continuations 1459–1486' (ed. N. Pronay and J. Cox) Gloucester 1986.

'An English Chronicle of the reigns of Richard II, Henry IV, Henry V and Henry VI' (ed. J. S. Davies) 1856.

'English Historical Documents' (ed. A. R. Myers) vol. 5 1327–1484 London 1969.

Robert Fabyan, 'The New Chronicles of England and France' (ed. H. Ellis) London 1809.

'Froissart's Chronicles' (ed. G. Brereton) Harmondsworth 1968.

'The Great Chronicle of London' (ed. A. H. Thomas and I. D. Thornley) London 1938.

William Gregory's Chronicle of London in 'Historical Collections of a Citizen of London in the Fifteenth Century' (ed. J. Gairdner) Camden Society vol. 17 1876.

Edward Hall 'The Union of the Two Noble and Illustre Famelies of Lancastre and Yorke', 1548.

'The Harleian Manuscripts' (ed. P. W. Hammond and R. Horrox) 4 vols British Library Harleian Manuscripts 1979–83.

'Hearne's Fragment' in 'Chronicles of the White Rose' (ed. J. A. Giles) 1834.

'Historie of the Arrivall of King Edward IV in England and the final Recoverye of his Kingdomes from Henry VI A.D. 1471' (ed. J. Bruce) Camden Society vol. 1 1838.

'The Household of Edward IV: the Black Book and the Ordinance of 1478' (ed. A. R. Myers) Manchester 1959.

'Knyghthode and Bataile' (ed. R. Dyboski and Z. M. Arend) Early English Texts Society 1935.

'A London Chronicle of 1460' (ed. G. Baskerville), *English Historical Review* vol. 28 1913.

Mancini Dominic, 'The Usurpation of Richard III' (ed. C. A. J. Armstrong) Oxford 1969, reprinted Gloucester 1984.

Sir Thomas More, 'The History of Richard III' in *The Complete Works of St Thomas More* (ed. R. S. Sylvester) vol. 2 New Haven and London 1963.

'The Paston Letters 1422–1509' (ed. J. Gairdner) 3 vols 1872–75.

'Plumpton Letters' (ed. T. Stapleton) Camden Society vol. 4 1839.

'The Priory of Hexham' Surtees Society vol. 1 1864.

'Rose of Rouen', *Archaeologia* 29 pp. 344–7.

'Rotuli Parliamentorum' (ed. J. Strachey et al.) 6 vols 1767–77.

J. Rous, 'Historiae Regum Anglicae' (ed. T. Hearne) Oxford 1716.

J. Rous, 'The Rous Roll' (ed. C. Ross and W. Courthope) Gloucester 1980.

Scottish Exchequer Rolls vol. 7 Ramsay ii.

'Short English Chronicle' (ed. J. Gairdner) Camden Society vol. 28 1880.

'The Stonor Letters and Papers 1290–1483' (ed. C. L. Kingsford) Camden Society 3rd series vols 29–30 1919.

Hans Talhoffer, 'Manual of Swordfighting' (trans. and ed. M. Rector) facsimile edn 2000.

'Three Fifteenth Century Chronicles' (ed. J. Gairdner) Camden Society 1880.

Polydore Vergil, 'Three Books of Polydore Vergil's English History' (ed. H. Ellis) 1844.

John Warkworth, 'A Chronicle of the First Thirteen Years of the Reign of Edward IV 1461–1474' (ed. J. O. Halliwell) Camden Society vol. 10 1839.

Jean de Waurin, 'Recueil des Chroniques D'Angleterre' (ed. W. Hardy and E. L. C. P. Hardy) 1891.

J. Whethamstede, 'Registrum Abbatis Johannis Whethamstede' in 'Registra quorandum Abbatum Monasterii S. Albani' 2 vols (ed. H. Riley) Rolls Series 1872–3.

William of Worcester, 'Annales Rerum Anglicarum' in 'Liber Niger Scaccarii' (ed. J. Hearne) 2 vols Oxford 1728.

'The Year Book de Termino Paschae 4 Edward IV' in 'Priory of Hexham', Surtees Society vol. 1 1864.

'The York Records of the Fifteenth Century' (ed. R. Davies) 1843.

Secondary sources

Allen, K., *The Wars of the Roses* (London 1973).

Allmand, C., *Henry V* (London 1992).

Archer, R. E. C., *Government and People in the Fifteenth Century* (England 1995).

Archibald, E. H. H., *The Wooden Fighting Ship* (London 1968).

Arthurson, I., *The Perkin Warbeck Conspiracy 1491–1499* (England 1977).

Attreed, L., (ed.) *York House Books* (Stroud 1991).

Bagley, J. J., *Margaret of Anjou, Queen of England* (London 1948).

Bain, J., (ed.) *Calendar of Documents Relating to Scotland 1108–1509* (1881–84).

Barbour, R., *The Knight and Chivalry* (London 1974).

Barnard, F., *Edward IV French Expedition* (London 1975).

Bartlett, C., *The English Longbowman 1313–1515* (London 1995).

Bates, C. J., *History of Northumberland* (London 1895).

Bean, J. M. W., *The Estates of the Percy Family* (Oxford 1958).

Bennett, H. S., *The Pastons and Their England* (Cambridge 1932).

Bennet, M., *The Battle of Bosworth* (New York 1985).

Bennet, M., *Lambert Simnel and the Battle of Stoke* (Gloucester 1987).

Bingham, C., *The Stewart Kings of Scotland 1371–1603* (London 1974).

Blackmore, H. L., *The Armouries of the Tower of London – Ordnance* (HMSO 1976).

Blair, C., *European Armour* (London 1958).

Boardman, A. V., *The Battle of Towton* (Stroud 1994).

Boardman, A. V., *The Medieval Soldier in the Wars of the Roses* (London 1998).

Brenan, G., *The House of Percy* 2 vols (England 1898).

Burne, Colonel A. H., *Battlefields of England* (London 1950).

Burne, Colonel A. H., *More Battlefields of England* (London 1952).

Carpenter C., *The Wars of the Roses: Politics and the Constitution in England c.1437–1509* (Cambridge 2002).

Charlesworth, D., 'Northumberland in the Early Years of Edward IV', *Archaeologia Aeliana* (4th Series 1953).

Charlesworth, D., 'The Battle of Hexham', *Archaeologia Aeliana* (4th Series 1952).

Chrimes, S. B., *Henry VII* (London 1952).

Clive, M., *The Sun of York, Edward IV* (London 1973).

Cole, H., *The Wars of the Roses* (London 1973).

Cook, D. R., *Lancastrians and Yorkists: Wars of the Roses* (London 1984).

Coward, B., *The Stanleys, Lords Stanley and Earls of Derby 1385–1672* (Manchester 1983).

Dockray, K. R., 'The Yorkshire Rebellions of 1469', *The Ricardian*, vol. 6, no. 82 (December 1983).

Dockray, K. R., *Chronicles of the Reign of Edward IV* (England 1983).

Ducklin, K., and J. Waller, *Sword Fighting* (London 2001).

Falkus, G., *The Life and Times of Edward IV* (London 1981).

Fiorato, V., A. Boylston and C. Knüsel (eds) *Blood Red Roses: The Archaeology of a Mass Grave from the Battle of Towton AD 1461* (Oxford 2000).

Foss, P. J., *The Field of Redemore Plain: The Battle of Bosworth* (Leeds 1990).

Gairdner, J., (ed.) *The Paston Letters*, 6 vols (Gloucester 1986).

Gillingham, J., *The Wars of the Roses* (London 2001).

Goodman, A., *The Wars of the Roses* (London 1981).

Grant, A., 'Richard III in Scotland' in A. J. Pollard (ed.) *The North of England in the Reign of Richard III* (Stroud 1996).

Grant, A., *Henry VII* (London 1985).

Gravett, C., *Medieval Siege Warfare* (London 1990).

Green, V. H. H., *The Later Plantagenets* (London 1955).

Griffiths, R. A., 'Local Rivalries and National Politics: The Percies, the Nevilles and the Duke of Exeter 1452–1455', *Speculum*, vol. 43 (1968).

Griffiths, R. A., *The Reign of King Henry VI* (London 1981).

Griffiths, R. A., *The Making of the Tudor Dynasty* (Gloucester 1985).

Griffiths, R. A., *Kings and Nobles in the Later Middle Ages* (Gloucester 1986).

Griffiths, R. A., *King and Country: England and Wales in the Fifteenth Century* (London 1991).

Griffiths, R. A., 'Patronage' in Griffiths (ed.) *The Crown and the Provinces in Later Medieval England* (Gloucester 1981).

Haigh, P. A., *The Battle of Wakefield* (Stroud 1996).

Haigh, P. A., *The Military Campaigns of the Wars of the Roses* (London 1995).

Hallam, E., *The Plantagenet Encyclopedia* (London 1990).

Hallam, E., (ed.) *The Chronicles of the Wars of the Roses* (London 1988).

Hammond, P. W. (ed.) *Richard III: Lordship Loyalty and Law* (Gloucester 1986).

Hammond, P. W., *The Battles of Barnet and Tewkesbury* (New York 1990).

Hammond, P. W. and A. Sutton, *Richard III – The Road to Bosworth Field* (London 1985).

Harvey, J., *The Plantagenets* (London 1948).

Hepple, L. W. *A History of Northumberland and Newcastle upon Tyne* (London 1976).

Hibbert, C., *Agincourt* (London 1964).

Hicks, M. A., *False, Fleeting Perjur'd Clarence, George Duke of Clarence* (Gloucester 1980).

Hicks, M. A., 'Edward IV, The Duke of Somerset and Lancastrian Loyalism in the North', *Northern History*, vol. 20 (1984).

Hicks, M. A., 'Warwick: The Reluctant Kingmaker', *Medieval History*, vol. 1 no. 2 (1991).

Hodges, G., *Ludford Bridge and Mortimer's Cross* (England 1988).

Horrox, R., *Richard III: A Study of Service* (Cambridge 1989).

Horrox, R., (ed.) *Richard III and the North* (Hull 1986).

Horrox, R., (ed.) *Fifteenth Century Attitudes* (Cambridge 1994).

James, M. E., 'The Murder at Coxlodge on 28th April, 1489', *Durham University Journal*, vol. 42 (1965).

Johnson, P. A., *Richard, Duke of York 1411–1460* (London 1988).

Jones, M. K., *Bosworth 1485: the Psychology of a Battle* (Stroud 2002).

Keegan, J., *The Face of Battle* (London 1976).

Keen, M., *English Society in the Later Middle Ages 1348–1500* (London 1990).

Keen, M., (ed.) *Medieval Warfare – a History* (Oxford 1999).

Kendall, P. Murray, *Richard III* (New York 1955).

Kendall, P. Murray, *Warwick the Kingmaker* (New York 1957).

Kendall, P. Murray, *The Wars of the Roses* (New York 1957).

Kightly, C., *The Dukes of York and their Duchesses* (York 1987).

Lander, J. R., *The Wars of the Roses* (London 1990).

Lander, J. R., *Crown and Nobility 1450–1509* (London 1976).

Lander, J. R., *The Limitations of English Monarchy in the later Middle Ages* (Toronto 1989).

Lomas, R., *Northumberland – County of Conflict* (East Lothian 1996).

Lomas, R., *North-East England in The Middle Ages* (Edinburgh 1992).

Long, B., *The Castles of Northumberland* (Newcastle upon Tyne 1967).

Lynch, M., *A New History of Scotland* (London 1991).

Macdougall, N., *James III: A Political Study* (Edinburgh 1982).

McFarlane, K. B., *The Nobility of Late Medieval England* (Oxford 1975).

McFarlane, K. B., *England in the Fifteenth Century* (ed.) G. L. Harris, (London 1981).

McFarlane, K. B., 'The Wars of the Roses', *Proceedings of the British Academy*, 50 (1964).

Meade, D. M., *The Medieval Church in England* (Worthing 1988).

Mortimer, I., *The Greatest Traitor* (London 2003).

Myers, A. R., (ed.) *The Household of Edward IV: The Black Book and the Ordinance of 1478* (Manchester 1959).

Neillands, R., *The Hundred Years War* (London 1992).

Neillands, R., *The Wars of the Roses* (London 1992).

Nicolle, D., *Medieval Warfare Source Book* (London 1999).

Norman, A. V. B. and D. Pottinger, *English Weapons and Warfare 449–1660* (London 1966).

Northumberland County History.

Oakeshott, R. E., *A Knight and his Weapons* (London 1964).

Oman, Sir Charles, *The Art of War in the Middle Ages* vol. 2 (London 1924).

Pevsner, N. and I. Richmond, *Northumberland,* The Buildings of England Series, (London 1992).

Pollard, A. J., *North-eastern England during the Wars of the Roses: War, Politics and Lay Society, 1450–1500* (Oxford 1990).

Pollard, A. J., *Richard III and the Princes in the Tower* (Gloucester 1991).

Pollard, A. J., *The Wars of the Roses* (London 2001).

Pollard, A. J., 'Characteristics of the Fifteenth Century North' in C. Appleby and P. Dalton (eds), *Government, Religion and Society in Northern England 1000–1700* (Stroud 1977).

Pollard, A. J., 'Percies, Nevilles and the Wars of the Roses', *History Today,* (September 1992).

Prestwich, M., *Armies and Warfare in the Middle Ages* (London 1996).

Ramsay, Sir J. H., *Lancaster and York* 2 vols (Oxford 1892).

Ridpath, G., *The Border History of England and Scotland* (Berwick upon Tweed 1776).

Roberts, D., *The Battle of Stoke Field* (Newark 1987).

Robson, R., *The Rise and Fall of the English Highland Clans* (Edinburgh 1989).

Rogers, Col. H. C. B., *Artillery Through the Ages* (London 1971).

Rose, A., *Kings in the North* (London 2002).

Ross, C., *Edward IV* (London 1974).

Ross, C., *Wars of the Roses* (London 1976).

Ross, C., *Richard III* (London 1981).

Ross, C., (ed.) *Patronage, Pedigree and Power in Later Medieval England* (Gloucester 1979).

Rowse, A. L., *Bosworth Field and the War of the Roses* (London 1966).

Runciman, Sir Stephen, *The Fall of Constantinople* (England 1965).

Sadler, D. J., *Battle for Northumbria* (Newcastle upon Tyne 1988).

Sadler, D. J., *War in the North – The Wars of the Roses in the North East of England 1461–1464* (Bristol 2000).

Sadler, D. J., *Border Fury – The Three Hundred Years War* (London 2004).

Simons, E. N., *The Reign of Edward IV* (London 1966).

Seward, D., *Richard III – England's Black Legend* (London 1983).

Seward, D., *Henry V as Warlord* (London 1987).

Seward, D., *The Wars of the Roses* (London 1995).

Seymour, W., *Battles in Britain* vol. 1, (London 1989).

Scofield, C. L., *The Life and Reign of Edward the Fourth* 2 vols (London 1967).

Smurthwaite, D., *The Ordnance Survey Guide to the Battlefields of Britain* (London 1984).

Stapleton, T., (ed.) *The Plumpton Correspondence* (London 1977).

Storey, R. L., *End of the House of Lancaster* (London 1966).

Storey, R. L., 'The Wardens of the Marches of England towards Scotland 1377–1489', *English Historical Review*, vol. 72 (1957).

Summerson, H., 'Carlisle and the English West March in the Late Middle Ages' in A. J. Pollard (ed.) *The North of England in the Reign of Richard III* (Stroud 1996).

Thrupp, S. L., 'The problem of replacement-rates in late medieval English population', *Economic History Review* 2nd series, 18 (1965).

Tomlinson, W. Weaver, *A Comprehensive Guide to Northumberland* (Newcastle upon Tyne 1863).

Trevelyan, G. M., *A History of England* (London 1926).

Tuck, A., *Crown and Nobility, 1272–1462* (Oxford 1986).

Wagner, P. and S. Hand, *Medieval Sword and Shield* (California 2003).

Warner, P., *Sieges of the Middle Ages* (London 1968).

Watson, G., *The Border Reivers* (Newcastle upon Tyne 1974).

Weiss, M., 'A Power in the North? The Percies in the Fifteenth Century', *The Historical Journal*, vol. 19 (1965).

Williamson, A., *The Murder of the Princes* (Gloucester 1978).

Wise, T., *Medieval Heraldry* (London 1980)

Wise, T., *The Wars of the Roses* (London 1983).

Wolffe, B., *Henry VI* (London 1981).

Woolgar, C. M., *The Great Household in Late Medieval England* (London 1999).

Index

Edward, 239
Elizabeth, Queen of England, 160, 186,
  236, 237, 238, 241
Sir Richard, 1st Earl Rivers, 80, 127, 160
Wressle, Manor, 45
Wright, Professor William, 290
Wrotham Park, 194
Wrottesley, Sir Walter, 178
Wye, R., 245

York, Edmund of Langley,
  Duke of, 25
York, Richard, Duke of, 19, 28, 38, 48, 59,
  62, 72, 88–91,
York, Richard, Duke of (of the Princes in the
  Tower), 238, 287–91
Yorkist Land Revenue Experiment, 159